Yeats's G

Brenda Ma

"Maddox approaches Yeats with the insight and wit she brought to her lives of James Joyce's wife (1988) and D. H. Lawrence (1994). . . . The 'scary and the splendid' sides of Yeats's personality neatly appraised."
—*Kirkus Reviews*

"[A] splendid new biography . . . with the selective freedom of a novel."
—*Newsday*

"Sensible, discreet, and brisk. . . . Well done."
—*Boston Sunday Globe*

"Maddox is a brave and stern interrogator of the imposing Yeats, as well as a scrupulous, exacting, and well-qualified one."
—*San Francisco Chronicle*

"Readers will enjoy this book not only for its touching portrayal of an unlikely marriage but also for its evocation of the transforming magic that enabled Yeats's best-remembered poems to rise out of the daily clutter of a great mind."
—*Pittsburgh Post-Gazette*

"[A] biography rich with insight and feminist perspective."
—*Book*

"Maddox has been a leader in broadcasting biography into a popular genre by producing dazzling authentic, readable lives. *Yeats's Ghosts* is her usual tightrope performance—perceptive, close-focus, compelling."
—*Financial Times*

"Sparkling, racy, but always carefully considered."
—*Sunday Times*

Yeats's Ghosts

Yeats's Ghosts
The Secret Life of W. B. Yeats

Brenda Maddox

Perennial

An Imprint of HarperCollins*Publishers*

For John

Designed by William Ruoto

The Library of Congress has catalogued the hardcover edition as follows:

Maddox, Brenda.
 Yeats's ghosts: the secret life of W. B. Yeats / Brenda Maddox—1st ed
 p. cm.
 Includes bibliographical references and index.
 ISBN 0-06-017494-3
 1. Yeats, W. B. (William Butler), 1865–1939. 2. Yeats, W. B. (William Butler), 1865–1939—Knowledge—Occultism. 3. Yeats, W. B. (William Butler), 1865–1939—Marriage. 4. Poets, Irish—20th century—Biography. 5. Spiritualists—Ireland—Biography. 6. Occultists—Ireland—Biography. 7. Yeats, Georgie, d. 1968.
 I Title.
 PR5906.M278   1999
 821'.8—dc21   99-12858

ISBN 0-06-098504-6 (pbk.)

00 01 02 03 04   ❖/RRD   10 9 8 7 6 5 4 3 2 1

I have a great sense of abundance—more than I have had for years. George's ghosts have educated me.

—W. B. Yeats to Olivia Shakespear, December 27, 1930

Contents

Acknowledgments

In trying to understand the phenomenon of Yeats, I was fortunate to be able to talk with some who knew him as a friend or acquaintance: Brigid O'Brien Ganly, Elizabeth Curran Solterer, Patricia Boylan, Omar Pound, the late Sean O'Faolain, Anne Gregory de Winton, Francis Stuart, and Anna MacBride White.

Many others helped me in different ways. For their interest and hospitality, I would like to thank Richard and Priscilla Boger, Eamon and Ann Cantwell, Jane de Falbe, Paul and Helga Doty, Rosemary Hammond, Maureen Howard and Mark Probst, Desmond and Peggy Fisher, Declan and Beth Kiberd, Maura and Michael McTighe, Robert and Becky Tracy, and Susan Schreibman. I am especially grateful to all connected with the Yeats International Summer School at Sligo, including, for tours of the town and countryside, Martin and Joyce Enright and John Flynn. The Ashdown Forest Golf Hotel kindly showed me around the premises before renovation.

For permission to quote from unpublished material I would like to thank Hodder Headlines, the Estate of Edmund Dulac, and the Harry Ransom Humanities Research Center; the Estate of Richard Ellmann and the University of Tulsa; Julia O'Faolain, the Cambridge University Department of Psychology, and Anne Gregory de Winton. and A. P. Watt, the representatives of the Yeats estate, and Oxford University Press and Simon and Schuster who kindly gave permission for generous quotation of Yeats's published work of letters..

My British publisher, Macmillan, also Yeats's publisher, gave immense help by making available many works by and about Yeats. I am particularly grateful to Tim Farmiloe and John Handford for their efforts on my behalf.

Once again in my biographical quest I was sustained by the impeccable scholarship of Bernard McGinley. I am grateful to him also, as well as to Ann Fogarty, Declan Kiberd, and David Pierce, for reading some or all of the manuscript in its rough draft. Errors that remain are certainly not theirs.

Able research assistance was provided by Mary Aldridge, at the McFarlin Library, University of Tulsa, Oklahoma; by Linda Sneed, at the Lilly Library, Bloomington, Indiana; by Gill Shepherd, at the British Library Newspaper Library at Colindale, where she unearthed the Margot Ruddock stories from the papers of May 1936; and by Carey Snyder, at the State University of New York at Stony Brook, where she stoically submitted to the punishing regime imposed by its Department of Special Collections.

Many thanks are due also to Nesta MacDonald for the loan of her collection of newspaper articles by Edith Shackleton Heald, to Michael Carney for letting me read his unpublished biography of Hilda Matheson, to Geoffrey Elborn for allowing me to quote from his unpublished interviews with Francis Stuart, and to Jane Mulvagh, who gave me once more the benefit of her scholarly eye for early-twentieth-century women's fashion.

The Yeats archive is a scattered one, although the National Library of Ireland holds the greatest concentration. But the story of Yeats's complex life involves not only his own papers but the records of many organizations and institutions. It is my good fortune to live near one of the best public libraries imaginable. The resources of the Central Library of the Royal Borough of Kensington and Chelsea are exceeded only by the helpfulness of its staff. For almost daily assistance, I owe special gratitude.

Heartfelt appreciation goes also to the following libraries, archives, special collections, and individuals: BBC Northern Ireland (Austin Hunter); BBC Written Archives; Bancroft Library, University of California at Berkeley (Anthony S. Bliss); Bank of England (press office); Berg Collection, New York Public Library (Stephen Crook); Bodleian Library, Oxford University; Bord Fáilte/Irish Tourist Board; The British Library National Sound Archive; British Library Newspaper Library; John J. Burns Library, Boston College (Robert K. O'Neill); Cambridge University Department of Experimental Psychology (J. D. Mollon); Rare Books & Manuscripts Division, New York Public Library; Central Bank of Ireland; Channel 4 (the late Chris Griffin-Beale); the Eugenics Society; Woodruff Library, Emory University Special Collections (Steve Ennis); London Borough of Hammersmith and Fulham Archives and Local History Centre (Jane C. Kimber, Borough Archivist); Houghton Library, Harvard University (Denison Beach); Harry Ransom Humanities Research Center, University of Texas (Dr. Thomas Staley and Cathy Henderson); Huntington Library, San Marino, California (Sara S. Hodson and Jennifer Watts); Irish Embassy, London (Geoffrey Keating, cultural attaché); The London Library; Manuscript Division of the Library of Congress; National Library of Ireland (Colette O'Flaherty); National Museum of Ireland (Michael Kenny); Princess Grace Irish Library, Monaco; Firestone Library, Princeton University; Radio Telefís Éireann; University of Reading Library (Michael Bott); San Antonio *Express-News* (Megan Stacey); the Savile Club; Sligo County Library (Donal Tinney); Swedish Royal Academy; Trinity College Library, Trinity College, Dublin (Felicity O'Mahony); McFarlin Library, University of Tulsa (Sidney E. Huttner); University College Library, University College, Dublin (Norma Jessop); Beinecke Manuscript and Rare Book Library, Yale University; Yeats International Summer School; the Wellcome Library, and the *Yeats Eliot Review* (Russell Murphy).

For correspondence, answers to queries, and other assistance I am indebted to Humphrey Carpenter, Anthony Cronin, Anne Margaret Daniel, Jane de Falbe, Paul Dolan, John Flynn, George Mills Harper, John Harwood, Rosemary Hemming, Penelope Hoare, Mary Holland, Austin Hunter, John Wyse Jackson, A. Norman Jeffares, Ronan Keane, John Kelly, Michael Laffan, the late Mary Lappin, Paul Laskin, Sheila Lawlor, A. Walt Litz, James Longenbach, David McKittrick, Pat Murphy, Richard Nash-Siedlecki, John Naughton, Nigel Nicolson, Ulick O'Connor, Seán Ó Mórdha, Penny Perrick, James Randi, Ronald and Keith Schuchard, Patricia Smyllie, Colin Smythe, Diana Souhami and Shelley von Strunkel.

From the start, my publishers, Peter Straus, at Picador, Macmillan, and Gladys Carr at HarperCollins, New York, offered support and enthusiasm. Caradoc King at A. P. Watt in London and Ellen Levine of the Ellen Levine Agency in New York, were mainstays as agents and friends. Once more Bronwen, Bruno, and John Maddox gave encouragement and perspective.

Introduction

When I interviewed the aged Irish writer Sean O'Faolain for the London *Sunday Times,* I asked as I was leaving what Yeats had been like.[1] "There *was* no Yeats!" he exploded. "I watched him invent himself."

That Yeats invented so many selves so successfully has made him hard to capture between two covers. His elusiveness has been aided by the fact that one (at very least) of these selves has been an embarrassment. W. H. Auden called it "the southern Californian side of Yeats,"[2] the scholar Curtis Bradford, "the price we pay for his poetry."[3] It certainly drove off O'Faolain, who as a young contemporary well placed to write a biography of Yeats, tried but gave up:

> I found that W. B. had, in his time, dived down so many caverns of knowledge and as quickly returned, bringing many pearls with him, that if I were to write about him with any

authority of knowledge I should have to dive down the same caverns[,] stay much too long, and bring back very little—all to write about his voyagings with an assurance about things I could not be interested in for their own sakes. Blavatsky is one such. Indian philosophy is another. Occultism another.[4]

The academic world is less embarrassed by the paranormal than it used to be. The mystical Yeats is the focus of the first volume of the historian R. F. Foster's authorized biography, published in 1996 with the subtitle *The Apprentice Mage*. The long communication with supposed spirits conducted by Yeats and his wife was transcribed and published in full for the first time in 1992 by a team led by George Mills Harper of Florida State University.

The six scholars who edited and annotated the three volumes of *Yeats's "Vision" Papers* had no easy task. The Automatic Script, as they call it, covers 3,600 pages, produced in 450 sittings over 20 months. Some of the entries were written backward, in mirror writing, by Mrs. Yeats's supposedly "grasped" hand, illustrated by sketchy diagrams and obscure symbols. When the Script petered out, more messages emerged through her speaking voice as she slept. Yeats recorded them all as best he could in his *Sleep and Dream Notebooks*. These too form part of the three volumes of newly transcribed material.

Now that it can be read, this vast record can be seen not to be the chartless abyss feared by O'Faolain. Rather, it is a biographical gold mine, waiting to be worked. In order to extract what seems most valuable from it, and also to avoid a biography of excessive length, I have chosen to concentrate on Yeats's last 22 years. Even so, I have tried to cover the main events and relationships of the complex and productive life that he led until his marriage in 1917.

My book begins early in 1917, with the poet at 51, not yet married but determined to become so by an astrologically crucial moment in the coming October. He was unaware, when he was turned down in his first proposal of marriage that year, that his second, successful, offer was made to a young woman with unsuspected gifts as a spirit medium.

Yeats later made no secret of the swift appearance in his newly married life of what he called "Controls," "Communicators," or "Instructors" from the unseen world. "Four days after my marriage," he wrote, "my wife surprised me by attempting automatic writing . . ."[5] Of what he learned through her hand, he made *A Vision,* his esoteric book of personal philosophy. He also made his greatest poetry.

But his young wife, Georgie, or George, as Yeats came to call her, did more than merely attempt automatic writing. She turned out to be a virtuoso, her hand turning out page upon page, in long arduous sessions, sometimes two a day, for several years.

The full text of the Automatic Script forces new interpretations of Yeats's life and work. Elizabeth B. Cullingford, in her full-length feminist study *Gender and History in Yeats's Love Poetry* (1993), concludes that the Script helped Yeats make sense of his sexual life; she points out how it directs Yeats's attention to the need for sexual satisfaction of "the medium" (his wife).[6] Such an interpretation would not have disturbed Yeats. He refers to his sexual life freely in his work and did not demand reverence from posterity. When speaking in a lecture of the alcoholism of his late friend Lionel Johnson, he said, "I would wish to be spoken of with just such candour when I am dead."[7]

This book would not exist without the industry and imagination of recent Yeats studies or without the stimulation of the deservedly legendary annual Yeats International Summer School at Sligo. Important new work includes, along with Professor Harper's *Vision Papers,* the *Yeats Annual* series, with Warwick Gould, as general editor. I am particularly grateful to Deirdre Toomey's "Away" in *Yeats Annual 9* (of which she was also the editor) and, from the same volume, to David Bradshaw's "The Eugenics Movement in the 1930s and the Emergence of *On the Boiler.*" John Harwood's *Olivia Shakespear and W. B. Yeats* (1989), with its many previously unpublished letters, illuminates an important relationship in Yeats's life that has been overshadowed by his legendary love for Maud Gonne. *The Gonne-Yeats Letters* (1992), edited by Anna MacBride White, Maud Gonne's granddaughter, and by the doyen of Yeats scholars, A. Norman Jeffares, provides much new information, particularly on Yeats's fascination with Maud's beautiful daughter, Iseult. David Pierce's meticulously researched and beautifully illustrated *Yeats's Worlds* (1995) brings out the English side of Yeats and of the importance of the Englishwoman who became his wife.

Other new books set Yeats within the frame of a gifted family. William M. Murphy's *Family Secrets* (1995) adds to the impressive scholarship shown in *Prodigal Father* (1978), his award-winning biography of Yeats's dazzling father, John Butler Yeats. Yeats's able sisters, Lily and Lolly, receive overdue recognition in *The Yeats Sisters* (1996), by Joan Hardwick, and in *The Yeats Sisters and the Cuala* (1994), by Gifford Lewis. John Kelly's work in progress for Oxford University Press, the multi-volume *Letters of W. B. Yeats,* has set a new standard of grace and erudition in the collection and editing of the voluminous correspondence of a modern literary giant.

I came to Yeats first at Harvard, through Professor John V. Kelleher's seminar on Anglo-Irish literature and later, through my research for a biography of James Joyce's wife, Nora. I came to Irish politics through *The Economist,* where, as Britain and Home Affairs editor, I had the opportunity to write a tiny part of that troubled story. During many visits to the Republic and the North, I learned that the tradition of hospitality and humor covers the whole island of Ireland, and that cross-border cooperation existed well before leaders from both sides went to the considerable trouble of writing it into an agreement.

My book is in four parts. Part 1 traces, with backward glances, the events of 1917 leading up to Yeats's marriage in October. Part 2 covers the years from the end of 1917 to 1922, with a close examination of the Automatic Script and its coincidence with the gestation and birth of the Yeatses' two children. (Soon after the couple achieved the desired son, in 1921, the Script and the "Sleeps" that followed it came to a halt.)

The third section, chapter 10, jumps back to the mid–nineteenth century. Why did Yeats, born in 1865, find spiritual communication so compelling, and love and marriage so difficult? The answer appears to lie with the least examined of the important women in his life: his mother, Susan Pollexfen Yeats.

The last section of the book, part 4, looks at Yeats from 1922 until his death in 1939: the family man, the senator, the Nobel laureate, the defier of de Valera and—the words are his—"the wild old wicked man." The 1930s saw him fall into such follies as an operation for sexual rejuvenation, a flirtation with fascism, a slapdash enthusiasm for eugenics, and a succession of senescent love affairs.

Throughout I hope I have shown that Yeats was first and foremost a great poet, probably the greatest in twentieth-century English-language poetry. There are admirers of his verse for whom the unlovely side of Yeats is so prominent that they have to be reminded why they love his work. Yet there is no need to shy away from Yeats's faults. The words of Auden's great elegy "In Memory of W. B. Yeats" cannot be bettered: "You were silly like us: your gift survived it all."

Yeats wore his faults on his sleeve. Vanity, snobbery, intellectual sloppiness, and flirtatiousness coexisted with loyalty to family, friends, and country. In his constant assistance and encouragement to young writers he was a generous man.

Ghost-lovers, however, should be warned. The admirable enterprise and editing behind the published *Vision Papers* has, to my mind, a flaw. The commentary on the text appears to treat the phantasmal cast of the Automatic Script—"Aymor," "Thomas of Dorlowicz," "Democritus," "Leo," and the rest—as real. The introduction to the *Papers* glosses, for example, an ambiguous line in the Script with the suggestion that "Aymor [may] have been thinking of the Yeatses' imminent visit to Ireland."[8] Elsewhere, it declares that "Thomas informed the Yeatses that he was 'not nearly done.'"[9] The symbol of a lion's head is explained thus: "Leo's sign on blank page . . . suggests that he may have been at least partially responsible for George's inability to produce orderly Script during this period."[10]

Phrases such as these, even if used as a matter of convention, suggest that "Aymor" could think, that "Thomas" could inform, and that "Leo" could stay George Yeats's hand. I do not believe this. I see the Automatic Script as an oblique form of communication between a young wife and an aging husband who did not know each other very well and needed it for things they could say to one another in no other way.

My firm conviction is that, at all times during the Automatic Script—even when four or five "Controls" are recorded as gathered at the same time—there were only two people in the room.

Yeats believed he had multiple instructors. He certainly has had multiple biographers. In the introduction to his 1997 biography of Keats, Andrew Motion says that the lives of all important writers need to be reconsidered at regular intervals, no matter how familiar they might be, because their stories offer new attractions and new difficulties to each successive generation.[11] I do agree and am glad that the days are gone when the Great Archivist in the sky decreed only one "Life" per person.

Lives change with the eye of the beholder, Yeats's above all. He is a phenomenon, like the First World War or global warming. He looks very different to a literary scholar than to a journalist, to a woman than to a man, to a believer than to an unbeliever, to an English poet than to an Irish poet. There never will be a last book on Yeats.

The events about which Yeats wrote also change with time. The so-called revisionist approach to Irish history sets the Easter Rising of 1916 in the context of the First World War. The postcolonialist school of literary criticism, in contrast, places the rebellion within the twentieth-century pattern of resistance and revolt that brought independence to Algeria, Egypt, and India.

If feminism has yielded a new Yeats, so too has molecular biology. Advances in the understanding of genes shed a kindlier light on the promise that of eugenics held for pre-Holocaust generations.

What follows is one view of the life of Yeats. I see it as the struggle of a great poet to understand where the images that threatened to master him came from and to ensure that they kept on coming.

—*Brenda Maddox*
December 1998

Part 1

1

An Astrological Deadline

(January–March 1917)

ON AN ICY SPRING DAY in 1917, the year that was to change his life, the poet William Butler Yeats traveled from London to St. Leonard's-on-Sea on the Sussex coast. Yeats was a big man, over 6 feet tall, with a massive frame conspicuously well dressed. At 51, he had masses of gray-black hair slanting over his forehead, brown eyes, and a soft, full mouth that, in photographs, looks ready to cry.

With him were two friends, cultivated men: the orientalist Edward Denison Ross, and the painter and stage designer Edmund Dulac. On March 22, the Great War was in its third year and 231st day. Sixty miles away British troops were massing for an assault on Arras, in St. Petersburg crowds were celebrating the overthrow of Czar Nicholas II, while in Washington Congress was reconvening to endorse the United States' entry into the war. Yet the travelers' minds were fixed on a different reality: a talking machine sometimes known as the Metallic Medium, claimed in psychical literature to speak on spiritualistic matters and to answer questions in several languages.[1]

The bachelor Yeats was an animated, loquacious traveling companion, running his hands through his hair as he talked unstoppably on. If his listeners did not get many of their own words in, they rarely minded. Yeats was the best conversationalist many had ever heard—often (with due respect to his audience) ribald in his flow. For those not being preached at or patronized, he was fun.[2] Anyone who had been long in his company, moreover, knew the excitement of the supernatural world, especially when conveyed with hints of Arabian nights and desert sands. On such Eastern esotericism, Denison Ross, director of the London School of Oriental Studies, was expert. His school advertised on the front page of the *Times,* for applicants to its courses "in the Principal Languages of the Near, Middle and Far East, and Africa. Also Oriental Religions and Customs."[3] For his part, the artist Dulac shared Yeats's enthusiasm for the plays of Japan; the previous year he had designed the costumes and masks for *At the Hawk's Well,* Yeats's first Noh play.

At St. Leonard's, the robot's owner, David Wilson, happily showed off his invention: a square, copper-lined wooden box, containing a brass drum and a short brass tube with a lens called "the eye," which revolved around the drum. The visitors were invited to try experiments with cards; Yeats had brought his own pack for the purpose. But the machine did not cooperate. Wilson thereupon sat himself in front of it and dictated syllables that Ross vouchsafed could be transformed into Turkish. These elicited a long string of livelier responses, such as "MASALA KOUM/KOUM TOUM BOULA BLI YESH."[4]

Yeats then offered to use his mystical symbols to clear the room (presumably of interfering spirits), but the box needed no assistance. It kept spewing out words, switching to English. Asked to identify "the excellent one," it responded with some scorn: "Who are you when knoweth not that the excellent one is he whose name may not be branded upon the camel's neck?"

The visitors were not impressed. After more attempts with cards and envelopes, they left disappointed that the machine was not scientific. Yeats, however, who had made the journey to St. Leonard's once before on a similar quest, felt he had to try again. He went back, and this time, alone, got better results. At about eleven o'clock the tubed box began to speak. At first all it said was "Leo," a name Yeats knew well from seances. Then it confessed that it was not sure who it was— possibly Yeats.

"But *I* am Yeats," Yeats contradicted. Homunculus Metallicus was unconvinced, insisting, "No, Yeats has gone." Yeats tried another tactic. Sitting at a table with his long arm stretched out before him, he bent down to try to communicate through telepathy. Suddenly his arm began to tremble and throb as if under the influence of the machine, which gratifyingly appeared to obey commands to stop and start. But no more words emerged. Yeats went back to London, disillusioned. In the notes he kept of such investigations, he concluded, much as Dulac had, that the robot's owner was somehow behind the voice.[5] Indeed, he believed, drawing on nearly 30 years of ventures into the paranormal, "999 mediums out of 1000 never communicate other than subconscious experience."[6]

But the one chance in a thousand was, for him, worth pursuing. Long experience had left him convinced that the images that welled up before what he thought of as "the mind's eye" came from a source deeper than the individual memory or unconscious. Images came, he was convinced, from a universal store that he (and not he alone) called the Anima Mundi, the world soul.[7] The chance to draw on this pool of accumulated imagination and wisdom offered a way out of the solitariness of the self and, not incidentally, a rich source of poetry.

Yeats's concept of "the age-long memoried self"[8] suggests Jung's collective unconscious. Yeats had read Jung—just as he had read Freud, Nietzsche, Pythagoras, Plotinus, Swedenborg, and Buddha—randomly, with the voraciousness of the autodidact. The new psychoanalytic theories floated in a warm bath in his mind with Platonic and Neoplatonic ideas that reality is hidden, that image is all we see.

A more sustained influence was William Blake. In the early 1890s, in collaboration with Edwin Ellis, a Pre-Raphaelite artist and London neighbor, Yeats poured enormous energy into mastering and editing

Blake's prophetic and mystical writings, which appeared as *The Works of William Blake* in 1896. His own mysticism, Yeats felt, helped him to understand Blake and see that Blake was not mad.[9] Yeats, having rejected scientific rationalism as well as the religion of his childhood, was seeking to make his own creed out of poetic tradition and "imaginary people . . . created out of the deepest instinct of man."[10] And the unschooled, Swedenborgian Blake, he found, had done so before him, discovering in his humble London surroundings a vision of the eternal world "of which the Vegetable Universe is but a faint shadow."[11]

In a half century of alternating between Dublin, where he was born in 1865, and London, his intermittent home since childhood, Yeats had given a great deal of his time to groups dedicated to the investigation of the supernatural. But he had given his time to many groups. Unusually for a poet (and he had never had any other occupation, except for literary journalism, lecturing, and long, unpaid labors for Dublin's Abbey Theatre), Yeats was a man who loved organizations. Much as he loathed realism in art, in his public life he was a joiner, a clubman, and more: an administrator, a virtuoso of the committee table, an avid draftsman of constitutions and rules of membership, an intrepid writer of letters to the editor.

As a peripatetic bachelor, he relied on gentlemen's clubs for accommodation and conversation. In Dublin his clubs were the United Arts, the Sackville Street, and the Stephen's Green. (He was ineligible for the University Club because he had no degree.) In January 1917 he was about to exchange his London club, the Royal Societies, for the socially superior Savile, to which he was very pleased to have been elected.[12] His artistic affiliations were equally institutionally anchored. In Dublin, with his friend and patron Lady Gregory, he had founded the Irish National Theatre Company (which became the Abbey Theatre). He served also as editor for his sisters' Cuala Press. In London he was prominent in the literary establishment. He was an elected member of the elite Academic Committee of English Letters and, since 1910, the recipient of an annual pension of 150 pounds a year from the Civil List. This public subsidy, a guaranteed income for life to one who was recognized as being in the first rank of living poets, was a gift of the king and had been secured for him through the influence of high-ranking friends, English and Irish, including Lady Gregory and the prime minister, H. H. Asquith.

Socially, it follows, Yeats was well connected. In London he dined at Downing Street. He was a desirable catch for titled hostesses' dinner parties and country weekends. Indeed, he was a welcome guest at great houses on both sides of the Irish Sea. On Monday evenings in London, he was at home at his rooms in Bloomsbury—lively occasions that began at eight and did not break up until half-past one or two in the morning.[13]

His occult connections were intricate and overlapping. In 1885, when he was twenty and living in Dublin, he helped found the Dublin Hermetic Society with the aim of using Eastern symbolism to trace pathways between the individual consciousness and the cosmos. In 1887, with the family moved back to London once again, Yeats switched allegiance to Madame Blavatsky's Theosophical Society (Esoteric Section). Soon forced out because of his independent initiative and outspoken criticism,[14] he joined the cult that was to become the focus of his magical activities for the next thirty years: the Hermetic Order of the Golden Dawn.

The Golden Dawn was a middle-class, unisex secret society of mystics devoted to the practice of medieval and Renaissance rituals of magic. Through carefully graded steps, successful students might advance to the highest good, defined as "True Wisdom and Perfect Happiness." When the ultimate stage was attained, darkness would disappear and the light of understanding would shine through: the Golden Dawn. The order, founded in London in 1888, said to owe its origins to the discovery of a coded manuscript, claimed to have been lost for centuries, only to turn up on a bookseller's barrow in Farringdon Road in 1884.[15] (The rediscovered "lost book" remained a powerful image for Yeats.)

A basic text of the Golden Dawn was *The Kabbalah Unveiled*, by MacGregor Mathers, published in 1887, an English translation from the Latin of the Hebrew mystical interpretation of the Old Testament. Yeats owned two copies. Mathers, a Scot, a Freemason, a Rosicrucian, and an inventive theoretician, in collaboration with the Reverend A. F. A. Woodford, who made the lucky find on the Farringdon Road, concocted a loose amalgam of the supposed scientific knowledge of the medieval alchemist Christian Rosencreuz (hence "Rosicrucian") and the wisdom of the ancient Egyptian magician Hermes (hence "hermetic") and studded it with cabalistic, Masonic, astrological, and tarot symbolism.

The Golden Dawn, like Blake, saw the world as mirror: "as above, so below." It divided the ladder of ascent from the earthly (called Malkuth) to the heavenly (Kether), into nine steps of three degrees, or "orders," each. Successful progression to the top brought the title of Ipsissimus: the Very Self, who held the status of magus, or priest, a human conduit of wisdom from the supernatural to the natural.[16]

The elaborate rituals for entry into the highly secret Second Order, devoted to the study and practice of magic, were sexually charged: daggers, swords, and incense; cords and chains (initiates were bound to a cross). The heady atmosphere thus created was particularly attractive to the well-bred adventurous female. In 1901, however, the order drew much unwanted publicity from a rape scandal involving a sixteen-year-old girl which arose from a false initiation rite performed by a spurious group in the Golden Dawn's name. Several splits and changes of name followed. Yeats's allegiance went to the splinter of a splinter called Stella Matutina.

For Yeats, as R. F. Foster has shown, the Golden Dawn, with its progressive series of increasingly difficult examinations, was his church and his university.[17] Yeats did not go to university. With the encouragement of his iconoclastic (and impecunious) father, a painter who prided himself on having educated his gifted son himself, Yeats broke with family tradition by not attending Trinity College, Dublin. (He later said that he could not have passed the examinations.) Instead, like his two sisters, he chose to attend the less demanding, and less expensive, Metropolitan School of Art in Dublin. He left in 1886 when he was twenty-one—the time of his serious plunge into magic.

By 1893, at the age of twenty-eight, Yeats had climbed five of the ten degrees of the Second Order of the Golden Dawn and had attained the high rank of Adept (one skilled in secret knowledge of practical magic). His secret name was Frater "Demon Est Deus Inversus"— "D. E. D. I.," for short. Whether *Demon* is translated as *daimon* (Yeats's word for the individual's guiding spirit or *alter ego*) or more conventionally as *devil,* the name appropriately conveyed his lifelong commitment to the reconciliation of opposites.

Commitment to the Golden Dawn did not bar other roads to the supernatural. In London in 1913 Yeats joined the Society for Psychical Research, dedicated to the scientific investigation of the paranormal. This society, which still exists, emphasized the collection of empirical data and verifiable results. Advances in scientific thought at the time appeared to support the ideas Yeats was developing through his own intense private experiences. In 1909 Sir Oliver Lodge, a fellow of the Royal Society as well as a member of the SPR, published *The Survival of Man: A Study in Unrecognised Human Faculty,* summarizing the evidence, which he took to be proof, of the individual's survival of bodily death.[18]

Less cerebral, and more frightening, was direct communication with spirits. Since 1909 Yeats had been a regular attender of Julia's Bureau, a spiritualist center run by William T. Stead at his home, Cambridge House, in Wimbledon. Stead's main contact "on the other side" was a dead American journalist, Julia B. Ames. Before the turn of the century Stead had published a stream of her alleged posthumous correspondence, *Letters from Julia,* which he later reissued as *After Death.*[19]

At the regular Monday meetings of the bureau, a vacant seat was always kept for the absent "Julia." Various spirits (or "Controls," as they were known in psychic science)[20] would announce themselves, speaking through a long, tin trumpet kept on the table. They fell roughly into two categories: the recently dead, returning to console grieving relatives; and restless figures from the past seeking certain significant individuals among the living, such as William T. Stead or W. B. Yeats, to whom they had something of importance to say. (That these "Controls" were not clairvoyant was proved in April 1914 when Stead left for New York on the *Titanic.*)

It was at Wimbledon in 1912 that Yeats felt himself contacted by the spirit claiming to be "Leo," whom he vaguely recognized from a séance three years before. "Leo," even though his voice came through the trumpet with a strong Irish accent, announced himself as a Moorish writer and explorer; he said he had been with Yeats since childhood as his "opposite" and would like Yeats to write to him as if he were still living among the Moors and Sudanese. Subsequent research in *Chambers's Biographical Dictionary* yielded a "Leo Africanus," otherwise known as Al Hassan Ibn-Mohammed al-Wezar Al-Fasi, a sixteenth-century Spanish Arab poet, explorer, and, for a long period, Roman slave, who had left copious written records of his dramatic adventures to excite nineteenth-century anthropologists.[21]

"Leo" thereafter frequently reappeared to Yeats, who was so stirred that he began composing a correspondence with this alternative self, whom he came to associate with the zodiacal sign of Leo, and to regard as less of a benevolent teacher than a tormentor.

This imaginary dialogue was not wasted. It inspired the great antiphonal poem "Ego Dominus Tuus," written in 1915, in which "Hic" (the objective self) debates with "Ille" (the inner or subjective self):

> Ille
> By the help of an image
> I call to my own opposite, summon all
> That I have handled least, least looked upon.

> Hic
> And I would find myself and not an image.

> Ille
> That is our modern hope, and by its light
> We have lit upon the gentle, sensitive mind
> And lost the old nonchalance of the hand;

In the next to last stanza, "Hic," still unpersuaded, wonders why it is not preferable to try to understand one's self rather than an unseen reality. "Ille" has the answer:

Because I seek an image, not a book.
Those men that in their writings are most wise
Own nothing but their blind, stupefied hearts.
I call to the mysterious one who yet
Shall walk the wet sands by the edge of the stream
And look most like me, being indeed my double,
And prove of all imaginable things.
The most unlike, being my anti-self,
And, standing by these characters, disclose
All that I seek; and whisper it as though
He were afraid the birds, who cry aloud
Their momentary cries before it is dawn,
Would carry it away to blasphemous men.

Yeats freely confessed that his useful sparring partner "Leo" might come from his own imagination. As he explained in 1917 to Sir William Barrett, past president of the Society for Psychical Research, "I think that one should deal with a control on the working hypothesis that it is genuine. This does not mean that I feel any certainty on the point, but even if it is a secondary personality that should be the right treatment."[22]

Such varied approaches to the world beyond consciousness, easily confused by the skeptic, were seen as utterly distinct, even antagonistic, to the psychic student of Yeats's time. "Mental" mediums, who relied on their powers of concentration and trance, looked down on "physical" mediums, who employed theatrical props such as tables, trumpets, Ouija boards, mysterious lights, and crystal balls to obtain their results. To most of the Golden Dawn, for example, séances were vulgar stunts, designed to appeal to the lower orders and very far from their own scholarly endeavors.

But Yeats did not balk at vulgarity in his search for truth. He would sit among servant girls at séances in Soho, listening to a "fat old woman . . . tell in Cockney language how the dead do not yet know they are dead."[23] For him, gathering evidence that the soul lived on after the death of the body demanded ceaseless effort and observation, many lines of investigation, much correspondence, and terrible rows.

One internecine fight within the Golden Dawn has become legendary as "The Battle of Blythe Road." For several days in late April 1900, Yeats stood watch at the London temple of the Second Order of the Golden Dawn. The temple was located upstairs in dingy three-story premises otherwise occupied by Mr. Wilkinson, a builder, on Blythe Road in Hammersmith, West London (and today by a Greek takeaway). Yeats, with a fellow member who was an amateur boxer, lay in wait to block the expected forced entry of the flamboyant mystic and magician Aleister Crowley. Crowley, whom the order had rejected as an initiate, was intent on taking possession of the temple's secret rituals. In due course the invader arrived, suitably dressed for the adventure in a black mask, a MacGregor tartan kilt, a gilt pectoral cross, and a dagger at his knee. But Yeats and his companion repelled him—apparently by throwing him down the stairs. Crowley (who was acting as emissary for MacGregor Mathers, with whom Yeats and the Second Order Committee had fallen out) then took out a summons, with the consequence that, as Yeats wrote Lady Gregory, "for a week I have been worried to death with meetings & watching to prevent a sudden attack on the rooms. For three nights I did not get more than 4 H hours sleap [sic] any night."[24]

The conclusion that Yeats formally delivered to the Second Order Committee was that a change was required in the constitution.

Yeats knew that he was credulous, willing to believe when others would give up, that he favored supernatural explanations when rational alternatives were available. He simply preferred belief to disbelief even if he was laughed at. His lecture "Dreams and Ghosts," in Dublin in November 1913, in which he argued that dead souls return to relive the most passionate moments of their lives, was mocked in the *Irish Times.*[25] Yet he preferred ridicule to an over-rationality like George Bernard Shaw's, which, as he saw it, reduced drama to polemic, and the mystery of life to the dry and explicable.[26] Besides, he tried to balance gullibility with skepticism. He worked hard with what he felt was a researcher's detachment to put psychic phenomena to scientific test.

They rarely passed. Disillusion swiftly followed a research trip to France in May 1914. Yeats, accompanied by Everard Feilding, secretary of the Psychical Research Society, went to Paris to see a highly sensitive materialization medium; word of her work with spirit photographs and other physical paraphernalia had greatly excited Yeats.[27] They (or at least Yeats) stayed at the home of Yeats's old love and good friend, Madame Maud Gonne MacBride; now legally separated from her husband, she lived in Passy (when not at her country home in Normandy) with her two children.

Immediately upon arriving in Paris, the two men first looked in on a so-called musical medium and found her performance (playing instruments in a trance) boring. Next, the object of their journey, Madame Juliette Bisson, granted them two sessions. Both, Yeats reported sadly to Lady Gregory, were complete fiascos.[28] Undaunted, they pushed on. Taking Maud* with them, they made an overnight journey south to Mirebeau, a village near Poitiers. Feilding had a commission from the Vatican to investigate the alleged miracle of various religious pictures that appeared to stream with human blood.

At Mirebeau the trio was led on a long and muddy walk by the eager local abbé, who took them to a workman's shed. The visitors stood at last before a blood-stained oil print of the Sacred Heart of Jesus on which a few fresh drops of liquid were visible. Maud, a devout Catholic convert, fell on her knees, but the research-minded Feilding and Yeats handed their handkerchiefs to the abbé, who swabbed the exudate for a sample.

Two months later the Lister Institute in London delivered its verdict: there was no possibility that the blood was human. Hoaxed again. Yeats accepted the failure of another mission.[29]

Séances, vulgar or not, gave Yeats better results. What he felt to be spirits appeared to him, sometimes with terrifying force. His first, attended at the age of twenty-two, precipitated a minor convulsion.

---

*In the main, family and friends will be referred to by the names, first or last, that Yeats himself called them. The exceptions will be Yeats himself, who is "Yeats" except when "Willie" or "W. B." is appropriate to the context, and his father, John Butler Yeats.

He was in a poor emotional state when he presented himself for it on a winter visit to Dublin in January 1888. Still compelled for economic reasons to live with his family, the previous summer he had been dragged once more from Dublin to London; hardly were they all lodged temporarily in a dark, ugly house in Earls Court than in July his mother suffered a stroke. In December two more seizures sent Susan Yeats into a private world where she remained (as an invalid in an upstairs room) for the rest of her life. The following month her eldest son, entering a séance room for the first time, was so gripped by the atmosphere that he acted like a man possessed. His body convulsed into a rigid arc, his head banged up and down on the table, and gibberish emerged from his lips. (Later he explained that he was chanting "Paradise Lost"—"the nearest to a prayer I could remember"—to ward off evil spirits.)[30]

Not surprisingly, he shied away from repeating the experience for some years. At the turn of the century, however, he was drawn back as he began studying Irish myths and legends with his new collaborator, Lady Gregory, and looked to séances as a possible means of probing the supernatural origins of folklore.

A lull of nearly a decade in his spiritualist activities followed, as he immersed himself in the National Theatre and public life. His interest revived around 1909, with his acquaintance with Feilding and the SPR. In 1911, during his second tour of the United States, he was particularly impressed by a celebrated Boston medium who boasted an affinity with dead poets.[31] Once back in Britain, he then systematically tried supernatural communication in the myriad forms on offer.

Many mediums practiced "automatic writing" in which they took down the words of supposed spirit voices while in a trance. (The technique had been popularized by Stead as the means through which he received his "Letters from Julia.") Around 1913 Yeats became captivated by a young automatic-writing medium, an upperclass Englishwoman, Elizabeth "Bessie" Radcliffe, who had the gift of taking ghostly dictation in languages as remote from her experience as Chinese, Croatian, Provençal, and Welsh. Her achievements convinced Yeats that he had secured proof of the independent existence of dead souls.

By 1917 the séance was something more than a parlor game. After three years of war, grieving millions turned to the spiritualist movement, searching for messages from their lost men. As Sir Arthur Conan Doyle observed, "I seemed suddenly to see that it was really something tremendous, a breakdown of walls between two worlds, a direct undeniable message from beyond, a call of hope and of guidance to the human race at the time of its deepest affliction."[32]

At a séance in January 1917, Yeats felt himself contacted by a spirit representing the late Sir Hugh Lane, Lady Gregory's nephew. Lane, art connoisseur, dealer, and collector, had died when the *Lusitania* was sunk by a German submarine off the coast of Cork on its return journey from New York in May 1915. Since Lane's death, Yeats and Lady Gregory had been campaigning fiercely to persuade the British government to return to Dublin Lane's remarkable collection of French Impressionist paintings. Their campaign was based on a penciled and unwitnessed codicil to Lane's will discovered after his death; this reversed the terms of the original will, which bequeathed the pictures to England.

When Yeats sat himself down in that darkened London room, if there was any ghost with whom he needed a word, it was Hugh Lane's. As he was trained to do, he followed the skeptic's precautions of not giving his own name and of not asking for any particular spirit. Yet the "Control" who appeared at once, almost as if summoned, claimed to come from Lane.[33]

Its message, however, was surprising. In his afterlife, Lane seemed not in the least concerned with the disputed codicil, but rather with scotching an ugly rumor circulating about the actual manner of his death. An American survivor of the *Lusitania* had been telling people that Lane had virtually committed suicide by wedging himself into the companion ladder as the ship was sinking.

Yeats would have had no difficulty conjuring up the scene; he himself had crossed the Atlantic on the *Lusitania* in 1914 and was well acquainted with the layout of its decks and passageways. Since the sinking of the *Titanic*, moreover, there were few who had not mentally rehearsed the agonies of death at sea.

What the Lane "Control" asked of Yeats was to tell his aunt, Lady Gregory—immediately, in order to save her further distress—that he had tried as hard as all the rest of the passengers to save his life.

Yeats dutifully and swiftly passed the message on to Lady Gregory, his close friend and protector. The widow of the colonial governor Sir William Gregory, she lived in Galway when not in London, and her Galway estate, Coole Park, had been his second, and better, home for twenty years.

The Lane encounter strengthened Yeats's sense of an unseen world trying to break through. In the early months of 1917, he was working on a book of personal philosophy in which he would explain his belief that the "real self" that an artist attains in his art is "an antiself" speaking from the deeper reality accessible only through the magic of symbols.

When the short prose work *Per Amica Silentia Lunae* appeared in 1918, the *Times Literary Supplement*'s reviewer was bewildered. An admirer of Yeats's poetry, he acknowledged with regret, "The beauty that we see is the only thing common between his mind and ours. There may not be sense to us, but there is music; and in that there is a common language."[34]

Yeats's good friend, the young American poet Ezra Pound, was less charitable. He pronounced Yeats's theories "very very very bughouse."[35]

Belief in spirits ran strong in the Yeats family, a legacy of childhood summers in Sligo, Yeats's mother's birthplace in the west of Ireland. Even when they were well into middle age and separated by the Irish Sea, Yeats and his sisters conducted a lively exchange in portents, prophetic dreams, banshee cries, visions, and visitations. In January 1917, just as Yeats was communicating with Hugh Lane's ghost, both sisters reported to him that they had seen the death head; Yeats speculated on who the doomed person could be.[36] Their younger brother, Jack, a fine painter, had the facility too. His wife, Cottie, boasted that "Jack sees visions that Willy would give his ears for."[37]

Their widowed father, living in New York City, was a staunch rationalist and disapproved of this superstitious strain in his children, which he blamed on their late mother. (Susan Yeats died in 1900.) Early in his marriage John Butler Yeats had scolded his young wife for the otherworldly tendencies of her family, the Pollexfens: "Whether from your mother or from some old fashioned aunt or from some servant like Nellie, you have all learned to have a kind of half belief in dreams and so worry yourself and others with narratives of your dreams."[38]

All the same, the old man could not help but admire the psychic gifts of his elder daughter, Lily, especially as she maintained that there was nothing supernatural about her powers. He accepted her explanation that they were the result of a kind of electrical transfer of thought, perhaps by radio waves: "something which the Marconis of the future will make use of."[39]

In middle life Yeats was struggling to find his way back to visionary poetry after his long detour through the Irish theater. (Or, as Ezra Pound called it, the "Oirish TeeAter.")[40] The prolific young poet, who had poured out beautiful lyric verse from 1887, when he was only twenty-two, had published much less after the turn of the century when he threw his energies into the Irish Literary Theatre, and its successor, the Irish National Theatre Society (from 1904 housed in the Abbey Theatre). He fostered playwrights, notably J. M. Synge, wrote his own plays, defended the controversial theater against press and public attacks (including the celebrated riots in 1907 after the first performances of Synge's *The Playboy of the Western World*), all the while coping with the ceaseless internal wrangles over the plays (performed and unperformed), personnel, and finances of the Abbey.

Those were years of increasing confidence and sophistication. Yeats made his first lecture tour of the United States in 1903–4, and dined with President Theodore Roosevelt at the White House. He became an enthusiastic reader of Nietzsche and weathered the turmoil first of Maud's marriage in 1903, then of the ugly divorce case that followed soon after. When he did turn to poetry, he struggled to find a less flowery and more "masculine" style of expression than he had indulged in as a youth.[41] "Adam's Curse," written in 1901 about his own craft, is evidence of a new prosaic, self-referential voice.

> I said: 'A line will take us hours maybe;
> Yet if it does not seem a moment's thought,
> Our stitching and unstitching has been naught.'

Poems such as "Upon a House shaken by Land Agitation" in his 1910 volume, *The Green Helmet,* confirm this change of direction and tone. A few years later, under the influence of Pound's stern modernist nagging, Yeats's poetry was becoming even harder-edged and more autobiographical. Yet it was not magical or revelatory.

Both as a poet and as seeker of secret wisdom, Yeats was a man dependent on images. In the 1890s, under the influence of Havelock Ellis, he had tried mescal and hashish, and learned how "a hashish eater will discover in the folds of a curtain a figure beautifully drawn and full of delicate details all built of shadows."[42] (Maud too had used hashish.) Entering his active public life, however, he largely abandoned chemical stimulants to hallucination. Yet how was he to summon visions? Long years devoted to political and artistic activity, he feared, had dried up the sources of his inspiration. A mournful poem, titled "Lines Written in Dejection," composed (probably in 1915) in what he considered the dry form of free verse, laments that the wondrous and exotic had ceased to appear to him:

> When have I last looked on
> The round green eyes and the long wavering bodies
> Of the dark leopards of the moon?

Having reached his half-century in 1915, he felt his age weighing on him. He put that in the poem too:

> And now that I have come to fifty years
> I must endure the timid sun.

Sun and moon held great symbolic significance for Yeats. He was a fervent astrologer, for whom astrology was a science, not an art, requiring skill and knowledge that went far beyond the conventional association of personality type with zodiac sign and birth date. He practiced predictive astrology, using a highly sophisticated technique to cast a "horary," a question about the future that required projecting the natal horoscope—the position of the planets at the time and place of birth—with its place at a specific moment in the future.[43]

Such forecasts did not imply a belief in a fixed destiny and the absence of free will. Rather, they provided information through which favorable opportunities might be seized, dangers avoided, and hostile forces understood. Yeats took no important decision without doing his astrological homework; he attributed his changes in mood to the stars, used divinatory techniques to guide him through Abbey rows, and blamed Maud Gonne's unwillingness to marry him on the opposition of her natal sun to his Uranus.[44]

Yeats was born in Dublin at 10:40 P.M. on June 13, 1865. Just as significant to him as his birth sign (Gemini) was his first "house," the twelfth of the sky nearest the eastern horizon and a critical determinant of personality. At the time of his birth, the ascendant constellation Aquarius was entering the first house, with the moon due to rise in about an hour and a half. He interpreted this configuration as making him "moon-sensitive," one wary of the proud and distant sun.[45] This sun-moon dichotomy, and its gold and silver equivalence, runs through his poetry and reflects his conviction that his temperament, and the source of his poetry, lay "per amica silentia lunae"—in the friendly silence of the moon.

Maud Gonne complimented Yeats on not being obsessed by the war.[46] She was full of anger, her nephew having been killed at Neuve Chapelle: "all the young art and intellect of France is being killed in the trenches."[47] She turned the orchards at her Normandy home into patches of potatoes and beans, and, with her daughter, worked as a nurse in a military hospital. As a passionate Irish nationalist (owing to family roots and a childhood spent in Ireland) she was neutral in the conflict—apart from her great hatred of England. Her explanation for the war was that "[England], as usual is following her commercial self-ishness getting others to fight so her commerce of existence shall be ensured by the weakening of Germany."[48] Maud longed to be in Ireland but decided to stay in France, where she admired the French for their courage in enduring the zeppelin raids: "Some of the houses looked like the houses I used to see in our [that is, Irish] villages after the English battering ram had been at them—."[49]

The Yeats of 1917 saw himself as an Irish nationalist too, although he had moved far from his revolutionary youth when he had been a member of the secret Irish Republican Brotherhood. He had moved far also from the anti-Crown stance of his early middle age when he had publicly called for protests against the Dublin celebrations of Queen Victoria's Jubilee in 1897 and against her visit to Ireland in 1900. As one of the leaders of the Irish literary revival, he had helped to shift the focus of nationalism from the political to the cultural following the death of Charles Stuart Parnell in 1891. With his leadership of the Irish National Theatre, with his Cuchulain plays about the hero of divine origin, Chief Champion of Erin, and with poems such as his long heroic ballad "The Wanderings of Oisin," he did more than any single figure to awaken Ireland to the power of its pre-Patrick past.

But in the "new utterance" he sought for Irish national life, art, politics, and mysticism were indivisible.[50] For a long while he had dreamed that he and Maud would establish an Order of Celtic Mysteries, a Hibernian version of the Golden Dawn (to whose membership he had briefly recruited her). Together they crisscrossed Ireland, England, and the Channel in their dedication to their linked Celtic, occult, and nationalist beliefs. Maud helped him organize the Young Ireland Society of Paris and encouraged him to take the chairmanship of the '98 Celebration Committee to commemorate the 1798 Irish rebellion, aided by the French, against British rule. He performed this contentious task with great vigor. In 1902 their collaboration reached its peak with Maud's electrifying portrayal of the title role in his inflammatory nationalist play *Cathleen ni Houlihan*. But their dream of a new Celtic order had died with Maud's marriage to John MacBride in 1903.[51]

By the time war broke out in 1914, his political sympathies lay with the Irish Parliamentary Party at Westminster and with its goal of Home Rule under the Crown. That said, Yeats was cool toward the interests of the British Empire. Although he wished for an Allied victory over Germany he thought the British Army in France inept. He resented the government's use of the war as an excuse to halt its grudging steps toward giving Ireland its own legislature. (The Home Rule Bill, despite the opposition of the northern Irish counties of Ulster, was passed by Parliament in May 1914, then promptly suspended for the duration.)

Yeats was enough of an Irish patriot to turn down the suggestion that he might accept a knighthood from George V in the New Year honors list of 1916. He had no inclination for the rise in social status, and he shuddered at what his nationalist family would say if he accepted it.[52] The same fastidiousness did not prevent him from drawing his yearly Civil List pension. Having ascertained in advance that its acceptance would not prevent him from speaking out for Irish independence and accepting that he was mocked in Dublin as "Pensioner Yeats," he interpreted the subsidy as a tribute to his art, given from taxes paid by people in Ireland as well as in Great Britain.[53] Indeed, he considered that he had earned it.

Indifferent or not, he was hardly immune from the war. Sugar and paper were rationed. His London rooms in Woburn Buildings were rocked by bombs that destroyed houses in nearby Gray's Inn and Kingsway; his crossings to Ireland were troubled by minesweepers. Casualty lists posted daily in Dublin and in London brought news of grief to friends and friends' relations. The brother of Lennox Robinson, manager of the Abbey, had been killed in France. Yeats felt for Lady Gregory in her constant anxiety for her only son, Robert, who was serving with the Royal Flying Corps. The war invaded even his spirit life. At a séance in 1915 the ghost of his favorite uncle, George Pollexfen, had appeared to him; George had been Yeats's astrological and spiritualist collaborator, and a fellow member of the Golden Dawn, until his death in 1910. Now from beyond the grave George's ghost materialized to thank his nephew for having introduced him to magic: the knowledge was so useful in life beyond the grave that he was now helping in France.[54] (Yeats, writing to his sister Lily about this avuncular visitation, spelled *séance* as *sceance*. The great master of syntax never mastered spelling. The same weakness is believed to have dimmed his chances of appointment to the chair of English Literature at Trinity in 1910 because in his letter indicating an interest he put two *f*'s in professorship.)[55]

Yeats made no apology for giving precedence to the personal over the political. War was a way of forgetting the self; art was the way of facing it. He had declared in "Ego Dominus Tuus" that the artist should avoid the world of action if he sought "a vision of reality." From New York, John Butler Yeats, in one of his frequent philosophizing letters, entirely endorsed his son's aloofness from the conflict: "It is so much easier to carry a rifle and a knapsack than to try to write poetry."[56]

By 1917 Yeats was not only an important literary figure but a popular one. Lily boasted that one of his lectures in London in 1915 had attracted two hundred duchesses at a guinea each.[57] His works had been collected into eight volumes, his poems taught in schools and learned by heart. His words lodged in the mind as beautiful, musical, and true. Favorite lines were easily chanted in a happy singsong: "I *went*—out *to*—the *hazelwood*, Be-*cause*—a *fire*—was *in*—my *head*."[58] Among his poems, "The Lake Isle of Innisfree," written when he was twenty-seven, was the favorite it has remained. "The Stolen Child," written even earlier, captured the universal dream of recovering a lost innocence. James Joyce sang the lovely lyric "Who Goes with Fergus?" to his dying brother George in 1902. And thanks to the verse inspired by Yeats's unrequited love, Maud Gonne was a living legend as the "perfect beauty" with "cloud-pale eyelids, dream-dimmed eyes"[59] long before she trod on his dreams by marrying Major MacBride.

Yet in his poetry as in his psychic investigations, Yeats sought not only cosmic truth but inner peace. All his life he strove to locate himself between his mother's withdrawn dreaminess and his father's assertive rationality. His mother had ended badly. Three strokes piled upon an depressive temperament had left her, by the time of her death in 1900, dumb and somewhat deranged—a fate that was always before him, as he admitted in *Per Amica Silentia Lunae,* "I know my mind is abnormally restless."[60]

In the spring of 1917 his thoughts were racing wildly. He worried about his future and his health. He suffered from wild nightmares, nervous indigestion, and insomnia.[61] His anxiety was all the more acute because of the approach of a critical astrological deadline.

Yeats had long been aware that his natal horoscope presented inherent problems for his romantic life. At his birth, Venus, the planet of love, was at 90 degrees (or "square") to his Mars and "semi-square" his Uranus: a menacing aspect.[62] For ten years, moreover, he had known from learned advice that he could never expect a better time to overcome the liability of his stars than late in 1917 when the number of favorable planetary conjunctions would be quite extraordinary. In other words, according to astrological interpretation of the evidence, if 1917 was the year for his marriage, October was the month.[63]

2

Counting

(March–May 1917)

All is number.
—Pythagoras

SUCH AS YEATS'S THOUGHTS on Ireland were in the spring of 1917, they centered on a medieval tower in County Galway. It stood at Ballylee, about six miles north of Lady Gregory's Coole Park, beyond the village of Gort, on land once part of the Coole estate but acquired by the Congested Districts Board for redistribution among the peasantry. Each summer since 1897, for periods as long as four months, Yeats had sought refuge and inspiration in the deep peace and utter silence of Coole. He loved the seventeenth-century house, approached by an avenue of ilex trees, surrounded by tall woods, and bounded by a river and a long lake.

What Yeats translated grandly (from the Irish *thoor* or *tur*) as *castle* was a fourteenth-century, square-topped, four-story stone keep. It stood at the edge of a country lane, beside a small, fast-running river. A peasant cottage was attached. Yeats thought he could modernize it to accommodate friends and family, leaving the tower for writing and symbolic inspiration.[1]

The "castle" and marriage were entwined in his mind. When the prospect of buying it first arose early in 1915, Yeats assured Lady Gregory that he would want the place *only* if he were to marry. Otherwise, it would be useless to him. He saw himself as too gregarious to tolerate the isolation of the country alone; as a single man, he ought perhaps to conserve his capital to help his widowed father and his unmarried sisters. He headed this letter with a bold "*Private.*"[2] But he already saw himself as the owner, for it was enshrined in "Ego Dominus Tuus": "On the grey sand beside the shallow stream / Under your old wind-beaten tower."

Thoor Ballylee was thus a romantic advance gift for his bride—whoever she might be. But, ever cautious, he asked Lady Gregory if the property could not be put into government hands for awhile, for if he did not marry, he would prefer to take a flat in Gray's Inn in order to live with more elegance than Woburn Buildings allowed him.[3] Woburn Buildings (now Woburn Walk), a paved passageway off Upper Woburn Place in Bloomsbury, was a squalid address when he took two rooms at number 12 in 1895. Between the British Museum and Euston Station, it owed its atmosphere more to the latter than to the former. Over two decades of occupancy Yeats had taken more space and brightened up the place, yet with its black-and-orange color scheme and trestle table, it still had a bohemian air. In any event, the lease was due to run out in a few years.

Although the urgency to marry came from the stars, there was pressure also from a source closer to earth. In January and February 1914 the *English Review* had carried extracts from the witty autobiography of the Irish novelist George Moore. In the final volume in his trilogy *Hail and Farewell,* Moore, a quarrelsome bachelor, an old acquaintance, and sometime collaborator, laid waste to Yeats's reputation. He attacked him for vanity, snobbery, and a squandered life. Yeats's work was finished, said Moore, his long, futile love for Maud Gonne "the common mistake of a boy."[4]

Moore built upon the fact that Yeats, for all his recognized contribution to the Irish theater, was a figure of fun in Dublin. In his impoverished youth, Yeats had indeed been laughed at for playing too well the role of the absent-minded aesthete, with his flowing cloak, lank hair, shabby clothes, and floppy tie, walking along chanting to himself and gesticulating as he searched for the right rhyme. The later Yeats presented an easy target too, with his penchant for spooks and stately homes.

Moore penned some savage caricatures. An earlier volume had already drawn Yeats lost in meditation by Coole Lake in a huge black coat, looking "like an old umbrella left behind by some picnic party."[5] Now he added Yeats being spoonfed strawberries and cream by adoring ladies at Coole, and Yeats returning from an American lecture tour with "a paunch, a huge stride and an immense fur overcoat."[6]

Sharpest of all was the portrait of a snob. Yeats liked to pretend, Moore charged, that his ancestors were higher than middle class when they were "on one side excellent millers and shipowners [the Pollexfens of Sligo], and on the other a portrait painter of distinction [John Butler Yeats]." He called Yeats a poet in search of illustrious ancestry.[7] (Yeats's well-born friends could only agree. They thought of him one who, as Lord Dunsany put it, "though his descent was from parsons, dearly loved a lord.")[8]

Sage paternal words came from New York: ignore the attack. "No one really minds what Moore says."[9] Father and son, who had fought bitterly, even with fists, while Yeats was growing up, were good friends now that they were separated by the width of the Atlantic. Yeats took the advice and refrained wisely from responding in public (unlike Lady Gregory, whose threat to sue forced Moore to withdraw suggestions that as a young woman she had tried to force Catholic tenants to turn Protestant).

Moore's attack, so cruel, so near the mark, had been widely read. It followed Yeats in February 1914 onto the *Lusitania* where he argued with the diners at his table about it.[10] His bitterness went into a poem sent to the *New Statesman* before he embarked: all his efforts had been reduced to nothing *"but a post that passing dogs defile."*[11]

Moore cut more deeply than he could have known. Yeats was self-conscious about his long bachelorhood even though he had good reasons for forgoing marriage during the years in which men usually marry. As a young man he had little money. Then for a more than a dozen years after their meeting in 1889 he had dared to dream that Maud Gonne might marry him. He had proposed several times, only to receive her cryptic answer that there were reasons why she could never marry.

His sexual development had been slow. With a frankness remarkable for the time when he began the first draft of his autobiography (1915), he traced his late awakening to the age of fifteen when his first orgasm took him by surprise as he lay on a beach at Sligo: "At first I did not know what the strange, growing sensation was." Days passed, he said, before he realized how to repeat the experience. From then on, he said, life was a struggle against it."[12]

He had clung to his virginity until the age of thirty, when a beautiful, unhappily married woman relieved him of it. Olivia Shakespear was the author of six novels, along with short stories, plays, and translations. She was also, not the least of her attractions, a dabbler in west London parlor spiritualism, and she was fluent, as he decidedly was not, in French and Italian. She was trapped in a loveless marriage to an elderly solicitor, Henry Hope Shakespear. Their daughter, Dorothy, born nine months and five days after the wedding, was the only indication that the marriage had been consummated.

When Olivia and Yeats met at a London dinner party in 1894, their attraction was instant. Before long, she shocked him by introducing him to the passionate kiss. Shocked or not, he invited her to run away with him, even though he had no money. But neither did she, and they settled for adultery instead, although not immediately. A year passed before Olivia ran out of patience and helped Yeats find the rooms in Woburn Buildings. She even went with him to Tottenham Court Road to help him buy the necessary bed. "Every inch added to the expense," wrote Yeats in his *Memoirs*,[13] as if to remind more liberated generations that the inhibitions of his day were as much economic as moral.

The investment did not guarantee success. Yeats was impotent at first attempt, "out of nervous excitement," his *Memoirs* say. But once begun, the affair lasted a year, with "many days of happiness,"[14] until Maud Gonne tugged on her leash and Yeats realized that she was his only love. His poem "The Lover mourns for the Loss of Love," written in May 1898, describes the end of the affair with Olivia:

> She looked in my heart one day
> And saw your image was there;
> She has gone weeping away.

Almost immediately, as if in its place, he took up the close but filial relationship with Lady Gregory. (His *Memoirs* say he thought Lady Gregory had been brought to him by "faery power.")[15] In the summer of 1898 he went to Coole for his first visit and, although well looked after, found himself sexually no better off: "Often as I walked in the woods at Coole it would have been a relief to have screamed aloud. When desire became an unendurable torture, I would masturbate, and that, no matter how moderate I was, would make me ill."[16]

He tried to remind himself that, like Lancelot, he had loved a queen. Exhaustion (or perhaps masturbation) was his reward. As his *Memoirs* puts it, "The toil of dressing in the morning exhausted me, and Lady Gregory began to send me cups of soup when I was called."[17] For nearly seven years he did not even try to make love to another woman.

With hindsight it is tempting to argue that the mistake of Yeats's life was in not carrying off Olivia Shakespear at first impulse. But elopement was impossible. For one thing, she did not have enough money of her own with which to weather the social ostracism of divorce. Unlike Maud, who was an heiress with a considerable fortune sustaining her independence, Olivia relied on her husband's support for herself and her daughter.[18] For another, Yeats seems to have had a profound fear of the sexual connection. His belief that his reverence for Maud had made him puritanical and slow to develop[19] seems like the reverse of the truth: that his fear of sex had locked him into the safe pursuit of an unattainable woman.

The love poems in *The Wind Among the Reeds*, published in 1899, exude a dread of the smothering, strangling powers of female hair. (Olivia Shakespear's thick pre-Raphaelite chignon, when unbound, must have fallen like a heavy curtain over her nervous initiate.) The same poems, in their recurrent use of the word *odorous*, suggest a recoil from the physicality of love. In this light, earlier poems such as "The Lake Isle of Innisfree" and "The Stolen Child" read like escapist dreams of a world free from the ugliness of sex.

The affair with Olivia ended in February 1897. For the next two years he threw himself into his furious whirl of political, Celtic, and mystic activities, seeing "any number of spirits" (with the occasional help of a tab of mescal). He was often in the company of Maud, sometimes in Dublin, Paris, and London, and almost as often in visions and trances. His health was poor; in October 1898 he was laid up for an entire month with depression following a cold. Then in December 1898, the busy round of 1798 celebrations successfully completed, his relations with Maud moved to a climax.

On December 6, when both were in Dublin, he had a dream that he kissed her on the lips and proposed to her. Hurrying round to her hotel next morning to tell her about it, he found that she had dreamed the same scene, even more vividly. She had seen their wedding, where the ceremony was performed by the ancient Irish god Lugh. Then, in the light of day, she kissed him on the mouth for the first time.

Two days later she had something less ethereal to tell him: the truth of her secret life, the reason why she could never marry. She had borne two children to a French politician, a married man, with whom she had had an affair for ten years. Yeats was devastated. For years he had regarded her as an untouchable goddess and fought Dublin rumors of her scandalous life in Paris. When they were both in Dublin, to avoid compromising her, he had always insisted on staying at a separate hotel. Only two months before, he had written a poem, "He thinks of those who have Spoken Evil of his Beloved," which concludes, "Their children's children shall say they have lied." Added to the hurt that the gossipers had been telling the truth was the realization of the grotesque contrast between her experience of the flesh and his.

Even knowing all this, he immediately proposed marriage to her again. But she replied as before, claiming, with clenched hands, "I have a horror and terror of physical love."[20] Such was Yeats's credulity (at thirty-three) that he unquestioningly accepted her declaration of frigidity, despite the evidence to the contrary. Not long after, he joined with her in a ritual that they called the "Initiation of the Spear," solemnizing their marriage on the astral plane.

Even so, he proposed one more time—in 1902—and did not surrender hope until 1903 when she devastated him once again with a telegram from Paris announcing that she was marrying Major John MacBride. The small, wiry MacBride was a nationalist hero in Ireland for leading an Irish brigade against the British in the Boer War of 1899–1902. That Maud was converting to Catholicism for the marriage was an extra blow. Yeats begged her not to destroy their mystical work with this turn to Rome. This plea too fell on deaf ears.

A decade later, as he approached fifty and his finances were sound, Yeats had adjusted to a bachelor life. He had love affairs. He crossed the Irish Sea and the Atlantic with a freedom that would have been difficult for a man encumbered with a family. Many of his friends were unmarried. There was no obvious reason to change a comfortable status. Yet he was aware that he had nothing of a private life—no children, no home. He had an intense desire, he later recalled, "for a life of routine in which it would be possible to live undisturbed the life of imagination"; instead, he had "for long periods a kind of fright, a sense of spiritual loss."[21]

At the time of Moore's attack in 1914, Yeats was spending the second of three winters with Ezra Pound in the Sussex countryside, in a small Georgian country house called Stone Cottage. The young American poet with the leonine high cheekbones and tawny hair had agreed to serve as his secretary. This was a service Yeats unquestionably needed. His correspondence was vast, his handwriting impenetrable, his eyesight poor. He had no typewriter. Yet he looked to Ezra, as he told Lady Gregory, for much more. Although he found Ezra's own verse chaotic and experimental, he trusted him as an incisive critic of poetry and a reliable guide to lead him out of the Celtic mists. "He is full of the middle ages," Yeats explained to Lady Gregory, "and helps me get back to the definite and the concrete away from modern abstractions."[22] He also worked to improve Yeats's physique, by teaching him to fence.

Ezra nicknamed Yeats "The Eagle." Living in close quarters with the victim of Moore's attack, he wrote to his fiancée: "the Eagle does nowt but write lofty poems to his ancestors, thinking that the heightiest reply [to George Moore]."[23] Another form of reply to Moore were the memoirs Yeats began not long after. These were to be, he told Lily, an apologia for the Yeats family.[24]

As a student of magic, Yeats had long been aware of the power of number. He did not simply put "bean-rows" on his Lake Isle of Innisfree. He put "nine" ("Nine bean-rows will I have there, a hive for the honey-bee"). He took the evocative name of Coole Park's Seven Woods for his fourth volume of poetry: *In the Seven Woods*. In 1913, under stern Poundian tutelage, he began to tap the poetic potential of the calendar. He gave the title "September 1913" to a sardonic poem about the death of romantic Ireland at the hands of those who "fumble in a greasy till." In *Responsibilities*, published in 1914, he showed how sensitive Moore's attack had made him to his biological clock.

The introductory poem in *Responsibilities* opens with a plea for his ancestors' forgiveness, "Pardon, old fathers," and closes with a confession of exactly how he has failed them:

Pardon that for a barren passion's sake,
Although I have come close on forty-nine,
I have no child, I have nothing but a book,
Nothing but that to prove your blood and mine.

In a commentary some years later, T. S. Eliot called this poem "violent and terrible," for its unpoetic use of the poet's age and family genealogy and also for its portrait of a man who has taken half a century to come face-to-face with himself.[25]

Many of Yeats's readers in 1914 would have known to whom the "barren passion" referred. What they could not have known was the strength of Yeats's belief in ghosts. To the poet, his forebears were live presences to be appeased; Moore had spoken for them.

In asking *"Pardon, old fathers,"* did Yeats consider his own father to be on the list?

By 1917 John Butler Yeats, well aware that he had never made the first rank among painters, thought he was entitled to call himself a success because he had produced such brilliant children.[26] His younger son, Jack, was an established, admired artist who had exhibited at the celebrated Armory Show of contemporary art in New York City in 1913. His daughters were brilliant too—as brilliant, that is, as was permitted lives blighted by the need to support their family and care for an invalid mother. Their Cuala Industries were much admired for the quality of embroidery and printing done with Celtic motifs in the Arts and Crafts style (learned in London from William Morris and his daughter, May, for whom Lily had worked for a long time). His only disappointment, he wrote to his younger daughter, Lolly, in 1916, was that he did not have grandchildren.[27]

His children had grown up in the poverty brought upon them by his abrupt decision in 1867 to give up a promising and prosperous career as a Dublin barrister and to train as a portrait painter among the Pre-Raphaelites in London. By the time the eldest, whom the family called Willie, had *"reached the age of forty-nine,"* the sisters had reached the ages of forty-eight (Lily) and forty-six (Lolly). They were unmarried and, without dowries, unmarriageable. Jack, youngest of the four, had married at twenty-three, probably to get out of the difficult household. Jack and his much-older wife, Cottie, who had an independent income (carefully tied up so that her father-in-law could not get at it), were childless after twenty years of marriage.

Thus the faint hopes of an heir to pass on the family name rested on Willie. Moore's attack in the *English Review* touched this raw nerve of family frustration and stung Yeats into recognizing his obligation to reproduce himself.

There was one other spur to marriage. For five years, from 1908 to 1913, Yeats had had an affair with an amusing, relaxed single woman in her thirties, an occasional actress. Mabel Dickinson, the sister of a well-known Dublin architect and critic, was a middle-class Irish Protestant like himself who shuttled between Dublin and London. Her relationship with Yeats seems to have been his first that was prolonged, satisfying, and affectionate. He asked her views on plays, on Abbey politics, on his character, and on his health. He gave her astrological advice. When the affair began in the spring of 1908, he was exceedingly sympathetic over the imminent death of her mother and spoke of the pain of seeing a loved one suffer.[28] He missed her when they were separated; when together, they read Chaucer, and he gave her long intellectual lectures that, he joked, tended to end with something less abstract.[29] It was she, he said, who had given him the idea for the lyric in "The Player Queen" ending "as long as there is but fire / In you, in me."[30] He addressed her in his letters in the fond way he addressed Maud Gonne (and never Lady Gregory, who was always "Dear Lady Gregory") as "My dear Friend."

History has dismissed Mabel Dickinson as a masseuse. A better description would be physiotherapist—like nursing, at the time one of the few occupations open to well-bred young women wanting to work.[31] The Abbey players had benefited from her instruction, as did Yeats; she gave him some Swedish exercises to strengthen his muscles. From Coole in 1908 he wrote to assure her that he was doing these every day, with marked improvement. She had changed his view of the body. Writing to her from Paris, when their affair was new, he reported his new pleasure in paintings of "strong light bodies" rather than his old preference for the mysterious, the gothic, and the religious.[32] But she was not what he wanted as a wife.

The affair continued until May 1913, when she wrote to say that she thought she was pregnant. She was by then thirty-eight; it would be surprising if he did not sense that she felt time running out. He was so alarmed that he could neither eat nor sleep—nor stop himself from telling his women mentors of his difficulty. Maud Gonne was not surprised; a clairvoyant in Ireland, she said, had predicted four years before that a terrible crisis was approaching Yeats because he had forsaken his old ideals.[33] Lady Gregory grimly saw no alternative, if the rumor were true, to "an ugly undignified forced marriage."[34] The spirit world, consulted through Bessie Radcliffe's automatic writing, hinted that some deception was afoot. That was Yeats's theory too, and when, about six weeks later, he learned that there was to be no baby, he felt angry as well as relieved. With no thought for the uncertainties of the female menstrual cycle, he was sure that he had been tricked. Immediately he wrote both to Maud and to Lady Gregory with the news. He told Maud that he had "been given a piece of false information."[35] As for the affair, it came to an abrupt halt after a furious row in the Victoria and Albert Museum.[36]

There was all the same an unexpected consequence of two months spent imagining himself a father. It awakened the desire to become one.[37] A more immediate reaction to the prospect of fatherhood went into an angry poem written in September 1913, "The Dolls." It speaks of a cradle to which "The man and the woman bring . . . A noisy and filthy thing," and ends with the woman murmuring to her husband, "My dear, my dear, O dear / It was an accident."

Above all, the Dickinson trauma woke him up to the emptiness of his life. Wistfully he wrote to Maud in July 1913, "A mistress cannot give one a home & a home I shall never have."[38] He knew he was lonely, driven to dining out to fill dark evenings. Settling down, he now saw, was essential for mental peace and the resumption of poetry.

The following year, returning from his spring lecture tour of the United States, he detected new signs of deterioration in himself. He was ill a great deal with colds and with what he called variously exhaustion, fatigue, collapse, or nervous breakdowns. He felt that his brain was affected; at times he noticed he could not think or converse coherently. Subjects for poetry coursed through his head and he could not hold them still.[39]

Deepening depression at advancing age yielded, in October 1916, the magnificent autumnal poem "The Wild Swans at Coole." The emphasis once again is on number. The poet looking at the lake sees "nine-and-fifty swans" and thinks of the fleeting years: "The nineteenth autumn has come upon me / Since I first made my count."

Yeats had a tortuous way of composing. Often having written his first thoughts out in prose first, he put almost every poem through innumerable revisions—sometimes even altering them after publication, to the dismay of those who had come to love the original version. As he worked, as *Yeats at Work,* by Curtis Bradford illustrates, he constantly tried different words, tenses, and rhyme schemes. The reader, seeing him blindly struggling toward the goal, wants to cheer him on and save him from wrong turns along the way.

The first attempts at "The Wild Swans at Coole" show Yeats starting fairly far from his destination. He began "These / The woods are in their autumn colours / But the Coole Water is low."[40] He soon discarded "These" for "The," and dropped "colours" for "foliage." Then he fiddled with the second and third lines, "But the lake waters are low / And all the paths dry under the footfall." He crossed out *And all* and substituted *hard* for *dry.* But the line did not come right until well into the third draft when he returned to *dry,* with the appropriate connotation of desiccation, and hit upon *beauty* as the right noun to end the first line, throwing out *foliage* (as Ezra surely would have approved). At last he reached the order of words that, now found in his *Collected Poems* and on Irish Tourist Board postcards, seems perfect and inevitable:

The trees are in their autumn beauty,
The woodland paths are dry.

Even so, it was not until the fourth draft that he hit upon the brilliant choice of *clamorous* for the sound made by the swans in flight:

And scatter wheeling in great broken rings
Upon their clamorous wings.

From there he built to the fifth and final stanza and one of the great rhetorical questions with which so many of his poems end:[41]

Among what rushes will they build,
By what lake's edge or pool
Delight men's eyes when I awake some day
To find they have flown away?

Thus he achieved not merely a magnificent nature poem but a sorrowful acceptance of the fading of his creative powers. The real sadness of these lines is that he did not know how wrong he was.

The older women who cosseted Yeats kept a close eye on his plan to marry. At the time of the Dickinson episode, Lady Gregory had advised Yeats to marry to avoid similar difficulties in the future. During the months when she was in London—she had a flat in Queen Anne's Mansions, Victoria—she brought various well-born young ladies down to Stone Cottage for his inspection.[42]

By 1917, in spite of his late start, Yeats was an experienced lover, a man about town, an Adept at remaining uninvolved. Women thought him handsome; fame added to his appeal. The English benefactor of the Abbey Theatre, Miss Annie Horniman, was obsessively in love with him for years. He had had brief affairs with a fellow occultist, Alick Schepeler, and with the divorced actress, author, and fellow member of the Golden Dawn, Florence Farr, who had been the mistress of George Bernard Shaw among others. Yeats admired Farr for her beauty and sexual exuberance, but perhaps even more for her diction. She had mastered the special form of chanting he liked for the delivery of his verse, accompanying herself on a twelve-stringed psaltery. (Imitating the Farr performance, tucking imaginary robes carefully around him, plucking invisible strings with a loud "P'wang!" and intoning "Isle of Inisfree" in a throbbing voice, was a favorite party piece of D. H. Lawrence, a gifted mimic who had witnessed it as a young teacher in London.)[43]

In 1906 Yeats had suggested to the powerful Irish-American lawyer and arts patron John Quinn that he and Farr do a joint American tour, but Quinn vetoed the idea. An unmarried pair traveling together, Quinn said, would be misunderstood by provincial America.

By that time Yeats's flirtatious interest in pretty women was widely recognized. On his American trip in 1914, Yeats had at last healed a breach with Quinn, caused by rumors that had reached New York—that Yeats had boasted in Dublin of having made a conquest of Quinn's pretty mistress, Dorothy Coates, on a visit to Paris. Quinn, a man of fierce temper, had not spoken to Yeats for five years in consequence. However, when Yeats was in New York in 1914, the young woman urged Quinn to make peace, which he offered and Yeats accepted. (So Yeats told Lady Gregory.)[44] What actually happened between Yeats and Coates is unclear.

Yeats had also succeeded, at long last, in bedding Maud Gonne. In Paris, in the winter of 1908, her marriage over, Maud had allowed their relations to descend from the astral plane. The affair seems to have been brief, but it helped cement their friendship. When they parted that December, Maud once again offered spiritual union and extolled the creative rewards of abstinence. Although he felt more deeply in love with her than ever, Yeats was better fortified now to accept her terms. "My desires must go elsewhere if I would escape their poison," he wrote in his journal.[45] And they did. The Dickinson affair had just begun.

If in the two decades of their friendship the long-widowed Isabella Augusta Persse Gregory had ever nourished hopes of marrying Willie (as she called him), she had long buried them. Their long partnership made them at times rivals, even opponents, with periods of coolness and resentment. Lady Gregory believed, with some justice, that he obscured her own creativity, that he took too much credit for collaborative works that were primarily hers. She had, moreover, annually to endure the resentment of her son, Robert, and his wife when Yeats visited Coole. The younger Gregorys did not like the way he assumed the master bedroom as of right or the way that he would simply hold out his teacup wordlessly for the servants to refill.[46]

Lady Gregory, a stout, Queen Victoria-figure, born in 1852 and thirteen years Yeats's senior, was a sensual woman all the same. As the young wife of an old man (Sir William Gregory was a retired diplomat of sixty-three when she married him in 1880), she had a passionate love affair with the English poet and philanderer Wilfred Scawen Blunt.[47] Three decades later, at the age of sixty, in New York in 1912 with the Abbey Players on American tour, she had succumbed to the gaunt handsomeness of John Quinn—a man of forty-two, five years younger than Yeats. Quinn (Georgetown University, class of 1893, Harvard Law School, class of 1895) was exceedingly attractive to women. He broke the heart of William Morris's daughter, May, and even stirred the banked fires of shy Lily Yeats: "He was the only man except J. M. Synge that she took *that sort* of interest in," Lolly wrote her father.[48] A sworn bachelor, he urged on Yeats the advantages of a "visiting wife."[49] In the brief dalliance with Lady Gregory in Quinn's apartment on Central Park West, the passion was sadly one-sided, as her subsequent loving letters to him show.[50] During their brief closeness, however, the unlikely lovers had a chance to share grudges against W. B. Yeats.

The poet remained oblivious to these undercurrents. For him Lady Gregory was supremely a maternal, nurturing figure, his truest friend. In 1909 he was terrified when she was ill. He thought that she was going to die and wrote in his journal, "She has been to me mother, friend, sister and brother. I cannot realize the world without her . . ."[51]

Another interested bystander at the 1917 courtship drama was Olivia Shakespear, who had introduced Yeats to physical love. Olivia was still a handsome woman, elegantly dressed, with the chiseled features, wide, curving mouth, and serene dark eyes in a noble face that Yeats, only the previous year in the draft for his autobiography, described as being "of a perfectly Greek regularity."[52] There was no longer any question of marriage between them, although by then her daughter was off her hands (Dorothy Shakespear married Ezra Pound in 1914). Yet Yeats's London life revolved around Olivia. He gave her gifts and sought her advice. They seemed to enjoy the comfortable friendship of former lovers who occasionally find themselves back in bed.[53]

In the spring of 1917 Yeats confided to Lady Gregory that the tower in Galway might be absolutely essential to him, because, he said cryptically, a falling out with "O.S." had brought his current living arrangements to an end.[54] He suggested that Lady Gregory cross out those lines after she had read them. Such circumspection suggests that his relationship with Olivia was still unconventionally close—if not sexually, then socially. Her London home at 12 Brunswick Gardens, Kensington, was his to use when he wished. Obviously, as his letter shows, she was very angry with him about something—perhaps his protracted dithering over marriage.

By 1917 Yeats was no longer poor. Gone was the turn-of-the-century look, mocked by Moore and described by the Irish novelist Edith Somerville as that of "a starved R.C. curate—in seedy black clothes—with a large black bow at the root of his long naked throat."[55] His clothes were now well tailored, he carried a pince-nez, and at his evenings at home wore a black velvet jacket. The fur coat brought back from America was made of chinchilla.

Thanks to his Civil List pension and various American lecture tours, between 1913 and 1917 his total annual income only once dipped below a comfortable five hundred pounds a year. The sum was enough upon which to live quite respectably, especially if he found a woman with some means of her own. He had invested his American earnings and invested them sensibly—after paying off the debts of the lean years, including five hundred pounds in accumulated obligations to Lady Gregory (even though she claimed she did not really want the money back). He was so well off that when *Poetry* magazine in Chicago paid him a hefty fifty pounds for a poem, he sent back forty, asking that it be given to some poor writer.[56] He also sent money, generously and uncomplainingly, to offset the expenses of his wayward father's prolonged stay in America.

John Butler Yeats had gone to New York in 1907 on a trip with Lily and refused to come home. He lived in a pleasant boardinghouse run by two French sisters at 317 West 29th Street; when he was not holding court there with his sparkling wit and eloquence, he was being lionized elsewhere in Manhattan's artistic and literary circles. "Your father has introduced the art of conversation to New York," an American in Theodore Roosevelt's entourage told Yeats on a London visit.[57] His remarkable skill at portraiture attracted American commissions, yet any prospect of self-support was doomed by his fatal inability to finish a picture. His welfare was looked after by Quinn, who, as the son of Irish immigrants, took a special interest in fostering Irish writing and painting.

To cushion the paternal ego—John Butler Yeats was an old man of bullying, stubborn charm—Yeats and Quinn arranged to set up a trust funded by Quinn's purchase of Yeats's manuscripts. In addition Yeats sent substantial sums directly when he knew his father was hard up. On one such occasion, when Yeats had sent enough to cover a pile of debt, the old man thanked him profusely, while claiming blithely that he was quite prepared to meet all his obligations himself.[58]

In the spring of 1917 Yeats's sense of fiscal well-being was being shaken by the protracted war. His investments were yielding less than they had, and, with the imminent entry of the United States into the war, there was small prospect of crossing the Atlantic to replenish his funds. Loath to dip into capital for small expenses, he worried about the Savile Club's new-members' fee of seventeen pounds and the twelve pounds a year bank charges on his overdraft. He was also haggling with the Congested Districts Board in Gort about the cost of stepping stones across the stream and of repairs to the bridge at Ballylee. Distraught, he told Lady Gregory (in one of thirteen letters that March) that he would pay whatever the board asked rather than lose it.

By mid-May, however, the property was his. Lady Gregory finally secured it for him for thirty-five pounds, a bargain he gratefully accepted. He dismissed rumors reaching him from Galway that the tower was so damp that you could wash your face in the water running off the walls. All old stonework, he said, felt wet to the touch.[59]

On May 12, he wrote to his father that he was at Coole, about "to take over my Tower, Ballylee Castle."[60] It was to be an economy, a place to store his books, allowing him to rent smaller quarters than Woburn Buildings in London. "Jack," he suggested enthusiastically, "can come here when he wants Connaught people to paint."[61] To Olivia he explained that the place would allow him to live in the country, the only place he was in good health.

Yet the marriage question was still unresolved. In June 1917 he was still so upset, so torn, he feared he might break down as his mother had done.[62] If he was to fulfill his promise to his ancestors, keep the appointment with his stars, and secure his health and peace of mind, he had to catch a fertile, well-off young woman quickly.

3

Mother or Daughter

(August–September 1917)

COLLEVILLE, ON THE COAST OF NORMANDY, was remote from the fighting in the summer of 1917. Only an occasional green glass buoy floating ashore gave evidence of torpedoed ships, drowning men, and the war to end war.[1] Yeats had crossed to France early in August with some risk. German submarines operating out of Ostend and Zeebrugge were sinking coal ships and fishing boats, and civilian traffic took a poor second place to the ten thousand or more men convoyed across the Channel every day through an illuminated route. Passengers sometimes had to wait two or three days for a steamer to be allowed to sail.[2]

Yeats was no Francophile, yet Colleville was a French setting in which he felt at home. He had been coming there since 1910, and the beach, the wildlife, and the big, ugly villa called "Les Mouettes" ("The

Gulls") were well known to him. At his side on long walks among the low, scraggy dunes was a young woman, very tall—about six feet like himself—very pretty, and, to him, subtle and intriguing.[3] She let him kiss her. He was in love.[4] Shortly after arriving in early August, he asked her, not for the first time, if she would become his wife.

Iseult Gonne was Maud Gonne's daughter, the second child of Maud's long liaison with the married French editor and politician Lucien Millevoye. The affair had begun in 1887 when Maud was a dazzlingly beautiful orphan of twenty-two whose beloved father's death had left her financially independent and free to live where she liked, which, because of Millevoye, was in France. Two years later came the day Yeats remembered as their first meeting; she descended from a hansom cab at the family home in Bedford Park, west London, in January 1889, and, as he later declared, "the troubling of my life began."[5] That spring she became pregnant by Millevoye. During that first year of Yeats's infatuation with her, as he and Maud went about London together on her occasional visits, dreaming of the Celtic Mystical Order they would found, engaging with Madame Blavatsky and the Golden Dawn, he did not notice that she was pregnant. On his first visit to Paris, however, in February 1894, he did observe that Maud seemed unwell and climbed the stairs slowly.[6]

When, at the time of the death of Parnell, October 1891, she arrived in Ireland, shaken and wearing deep mourning, she said that she was grieving for a child she had adopted who had died. Yeats accepted her explanation and, loving her all the more, made his first proposal of marriage. She refused him gently, saying (what he was to hear repeatedly until seven years later when she told him the truth about her secret life) that there were reasons why she could never marry. His lovely lyric beginning "When you are old and grey and full of sleep" was written in October 1891 following that rejection.

The child who had died in August was her own: Georges, born in January 1890. Yeats never suspected—not even when he heard her during that Dublin visit question closely his mystic friend George Russell, after several séances and visions, whether it was possible to reincarnate a dead child through a new birth to the same parents. From

Russell's encouraging answer, Maud determined a course of action: she and Millevoye would attempt a new conception in the little memorial chapel she had built for her beloved "Georgette." The result of this sepulchral sex was Iseult, born in August 1894.[7]

Iseult Gonne, although not of her mother's classic beauty (which, to Yeats, was descended straight from Greek and Celtic antiquity: "beauty like a tightened bow, a kind / That is not natural in an age like this"),[8] was lovely to look at. On his first visit to Colleville (the villa was Millevoye's gift to his daughter), he noticed that Iseult had become tall and very pretty. By then he and Maud were drifting apart,[9] and Maud was actually getting old and gray, while Iseult offered the erotic charm of nubility. Soon she too was getting the tribute of poems. Yeats exaggerated her youth. "To a Child Dancing in the Wind," admiring her innocence of desire, was written when the "child" was eighteen; "To a Young Girl," recognizing her sexual awakening, was written when she was twenty-one.

Yeats liked young women, and such was his reputation, his elegant bearing, and his flirtatiousness, they liked him. On his American tours he had been idolized at women's colleges, particularly Wellesley and Bryn Mawr.[10] In 1913, when Iseult was in London visiting her aunt Kathleen in Chelsea, Yeats had enjoyed showing her off to friends. His artist friend T. Sturge Moore admired her, and Arthur Symons found her "strangely exotic."[11] Lady Cunard's comment has been much quoted: "Never have I seen such a complexion."[12] That summer Pound had laughed to Dorothy Shakespear, his fiancée, that "The Eagle" was "burning tapers to some new scion or scioness of the house of Gonne."[13]

Iseult accepted, even indulged, admirers with the matter-of-factness of the female of indeterminate social status who takes what life sends. She accepted that her bastardy was an embarrassment to her mother and to her legitimate brother, Sean MacBride. Without complaint, she obeyed Maud's insistence on being called "Moura" rather than any variant of "Mother."[14] She was not talkative, but quiet and of a literary bent. Her essays on Huysmans and D'Annunzio were (so her mother thought) remarkable.[15] There was a charming French catch in her *r*'s when she spoke in English, her second language.[16]

In many ways, Iseult suited Yeats. She had youth, occult interests, and, through her mother, independent means. Maud and her sister, Kathleen, had inherited the considerable sum of forty thousand pounds from their father, a British Army officer, Colonel Thomas Gonne, plus diamonds and valuables (and indirectly) from their mother, who had died early in their childhood. The income from this wealth* allowed Maud to live as she liked, crusading for Irish causes and disdaining convention.

Iseult, like her mother, was a Roman Catholic, but neither of them found their religion a bar to the kind of paranormal experience that fascinated Yeats. Maud, who believed that Yeats paid astral visits to her in her sleep, was haunted by a malevolent "Grey Woman" who hovered in and out of her life at will. Iseult, for her part, had seen the eyes on her mother's portrait open and shut while the face grew black, then green and contorted.[17] Together the two women communicated with spirits by planchette. In the summer of 1913 they visited a French village to observe peasant women taking down long inscriptions in Latin from scrolls in the sky. Although they could see nothing themselves, Iseult took notes with Yeats in mind.[18] She was flattered when Yeats praised her wisdom to Maud; she looked forward to the visits of "Uncle Willie" and promised to look out for a ghost for him.[19]

As Iseult matured, Yeats gave Maud advice on her development. Thus she began learning Bengali in 1914, but the lessons stopped when the young Indian (nephew of the poet Tagore) who was helping her with translations fell in love with her. Yeats, prodded by Maud, worried about her smoking: "She smokes a paquet of cigarettes a day," Maud wrote beseechingly during one of Iseult's London visits, "and *it is killing her.*"[20]

Iseult did give her mother a lot of worry. She refused to eat meat, had fainting fits, and seemed lazy. In 1915 she began work at the French equivalent of one hundred pounds a year for a large aviation company, a job probably secured through the efforts of Millevoye. (Maud said that at least it would help the girl pay for her clothes.)[21] She

---

*The Bank of England considers that one pound sterling in 1889 had the purchasing power of £52.71 in 1998.

also assisted Maud in nursing the wounded in four military hospitals in Paris, although Maud reported Iseult's enduring "some nasty moral shocks" in the process.[22]

Iseult was no stranger to approaches from older men. Her large brown eyes, wide firm mouth, willowy figure, and vulnerability aroused their attention. When she was a mere ten, she had been sexually assaulted by her drunken stepfather, John MacBride. The attack traumatized her: for years afterward she had nightmares that MacBride was running after her; even in the daytime she was afraid to climb the stairs for fear that he was waiting to jump out of dark places.[23] Fortunately, as a child she did not have long to spend in her stepfather's company, for MacBride matched this outrage by seducing (or raping) Maud's teenaged half-sister, Eileen Wilson. Maud headed for the divorce court late in 1904 when the marriage was in its second year and her son less than a year old.[24]

Helping Maud through the squalid case that followed over the next few years shook Yeats free of any residual squeamishness on sexual matters. MacBride fought hard to get control of his son. He suggested to the court that his wife had had many affairs (including one with Yeats, a charge that at that point was untrue). He claimed also that she was addicted to morphine, a charge that infuriated Maud, who angrily wrote to Yeats, "As a matter of fact I have taken morphine 21 *times* in all my life!"[25] In Dublin MacBride moved to undermine the support Maud might have enjoyed from nationalists in Ireland. He declared that her claim to Irish origins was bogus and that she was ineligible to be a member of the nationalist Cumann na nGaedhael which she had helped to found in 1900 and through which they had met. Stung, Maud in self-defense sent a copy of her pedigree to the great radical nationalist leader John O'Leary, president of the organization, to prove that her family had been in Ireland since 1560. It did no good. She was expelled anyway, for lack of Irish birth or descent.[26]

MacBride had many friends. When Maud enlisted John Quinn to collect affidavits of MacBride's drinking bouts in New York, Quinn could find no Irish Americans willing to give evidence for fear of damaging "the cause."[27]

For her part, Maud was eager to conceal the sexual aspects of her case. She feared the scandal could have reached international proportions. A sexual assault against a child, if proved, carried a sentence of over twenty years in France, and MacBride was a hero in Ireland. Millevoye, more-over, Iseult's unacknowledged father, was a prominent figure in French public life. Maud was concerned also to protect Iseult, then eleven, from having to appear in the witness box. In any case, quite without the assault incidents, she had sufficient grounds for divorce in wife-beating, adultery, and debauchery. When the charges against MacBride were read out in court, the offense against Iseult was veiled under drunkenness—*"cette ivresse devait conduire MacBride aux pires immoralitées"*—but the English papers managed to reveal it anyway.[28]

The long-drawn-out wrangle was not finally settled until 1908 when Maud had to accept a judicial separation because MacBride had proved Irish domicile and the French courts could not grant a full divorce because of the international complications. She was awarded custody of Sean and thenceforth took care to remain in France lest the venge-ful MacBride try to steal the boy away.

It was in the aftermath of this case that Maud let Yeats into her bed. Their brief liaison was the only time in their long correspondence when she addressed him as "Dearest" rather than as "Willie" or "My dear Friend." However, when she told Yeats that she preferred to revert to the spiritual plane, she maintained that she had a distaste for physical love. This much-professed frigidity, however, may have been a diplomatic excuse to spare his feelings.[29] As a young woman, she clearly had been violently attracted to Millevoye. Indeed, the sight of him with a new mistress is thought to have catapulted her into marry-ing MacBride.[30] Yeats, moreover, in one of his poems to Iseult, "To a Young Girl," suggests that Iseult was beginning to know "the wild thought" and "blood astir" that her mother "denies / And has forgot."

In the event, shortly after the end of their affair, Yeats began to shift his interest from mother to daughter. He sent Iseult a fan made by one of his sisters. They went to the beach together. Yeats was a good swim-mer, thanks to his boyhood summers on the beaches near Sligo, and could go long distances underwater. Iseult laughed to see him dive under the waves, with his long legs and long hair. In 1909, when she was fifteen, she had teasingly proposed that he marry her. He dismissed her lightly with an astrological excuse: there was too much Mars in her horoscope.[31]

The Easter Rising of 1916 changed all their lives. Easter fell late in 1916. At noon on the warm spring Monday of April 24, some sixteen hundred nationalists from the Irish Volunteers and the Irish Citizen Army rose up against Britain. In Dublin they occupied a number of public buildings. Their leaders—John MacBride among them—seized the General Post Office on Sackville Street in Dublin, where the poet and schoolmaster Patrick Pearse proclaimed, to "Irishmen and Irishwomen: In the name of God and of the dead generations from which she receives her old tradition of nationhood," the independent Irish Republic. The insurgents held out for five hopeless days in the Post Office and other buildings until forced to surrender by British troops backed by artillery and a gunboat on the Liffey. Court-martials followed swiftly. By May 12 fifteen of the men had been executed. MacBride was the eighth to die. When his turn came to face the firing squad, on May 5, two days after the rebels' leader, Patrick Pearse, MacBride waived away the blindfold, saying that he had been staring down gun barrels all his life.

Maud learned about her husband's death only from a Sunday paper. Her future changed in a flash. She decided that both children would be better off in Ireland than in Paris; she would take them there to live as soon as she could arrange it. For years she had longed to bring her son to Ireland, to have him educated at the bilingual school, founded by Pearse, St. Enda's, but had feared to put the boy within MacBride's reach. Now MacBride was better than out of the way: he was a glorious martyr.

Yeats's early reaction, dispatched to Lady Gregory from the Royal Societies Club in London, was that the Rising was brave but foolish, and the executions just one more example of British incompetence.[32] If the coalition government had only declared that it would honor the

Home Rule legislation passed before the war, he thought, there would have been no rebellion.

His sisters, although passionate Irish patriots despite their long years in England, shared the dismay of most of the Irish populace at seeing the center of their fine city pointlessly destroyed. Lily, from the home she shared with her sister, Lolly, outside Dublin, wrote to John Quinn in New York, "Did you ever hear or know of such a piece of childish madness? There is not one person in the whole of Ireland that is not the worse for this last fortnight's work."[33] From New York, Yeats's father grasped the tragicomedy of the doomed operation. He called the rebels featherheads and their action foolish but saw that some good for Ireland might come out of it.[34]

The Rising *was* madness. The choice of the General Post Office, an imperial building, was dramatically symbolic but, right in the center of Dublin and so easily surrounded, strategically suicidal. The theatricality of the event, much remarked on in retrospect, was noticed at the time. On May 9, 1916, the London *Daily Chronicle* asked, "Has not this revolution in some sense a genesis in the Irish Theatre?" Yeats himself mused to Quinn (as he would do in a poem at the end of his life) over his personal responsibility for romanticizing insurrection: "I keep going over the past in my mind and wondering if I could have done anything to turn those young men in some other direction"; he resolved to give up his London rooms and return to Ireland "to begin building again."[35] As the weeks went by, Yeats realized that he had been more moved by the Rising than by any public event in his lifetime. He told Lady Gregory that he had sketched the outline of a poem about the executed men along the lines of "terrible beauty has been born again."[36]

The Rising threw his own life into turmoil. Iseult unexpectedly turned up in London, asking him to join them at Colleville to console her mother, who was upset, lonely, and unable to sleep. She herself was having passport difficulties because, she thought, she had no legal name. Yeats took the opportunity to question her about her feelings about her illegitimacy. She replied that it might bother other girls but, apart from such inconveniences, she did not mind. However, she amplified, because of her irregular status, she felt she could not risk bohemian behavior in any way. She was furious, she said, with her natural father, Millevoye, with whom she had been on good terms, because he had advised her that the happiest and most powerful life for a woman was as an "Aspasia" (the name of Pericles' mistress, a friend of Socrates)—in other words, as the cultivated mistress (*hetaira*) of an important man.[37] Millevoye was thus guiding his daughter into the very role her mother had played for him until her marriage.

Iseult planned to linger in London for three weeks. Yeats noticed admiringly that she had suddenly grown up and was "quite a commanding person now," self-possessed and elegant.[38] He gave her lunch at Woburn Buildings, lent her books, introduced her to Ezra and Dorothy Pound, and took her to Sir William Rothenstein to have her portrait painted, thinking to himself that if she lived in London, society would hail her as a beauty in no time.[39] Yet when they set out to cross the Channel together late in June, he was determined to propose marriage to her mother.

Keeping Lady Gregory fully informed, he swore upon leaving, as if in a contract (he joked), that he would not undertake the marriage unless Maud vowed to give up politics and devote herself to charity.[40] The stage was set, therefore, for Maud to hear his fourth (or fifth) proposal. The last time she had turned him down, he had asked why she would not marry him and let him make a beautiful life for her among writers and artists; she had replied tartly: "The world should thank me for not marrying you."[41] During the actual affair in 1908, the question had not arisen because, as a Catholic, Maud would not consider remarriage while her spouse was still alive.

The proposal of July 1, 1916, was over and done with fairly quickly. Did Yeats really want Maud to say yes? She was then approaching her fiftieth birthday—not the likeliest age to help him keep his promise to his ancestors. He may have felt that, as the British executioners had set her free, courtesy and old friendship required him to repeat his long-standing offer. There was little danger of his being accepted. His precondition—that she give up politics—was hardly likely to tempt Maud now that she saw a new great role for herself in Ireland as a martyr's widow. With her impassioned piety, she was, in a sense, more married than ever. MacBride was now "my husband." He had died for Ireland, leaving a name for Sean (or Seaghan, as she was then spelling it) to be proud of. Conjugal sins were forgiven as she announced to Yeats that MacBride "has entered Eternity by the great door of sacrifice which Christ opened."[42]

That settled, Yeats asked Maud's permission to put the same question to her daughter. She consented but warned him his proposal was unlikely to be taken seriously. In her heart, she knew how she and Iseult laughed at Willie Yeats behind his back, how they thought he was mean and a snob, and how they had personally persuaded him against accepting a knighthood.[43]

As Yeats turned to Iseult, her illegitimacy did not concern him. If in some ways a snob, he was no prude. He had remained a loyal friend to Oscar Wilde throughout the scandal of the trials. As one who had lived long among artists, the bastards and promiscuities of his friends amused but did not offend him. As the summer of 1916 drew on, his admiration for Iseult grew. Impressed with her writing, he began to think of her as a near-genius—and a paragon of modesty and gentleness as well. He took charge of her smoking, rationing her to one after every meal and two when she was writing. They read Péguy together (she translating), and he listened to her blithe confession that she had given up her Catholic faith, being more in love with creation than with the Creator.[44] But when it came to his proposal, she was flattered and touched, but evasive. He could see that she thought of him only as an aged friend of her mother's. He reported sadly to Lady Gregory, "As father, but father only, I have been a great success."[45] Still, he could not tear himself away. He had stayed so long, he realized with some anguish in mid-August, that he was missing his first summer in nineteen at Coole. He told himself he needed to stay for Iseult's sake.

Back in England in September, he completed the great poem "Easter 1916." In it he used the incantatory power of the list to elevate MacBride to the Irish litany of saints.

> I write it out in a verse—
> MacDonagh and MacBride

And Connolly and Pearse
Now and in time to be,
Wherever green is worn,
Are changed, changed utterly:
A terrible beauty is born.

This poem, like the French court proceedings, hid MacBride's sexual crimes under a fine phrase and the sociable vice of drink. Thus a wife-beating alcoholic child-abuser came to be known by posterity as "a drunken vainglorious lout." / and one who "had done most bitter wrong / To some who are near my heart."

High on the list of all that was changed utterly by the magic of Yeats's words must stand John MacBride's reputation. Even so, Maud did not like the poem, which Yeats read to her on the beach at Colleville. She could not agree that too long a sacrifice could turn a heart to stone.

Yeats spent the next twelve months hoping to persuade Iseult to change her mind. He hoped that Lady Gregory would invite her to London for the winter.[46] (Lady Gregory declined to have her to stay; she would have her for tea only.)[47] He sent Iseult a tempting photograph of Robert Gregory's drawing of his castle. So well did his campaign seem to be succeeding that in November, invited for tea at Dunsany Castle, he was preceded by the rumor that he was going to marry Maud Gonne's young daughter.[48] George Moore had also taken account of Yeats's fixation when, in his caustic memoir, he alluded to his "pursuit of the golden-haired Isolde, whom, perhaps, the poet missed or found in Britanny or Passy."[49]

The whole time, however, Yeats fought the fear that he was too old for Iseult and that, as her mother's former lover, he carried, in his approach to the daughter, some of the incestuous taint of MacBride's. He was gnawed too by the suspicion that he was not passionate or potent enough to claim her: "O heart, we are old; The living beauty is for younger men." To Yeats, sexual and poetic potency were always equated, and he grew increasingly explicit about the connection, allowing himself, in the same poem ("The Living Beauty") coarse sexual symbolism: "the wick and oil are spent." He mocked himself in another poem ("A Song") for thinking (with obvious reference to the efforts of Ezra Pound and Mabel Dickinson) that all that he needed "Youth to prolong" were "dumb-bell and foil." "The Wild Swans at Coole" was a product of that same period of sexual doubt; it became the title poem of his next collection. Over the winter of 1916–17, however, he was also working hard at his book of essays on lunar reality, *Per Amica Silentia Lunae,* and when he finished the book on May 11, 1917, he dedicated its prologue to Iseult, using his private name for her, "Maurice."

August 1917 saw him back at Colleville (after a visit to Coole) for a renewed attempt to win Iseult's hand. Welcome as ever, he arrived the day after her twenty-third birthday. He made his offer and waited. Five days later, he told Lady Gregory he did not think she would accept.[50] All the same, he enjoyed the Pre-Raphaelite anarchy of Maud's household. Her menagerie included a parrot, a monkey, two guinea pigs, two rabbits, two dogs, and cages of singing canaries—"three and thirty," as Yeats counted them for Sturge Moore[51]—with their doors kept open so that the birds could hop about the long table, sit on the plates, and peck at the food. He also enjoyed the spectacle of the now-adolescent boy criticizing his mother's politics. Yeats had much to do, preparing lectures to deliver in Paris in a few weeks, but by August 21 had to report to Lady Gregory the negative if inconclusive verdict: "Iseult and I take long walks, and are as we were last year affectionate and intimate and she shows many little signs of affection but otherwise things are as I wrote."[52]

The family moved back to Paris at the end of the month, Yeats with them. He took his meals at Maud's apartment at 17 rue de l'Annonciation in Passy, but stayed at a small private hotel in the nearby rue Gavarni where the proprietor spoke English. For years he had struggled to learn French but failed, owing, he said, to lack of "the little words I should have learned at school."[53]

Maud was still struggling to clear her way back to Ireland. She was more eager than ever, seeing that, the United States having entered the war, Ireland would have an ally in claiming recognition as a new, small nation in the realignment of national boundaries at an eventual peace table. Her old hatred of England blazed. As Yeats reported to Lady Gregory, she was in "a joyous and self forgetting condition of political hate the like of which I have not yet encountered."[54] But she needed a passport from the British authorities.

An old army friend of her father's, now in charge of the British Passport Office in France, got her one but warned her against traveling, as, once in England, she might not be allowed either to go to Ireland or to return to Paris. Maud could not understand the reasoning. Her rebel friend the Countess Markiewicz (born Constance Gore-Booth, near Sligo), arrested as a sniper during the Rising and saved from execution only by her sex, had just been released from Aylesbury Prison in England and had gone immediately in triumph to Dublin. Why, Maud asked her father's well-placed friend, should the countess be allowed to return and not she? "Perhaps the authorities do not want to have two such mad women on the loose in Ireland" was the reply.[55]

By September 8 Yeats, still in Paris, was trying to convince himself that he was not mad with love for Iseult but merely worried about her welfare. As he had stood *in loco parentis* for so long, he told himself, he was not personally too downcast by her rejection of him. He had agreed to become—indeed Maud Gonne had insisted—Iseult's guardian. Yet the assumption of this responsibility presented a new difficulty. He was still determined to marry by his urgent astrological deadline in October. Would a new wife appreciate a husband with a beautiful young ward on his hands?[56] A jealous wife would hardly give him the tranquillity he craved.

Thus torn, he escorted mother, daughter, son, ten canaries, one monkey, one parrot, and one cat aboard the Channel boat at Le Havre. They made a tense party. Maud was leaving Paris for good; she had realized all her assets in the hope that, once in London, she might get the government refusal for her to go to Ireland withdrawn. Iseult was in tears because, she said, she did not want to marry Yeats but she did not want him to marry anyone else either. Yeats snatched at this straw as the ship plowed toward Southampton, to offer her one last chance and a week to think about it.

England was not welcoming. On landing, the boat train was held up while both Maud and Iseult were searched under suspicion of being spies. In London the two women were then served with a formal notice under the Defense of the Realm Act (the notorious "DORA") that they were prohibited from landing in Ireland. The finality of this rejection sent Yeats into gloom. He had rather counted on Iseult's being in Dublin, out of sight, off his hands. Instead, it looked as if she would remain to trouble him in London for as far ahead as he could see.

In utter confusion, he humbly wrote to Lady Gregory and asked for counsel. Unsettled by having to stay at the Arts Club (as his rooms in Woburn Buildings were let and the Savile Club was being cleaned), he arranged to meet Iseult at an ABC tea shop to learn his fate.

Her answer did not surprise him. With a new firmness, he accepted her decision, warmly reassuring her that nothing would break their friendship. However, he was very tired and had a great longing for order.[57] He could wait no longer.

Part 2

4

Soror and Frater

(October 1917)

FIVE WEEKS LATER, on Saturday, October 20, 1917, Yeats stood at the Harrow Road Register Office in the drab London borough of Paddington and married Bertha Georgie Hyde-Lees, spinster, of 21 Kildare Gardens, W2. It was three days after the bride's twenty-fifth birthday.

The witnesses were Ezra Pound and the bride's mother, Ellen (or Nelly) Tucker. Nelly Tucker was the sister-in-law of Yeats's ex-mistress, Olivia Shakepear. Ezra's wife—Olivia's daughter, Dorothy—was the bride's best friend. Yeats was binding himself into a tight and familiar circle.

Yeats told no member of his own family until a few days before the wedding, even though they were all in regular contact. His sister, Lolly, had a note from Paris early in September, in which her brother had mentioned the lectures he was preparing for delivery in Paris in the winter, but nothing about his personal life.[1] She had another letter on September 30, six days after Yeats had gone to Sussex to become engaged to Miss Hyde-Lees; this letter said that he had been in Sussex to avoid the air raids.[2] He never hinted that the momentous event for which his family had been waiting a quarter of a century was about to occur. This secrecy was remarkable, for reticence was never Yeats's forte. As she had remarked in a letter to their father only that month, "I tell people too much and Jack too little and Willie tells *almost* all his own affairs but generally with great apparent secrecy—and then finds out he has told so many other people the same thing (as a secret)."[3]

John Butler Yeats in New York did not learn of the engagement until after the wedding. The family, however, forgave the surprise in their pleasure; eagerly they shared the scraps of information they had gleaned from Willie. Lily wrote her father: "He says she is comely, so this may mean not good-looking."[4] For his part, the paterfamilias was concerned about the bride's age (too young) but pleased about her independent means. To Quinn he brandished the facts "that her father was educated at Eton and Oxford, and that her family owns Gainsboroughs and Romneys; which all means money."[5] Willie spelled it out a bit further: his wife had money of her own but (perhaps thinking of Maud's wealth) not too much; her annual income was slightly larger than his, and the joint sum would keep them free from worry.[6] Proud of her youth, he told his father that his bride was "joyous & aged but 24," even though she would turn twenty-five before the wedding.[7] When the bride herself wrote to her new father-in-law, expressing her pleasure at being united with such a gifted family, John Butler Yeats astutely assessed the letter's writing style for Quinn as very British—brief but direct and friendly.[8]

The choice of a civil ceremony underlined Yeats's determination to avoid publicity. Register office weddings were the choice of only a quarter of the population at that time and rare for people of social standing who had not been divorced.[9] Yeats's family were Church of Ireland Protestants. In 1863 John Butler Yeats and Susan Pollexfen had been married in Saint John's Church, Sligo; Jack had married his wife, Cottie, (Mary Cottenham

White) in Emmanuel Church in Gunnersbury, west London. Even Ezra Pound had been forced into church in order to marry Dorothy Shakespear. Dorothy's elderly father, whose cold indifference had driven the passionate Olivia to the hard labor of getting Yeats into bed, was outraged when his prospective son-in-law suggested that a polytheist like himself would prefer a civil ceremony:

> **When my consent was asked to Dorothy being married noth-ing was said as to her wishing to be married otherwise than in the manner in which people in her station of life are usually married & it came as a shock to me much later to learn that she contemplated being married other than in Church.**[10]

A church wedding, Shakespear expanded, would show that his daughter was entering the solemn obligations of marriage "in the sight of & seeking the assistance of the Divine Powers." "The one thing definitely indicated by a merely Civil marriage is the precise negation of this."[11] On April 20, 1914, therefore, Ezra presented himself at the altar of the Victorian Gothic Saint Mary Abbots, Kensington, to claim his bride. Yeats stood beside him as best man. Yeats's own views can perhaps be found two years later in the poem "The Collar-Bone of a Hare," in which he dreams of escape from "the old bitter world where they marry in churches."

Yeats had come back from New York for Ezra's wedding. Two days later, visiting a friend (and medium), Mrs. Eva Fowler, he had to listen to her and her sister denouncing Ezra's eccentricity for the entire morning.[12]

At the time Dorothy wrote Ezra that she was worried about Georgie:

> **She was pleased, I think . . . She didn't say much—I particularly don't want her to feel "deserted" by my marrying—I know how it is when one's girl-friends marry. Of course it can't be helped in a way—but you can help, if you like her—which I believe you do?**[13]

Was this a veiled plea for Ezra to get his best man to marry her best friend, who had had a crush on Yeats for years?

Georgie Hyde-Lees had no father to rage on her behalf. William Gilbert Hyde-Lees had died in November 1909 at the age of forty-five. Since Eton, Wadham College, Oxford, and the army, he had led a life tainted by scandal.[14] His marriage to Ellen ("Nelly") Woodmass was, like that of the MacBrides and the Shakespears, over in all except name in a very short time. Nelly's brother, a clergyman, refused to have "that man" in his house.[15] The late Hyde-Lees's unnamed offenses seem to have included drinking and introducing his son to Parisian night life.[16] Yet even if her father was the black sheep of the family, Georgie had loved him very much. Eight years after his death, she was still mourning him, and the very sight of a telegram gave her a shock.[17]

Money may have been the cause of Hyde-Lees's downfall, for when left modest wealth by a rich uncle, he had resigned his army commission and ceased to work. His means were sufficient for his estranged wife and his daughter to live comfortably, with none of the hardship that had forced Yeats, in his London youth, to walk from Trafalgar Square to Bedford Park to save the fare.

Georgie was better educated, if somewhat erratically, than many of the other women in Yeats's life, certainly better than he was. She had attended private day schools in London and later was a boarder at Malvern College in Worcestershire. She was widely traveled and at ease in French and Italian. With her mother, and later with Dorothy Shakespear, she had enjoyed the life of a leisured Edwardian woman, wandering through Italy with sketchbook and language dictionary and scrambling adventurously over beauty spots of the English countryside. She and Dorothy were constant companions in the years before Dorothy's marriage in 1914. Reports of Georgie's dreams, insights, and moments of depression filled Dorothy's letters to Ezra. "She is awfully intelligent . . . Alarmingly intuitive at 18," said Dorothy, who was older, to her fiancé.[18] All in all, it is not surprising that Georgie followed the lead of her best friend and snared an even greater poet for herself.

When in 1912 Georgie's mother, a pretty woman released at last from marriage to a rich wastrel, married Olivia Shakespear's brother, Dorothy's uncle became Georgie's stepfather. Georgie joked that she and Dorothy were now related, and signed her letters to Dorothy "Yr step-pest."[19] By 1917, however, having lost the close companionship both of her mother and of her best friend, she was ready for a fresh start. As a young woman much missing her father, she did not recoil from a much older man as Iseult Gonne had done.

A register office wedding suited her temperament: "an inclination to the bohemian and slightly rackety" is how Foster, Yeats's official biographer, describes the family background.[20] Nelly Tucker's own mother had produced five children in her marriage but only two of them fathered by her husband. Nelly was assured that she was one of the lucky two.[21] Georgie herself was a free spirit. She was capable and practical, liked pranks, and lived separately from her mother and stepfather. She smoked and drank. Her conversation was peppered with the "Christs," "hells," and "damns" of the liberated woman.[22] Her clothes proclaimed her a woman of advanced ideas. She favored an Arts and Crafts look with a touch of orientalism, displayed in button-less wraparound fur-trimmed coats, turbaned headpieces, dramatic capes, and shawls. Yeats, describing her style to his father, who savored such visual details, spoke of her bold earrings and love of strong colors, especially a dark green that suited her complexion.[23] Maud Gonne, in her letter of congratulations to Yeats, also paid a double-edged compliment to Georgie's clothes: "With her bright picturesque dresses," said Maud, "she will give life & added beauty to the grey walls of Ballylee."[24] It was perhaps a polite way of saying that Georgie dressed to be noticed.

The bride was indeed comely—that is, pleasant to look at, what would now politely be called "attractive." She had piercing, intelligent eyes, heavy brows, an arched nose, a wide, thin mouth, a strong chin, and square jaw. Ezra and Dorothy, in their letters, used a hollow square to represent Georgie. She had curly, reddish brown hair and brown eyes and markedly high color.

Georgie Hyde-Lees was certainly not beautiful in the manner of the two Gonne women, who made men catch their breath in the street.[25] That the man whose poetry celebrated women's beauty almost as if it were a distinguishing mark of their sex should choose a wife who was not conventionally pretty was a sign that Willie Yeats (to borrow a vivid image from a later essay) had got down off his stilts.[26] That he did so ought to offset some of the late-twentieth-century feminist criticism that disapproves of the many lines in Yeats suggesting that women have a duty to be beautiful.[27] There seems little point in retrospectively reproaching Yeats, who died in 1939 and who was such an ally of gifted and intelligent women, for clinging to a Pre-Raphaelite idea of female beauty.

In her letter of congratulation, Maud Gonne also reminded Yeats that his wife had "an intense spiritual life of her own."[28] The reality covered by this vague phrase was that Georgie Hyde-Lees was psychic, a believer in clairvoyance, poltergeists, and spirit communion. Georgie's aquiline features and penetrating gaze served to accentuate her mediumistic proclivities. Yeats acknowledged this quality of strangeness when, trying to arouse Iseult's jealousy, he said that he had in mind marrying a woman who was "strikingly beautiful in a barbaric way."[29]

Yeats knew Georgie Hyde-Lees through Olivia. Accounts of the date of their meeting vary. One version attributed to Georgie, has her first seeing him in 1910 when he rushed past her one morning at the British Museum when her mother thought she was at art school, and then being properly introduced to him at tea at Olivia's that very same day.[30] Another also attributed to her, places the date in May 1911.[31] By December that year, she was accompanying him to séances and performing small tasks of historical research for him. Subsequently, he visited the Tuckers in the country and at the seaside, on visits at which Georgie was undoubtedly present.[32]

Drawing them together, in addition to their friendship with the Shakespears, was the Order of the Golden Dawn. Georgie was indeed, as Yeats was to write to many people in the months to come, "a student of all my subjects."[33] She was one of the unconventional women whom the Golden Dawn attracted. Yeats had been her sponsor in 1914 when she was initiated into the Amoun Temple of the Stella Matutina branch of the order. Blindfolded, wearing red shoes and a black gown, with three strands of rope twisted around her waist, she intoned the oath:

> I solemnly promise to persevere with courage and determination in the labours of the Divine Science . . . if I break this, my Magical Obligation, I submit myself, by my own consent, to a Stream of Power, set in motion by the Divine Guardians of this Order.[34]

With Yeats as Frater D.E.D.I., standing beside her at that solemn moment, she may well have felt herself half married already.

"Nemo"—"No one"—was her secret name. As Soror Nemo, she swore, as a dagger dipped in wine was held before her, that her membership would remain secret all of her life: never would she reveal it.[35] Over the next few years, she diligently climbed the order's ladder of knowledge, learning the paths connecting the Sephiroth (the ten emanations of God) with the twenty-two letters of the Hebrew alphabet. She mastered the alchemical principles of sulphur, mercury, and salt; the suits of the tarot pack; and the symbolism of the cabala. She applied herself. In her notebooks, she drew careful diagrams of the cabala Tree of Life and the Brass Serpent (a spiral of ascent to God), made badges of yellow silk, learned pre-Christian Hermetic rituals of swords, passwords, and paces, and read ancient books of magical rituals.[36] She used her Italian to translate Pico della Mirandola, the fifteenth-century Neoplatonist with ideas about the reality beyond reality. She acquired her own tarot pack of the Marseilles design.

As she rose to higher levels and was admitted to knowledge of what were considered dangerous practices, she was invited to meditate on five Hindu symbols, such as the black egg of the spirit, to sharpen powers of clairvoyance. At the ceremony to receive the degree known in the order as the "4 = 7," she became very upset, apparently at the prospect of the intensification of her psychic powers.[37] But she studied on. By 1917 she stood equal with Yeats at 6 = 5 degrees.[38] Thus the couple who stood at the Harrow Road Register Office on October 20 were Frater and Soror, both Adepts Major and sharers of the inner secrets of the Second Order of the Golden Dawn.

Keeping a wary eye on her daughter's fascination with the flirtatious middle-aged poet, Nelly Tucker feared as early as 1915 that he was about to propose and was relieved when he did not. Georgie, however, was disappointed, and when, in February 1917 she bumped into Yeats on St. James's Street while on her way to a séance, her hopes revived.[39] The next month, when he began to drop hints of marriage, she decided that voices had guided her to turn in the right direction.[40]

Yeats seems to have held Georgie in reserve all year while negotiating with Iseult. When he wrote to Nelly asking if he might come down to Sussex to speak to her about her daughter, Georgie believed that her long patience had been rewarded, that Yeats's long interest in her had gone beyond hermeticism and had ripened into love.

Lady Gregory was his only confidante. He had told her that he intended to propose to Miss Hyde-Lees "unless she is tired of the idea."[41] However, when the time approached to carry out his intention, he confessed that he was having nightmares. Words on stone and on parchment had appeared to him. Spirits, he felt, were trying to tell him something about his marriage, but he could not decipher the writing. He could only pray he was doing the right thing.[42]

He hung about London, coping with the Gonnes. Maud was now in the grip of an unhelpful conviction that Iseult was his child, on the grounds that when she was born Maud had been full of his ideas.[43] Iseult, much like her mother in not wanting Yeats but not wanting to let him go, teased him with the statement that even if she loved him wildly, she would not marry him because it would upset her mother.[44] Trying to keep his head, Yeats told Lady Gregory that a friendly, sensible girl might help him settle down and that if they had enough common interests, they might be happy.[45] He then left for Crowborough in Sussex. On or about September 24, he proposed marriage to his third choice in fourteen months. This time he was accepted.

*   *   *

Georgie Hyde-Lees, a sophisticated young woman, was well aware that she was embarking on a risky and ambitious marriage. Herself a passionate believer in the stars, she accepted the astrological argument for haste. Yet, every bit as intelligent and intuitive as Dorothy had described, five days after the proposal, she sensed that something was wrong. Her mother had a long talk with Yeats and then, without (so she claimed) telling Georgie, took action. On September 30 from Crowborough Mrs. Tucker wrote to Lady Gregory, asking her to advise Yeats to break the engagement and to tell him to consider himself free to do so: "If he wishes his release this letter is it."[46] Implicit in these formal words is the knowledge that breach of promise of an offer of marriage was ground for legal action.

The letter was poised and well phrased, one woman of the world to another. Mrs. Tucker did not want to see her daughter trapped into a loveless marriage. She saw how the engagement had come about: "The idea occurred to him that as he wanted to marry, she might do." Georgie deserved better. She was only twenty-four and the very next month about to begin a good job at the Foreign Office. She was "under the glamour of a great man 30 years older than herself & with a talent for love-making." (Even if "love-making" was a conventional phrase for flirtation, it conveyed that Mrs. Tucker was aware of Yeats's past, particularly the affair with Olivia Shakespear. What woman could welcome her daughter's marrying her sister-in-law's ex-lover?) In short, said Mrs. Tucker, the match was undesirable from every point of view. She concluded ringingly: "If George had an inkling of the real state of affairs she would never consent to see him again, if she realized it after her marriage to him she would leave him at once."[47] Georgie went up to London the following day for the publishing of the marriage banns. Dorothy, who accompanied her, was astonished at the nervousness of her usually composed friend.[48]

Three days later, Yeats left for Ireland in such haste that he forgot his sugar rationing card and had to ask Georgie to send it on to him.[49] When he reached Coole, it took exactly one hour for Lady Gregory to set him straight. She hurt his feelings by saying that he was getting married in the clothes he bought to court Iseult in.[50] Then she said that he and his fiancée should marry as soon as possible and that he should bring his bride to see Ballylee before the cold weather and winter rain set in.

Yeats then settled down to some peace, reading plays and tending to other Abbey business, and rowing the Gregory grandchildren on the lake. He also wrote dutiful daily love letters. These are curiously reminiscent of those his father wrote to his mother during their betrothal, as perhaps he knew. (John Butler Yeats's love letters to Susan Pollexfen are among the family papers deposited at the National Library of Ireland.) Yeats wrote to Georgie, as his father had done, that he dreamed of their future together, of how he would find her waiting for him at the end of his day's work, sitting by the fire or dealing with his household.[51] A sign of his agitation in the initial love letter from Coole is that it is, more than usual for the maladroit penman, spattered with inkblots.

On more immediate matters, he informed her of the progress of repairing the roof on Thoor Ballylee. The tower that he had thought might tempt Iseult was swiftly converted in his mind to a place for Georgie. He passed on another of Maud Gonne's dubious compliments: that not only did she and Iseult approve of his choice, but also that "Iseult likes her very much & Iseult is difficult & does not take to many people."[52]

Yeats delicately sounded the sexual note: he expected Georgie to bring him peace and strength and, through these, desire. He spoke of the physical longing stirred in him by her strong bones ("bones" was always a powerful word for Yeats) but also by the magnetism of her spirit.[53] She would read for him to help his tired eyes. He looked forward to a quiet life of common interests studied in country places. He thought that they might go to Italy and remain there until the end of the war. He feared the malice of Neptune, but the letter that Lady Gregory was writing to Mrs. Tucker would defeat that meddlesome planet. He addressed her as his beloved and his dear child.[54]

Neptune was indeed driven off by Lady Gregory. Briskly she rejected Mrs. Tucker's offer of an amicable end to the engagement, and assured her of the sincerity of Yeats's wish to marry Georgie.[55] There followed a courteous letter from Georgie, thanking Lady Gregory for her congratulations. All was settled.

However, the healing power of Coole faded as soon as Yeats returned to London. With ten days to go to the wedding, he found himself still obsessed with Iseult. He felt it was his personal duty to cure her depression, erratic behavior, and chain-smoking. He tried to match her with a mystical friend, William T. Horton, suggesting that the two might meet in the British Museum Reading Room, where Horton was regularly occupying Yeats's old seat, K4.

Horton declined. He was still in love with his dead sweetheart, he was about to turn Catholic, and was he not a bit old?[56] (He was sixty-three.) He pressed another blunt question on Yeats. Was Iseult perhaps Yeats's daughter? No, replied Yeats firmly, she was not.[57] Another friend, however, came to the rescue, Edward Denison Ross, with an offer of a job as assistant librarian at the London School of Oriental Studies. Overcome with relief and gratitude, Yeats burst into tears.

At this point Georgie showed what strong stuff she was made of. Rather than indulging in jealousy or possessiveness, she briskly accepted Iseult as the young daughter of an old friend to whom he felt a personal obligation. She encouraged Yeats to spend time with Iseult and declined to be present herself, saying that the two of them needed to be alone.[58]

She took a graver risk than she realized. Yeats was more besotted than ever with Iseult. One week before the wedding, in a despairing letter to Lady Gregory marked *"Private,"* he poured out his anguish: how he had thought that once the wedding date had been fixed he would feel better, but instead he felt worse. He was in a state of "wild misery."[59] He might not even be able to go through with the ceremony. Perhaps, he lacerated himself, he had simply proposed to Georgie to stop himself from pursuing Iseult. He was in love with Iseult and believed he would remain so as long as he lived. But above all he wanted to be fair to Georgie, who was noble and unselfish. She must not guess his thoughts.[60]

Waiting anxiously at Coole, Lady Gregory asked to be sent a telegram when the wedding was over. Ezra, as best man, was instructed to send it—discreetly worded, Yeats urged him, as the village of Gort was the kind of place "where the parson goes down to the post office every day to get the news off the post cards."[61]

The night before the wedding, Yeats fell ill and feverish. Yet when the time came, he dragged himself to the appointed place and said the appropriate words. Afterward he felt drained and exhausted. But the deed was done. D.E.D.I. had married Nemo; Soror and Frater were husband and wife.

Yeats was determined to avoid the attentions of the press at his wedding. So prominent a poet—his name had even been suggested for the poet laureateship before Robert Bridges was appointed in 1913—was well aware of the unwelcome treatment that the London press, then as now, afforded people in the public eye. However, on Tuesday, October 23, there was a notice in the *Irish Times* and the *Freeman's Journal* in Dublin carried a news report: W. B. YEATS MARRIED. Under the subheadline "Quiet Ceremony in London: Sketch of the Poet's Career" it emphasized his fame:

> Mr. Yeats is perhaps the greatest figure in Anglo-Irish literature, and is by general consent of his literary critics first among the poets of his time. His latest work in prose, "Reveries on Childhood and Youth" tells the story of his early years. He was born in Dublin in 1865, into a family of artists.[62]

The *Freeman's Journal* went on to say that *Cathleen ni Houlihan* was first in the affections of all patrons of the Abbey Theatre, but that his fame in the Irish dramatic world grew less from his personal achievement than from his founding of the Abbey, as well as his zest, as the 1907 controversy over *The Playboy of the Western World* had showed, for taking on a literary fight. The *Journal's* four-paragraph article omitted the age of the bride; neither did it give any details about either of the families or the location of the "quiet ceremony." Lily wrote to her father how their maid Rose had sniffed: "He did not say whose son he was, or nothin'."[63] Once the story appeared, reporters thronged the Abbey for more news, but there was none to be had.

Unperturbed, John Butler Yeats wrote his son a warm letter of congratulation.[64] The old man retained a touching faith, considering the bleakness of his own experience, in the healing power of matrimony. Willie, he promised Lily, would be molded by marriage: "I contend that every man is a kind of wild animal . . . until a woman has laid on him her hand. . . . Willie won't need a heavy hand, but his abstract and self-concentrated mind has produced a kind of *personal isolation.*"[65]

When they heard of the unexpected marriage, Yeats's friends laughed. There was something Chaucerian about an aging bachelor marrying a much younger woman, and they did not make too little of the joke.

Dublin, ever cruel, had long diagnosed Yeats as afraid of sex. His predilection for masturbation, so secretly confided to his memoirs, was no secret to his mockers. It was the subject of a wicked limerick based on the well-known unsatisfied passion of Miss Annie Horniman, the Abbey's financial patron, for the floppy-tied poet:

What a pity that Miss Annie Horniman
When she wants to seduce or suborn a man
Should choose Willie Yeats
Who still masturbates
And at any rate isn't a horny man.[66]

His friends were no more generous. "What of La Beale Isoud with the White-face whom we saw at your house, and to whom Yeats had such a charming and delicate avuncular bearing?" a painter, Gordon Bottomley, asked Sturge Moore.[67] Arthur Symons, Yeats's former flatmate, passed along to Quinn the true thoughts of Maud Gonne and Iseult: how they had said to each other that Yeats had made a dull marriage, and how Maud had remarked that Yeats had found for himself "a good woman of 25—rich of course—who has to look after him; she might either become his slave or run away from him after a certain length of time."[68] Another London friend, the painter Charles Shannon, who did Yeats's portrait, commented to Quinn, "It all seems very sudden and suggests that she is furniture for the Castle."[69] George Russell told Quinn that no doubt Yeats's new wife "would communicate with the dead and the living for him."[70]

Quinn could enjoy the spectacle. Happily heterosexual, he enjoyed steady mistresses, plus regular sprees on his trips to Europe, taking in Paris night life, and, on at least one occasion, in the company of Augustus John, a Marseilles brothel, but he went a bachelor to his grave.[71] Ezra was less caustic. He wrote Quinn to say that he had known the bride almost as long as he had known his wife and found her sensible and level-headed. He added the hope that she might steer Yeats out of some of his spookiness.[72]

Ezra, it seems, did not know the new Mrs. Yeats as well as he thought.

For their honeymoon, Yeats chose Stone Cottage in the Ashdown Forest in Sussex, where he had wintered with Ezra. The venue was a clear signal of what his bride had probably guessed already—that she was taking over from Ezra as Yeats's secretary. The pleasant, if practical, honeymoon choice was more house than cottage, a neat, double-fronted limestone building, with rolling views over heathland and the Weald of Kent, just along the dirt lane from "The Prelude," the large brick house Nelly and Harry Tucker sometimes rented. The East Grinstead railway station was nearby for quick trips up to London.

As Stone Cottage was booked until early November, the newlyweds went at first to the Ashdown Forest Hotel, a gabled, late-Victorian establishment of half-timber and stucco which called itself "a golfing hotel." With separate golf courses for men and women and the kind of dining room where guests spoke in hushed whispers, it was as staid a venue as honeymooners could find. They planned to spend a few days there, then go on to Ireland, which Georgie had never seen.

Yeats arrived at the hotel weak and despondent, complaining of neuralgia and a total lack of energy. Iseult haunted his mind. How was she getting along at the School of Oriental Studies? Four days after the wedding, he indulged in an outpouring to Lady Gregory. Lodged in his head, he wrote, was the ineradicable image of another woman. All he could hope was that his new wife, loyal, selfless, patient, did not notice. When he felt well, he could see the future, but the slightest fatigue sent him back into depression.

The letter sounds like a discreet and despairing confession of non-consummation. He had made a marriage of convenience; the task was to eroticize it.

The same day he wrote a short poem confessing how his love for Iseult was driving him mad. Usually Yeats wrote slowly, but "The Lover Speaks" came fast. Wherein lay the madness? A companion piece, "The Heart Replies," written three days later, contains a clue: it refers to Iseult as a child and Georgie as a woman. A strong current of incestuous guilt in Yeats's obsession with Iseult runs through the poems written for her. After all, he had known the girl since she was an infant; he had slept with her mother, and he had played a part in her upbringing. At a time in her life when as a guardian he should be trying to help her find a suitable mate, he was trying to claim her virginity for himself. He had all the more reason to reproach himself because Iseult, immature, Latin-bred, unstable, unpredictable, could offer him none of the stability promised by the wife he had chosen. In the second poem he tried to mock the unsuitability of his wish for "that young child:"

How could she mate with fifty years that was so wildly bred?
Let the cage bird and the cage bird mate and the wild bird mate
    in the wild.

Then, a few lines later, there was remorse, and a sign of a growing love for his wife:

I did not find in any cage the woman at my side.
O but her heart would break to learn my thoughts are far away.

It is strange that Yeats, in these poems, treats Georgie as so much older than Iseult when there was only two years' difference between the two. In his betrothal letters he had occasionally referred to

Georgie as his dear child, but he had no cause to say of her, as he had of Iseult, "she has always been something of a daughter to me."[73] The guilt he felt toward his new wife sprang from a sense of marital disloyalty, less disturbing than an abuse of quasi-paternal trust.

These two poems (published in 1924 as one poem with two sections under the title "Owen Aherne and his Dancers") were not all he wrote in those bitter days. Against his better judgment, he got in touch with Iseult to let her know how unhappy he was. On Friday, October 26, writing from her flat on the King's Road, Chelsea, Iseult replied.[74] Her letter almost certainly reached the honeymoon hotel the following morning.

In the interval between her writing and the letter's arrival there was a night of unusually severe gales. Trees were uprooted as storms lashed the southeast of England. The scene inside the hotel can be imagined: Yeats as miserable as he had ever been since Maud Gonne's marriage, the new bride confined to a hotel room with an elderly poet in the depths of gloom who sat silently writing poems while the trees shook and bent outside.

When Yeats read Iseult's letter, he found a new maturity in tone. Gently, as if it were she who was *in loco parentis,* Iseult assured him that the distress he was feeling was quite natural. "An abruptly new condition," she wrote, "is bound to have a little of the fearfulness of a birth." She could assure him, she said generously, "that I share your sadness and will share your joy when you will tell me, 'All is well'."[75]

The new Mrs. Yeats learned of the letter because, true to form, Yeats told her. It was the worst moment of her life.[76] Any illusion that Yeats loved her was shattered. Her mother had been right. She had been taken on the rebound. Just as her mother had foreseen, she thought of walking out.[77] What she did instead, in the afternoon of October 27, 1917,[78] saved the marriage—at a price.

5

Folie à Deux

(November–December 1917)

Ghosts are troublesome things . . . There is only one way to appease a
ghost. You must do the thing it asks you.
—Patrick Pearse, December 25, 1915

SOME HOURS LATER on that Saturday—looking back, Yeats placed the time at 6:40 P.M.—Georgie began writing too.[1] In their hotel room, seated at a table, she picked up a pencil and, keeping up a stream of conversation, let her hand wander over the paper, scrawling words with no break between them which ran right off the edge of the page. Something was being written through her, she said. The first words that came (according to Yeats's unreliable memory) were "with the bird all is well at heart." Yeats took "the bird" to be Iseult. Next appeared "your action was right for both but in London you mistook its meaning." Then, just as Yeats was asking himself whether he would ever attain peace of mind, the moving hand, as if reading his thoughts, formed the sentence, "You will neither regret nor repine."[2]

"All is well"—that these were precisely the words that Iseult in her letter had said she waited to hear did not occur to him. Rather, as his letter told Lady Gregory, he had had "an incredible experience," an intervention from the spirit world to tell him that in marrying he had done the right thing. Suddenly all *was* well. Within a half hour, his aches, depression, and utter weariness had vanished.[3] So too, it sounds, had impotence. He could love his wife and, presumably, make love to her too.

Yeats wrote the joyful news to Lady Gregory on Monday. "The last two days Georgie and I have been very happy. Yesterday we walked to a distant inn on the edge of the Forest and had tea."[4] He repeated that he was happy—"extremely happy"—and believed that he would never in his life have a moment of regret again. He enclosed for safekeeping the two poems he had written in his misery.

The burst of miracle changed all his plans. Excitedly, he abandoned thoughts of France or Italy; even the trip to Dublin was postponed. He and Georgie remained at the Ashdown Forest Hotel, where she found she could repeat this feat of free association by hand again and again; great truths seemed to emerge. After the first few dazzled days, Yeats the executive and psychical researcher took over. He began to prime the pump, putting difficult questions into the void to which he demanded answers. He had Georgie save and date the pages and record the place and time of sitting; he wrote down his questions in one book and had her keep her answers in another.

Sitting down twice on most days, in the little over a week, Georgie's hand yielded ninety-three pages. Confirmation that the newlyweds were indeed being blessed with supernatural messages came from the medium Elizabeth Radcliffe in a letter that included the pregnant sentence "And they departed with the rewards of Divination in their hands."[5]

For Yeats the rewards of divination were immediate. He saw the information he was receiving as the foundation for a personal system of philosophy and a font of symbols for his poems. He believed, as he reported to Lady Gregory, that Georgie did not know the meaning of what she wrote. He saw his wife literally as a medium: a conduit through which spirit masters were delivering personally to him hidden truths from the unseen world. When (as he later wrote) he volunteered to spend the rest of his life "explaining and piecing together those scattered sentences," his offer was turned down. "We have come to bring you metaphors for poetry," he said they said.[6]

If poetry was the intention, the mission was a success. Many of Yeats's best-known images—"the widening gyre," for example—are a direct legacy of this ghostly beneficence. Yet as muses, the spirits were highly inefficient. Three-quarters of what was delivered was devoted to matters so personal as to be unusable in the book of philosophy, *A Vision*, that he was to make out of it. The "scattered sentences" were strangely preoccupied with Yeats's sexual life; indeed the messengers seemed at times to have been reading Marie Stopes's *Married Love*, a highly popular book that stressed the husband's duty to give his wife sexual satisfaction.[7]

As ghostly marriage therapy, however, to help a man who much of his life had suffered from sexual inhibition and to whom the female's nether regions were "dark declivities,"[8] Georgie's burst of magic was a brilliant stroke, one of the most ingenious wifely stratagems ever tried to take a husband's mind off another woman. Yet it was also a move of desperation. Like Scheherazade, Georgie Yeats staved off her fate by captivating her master but at the price of being unable to stop. Yeats later acknowledged the parallel with *The Thousand and One Nights* in the poem that most clearly refers to his wife, "The Gift of Harun Al-Rashid," written in 1923. An old scholar praises the mysterious magical wisdom of the young bride the Caliph has given him as a gift:

> I heard her voice, "Turn that I may expound
> What's bowed your shoulder and made pale your cheek";
> And saw her sitting upright on the bed;
> Or was it she that spoke or some great Djinn?
> I say that a Djinn spoke. A livelong hour
> She seemed the learned man and I the child;
> Truths without father came.

One way to keep the script coming was to introduce new characters. The first of what the Yeatses called their "Communicators" announced his name on November 5, making plain that Georgie's interests were uppermost.

> I am here for a purpose & must go when that is done
> I am here for her only . . .
> my name is Thomas of Dorlowicz as I said—as I said . . .
> Goodbye[9]

"Thomas" warned them, as they moved from the Ashdown Forest Hotel to Stone Cottage, that the magic writing would be temporary because it would be harmful for the medium. "Thomas" seemed to know the principal characters in Yeats's life: Maud, Iseult, and Lady Gregory, and in Georgie's too; her father, her brother, and alleged hereditary faults all were mentioned.[10] "He" also seemed to know the details of the marriage bed, introducing a code of instruction as to when and how often they were to make love. On Georgie's pages, the symbols of the sun and moon and of Saturn and Venus frequently instructed when the sun (male) was to go into the moon (female) and Saturn to melt into Venus. In the Script "sun-in-moon" eventually became a private code for the Yeatses' acts of sexual intercourse.[11]

That the Yeatses practiced automatic writing is well known. Yet for decades after Yeats's death in 1939 little was known of its contents apart from what he chose to reveal in the second edition of *A Vision* (1937) and what Georgie Yeats, when a widow, chose to tell the American scholar Richard Ellmann in 1946. Hints that much had been left out of *A Vision* were dropped in the first edition, published in 1926, (but dated 1925), when Yeats openly confessed that he had not dealt adequately with the important subject of sexual love.[12]

In 1987, however, with the publication of *The Making of Yeats's "A Vision,"* by George Mills Harper, followed in 1992 by the full transcript of the *Vision Papers* in three volumes, the Automatic Script was revealed for what it was: a circuitous method of communication between a shy husband and wife who hardly knew each other, whose sexual life had got off to a troubled start, and for whom the occult and the sexual were virtually indistinguishable.

That the Script had another purpose is transparently obvious now that Yeats's *Vision Papers* can be read in detail. It handed Georgie the levers of control over the marriage. The couple had married so precipitately that the basic decisions about their future remained to be taken: where they would live, how they would organize their finances, and even whether they were to have a family. By falling into her stenographic trances, Georgie was doing more than hold her marriage together. She was preparing Yeats to father a child. Whether from her own wish for a baby, from her awareness of his determination to placate his ancestors, or from her eagerness to cement the marriage (probably from all three), her pages gave procreation a high priority—as if she sensed that it was going to be difficult. Yeats's "incredible experience," whatever else it was, was a preliminary to conception.

The effort was enormous. Few new wives can have been pressed as relentlessly by an overeager husband. Yeats insisted often that Georgie perform her magic for him twice a day. In physical relations, however, the text of the Script suggests that the pressure came from the other direction.

Yeats, worried constantly over his health as he aged and concerned about the possible debilitating effect of frequent intercourse, soon learned that he had married a young woman with an unabashed sexual appetite. A danger of Georgie's campaign to invigorate her husband was that he got so caught up in spiritual excitement that he was unfit for his conjugal obligations. With the marriage less than three weeks old, "Thomas" had to give Yeats some cautionary advice:

> not very good—yes
> that depends on your physical vitality
> you are tired 2 days later once is enough
> if your fatigue lasts over two days once a week is enough
> yes

cant do anything but wait—dont eat indiscreetly . . .
you wont be able to do more than you can
yes on one night
quite—don't do too much

no use having a theory if it tires you
The fatigue is the safeguard against excess[13]

Isolated Stone Cottage on the heath at the edge of Ashdown Forest, with its small, quiet rooms and where their meals, prepared by the owner's sister, were taken alone, was a happier environment for secret work than a golfing hotel. "Thomas" now suggested that they burn incense before a sitting.

Yeats had not lost interest in the power of hallucinogens. Among his papers he kept an article from the *Occult Review* of 1906, "Visions Induced by an Oriental Powder," which describes the brightly colored mystical hallucinations that could be induced by burning a substance "similar to incense" and inhaling the fumes.[14] Both Yeats and his wife, moreover, were familiar with incense from their Golden Dawn observances. Whatever form of incense they used after 1917, it was to play a regular part—frequently at the insistence of their "Communicators"—in putting them in a receptive mood.

Was Georgie faking? Deliberately deceiving her husband in order to hold him? In 1946 she gave Ellmann, Yeats's first postwar biographer, an ambiguous account of her role in the Script. On that first afternoon in the Ashdown Forest, she said, she had simulated automatic writing to try to lift her husband out of his gloom but then felt her hand "grasped and driven insistently on."[15]

There are good grounds for suspecting that she was in conscious control throughout—both during the Automatic Script and the "Sleeps" (ghostly voices speaking aloud through her while she apparently slept) that followed. Her "Communicators," the Script shows, were assiduous from the start in cutting Yeats off from his other occult associates and making him wholly dependent on her. He was ordered not to read any philosophy until the work underway was done. He was not to attempt automatic writing himself (even though he had done so in the past). He was forbidden to enlist any other medium or to permit any third party to watch. This last stricture is particularly suspect, for it was contrary to Yeats's wishes. Good psychical research, he well knew, insisted on neutral observers as witnesses to any claimed paranormal phenomenon. Yet among the most conspicuous features of the Script are the fierce repeated reminders of the need for absolute secrecy.

Conspicuous too is the way the supposed instructors follow Georgie's personal agenda, invariably taking her side, praising her, criticizing him. Yeats is alerted to notice when the medium is lonely, hungry, or tired, or when she needs more attention or more sex. He is led, as by a clever fortune-teller, to volunteer much of the material subsequently fed back to him.

Illustrations in the *Vision Papers* also make it apparent how Georgie dramatized the automatism of her writing: sending words careening across the page, varying the size of the letters wildly from small to large, interspersing odd sketches and signs of the zodiac along the way. For messages of particular personal importance to herself, she wrote backward, in reverse, or "mirror," writing. For extra emphasis, she would copy these crucial lines several times over. The whole performance suggests rehearsal.

Against these arguments for deliberate deception must be set the patent honesty that impressed both Ellmann and Virginia Moore, author of *The Unicorn,* an account of the Yeatses' spiritualist activities, and the considerable evidence of Georgie's deep and lifelong belief in ghosts. When Ellmann confessed to her that he himself was a skeptic, she snapped, "That's the trouble with you."[16] Often the automatic writing shows her putting her own independent questions to the spirits, addressing them as if they were quite separate persons in the room from whom she genuinely expected answers.

Her mother's family had long believed that Georgie was psychic.[17] By the age of twenty-five she was well versed in the ceremonies of mysticism. Her allegiances included the Anthroposophical Society and a German-based Rosicrucian rite of Freemasonry.[18] Within the Golden Dawn, her high grade in the mystical Second Order entitled her to practice magic and to invoke spirits. In her daily life she was alert to the work of poltergeists and ghosts announcing themselves through strange noises, aromas, and cryptic messages. She enjoyed a rich dream life. When in 1920 Yeats told John Quinn, "My wife is a witch," he was only half joking.[19] His poem "Solomon and the Witch," written two years earlier, says the same thing in earnest.

If there was any deception, it was perhaps exerted on Ellmann. To him Mrs. Yeats underplayed her involvement in the Automatic Script, claiming that she had persisted only to humor her husband and to shift his mind away from its obsession with mediums. Ellmann accepted this quiet ruse as the full story and passed it to posterity in his *Yeats: The Man and the Masks* in 1948.[20] The voluminous text of the *Vision Papers,* however—3,600 pages accumulated in 450 sittings over two and a half years—reveals Georgie to have been a far more active and intense partner. The sheer volume of the Neoplatonist and Rosicrucian lore that she supplied reflects her years of reading and occult study. Had she been as exhausted and bored as she maintained to Ellmann, she could not have contributed so much.

What the rationalist Ellmann underestimated was the solemn vow of silence under which she labored. No more than a Freemason would Mrs. Yeats have divulged occult secrets to an outsider. The ritual for the neophyte ceremony of entry into the Order of the Golden Dawn threatened oath breakers with "a deadly and hostile Current of Will" by which they might "fall slain or paralysed without visible weapon, as if blasted by the Lightning Flash."[21] Their personal "Communicators" were hardly less demanding. From the start and throughout, the Controls warned them to conceal the spiritual origin of the truths being handed on. "Imply *intervention* if need be . . . but *not guidance of spirits in your life.* That is always wrong—because you speak to unbelievers you destroy our help."[22] The Yeatses were to say that they imagined, invented, or deduced it—but not that they had received it as revelation. Above all, each had taken a solemn oath not to tell the secrets.[23] It was a considerable favor to Ellmann, therefore, that she even lifted the veil to the extent of telling him that the one serious row she had ever had with her husband had come when, preparing a revised edition of *A Vision,* he had insisted on revealing her part in the automatic writing.[24] Ellmann interpreted this anger as the widow's modesty. A more likely explanation is her fury at Yeats's breaking his promise to conceal the spiritual origin of the truths being handed to them. In any event, Ellmann respectfully did not divulge this revealing confession until the second edition of his biography, published in 1979, eleven years after Mrs. Yeats's death.

If Georgie Yeats had been attempting automatic writing for the first time on her honeymoon in 1917, she knew how to do it. So voguish was the practice that the Society for Psychical Research's index for 1917 contains pages of listings of its various forms: subheadings include "script," "speaking," and "table-tilting." Thanks to automatic writing, the Irish novelist Edith Somerville was able to continue as "Somerville and Ross" long after the death of her beloved collaborator Violet Martin.[25] Olivia Shakespear had a cousin whom she described to Yeats as "an automatic writing medium."[26] Another of Yeats's Dublin contemporaries, Hester Dowden Travers-Smith, found such a facility for automatic writing when she moved from Dublin to London after the breakup of her marriage that she built up a professional clientele of thousands.[27]

Besides, if Georgie had been hoping, as her mother had suggested to Lady Gregory, for at least two years to become Mrs. Yeats, she would have done some homework. The script that flowed from her "grasped" hand closely resembled that of Elizabeth Radcliffe, of whose automatic writing Yeats had been an enthralled student since 1913. (Indeed, he was in the first grip of this enthusiasm when he spent two long weekends in the country with Georgie and the Tuckers.) Georgie's script, moreover, contained an image of two winged horses, one dark, one white, which, she knew, much excited Yeats because he had been supplied it on two separate occasions by two occultist friends, Lady Lyttleton and W. T. Horton. Yeats took this double picture to represent the objective and subjective selves in symbolic animal form. It is a measure of Yeats's wish to persuade himself of the uniqueness of his wife's gifts that he did not see her Script as a direct replica of what he had babbled about in the years when she was silently hoping to catch his attention.

Georgie's automatic writing can also be interpreted as a sign of love. She had married a great poet and believed that it was her role to help him continue. Intuitively or deliberately, she was giving Yeats exactly what he told Lady Gregory he hoped to derive from his marriage: a new life built on his and Georgie's common interests to make them both happy and banish the surges of longing for Iseult.

If at times she was consciously hoodwinking him, she was only acting in the way that Yeats accepted as normal practice. In 1913 he wrote: "Because mediumship is dramatisation, even host mediums cheat at times either deliberately or because some part of the body has freed itself from the control of the waking will, and almost always truth and lies are mixed together."[28]

All his life, Yeats retained what some might consider a very Irish facility for tolerating ambiguity and for sustaining belief and disbelief at same time. In his encounters with the paranormal, Yeats also kept a degree of skepticism—the father in him balancing the mother in him. His wife, on the other hand, was a forthright Englishwoman who was less ambivalent about the supernatural. She was, it seems fair to conclude, never skeptical, a true believer in her own powers.

Although Georgie was in charge of the answers, Yeats was controlling the questions, and she found herself writing down an unwanted name much oftener than she can have liked. His most arcane conjectures about the primary and antithetical self or the sexual attraction of opposites quickly boiled down to the matter of "the bird," Iseult. While enjoying the first experience of regular, sanctioned sexual relations, Yeats was still torn with thoughts of what might have been:

> Maybe the bride-bed brings despair,
> For each an imagined image brings,
> And finds a real image there;[29]

With the masochism of the plain Jane Eyre sketching from the windowseat the beauty of her rival for Mr. Rochester's affections, Georgie forced herself hour after hour to deal with questions about Iseult's desirability and sexuality—fifty-eight questions in one day on this subject. Yeats was keen to know what might be done about Iseult's "sex complex."[30] As Iseult was then still a virgin, her "complex" referred to the assault on her as a child by John MacBride, an incident that, according to "Thomas," was still on her mind. The suggested remedy was Freudian: Iseult, said the script, could most likely rid herself of the memory by talking about it to Yeats.

One subject on which Yeats repeatedly sought spiritual guidance was the relation of physical desire to female beauty. He was trying to understand his long obsession with Maud. "Thomas" worked hard to disentangle the longing for ideal beauty from "the outburst of desire at the loins" and sagely counseled that female beauty was not a prerequisite for sexual arousal.[31]

From the early days of the Script, "Thomas," although the dominant voice, had to battle to get through the opposition of "Frustrators." Yeats and Georgie believed that spirits of evil intent were trying to disrupt the flow of communication with false information and lies. Chief among these tormentors was "Leo," a variant of his old antagonist "Leo Africanus." "Leo's" intrusion into the script was signified by his astrological sign or by a rash of triangles drawn like daggers on Georgie's pages.

At this point if not before, the skeptical reader may wish to question the couple's sanity. The Script was consuming several hours a day of their honeymoon, Georgie writing, Yeats prodding with questions, then codifying and organizing the information. In the times when they were not actually engaged in its production, they reread the pages, discussed their meaning, and devised ways to prevent an attack by "Leo." This massive joint endeavor has been called "possibly the most extensive series of psychological researches ever recorded by an important creative mind."[32] It can also be called a folie à deux. While their automatic writing may have been no farther from reality than were the ceremonies of the Order of the Golden Dawn, the aberrant element was their conviction that spirits had chosen them personally to receive the hitherto unrevealed secrets of the universe.

✦   ✦   ✦

The foundation of what Yeats came to call his "System" emerged early in this honeymoon period. There were three main concepts: that civilization moves in cycles of two thousand years, heralded by a kind of messiah; that the range of human personality can be represented by the twenty-eight phases of the moon; and that the individual soul, through a series of incarnations, passes through each of the phases, from the complete objectivity of infancy (phase 1) to the complete subjectivity (phase 28) of the Fool.

This System, in short, described movements. Part of the information Yeats was trying to wrest from his spiritual mentors was how these movements took place. Early in the Script, therefore, references appear to "dreaming back," a process Yeats had learned of in his early flirtations with Indian philosophy and had lectured on in Dublin. "Dreaming back" for him described the way that wandering souls could lodge themselves in a new soul—perhaps that of a coming child—in order to relive their past lives from death to birth. The soul, Yeats came to believe, could achieve no rest until the major crises of its former life had been relived and forgiven.

A useful aid to this spiritual return appeared on December 6 in the form of the symbol of a funnel (or cone, or gyre) in the Script. This metaphysical appliance, like its household counterpart, had a wide end and a narrow end and the function of transferring large to small, general to particular, or spiritual to natural. Yeats came to envisage the funnels as working in pairs, interpenetrated and turning.

Yeats had no need to shrink from the obvious sexual significance of interlocked, gyrating cones. At one point in the Script, he stated baldly: "The overlapping cones Man & Woman—Father & Mother being the two cones inverted into each other."[33]

One scholar considers Yeats's entire System a cosmology founded on the sexual metaphor for the purpose of resolving the poet's five decades of conflict about sex.[34] Yeats would probably not have disagreed. The conflict was for him lifelong. He believed that all arts sprang from sexual love. The young hero of his early unpublished autobiographical novel, *The Speckled Bird*, wants to reconcile Christianity with physical passions, while his poem inspired by Georgie, "The Gift of Harun Al-Rashid," acknowledges the sexual source of the System:

All, all those gyres and cubes and midnight things
Are but a new expression of her body
Drunk with the bitter sweetness of her youth.
And now my utmost mystery is out.

He said it again in *A Vision* in 1925: "All these symbols can be thought of as the symbols of the relations of men and women and of the birth of children."[35]

All may have been well "for the bird" but not for the bird's mother. Maud Gonne, virtually imprisoned in London by the order served against her under the Defense of the Realm Act, was desperate to get to Ireland. While the Yeatses were communing with their spirit masters in the Ashdown Forest, the first Sinn Fein convention was meeting in Dublin.

Sinn Fein, whose name in Irish means Ourselves, or Ourselves Alone, was neither revolutionary nor radical when founded in 1905. It sought to give Ireland its own parliament but to retain the British monarch: a dual monarchy along Austro-Hungarian lines. After 1916, however, Sinn Fein was determined to establish the republic proclaimed by Pearse and Connolly from the General Post Office. In early 1917 the party began to contest—and win—by-elections for Irish seats at Westminster; its candidates refused to take their seats when elected. When the British government called a convention to prepare for a self-governing Ireland within the empire, Sinn Fein boycotted it and held its own. Anticipating the redrawing of the European map at the end of the war, as Poles, Yugoslavs, Czechs, and others pressed their national claims, Sinn Fein demanded complete independence and elected as president of its putative republic the able Eamon de Valera. De Valera, one of Sinn Fein's elected but abstaining MPs, was newly released from an English prison. (One of the 1916 leaders, he was saved from execution by his American birth and citizenship, or rather, by British fear of the American reaction if they shot him.)

Maud burned with frustration. While she read of Sinn Fein cheering de Valera's message that Ireland was as entitled to be free as any nation in the world,[36] she was stuck in a flat on the King's Road, Chelsea, trying to keep peace between her uprooted children. Sean, now thirteen, plucked from his French school, was being tutored fitfully by Ezra Pound. She wrote Yeats that in England nothing seemed alive but the air raids.[37]

Returning to London briefly two weeks after his wedding, Yeats visited the restless family and returned to Sussex with reports of Iseult's melancholy. "Thomas" thereupon advised charging a small object with a magical charm, then sending it to Iseult as a talisman to strengthen her daily self and defeat her antithetical self.[38]

On Yeats's next trip to London, Georgie went too. The object of his mid-November visit was to introduce his new wife to his London circle, and also to attend séances as part of the continuing search for a witnessed codicil to Sir Hugh Lane's will. At the party he gave for her at Woburn Buildings, Georgie could not have been happy to hear him expounding on the subject of his new spiritual experiments.

From his old friend in mysticism W. T. Horton, Yeats did not get the enthusiastic response he expected. Horton, reconverted to Catholicism, wrote Yeats a fierce rebuke the next day, telling him to give it all up. No wisdom could come from unconscious means. "Automatism etc. lead to obsession, depletion, hallucination, utter lack of self reliance & self control, weakness & moral disintegration," said Horton.[39] He urged two books on Yeats, in one of which he recommended the chapter on "Narcotics, Alcohol & Psychism."

News of Georgie's abilities was gaining circulation. The bimonthly *Irish Book Lover*, in its November–December 1917 edition, carried, perhaps at the prompting of Yeats's sisters, the following item:

Congratulations to Mr. W.B. Yeats on his marriage, and best wishes for the future. The bride, I understand, is Miss Hyde Lee, of Pickhill Hall, Wrexham, an accomplished lady who speaks many languages, is a good classical scholar, and shares her husband's passion for astrology. I note that a new book

from his pen, "The Wild Swans at Coole" will shortly be
issued, in an edition limited to 400 copies at 11s. 6d. each.

In writing to his friends about his new wife, Yeats asked them to call her
"George." He wanted, he said, to avoid using "Georgie"—a name he found
unendurable and she had always disliked.[40] And perhaps she had, although
she made no effort to deter her best friend, Dorothy, from calling her
"Georgie," which was the name following "Bertha" on her birth certificate.

Yeats was not the first to call her "George." Her mother used it from
time to time. Her father had named her as "Bertha George" in his will.
Yeats himself at first used "Georgie" and "George" interchangeably.

A deeper loyalty was possibly at work. In the back of his mind, dur-
ing those months when his newly purchased tower was being refur-
bished, the rhyming possibilities of the monosyllabic version of her
name were very likely forming in his mind. Rhyme was supreme to
Yeats. When writing a stanza, his habit was to pick his rhymes first,
then choose the rest of the words to fit. Literal facts were secondary.
When it was pointed out to him, for example, that the vernacular for
the tax paid by his mercantile ancestors was "the eight and six" and
not, as he had written in *"Pardon, old fathers,"* "the ten and four," he
shrugged off the error. He confessed that he could not change the
words without more rewriting "than I have a mind for."[41]

The little poem that emerged in the summer of 1918, "To be
Carved on a Stone at Thoor Ballylee," was a significant statement of
his new persona. It would be the first in which he referred to himself
by name. Although the exigencies of rhythm forced him to omit the
otherwise essential "Butler," the first four of the six lines now serve as
caption for one of the most photographed tourist sites in Ireland:

I, the poet William Yeats,
With old mill boards and sea-green slates,
And smithy work from the Gort forge,
Restored this tower for my wife George.

"For my wife Georgie" would hardly have had the same ring. Besides, the most obvious rhyme for his wife's real name was, as any child knows, "porgie." Moreover, if he had to call his wife by a man's name, "George," the name of his late and closest uncle, was highly appropriate. Before long Yeats's efforts were rewarded. "George" stuck.*

Lady Gregory did not like the change one bit. "Can I stretch my loyalty so far as to call her 'George'?" she asked. She wondered if she could not compromise with something completely different, such as Mary. But more important matters were pressing, such as their forthcoming visit.

> We will be glad to see you as soon as you like after Xmas for a fortnight—I think we shall all scatter by the middle of Jan—the children want regular teaching.
>
> I am glad you can come now (though I would rather have had Ballylee seen under sunshine).[42]

The children she referred to were her three grandchildren, who had had been living on the estate, where she had been teaching them to read and write, leaving Margaret Gregory free to join her husband, Robert, stationed in England with the Royal Flying Corps. Robert, however, had recently been posted abroad. The war was far from over.

In any event, Lady Gregory said, she would not be able to have them at Coole later than March because Margaret was expecting her fourth child early in June and they could not have any visitors in the time before or after the confinement:

> She [Margaret] was seriously ill in London (threatened miscarriage) and has to keep v. quiet—poor thing—a trying time for her—we don't know where Robert is and his squadron have been sent except that it is a place with "icy winds and no

---

*It is as such that Mrs. Yeats will henceforth be called in this book.

fuel"—that sounds like Italy—Don't think by all this that you are not very welcome. You will cheer us up. . . . Please bring your own sugar and stationery.[43]

Yeats promised they would be there at the end of the first week in January. He was eager to show George her tower.

When they returned from London to Stone Cottage, the automatic writing resumed with new intensity. If Yeats was too tired for sex, he was not too tired for Script. He was persistent and relentless. The three sessions of November 22 began sometime in the afternoon and resumed at 5:35 P.M., when Yeats put seventy-three questions and Georgie provided seventy-three substantial answers; there was more work later in the evening. That Yeats had now determined to make a book out of the revelations only increased his single-mindedness. For the seventy-third question he asked what might have come first of all: "Why were we two chosen for each other"?[44]

The answer, written backward and repeated five times, was: "One needs material protection the other emotional protection"—a fair, if cold, summing up of their quid pro quo. The emotional protection, the Script amplified, was for the medium, who suffered from "her own distrust of self and moods."[45]

The Script gave him little emotional shelter. While together he and George were "the collaborators" and she herself was "the medium," Yeats on his own was addressed bluntly as "you." But he did not ask for respect. The work was too absorbing. Together they were creating, with the help of the rituals of the Golden Dawn, the symbols of the tarot pack, lashings of Blake and bits of Freud, Boehme, Swedenborg, and Nietzsche, their own religion.

Arrogant, perhaps, but poets need no apology. Yeats was as convinced as Plato that what we know as reality is just a shadow of the real world. If he could get the right metaphors, he could break through to this over-arching reality, and he trusted his fantasies to lead the way. Reverie was the very foundation of his poetry: "*In dreams begins responsibility*," declares the epigraph to his volume *Responsibilities*. He had also written, to explain his fascination with the old carvings of faces that Ireland had in abundance: "These imaginary people are created out of the deepest instinct of man . . . whatever I can imagine those mouths speaking may be the nearest I can go to the truth."[46]

This confidence in reverie appeared in his response to a questionnaire on creative effort sent him sometime between 1926 and 1927 by the Psychological Laboratory of Cambridge University as part of a visiting Harvard doctoral candidate's statistical and experimental study of "the process of scientific and artistic creation." One question asked about "activities during the period of productive inclination:" "What are your intellectual activities during this period?" Were they "vague day-dreaming along lines determined by the nature of the work?"[47]

Given the choice of "Always—Usually—Seldom—Never" Yeats struck out the last three, chose "Always," and firmly underlined it. "Reverie," however, is not the word for the intellectual activity that went into the System. Yeats expended a vast amount of time assigning great men of the past to the appropriate phase of the moon. He would feed the names to George; her writing would deliver the decision. This involved much discussion between them, for determining a classification was not a matter of intuition but rather of assessing the balance between opposing forces in the personality in question—opposites that Yeats came to call the Ego and the Mask. (Later he replaced "Ego" with "Will.") He treated his assignments with the utmost seriousness. Should William Blake be moved to phase 13 and Aubrey Beardsley allowed to remain there? Was it right to move Keats (named more than any other writer in the Automatic Script) from phase 12 to phase 14?

Because the Script was a completely private exercise, the need for logic and consistency was minimal. If George's answers sometimes were vague, fragmentary, or contradictory, Yeats had no recourse but to try again. When he asked "Thomas," for example, whether he came only when questioned or whether he lodged in their thoughts, dreams, and imaginations at other times, the answer was havering, to say the least. To Yeats's "Does it sometimes happen that a spirit returns & communicates because in his dream life he has come to crisis which accords with that of those with whom he communicates," George's hand returned an unhelpful "No in such a crisis he has to get in touch with some medium who may unconsciously help him through that crisis But it may happen that a spirit is sent to communicate with someone who is passing through crisis similar experience."[48]

George did not take dictation only from spirits. "I am dictating this to my wife" was a standard opening on Yeats's letters after October 1917. Being Mrs. Yeats, so George was learning, was a full-time job, and she had not yet encountered his sisters' shaky business enterprises or his father's incessant bills. Among the duties she took over was the correspondence with Rafferty, the builder who was renovating Thoor Ballylee. She did more. She paid, from her own bank account, the bills for the tower she had never seen in the country she had never visited.[49] Yeats uneasily felt that she should not spend any more on the tower until she had seen it. When he wrote warmly to Lady Gregory in mid-December, "My wife is a perfect wife, kind, wise, and unselfish . . . She has made my life serene and full of order," he was not exaggerating.[50]

George was amanuensis as well for a play that sprang into Yeats's mind simultaneously with his marriage and the arrival of his System. *The Only Jealousy of Emer,* based on the Irish legend of Cuchulain's marriage,[51] is in the spare style of the Japanese Noh, with masks, musicians, and an encounter with the supernatural. Transcribing its dialogue was a real test of George's composure, for the plot dramatizes the triangle at the heart of her marriage and leaves the rescuing, self-sacrificing wife as the loser.

The two male characters in the play illuminate Yeats's divided view of himself. On the one hand, there is the ancient Irish hero Cuchulain ("amorous, violent, renowned Cuchulain"); on the other, Cuchulain's anti-self, a twisted cripple, Bricriu. As the play opens, Cuchulain is believed to be dead and is mourned by his new wife, Emer. His place is taken by Bricriu, who looks like him except for a grotesque face and a withered right arm. (This deformity seems as vivid a warning of the dangers of masturbation as a dramatic poet could devise: the arm has withered as the result of "too great an absorption in the antithetical self."[52]

Three women are struggling over Cuchulain in roles not very different from those played by George, Maud, and Iseult. Queen Emer is robust, worldly, and decisive, fighting to reclaim her husband from the spell of the mesmerizing, statuesque moon-goddess Fand. But she finds she must also rescue him from his desire for his young mistress, Eithne Inguba. Both Fand and Eithne Inguba are described as exquisitely beautiful.

The Queen nobly struggles to forgive the young mistress:

Come hither, come sit beside the bed; do
Not be afraid, it was I that sent for you.

But Eithne Inguba is too guilty to accept:

No, madam. I have wronged
You too deeply to sit there.

As the short play ends, Bricriu shrieks at Emer that she must renounce her husband's love if she wishes to rescue him from Fand's other world. The noble Emer makes the sacrifice, only to see Eithne Inguba come in and take Cuchulain back into her arms.

Emer clearly has much to be jealous about.

Undeterred by the unhappy ending of this allegory, George strove to enact it. On the eve of another trip to London in early December, "Thomas" addressed Yeats directly in the imperative and ordered him (after telling him to take more exercise) to take Iseult with him and his wife as they made their social rounds.[53] Their company might help her solve her problems.

The couple obeyed "Thomas." One evening when Iseult was summoned to dinner at Woburn Buildings (where George had brightened up the rooms with modern furniture and purple pottery dishes), they suggested to her that she seemed tired and invited her to stay the night. Next morning—as if he had not read his own play—Yeats marveled at the growing closeness between the two young women. Watching them gossiping away about fashion and oriental languages, he was pleased to think that their friendship was both genuine yet formed to please him.

*   *   *

George then surpassed her own selflessness. She rejected their plans to spend the holiday with Edmund Dulac, and instead invited Iseult to spend Christmas with her and Yeats in Sussex. Iseult needed country air, she said. Further, to Yeats's great satisfaction, she bought Iseult a dress.

The first Christmas of the Yeatses' married life, therefore, found them *à trois* in the Ashdown Forest (in a different house, as Stone Cottage was booked up). The Automatic Script returned with vigor. A host of new names began to hover through George's automatic pages: "Isabella of the Rose" (or "Rose"), "Leaf," and "Aymor," in addition to the ever-faithful "Thomas." Two days before Christmas, following an exuberant burst of scratchy sketches of a cat's head, a house with a boat inside it, and a star, there was a command to Yeats—in mirror writing, repeated three times—to watch out that his love for Iseult did not prevent her from getting married.[54] "Thomas," speaking collectively for all the assembled spirits, then offered what was tantamount to a ghostly Christmas gift for George. It was a drawing of a ring, accompanied by a prediction for Iseult's future that was so important George wrote it four times, backward:

It will be a marriage ring soon to be on her hand . . . We do not err when we make judgement on these matters.

It will be a marriage ring soon to be on her hand . . . We do not err when we make judgement on these matters.

It will be a marriage ring soon to be on her hand . . . We do not err when we make judgement on these matters.

It will be a marriage ring soon to be on her hand . . . We do not err when we make judgement on these matters.

Thus ended the eventful year of 1917. If Lady Gregory expected them at Coole by the end of the first week in January, as Yeats had promised, she was due to be disappointed. George's ghosts had other plans.

6

An Adventure

(January–March 1918)

When one reads these strange pages of one long gone one feels that one is
at one with one who once . . .
—James Joyce, *Ulysses*

THE TURN OF THE YEAR into 1918 found them not in Ireland but in
Oxford, installed in a pleasant rented house at 45 Broad Street across
from the Bodleian Library. Yeats believed that spirits had brought them
there to continue their mystical explorations. There were other advan-
tages. In a stroke they had gotten out of reach of the zeppelins, found
a place where they could entertain weekend guests, and provided
themselves with a cozier equivalent of the British Museum.

The move to Oxford was accomplished with the easy mobility of
their times. The Yeatses, like many of their friends, shifted from one

rented place to another with no apparent disequilibrium. Renting out their own rooms in Woburn Buildings, they furnished their Oxford quarters with the contents of George's mother's London house, which had just been let to tenants unfurnished. They then set to work. Their discovery of what Yeats described to Lady Gregory as "a very profound, very exciting mystical philosophy . . . which makes me feel that for the first time that I understand human life"[1] left masses of work to be done: the blend of magic and scholarship that Yeats loved.

Bolstered now by a wife who read Dante and Pico della Mirandola in the original and who owned the complete works of Plotinus, Yeats mimicked once again the university education he never had. Quickly he found himself a corner of the Bodleian and covered a desk with old etchings and woodcuts. The Bodleian was, he declared, "the most friendly comfortable library in the world and I suppose the most beautiful . . . One can leave one's books on one's table and read them at odd moments."[2]

The long-postponed trip to Ireland was postponed once again. Yeats warmed to the idea of working without interruption; that was why he had married. For her part, George had no great eagerness to get to Coole to stay with Lady Gregory. The matchmaking Augusta had cut her dead several times in the Stone Cottage years, seeing her as a rival to the prospective brides she was presenting for Yeats's attention.

Oxford had many attractions. George's cousin, Grace Spurnaway, with whom she was on affectionate terms, was in her second year at the Oxford women's college St. Hugh's. As luck would have it, the principal and vice principal of St. Hugh's were the authors of a psychic book that had greatly excited the Yeatses. *An Adventure,* a highly popular book, first published in 1911 under pseudonyms by Charlotte Moberly and Eleanor Jourdain, and under their real names in 1913, went into many editions with its account of their visionary encounter during a visit to Versailles in 1901 with Marie Antoinette and other eighteenth-century figures wearing the dress of the court of Louis XVI. The authenticity of their experience was confirmed when the authors later discovered old documents attesting that certain landscape features they had observed that remarkable day in 1901 had disappeared from the gardens long before. Library research was the key to their *Adventure*. The book vividly conveys the excitement of coming across historical evidence in the Bodleian.

The two academics (whom Yeats hoped to meet while he was in Oxford) did not consider themselves occultists in any way. Rather, they believed that their glimpse of Marie Antoinette, just like their sighting of the ghost of the emperor Constantine in the Louvre on another trip to Paris, was no hallucination but a genuine instance of transportation back in time. The Society for Psychical Research supported their view, after initial skepticism, and accepted their Versailles experience as "a singular instance of retrocognitive vision."[3] Influenced undoubtedly by Albert Einstein's recently published general theory of relavity, the Society seemed now to appreciate that space and time were somehow interchangeable and that there was therefore no scientific reason why people of the twentieth century should not have physical encounters with those of the past.

The move to Oxford did not halt the Automatic Script for even a day. On New Year's Eve George recorded a new Communicator called "Fish," who began peremptorily: "Well ask questions." Yeats obliged by asking for help with a new definition of beauty. "Fish" did not bite. "That is a thing you must write for yourself" was the reply.[4]

"Fish" was what George considered a Guide. In her explanations to Yeats about the messages coming to her from the spirit world, she differentiated between Controls, spirits who once were human and who offered wisdom, and Guides. Guides bore the names of natural objects and gave advice on practical matters, as "Fish" demonstrated by briskly ordering the couple not to make their Irish trip until after a long period of rest. Immediately, George wired Lady Gregory to say that they would not come to Coole until spring.

"Fish" was joined by "Leaf"; then "Thomas" reappeared. The names of all three were in George's script on January 6, 1918, when Yeats meekly sought spiritual confirmation of their revised timetable. "Will it suit your plans if we go to Ireland at the end of March?" he asked. Yes, he was told, if his health permitted. Then, getting down to the matter at hand, Yeats asked how much automatic writing he and

George might safely do. The answer came back confidently. "As much as medium likes." Mental fatigue, the Script amplified, was to be avoided, but sexual fatigue was nothing to worry about unless the medium was otherwise tired.[5]

Once more George's rapport with her invisible messengers did nothing to lighten her duties. On New Year's Day alone, in spite of having moved her household fifty miles from London to Oxford, she produced answers to fifty-six questions. The exercise must have been nerve-racking, for what she wrote down vitally affected her own life and Yeats's feelings about Iseult. He posed questions about abstruse concepts for which she had no clearer grasp of the answers than he had of the questions. To his "Do mortal & immortal share a very different life in dreaming?" for example, she came back with "Not in all cases but often."[6] And there were eighty-five more such exchanges (thirty-one before dinner, fifty-four after) the next day.

Not surprisingly, the medium was often tired. Yeats, while in awe of his wife's learning and attunement to the unseen world, was also bullying. He prodded and prodded. He complained when "Thomas" contradicted himself. Time and again the Script pointed out that the medium was exhausted, and it began to contain instructions on how Yeats should organize his day: to take a nap, to avoid sessions that went on for more than an hour without stopping, and occasionally to take a long break. These respites, however, seldom lasted as long as ordained. The indefatigable Yeats, in spite of the move and a bad cold, managed also to finish *The Only Jealousy of Emer* and form the idea for a new play.

From the time of the move to Oxford, the Automatic Script may be read as an exotic exercise in family planning. The couple, to judge from the notes Yeats kept as a commentary to the script, had decided to have a child. Trying to work out the astrologically propitious moment to stop using contraception, they cast a horary for their child's possible birthdate and presented it to "Fish." Once again "Fish" was dismissive: if conception were to occur, the forecast would be correct, "but I am not a doctor."[7] In the next breath, "Fish" was more forthcoming, pointing out that when George had cast a horary the previous March, her marriage had not immediately resulted. (These lines in the Script revealed that George had been using the stars the previous year to try to catch Yeats; they constituted such a personal confession that the pages on which they were written were removed from George's notebook—either by her or by her husband—and filed away separately.)[8]

By the end of their first month in Oxford the planned child had grown in their imagination to something much grander than an ordinary baby. It was to be a new messiah, redeemer, or initiate who, like Christ or Buddha, would introduce a new cycle of history. This approaching redeemer and new era was fundamental to Yeats's "System" and (more important to his readers) to the powerful poetry he was to make out of it.

Thoughts of birth were interrupted by death. On January 23, 1918, Robert Gregory was killed in action in Italy. He never received his mother's last letter, which was returned to her unopened. A clipping in her files reads:

Major Robert Gregory, R.F.C., of Coole Park, Co. Galway, killed in action on January 23rd. The only son of the late Rt. Hon. Sir William Gregory, he was educated at Harrow, where he took the first classical scholarship of the year, and at New College, Oxford.[9]

From Coole came a brief note from Lady Gregory to say that the dreaded telegram had arrived.[10] She asked Yeats if he would write something in commemoration.

It was a difficult assignment, and the Script faltered for a time. Yeats's own relations with the heir of Coole had been strained. While he praised Robert unreservedly in a grieving letter to Quinn and had sincerely admired the work Robert had done as a painter and as stage designer for the Abbey, Yeats had long held reservations about Robert's intellect and ambitions. (Unaware at that point that Robert had been shot down in friendly fire by an Italian pilot on the Allied side, Yeats assumed that he had met a hero's end in combat with the enemy.)

The death threatened to dislodge Yeats from his privileged position at Coole. Robert had been the estate's legal owner since 1902 when he turned twenty-one. He had, somewhat grudgingly, allowed his mother to live there for her lifetime while he and Margaret, both painters, spent most of their time either in Paris or in London, where they had a house. Lady Gregory clung to Coole, in part because it was the basis of her strong position in the Irish literary revival, but also because she was determined to preserve Coole for her grandson Richard. However, as Richard was only eight when his father was killed, his mother became his guardian, making Coole's future highly uncertain. Margaret, a pretty young woman from Wales with a taste for social life, did not share her mother-in-law's attachment to the estate; she felt that her three children should be brought up in a livelier setting than remote Galway. At the time of Robert's death, Lady Gregory, sensitive to the realities of property, volunteered to move out of Coole at once. Happily for her, the offer was refused.

To help his old friend in her grief, Yeats suggested that he and George come to Ireland immediately, take up Lady Gregory's earlier offer of a house on the estate and assume some of the burden of administration of the Abbey and the campaign for the return of the Lane pictures. Lady Gregory, who kept her composure remarkably throughout her mourning, would not hear of it. She asked him to remain in England and continue the Lane work from there. Yeats was only too happy to agree; he was more worried about the Lane pictures, he said, than about Home Rule.[11] On February 17 his "Note of Appreciation" appeared in *The Observer* and conveyed with exquisite delicacy his mixed feelings for Robert Gregory: "He had so many sides . . . that some among his friends were not sure what his work would be. To me he will always remain a great painter in the immaturity of his youth."[12] He also began about that time what was to be the first of four poems in Robert's memory.

His new System showing its worth, he drew upon his idea of "dreaming back" from death to birth to say of Robert in "Shepherd and Goatherd":

'He grows younger every second . . .
Till, clambering at the cradle-side,
He dreams himself his mother's pride. . .'

"Dreaming back," as it was developing in the automatic writing, was (theosophic touches apart) not unlike the new psychoanalysis then gaining vogue: a process of reliving the past in order to understand it and to forgive it. Both Yeats and George were fascinated with Freud. The Script is dotted with references—to the significance of forgetting, for example, and the need to clear the unconscious. In his first appearance "Thomas" had told them that the "unknown & unconcealed complex" remained "like a tumour or growth in the subconsciousness which grows as does the physical disease."[13] The cure was talking on an intimate basis with one or more trusted friends.

By the time they reached Oxford Yeats had worked out the ruse by which he would conceal the spiritual authorship of the philosophy he was already writing into a book. He described to Lady Gregory how he would pretend that the truths derived from an old medieval book written by Giraldus and based on the mystical patterns danced into the sand by a sect of Arabs called the Judwalis, or diagrammatists.[14] His friend and Iseult's employer, Denison Ross, (now Sir) helped him with the Arabic lore. Edmund Dulac, who was to do a woodcut of the said Giraldus, clarified that the bony face Yeats had in mind for an illustration was not that of the twelfth-century Welsh mystic and traveler Giraldus Cambrensis but of the more appropriate Gerard of Cremona, Latin translator of Arabic scientific treatises.

Such an undertaking required a strenuous contribution from George. Displaying her mastery of astrological science and of the difficult geometrical and color symbolism of the Golden Dawn, she filled her pages with intricate calculations about celestial movements and with long strings of planetary and zodiacal symbols. She and Yeats conversed fluently in this private language. Working to the Judwalis theme, she wrote words in imitation Arabic.

Her attempt is testimony to the Arabist fantasy so prevalent in late-nineteenth- and early twentieth-century England. Leighton House in

Kensington, the London borough that was to theosophy and occultism what Hampstead was to psychoanalysis, is an architectural monument to Victorian dreams of Araby, with its gold-bordered peacock-blue tiles, sumptuous mosaics, and marble arches. Some of Yeats's fellow Irish authors took a cool view of this yearning toward the mysterious Orient. The poet James Clarence Mangan described it as "the love of many lands . . . eastern tales and the memory of curiously printed books," while the jesuitical James Joyce presented it as tawdry illusion in the *Dubliners* short story "Araby."[15]

At 45 Broad Street, the effort intensified to assign personalities to their appropriate phase of the moon. According to the schema the Yeatses had employed since George wrote it at Stone Cottage, no personality type could be allotted to phases 1, 15, and 28. Phase 1 marked the dark of the moon, when no life is possible; phase 15 represented the full moon (or, as Yeats held, perfect beauty); while phase 28, with the waning moon virtually vanished, could hold only the nearly extinguished personality, the Fool. All Yeats's assignments thus had to fall between phases 2 and 27. In his eyes, the phases on the far side of 15 were more desirable, representing creativity and imagination. On the rising side of the moon, phases 2 to 14 stood for a gradual assertion of individuality, increasing to a love for action and adventure, and intensifying into recklessness and exaggerated self-importance.

The scripts done at Oxford in January and February 1918 produced an untidy jumble of the great and the familiar. Nietzsche was declared a phase 12, as was (no surprise) Ezra Pound. Maud Gonne and Helen of Troy were just past perfection at phase 16, while Iseult also came close to ideal beauty at 14, a phase she shared with Tennyson and Wordsworth. The flaw that kept Maud from perfection was specified: an antithetical self given to fanatical obsessiveness, even violence.

George Yeats was placed in the intellectual and loving phase 18, along with Zarathustra, Titian, and Plutarch, while Yeats appeared in the subjective and poetical phase 17, with Shelley and Dante. Day by day the names and numbers whirled through the Script: Schopenhauer, Virgil, Shakespeare, Homer, Chaucer, Parnell, and many others drew their classifications in turn. When Verlaine drew an understandable phase 13 (sensuous) and Pascal phase 27 (the Saint) but Tolstoy a mere phase 6 (artificial individuality), Yeats halted. Why so early? "Fish's" reply was odd: "It is not a novelist from intellect or objectivity of intellect."[16]

As convinced as ever that these assignments were being made with otherworldly direction, Yeats then asked "Fish" to place his former lover, the actress Florence Farr, on the circular scale. "Fish" was forced to admit that he could not obey because the medium had seen Farr only once.

Richard Ellmann, Harold Bloom, and other scholars have traced the many resemblances between Yeats's phases of the moon and occult systems found around the world. George Yeats is known to have been influenced, when she made her own list, by Chaucer's "Franklin's Tale," with its description of the "eighte and twenty mansiouns" of the moon. The cultural parallels are clear, if wobbly. However, there should be little need to search deep into anthropology or world literature to comprehend the universal magic of the number twenty-eight. Yeats, as his mind raced round and round the lunar calendar, was for the first time in his life in the hands of a woman who was trying to have a baby.

Iseult was one of their first visitors. Another guest was the physician and occultist scholar Frank Pearce Sturm, who assured Yeats that postwar Oxford was becoming a center of a great revival of spiritual learning. Sturm, hearing Yeats sound off on his dislike of children, formed the impression that the great poet was unlikely to become a family man. Perhaps for this reason, George Yeats took a dislike to Sturm and pronounced him "too mediumistic;" one of her Controls later said that he had brought frustration to the Script.[17]

Yeats seems to have been thwarted in his wish to meet the authors of *An Adventure,* even though he believed that such a meeting might have been the purpose of spirits' summoning him to Oxford. In an automatic writing session one day he demanded an explanation of the sighting of Marie Antoinette. The unnamed communicator of the day replied that the queen had been "dreaming back" and all the other figures seen in the garden were part of her dream. And what of the same women's sighting of the shade of the emperor Constantine in the Louvre? A new and didactic Control called "Aymor" explained it readily as the power of great personalities to remain in the Anima Mundi for centuries.

Yeats then wrote directly to Miss Moberly, the principal of St. Hugh's, telling her, somewhat ingratiatingly, that his occultist friend Elizabeth Radcliffe had seen her late father, the bishop of Salisbury, at a séance. He received a brisk rebuff. The bishop had been dead for thirty-three years, Miss Moberly replied, with nothing having been heard for him for twenty-six of those years. However, after she published in the same year both *An Adventure* and a family memoir, she began to hear from a great many mediums that her late father was making "communications." As a Christian woman, she went on to say, she heartily disapproved and saw séances as a departure from the approved path of faith. On a more kindly note, she added, undoubtedly respectful of the great poet, that if she or Miss Jourdain could help Yeats in his own "great anxiety to unravel all the truth," they would certainly do so.[18]

An additional function of the Automatic Script was to relieve the depression that descended on both husband and wife from time to time. George's inner anger broke through on January 22. "Leo" appeared, forcing her to draw his symbol all over her page and to write that he hated the medium. This Frustrator entered another day in the form of daggers, drawn as triangles, spattering the paper. By mid-February the medium was in such a black mood that, writing backward five times, "AR" (a Control who may or may not have been the same as "Aymor") said "he" could not come until her depression was gone. There was then no Script for seven days.

On February 23, the gloom lifted. In an astonishing change of direction, the Script announced the name of the seventeenth-century aristocrat who had chosen the Yeatses to reincarnate her dead child. This spiritual ancestor was announced by "AR" with such detail as to suggest prior research by the medium:

She calls herself Anne Hyde Duchess of Ormonde and gives
you both her dear love . . .

    1681 married James—now I will try and send her away . . .
died in childbirth

The rest of "Aymor's" long communication that evening had to do with
the astrological grounds for predicting the war's end in July or August, but
Yeats was far more interested in the news of his child's interesting forebear.
Next day he rushed to the Oxford Union to look up Anne Hyde in *Burke's
Peerage*. Gratifyingly, the name was there, but "Aymor" had overstated her
lineage and given the marriage date wrong by a year. Anne Hyde had been
a mere countess, not a duchess; her husband, James Butler, became duke
of Ormonde three years after she died in 1685. The errors were mistakes
that could have been made by anyone, such as the medium, hastily look-
ing up references in an encyclopedia. Yeats corrected them, through fur-
ther checking, without a qualm. He read further about the Ormondes in
the *Dictionary of National Biography* and also, the Bodleian not letting him
down, in the six volumes of *An History of the Life of James, Duke of Ormonde*,
by Thomas Carte, published in 1851, where he learned more. Anne's death
had come unexpectedly after a miscarriage. George then furthered the
research that night with a dream yielding more biographical information;
Anne Hyde had died very young, not after a miscarriage but after giving
birth to a child who lived only a few days.

    The surnames thus provided could not have been more welcome.
Yeats liked to claim a connection with the ancient Irish clan of Ormonde,
whose family name, Butler, was proudly sprinkled throughout his own
family tree. The distinguished name traced back to a great-great-grand-
mother, Mary Butler, who married the linen merchant Benjamin
William Yeats in 1773. The Butlers, wealthy and powerful, had come
from England to Ireland in the twelfth century, and were far more distin-
guished than the humble Yeatses, who had arrived from Yorkshire much
later, as tradesmen. In the words of William Murphy, historian of the
Yeats family, "In the peculiar logic of the class conscious, Ireland's great-
est poet would have been held in higher regard if the surnames of his

great-great-grandparents had been reversed."[19] Yeats's friend George Russell knew that Yeats felt much the same way. Russell wrote to John Quinn in 1911, "W. B. Yeats believes he is the Duke of Ormond."[20]

That George's Script had revealed a spiritual mother for their own child who also bore her own family name, Hyde, added to their sense of having been chosen. (It may be worth noting that two of the names of her Guides, "Rose" and "Leaf," can also be found on her family tree; Herbert and Rosie Leaf were relatives by marriage of her stepfather, Harry Tucker.)[21]

The way seemed set for "Anne Hyde" to use the Yeatses for dreaming-back purposes. However, after a five-day hiatus in the Script, "Leo the Frustrator" reappeared, with a frenzied attack of sketchy daggers shattering pitchers. Shaken, Yeats asked for spiritual guidance on how to prevent another attack. The only defense, replied "Aymor," was calmness, prayer, and meditation, adding the rebuke that the medium meditated more than Yeats did.

The first week in March was set for the trip to Ireland. The thought was to visit for several months, taking Ballimantane House near Lady Gregory until work on the tower was done, then to return to Oxford for the winter months. The decision to depart at last for the country of Yeats's birth found the medium very nervous.

With a sense of finale, as if in the closing chorus of an opera, the whole cast, "Thomas," "Rose," "Fish," "Leaf," "Aymor," and "AR," appeared together on March 4. In unison they gave a long exhortation to secrecy. They scolded Yeats for talking too freely. Any ruse could be used, they said, to conceal the truth that he was receiving direct and active guidance of spirits in his life. "Aymor" then made a declaration that must have come as a surprise to the poet, who believed that the spirits' primary interest was to transmit the secrets of the universe. Of all their messages, said "Aymor," most important by far were those concerning his personal life. These above all must never be disclosed. Nor (again the self-serving catch) must Yeats ever disclose the restrictions the spirits imposed on him. The command to secrecy was the most secret of all.

Either "Rose" or "Aymor" (the Script is unclear) then delivered a simple message in plain words that left no room for misunderstanding. The Yeatses were to have a son.[22] But only if Yeats wanted one. He would have to make up his own mind within three months—and do so without telling his wife. (This important message was written backward, as if it were private communication between Yeats and his Controls and as if George could not read her own mirror writing.) Then, as if to absolve George from any charge of pushing him into fatherhood, came another message so important that it was repeated, in reverse writing, an eye-catching five times:

**she will on the whole be equally happy during your life
whether you want a child or no**

it will always be you she will love in the child

To have a child against his will, in sum, would destroy the link between him and George. But his decision must be free and unforced. He was to remember, however, that if he decided in the negative, his son would never be born. Then, backward script continuing, came the admonition

**you must not wait till you are growing old—remember a child
will not make her any more happy now—**

The messenger then began to sound impatient and, falling into the first person, positively wifelike. It reminded Yeats that children might be a nuisance at the start but that they grew up eventually:

**neither of you like parrots or weasels parrots become peacocks
& weasels lions five or six years of a weasel than it is a mina-
ture lion . . .**

oh no but youll go on meandering for 10 years if I dont fix a time[23]

The warning about secrecy now hit home. Yeats and George ripped out of their respective notebooks these pages concerning his indecision over the possible child. George probably destroyed hers. However, Yeats, the writer in him predominating, put his possible literary needs against spiritual warnings, stored his own pages, and labeled them.[24] Only when they were discovered in the late 1980s by a librarian in the Yeats Archive at the State University of New York at Stony Brook was it revealed how a reluctant Yeats came to embrace parenthood on the orders of his Automatic Script.

Two more Script sessions took place the following day. "Aymor" returned to give them the specifics of what "Anne Hyde" required: that they should recreate her boy in order that she could separate from him. More than that (in an oedipal twist that suggests a son's fantasy of marrying his mother in order to give birth to himself), "Anne" told "Aymor" that she saw herself as the medium and looked upon Yeats as her husband.

Yeats at long last reawakened the skeptic in himself. He inquired whether this insistent "Anne Hyde" might not have learned about herself from his own memory of what he had read in *Burke's Peerage*. This plausible suggestion was rejected. "Anne," said "Aymor," had come through the medium and also through his sisters' minds (Lily and Lolly Yeats being very eager that the family line be carried on). Her overriding goal was that the Yeatses reincarnate the dead son who had had no chance of life. In conclusion, as if in anticipation of the garrulous family and friends waiting in Dublin to welcome the irrepressible Yeats, "Aymor" added:

> Remember warning—also personal secrecy Always
> Goodbye.[25]

These were the last words of Automatic Script to be written in England for the next fourteen months.

7

What Rough Beast?

(March 1918–February 1919)

WAITING IN IRELAND were Yeats's sisters, the quiet, witty Lily (or Susan, named for her mother) and the unquiet, managerial Lolly (Elizabeth, named for her maternal aunt). The sisters were similar only in nickname; no one who knew them ever confused them. Lily, the elder, was Yeats's favorite sibling; Lolly was difficult for everyone, especially Lily, her temper and restlessness often leading close relatives to fear that she was about to succumb to the Pollexfen madness. Another explanation for this irritability was that, unlike Lily, the fifty-year-old Lolly had not extinguished her hopes of marriage.

The two women lived in Dundrum, a village south of Dublin, in the modest house, Gurteen Dhas, that they had shared since leaving Bedford Park in London in 1902. Not far away was the cottage that housed their Cuala Industries. Cuala (pronounced Cooala) employed only women, mainly girls (some as young as fourteen), over whom the Yeats sisters presided like benevolent governesses. They not only trained their staff in the required crafts but taught them Irish, and encouraged them to read, attend the theater, and learn Irish dancing. Photographs taken in the workrooms of Cuala's predecessor, Dun Emer Industries, showing the serious young females with long smocks and shimmering hair at their machines, are an Edwardian feminist vision of a world without men.

One man squarely in the middle of the sisters' enterprise was their brother. The Cuala business card and letterhead said:

EMBROIDERY LILY YEATS
HAND PRESS ELIZABETH C. YEATS
EDITORIAL DIRECTOR W. B. YEATS

He had total editorial control. He exercised it by allowing them to bring out mainly first editions of his own books, hand-printed in eighteenth-century Caslon type on thick, unbleached Irish paper with a high rag content, before passing them along to the more commercial hands of Macmillan in London. The contrived archaism of the inscription of a Cuala book is mocked in the opening scene of *Ulysses* as "Five lines of text and ten pages of notes about the folk and the fishgods of Dundrum. Printed by the weird sisters in the year of the big wind."

Yeats did steer other works Cuala's way, but not as many as the sisters would have liked, and for the privilege of publishing his own, he extracted what they considered an excessive share of the royalties. It was no fun, Lolly, who handled the finances, complained to her father, being in business with Willie. You had to be as wily as a serpent.

Maud Gonne had reached Ireland before Yeats and George did. In January 1918, defying the British order against her, she crossed to Ireland from Holyhead disguised in a pious variation of her old Cathleen ni Houlihan costume: long black skirt, shawl over her head, rosary beads in her hand, and suitcases tied with string. No one pursued her once she was there. She went to Coole to offer condolences to Lady Gregory, bought a Dublin townhouse at 73 St. Stephen's Green, and went to work for Sinn Fein. The nationalist party was gathering strength from Britain's attempt to impose military conscription in Ireland. Until that time, a great many Irishmen, Robert Gregory among them, had fought in the Great War as volunteers. The move of Lloyd George's government to extend "the Compulsion" to Ireland was intended not only to raise manpower for the western front but to increase Irish patriotism and loyalty to the Crown. The move backfired, to the great benefit of Sinn Fein.

While house-hunting, Maud went out to Dundrum to visit the sisters. They had long disliked her strident theatricality. Lily was now incredulous at the spectacle of Maud's calling herself Madame MacBride and sporting widow's weeds and veil for the late husband everybody in Dublin knew she did not lament. Maud, however, needed the martyr's name for political purposes and for her son's sake. Sean MacBride had come over from London to join her and was enrolled in Mount St. Benedict School in County Wexford, while her "adopted niece," as the illegitimate Iseult would continue to be known in Ireland, remained in London. But Maud had her uses, as Lily told her father: "She told me more about Georgie in five minutes than all others or all letters."[1] Her information was, in effect, that Georgie's color was dark and high, almost too high; that her life had not been happy because of a charming but neurotic mother, that she had serious tastes and would be a good anchor for Willie and that Willie did not like his brother-in-law, Harold Hyde-Lees.[2]

The sisters, therefore, were well briefed when word came from Liverpool that Yeats and George were on their way and from Saturday, March 9, would be staying at the Royal Hibernian Hotel on Dawson Street. Lily and Lolly set aside the corned beef they had planned for Sunday, got a joint of beef, arranged a large bowl of spring flowers, and invited their brother Jack and his wife to join them for the first look at Willie's bride. Their loyal maid Maria, who had been with them since Bedford Park days, went down on her knees and polished the already-polished floor.[3] By Monday Lily's verdict was on its way to John Quinn:

She is not good looking, but is comely, her nose too big for good looks; her colour ruddy and her hair reddish brown; her eyes very good and fine blue, with very dark, strongly marked eyebrows. She is quiet but not slow, her brain, I would judge, quick and trained and sensitive. They are most happy together. Willy I never saw looking so well.[4]

George, in the next few days of beautiful weather, was introduced to the Abbey Theatre company and to various Yeats relatives such as Uncle Isaac, Aunt Jenny, and Aunt Grace. There was much subsequent debate among them whether George was less or more handsome than her photograph; all agreed she had a beautiful expression. All undoubtedly also noticed the clipped, upper-middle-class Englishness of her voice.

There was quiet consternation over her clothes.[5] Although the Yeats sisters admired the aesthetic look in William Morris wallpaper and Liberty textiles, they were less happy about its use in fashion. Lolly in particular always dressed extremely well, and both shared the prevailing view that unconventional dress in women was a sign of free-thinking, aggressiveness, even socialism.

But they did not have to worry about her religion. Englishness signified Protestantism and its associated traits, thrift, common sense, and responsibility. Catholics, in Anglo-Irish eyes, were financially feckless. When Lily sent her father news of a local garden fête held on behalf of the district nurse, she reported that, as the event had been run by Catholics, no one had any idea of how much money was made.[6] Yeats himself was of much the same mind; Catholics of the best sort, he told Lady Gregory in 1915, were loyal and generous as individuals, but they lacked any sense of community spirit and the common good; it was the Protestants who had kept public life alive in Ireland.[7]

In their regular vivid letters to 317 West 29th Street, Lily and Lolly were doing more than keep John Butler Yeats up to date on the old country. They were preparing him for his return. As he was nearing eighty, they confidently expected that he would come home to Dublin where they could look after him. When that spring he said he would possibly arrive in the autumn, they told him that his chair was waiting for him, as was the little space in the bookshelf where he kept his tobacco box.[8]

His prolonged stay in the United States was, on the face of things, no mystery; he loved the place, found it "the most intelligent country in the world," where he had "realized for the first time the meaning of the words 'human destiny,'" where people were always willing to talk seriously and where they liked old men "as if they thought it was jolly to be old . . ."[9] Yet he was undoubtedly held in New York by a fear of seeming inferior to his famous sons; Willie's and Jack's success underlined his own failure. He kept inventing excuses for postponing his departure: he did not want to travel in winter, he had to finish his self-portrait first. But his finances in the United States were parlous, while in Dublin a book of his published essays had been warmly received and he had great hopes for his autobiography, which was about to come out. At last he seemed to accept, as Lily teased him lovingly, that he was too old to remain so far from his own family and that he could have an entertaining, interesting life if he returned.[10]

The Irish Sea was no barrier to the "Communicators." Yeats and George resumed the Automatic Script at the Royal Hibernian Hotel, but briefly. "Anne Hyde" now appeared as a Control in her own right, to write on "unphilosophic things," which appeared in mirror writing, because (can Yeats *really* have believed this?) "I do not wish medium to know and if you say name familiar she will know at once Anne Hyde is writing."[11] Two days later Yeats and George left Dublin for Glendalough, an ancient religious site in the Wicklow mountains southwest of Dublin. A high, wild, archaeological paradise, its lakes are bounded by jagged rocks, tumbling rivers, and the ruins of the sixth-century monastery founded by Saint Kevin. Its most dramatic feature, an ancient round tower, was a fitting backdrop to their spiritualist studies and, if the poems written there are any hint, to their increasingly satisfying conjugal embraces. Not surprisingly, Yeats thought the spirits had brought them to Glendalough, as to Oxford, for revelatory purposes. He and George checked into the Royal Hotel for a fortnight and bought fishing rods but were warned by "Rose," "Fish," and "Apple" not to let the medium do too much walking and get overtired.[12]

The basic question Yeats was now posing in the ensuing lengthy sessions full of mathematical, geometrical, and zodiacal shorthand was, in its way, straightforward. It concerned the symbol of the cone, or gyre. What was the relationship of the individual cone to the world cone? How, that is, did the cycle of an individual life fit into the cycles of history? He had decided—or rather George's Script had told him—that a cone equaled fate.

The concreteness of his questions is astonishing, considering that he was probing the invisible world. Like an engineer, he was trying to work out the mechanics of the various processes on which his new System was based. Indeed, he used the word *mechanical* again and again.

How *did* a spirit dream back to its childhood after death? Did it start immediately, relive its life in reverse chronological order or by the most passionate moments? Did it pause on the way? How many reincarnations did it have—eight? Or more? How did an individual soul disengage from the world soul, the Anima Mundi? As for the interlocking cones, gyres, or funnels (he asked one day if he might refer to them also as "spindles"), did these lie horizontally or vertically? He had decided that the soul traveled with a spiraling motion through its cone, but was the movement up and down or in and out? Did it start at the narrow end or the wide end?[13]

The answers were duly delivered, with George's hand setting out long tables of numbers and astrological signs, accompanied by more exhortations to secrecy. The wonder is not that she had the energy for these difficult exercises but that she was able to find answers at all. On Saint Patrick's Day 1918 the Guide called "Apple" recommended, "She must not write today if she is to write on funnells tomorrow."[14]

Absurd as many of the questions seem, they covered a great deal of psychological ground. Toward the end of March the couple moved to the nearby village of Glenmalure. There, in a smaller hotel, their questions and answers grew more personal and autobiographical. "Anne," "Apple," and "Aymor" took over. Yeats wanted to know why some children died young. "Aymor" explained. Deaths at or around birth were caused by weak sexual desire at the moment of conception; the strength of the child, accordingly, depended on the strength of the desire of its parents at the time.[15] Yeats then asked, reaching back consciously or unconsciously, into his childhood memories of his two-year-old brother Robert who had died suddenly when he was five and an infant sister who died a few years later, "Are there not bad children who die young?"[16] The answer blamed "intense evil" in an earlier phase of the soul. Yeats asked these curious questions because he believed he needed to know whether the souls of children, or those of the insane, for that matter, went through the same twenty-eight phases as the rest. (Over this session, he noticed wonderingly, there hovered a smell of incense.)

It was a productive time of retreat. The Script clarified concepts important to Yeats such as "the shiftings" (the state a soul entered after it had completed its return to its former life) and what he called the four "Principles" of Eternal Man: the Passionate Body, the Celestial Body, the Physical Body, and the Spirit Body. To the poet and his wife, working high in the Wicklow mountains in 1918, these abstractions were so real and familiar they could be referred to by initials. Yeats, puzzled about the "PB" ("Passionate Body"), asked "Rose" what the "PB's" relation was to sex. He got a clear answer: "It is sex."[17] "Rose" then scolded the poet for his passivity and called for a halt of three weeks in the Script to enable him to extract and codify what had been set down.

This deciphering was no small matter. The automatic writing continued dreamily to meander over the page, barely legible, with no breaks between the words. Nonetheless, Yeats worked over the growing text diligently, extracting what he wanted, either to use in his book or to add his own comments; he wrote at times in a manuscript book or, later, on hundreds of three-by-five-inch file cards (which he made out of blank postcards). He arranged the cards alphabetically according to his unique classification system. Entries under "B" included "Beatific Vision," "Birth," "Before Life," and "Berenices Hair." All diagrams went under "D."

Yeats's attraction to the Glendalough round tower intensified his attachment to his own tower and if he never used the word "phallic" in describing either, he had no need. The high black column at Glendalough was in itself a symbol of the "PB," as two Controls, who often appeared in tandem, "Aymor" and "Arnaud," explained: "It is a symbol only in life—abundant flowing life."[18] George then drew a round tower broken by jagged lines, a diagram suggesting that the halves needed to be joined together.[19]

Yeats was extremely pleased with their work done in that ancient spot, and so he should have been. The homemade philosophy was yielding wonderful poetry. The frolicsome "Under the Round Tower," with romantic glimpses of a prancing "golden king" and his "silver lady" (who was also described as "that wild lady"—*wild* being one of his favorite adjectives of approbation), was finished, the long philosophical dialogic poem between Michael Robartes and Owen Aherne begun. The poem "The Phases of the Moon" remains a useful guide to Yeats's System:

> Twenty-and-eight the phases of the moon,
> The full and the moon's dark and all the crescents. . .
> From the first crescent to the half, the dream
> But summons to adventure . . .
> And after that the crumbling of the moon,
> The soul remembering its loneliness
> Shudders in many cradles; all is changed,
> It would be the world's servant.

In the autobiographical "Solomon to Sheba," Yeats produced as near an epithalamium as he was to write for his bride. He cast her (recording her high skin color) as a "dusky" Queen of Sheba to his King Solomon, and proclaimed proudly:

> There's not a man or woman
> Born under the skies
> Dare match in learning with us two.

He also kept to his promise to write something about Robert Gregory. "Shepherd and Goatherd," the first of his four poems, was an elegy in the manner of Spenser's ode to Sir Philip Sidney and paid a tribute direct to the mother of the fallen man:

> How does she bear her grief? There is not a shepherd
> But grows more gentle when he speaks her name.

The poem was less kind to Robert, comparing him to a cuckoo who only fitfully rested in his father's house before moving on, leaving no trace of improvement behind. This brazen image covers the counter-truth—that Yeats had been considered the cuckoo in the Coole nest.

Another poem in eulogy, "In Memory of Major Robert Gregory," is more conventional, incorporating all the traits the family wished mentioned. Lady Gregory, herself nearly as ambivalent as Yeats about Robert's achievement, is thought to have advised on its contents: "Soldier, scholar, horseman, he,/And all he did done perfectly."

With these two poems alone, Yeats repaid his debt to Lady Gregory. His third poem, "An Irish Airman Foresees His Death," immortalized her son. In it he found voice for his own, very Irish, indifference to the struggle between England and Germany:

> I know that I shall meet my fate
> Somewhere among the clouds above;
> Those that I fight I do not hate,
> Those that I guard I do not love;

So why fight? The poem answers that universal mystery, drawing on a comment that Robert had made to Bernard Shaw that his army years had been the happiest of his life:

> A lonely impulse of delight
> Drove to this tumult in the clouds;
> I balanced all, brought all to mind,
> The years to come seemed waste of breath,
> A waste of breath the years behind
> In balance with this life, this death.

If willingness to gamble everything for one sublime moment is the measure of heroism, then the poet and the lover too are heroic. "Though we cannot make our sun/Stand still," wrote Marvell, "yet we will make him run:" daring is the only response to the brevity of life. That Yeats could produce such profound and enduring poetry while absorbed in a new marriage and in the grip of an occultist obsession shows the strength of his confused genius.

Early in April 1918 the Yeatses at last arrived at Coole. It was a household in shock. Robert was scarcely two months dead; his wife had lost the baby she was expecting (whether from an early miscarriage or from the news of his death is not known).[20] The three young Gregorys—Richard, nine; Anne, seven; and Catherine, four—were scampering about stables and gardens, needing lessons and entertainment. It was not the ideal time for visitors, and George soon felt depressed and excluded by the Big House rituals so familiar to Yeats.

At her best Lady Gregory was the sort of woman who is cold to other women; her warmth and wealth were directed toward men. Lily and Lolly Yeats both complained that she ignored them. So did Jack's wife, Cottie.[21] Robert's wife, Margaret, an outspoken young woman, had never found relations with her mother-in-law easy, and following Robert's death the traditional tensions were exacerbated by the uncertainty about the estate.

In such an atmosphere, it is hardly surprising that the Communicators, so forthcoming at Glendalough and Glenmalure, had much less to say. When Yeats and George sat down to evoke their spirits, "Leo the Frustrator" intruded on Yeats's efforts to develop a theory of history. "Thick air joyless heavy" was "Aymor's" disgruntled judgment on Coole.[22]

Margaret Graham-Parry Gregory had always irritated Yeats, who found her habitually combative. (Lily too disliked Margaret Gregory; she called her a suburban minx who had no appreciation of landowning traditions.)[23] One evening in the second week of their visit, Yeats decided to pay Margaret back in kind. Afterward, he was so pleased with his performance and its unexpected consequence that he confided it in full to his *Vision* notebook:

> One night . . . she [Margaret] began at dinner to contradict as usual every thing I said & instead of avoiding reply as I had done hitherto I turned on her. I had come down to dinner in the highest of spirits with this wicked intention & at the end of dinner went up stairs in the highest spirits. George told me I had behaved badly but had so much sympathy with me, that we omited our usual precaution against conception. . . . From then on we expected the conception of a child. We had not waited quite as long as the spirit had advised thanks to Margaret Gregory.[24]

Yeats was familiar with the mechanics of contraception. Fumbling with a nineteenth-century condom was part of his education from Olivia Shakespear. George too, as a free-thinking woman of the upper middle class, was aware of the favored techniques for family limitation. What is more, they were both delighted to see that anger had released what they saw as "the Mars" in him.[25] The occasion of April 17, 1918, was so memorable for them both that, although it did not result in a pregnancy, its anniversary a year later saw no fewer than five Communicators jostling for space in the Script in celebration. The irony of the incident, a burst of sexual exuberance triggered by anger at a young woman who had just lost her husband and a baby, went unnoticed.

As the Yeatses seem never to have resumed contraception, horoscope casting took on a new urgency. Begetting a child was a momentous act: opening the door for a dead soul to re-enter the world. The word "child," accompanied by references to myrrh and frankincense, indicating the Christ-child, appeared in the Script a week later. Accepting Lady Gregory's offer of Ballinamantane House as a more convenient place from which to supervise the work on Ballylee, they freed themselves from Coole's entanglements and settled back into serious Script. Renewed effort went into assigning geniuses of the past, such as Napoleon and Byron, to their proper lunar phases, and the cycles of history to their turning points, marked by the birth of their leaders,

Christ and Buddha. A new, ecclesiastically knowledgeable Control named "Zoretti" appeared.

Yeats was now trying to apply his image of the cone to the rise and fall of civilizations. He wanted to calculate where the coming of Christ fitted into his picture of the Great Wheel of human history; this wheel was also divided into twenty-eight phases. More specifically, he was trying to calculate the date of the second coming of the variously named new redeemer. The numbers were proving difficult. If history ran in cycles of 2,000 or 2,100 years, as the Script was revealing to him, how to explain the fact that 1920—or even 1919—as was beginning to seem possible, was the fateful year?[26]

The late spring and early summer of 1918 should have been a happy time, with the renovated tower and cottage nearly ready and pregnancy in the air, but the medium's depression had returned. In the backward writing she used for her most direct marital lectures, George's "Thomas" spoke of "your boredom and coldness of heart to her and your thought all within." "Thomas" observed Yeats's indifference to the effect his saturnine moods had on the medium, and mentioned despair and the possibility of hatred arising out of the medium's growing depression and loneliness. "Thomas" reminded Yeats of the need for kindness, and cited an incident that morning that made the poet's relationship to the medium seem no more than a legal formality. At the same time Yeats was scolded like a child for asking questions that were no more than "why a dog has a tail." Once "Thomas" had to go and fetch "Rose." Meanwhile, sketches of the funnel of life began to look more and more like those of the womb and birth canal. On June 18 Yeats asked: "Does birth take place in centre or one of ends?" Answer: "At one of ends."

Despite the entry of the United States, the war with Germany was by no means over. In April 1918, despite powerful opposition, including Yeats's, the British government passed the bill introducing conscription for Ireland. The German offensive launched in March made more troops essential. With married men in their late fifties being called up in England, the British government was hoping to raise 150,000 from

Ireland without sparking another Rising. Lloyd George, the prime minister, reasoned that if Ireland wanted the promised Home Rule after the war, it ought to be willing to share the burden of winning the peace.

Lloyd George was wrong. So unanimously outraged was Irish opinion that the Irish members of Parliament walked out of Westminster and returned to Dublin to join Sinn Fein in protest. The country was in uproar. A general strike on April 23 affected every part of Ireland outside of Belfast. Yeats told Maud that he did not think the government would be mad enough to try to enforce conscription, but considering the public mood, he thought it wise to cancel a lecture and a play.

Yeats too was wrong. In May the government sent out a military lord lieutenant from London, who began by declaring all members of Sinn Fein traitors and German conspirators. Immediately an order went out to arrest the party's leaders. Among the first to be caught, after Eamon de Valera, was Maud Gonne. She was apprehended one evening as she walked home from the tram with her son, Sean, and an English MP. Taken to London and put into Holloway Prison, she was held with Constance Markiewicz. The Irish contessa had been rearrested in Dublin, where she had been living since her triumphal return from an English prison the previous year.

Yeats was as angry at the two women as he was at the authorities. Nevertheless, he was exceedingly sympathetic to Maud's plight when he received a letter describing her cell: seven feet by thirteen, with one small window too high to see out. "Do what you can for Seagan & Iseult," she pleaded.[27] She was not allowed even to send the boy money.

The kindly letter with which he replied shows that he remained, just as she signed all her letters to him, "Always your friend." He told her that, knowing she was threatened with tuberculosis, he had gone to see Edward Shortt, the chief secretary for Ireland, to try get her release on medical grounds. He had even asked a second favor—that Maud be released without having to swear that she would not try to go to Ireland; such an oath, he asked Shortt to understand, would violate her conscience. He went further. If the government could not allow such a dispensation, he would then request that Maud be allowed to return to

France, where Sean could return to his old school. Relating all this to Maud, Yeats urged her to take whatever concession the government offered. She should put her children above principle: "The matter of most importance to them in the world is that your health shall not break down and that you will be able to watch over their start in life."[28]

Awaiting the government's answer, Yeats, adding to his burden as family guardian, invited young Sean MacBride to live with him and George in Ballinamantane House over the summer holidays. For George, the boy made another ménage à trois, but fortunately, at least as Yeats saw him, the boy was well behaved: "self-possessed, and very just, seeing all round a question and full of tact."[29] He was pleased that Sean accepted tutoring from the schoolteacher in Gort.

Yeats was delighted with the progress on his tower. He saw it in modernist terms, as a setting for himself and a symbol for his poetry: "A place to influence lawless youth, with its severity and antiquity," he told Quinn, adding exuberantly, "If I had had this tower when Joyce began I might have been of use, have got him to meet those who might have helped him."[30] Yeats was ignorant, it seems, of the urban Joyce's distaste for nature in any form wilder than Saint Stephen's Green. He had, however, read enough of the excerpts from *Ulysses* that had appeared in the *Little Review*, an avant-garde American publication subsidized by Quinn, to be awed at Joyce's intensity and innovation. He welcomed the interior monologue, he told Quinn, as "an entirely new thing . . . what the rambling mind thinks and imagines from moment to moment."[31] Yeats had also read enough to see in *Ulysses* the caricatures of his sisters and of George Russell, and by extension himself, as theosophists who haunted libraries in search of lost truths in ancient books. Lampoon seldom bothered Yeats, certainly not when it appeared in a serious work of art. Unwillingness to censor was one of his nicest characteristics.

With his Arts and Crafts tastes and his eye for design, Yeats dreamed of having his castle free of "ugly manufactured things."[32] In June George went to Dublin to discuss the hand-hewn unpolished furniture being made for Thoor Ballylee by the architect Michael Scott and also to see the dentist. Her visit gave the sisters a chance for closer acquaintance. They marveled at the daily letters Willie wrote her and how he reported dutifully that he was watering her seedlings. Sharp-eyed Lolly noticed how George enjoyed giving her name in the shops as "Mrs. W. B. Yeats"; Lolly was pleased to hear one tradesman reply that no one in Ireland should have difficulty in spelling that name.[33]

Lolly now retracted her averse reaction to her sister-in-law's looks and blamed it on George's bad cold in March. George, she reported to her father, was glowing, and grew prettier every time one saw her. Lolly took back too everything she had originally said about George's eccentric clothes; those she was now wearing, although admittedly brilliant in color, were clearly expensive and fashionable.[34] Perhaps, Lolly reasoned charitably, what George had worn for their first meeting was what she had imagined Yeats's artistic sisters would like. Anyway, her appearance hardly mattered. George was in love with County Galway and was admirably sensible. With so many neurotic women about, Lily added in her own letter, Willie was a lucky man.[35]

For a young woman of twenty-five, however, being Mrs. W. B. Yeats was not an unmixed blessing. George's accumulated resentments of the past nine months burst forth in a letter to Ezra Pound, a friend of her own generation. Writing from the Royal Hibernian Hotel, George referred patronizingly and flippantly to "W. B." as if he were a geriatric patient in her care. In breezy prose very far from the tone of the Automatic Script, she told Ezra about the mass of work Yeats had lying around unpublished waiting for him to recover from exhaustion. She was not polite on the subject of Iseult (whom she referred to as "Maurice"). "W. B.," she suggested, was all too prone to fears about the moral dangers that London presented to the distressed beauty, fears that Iseult was only too eager to stir up. As far as she, George, knew, Iseult and her brother had enough money to live on, but the young woman would have to find more work. However, George disapproved of Iseult's idea of leaving the School of Oriental Studies and working for Pound in his capacity as London agent for the *Little Review.* The reputation of the *Little Review* was too suspect. Perhaps some other out-of-the-way rag would take her—*The Bookman* perhaps. In any case, George said, it would not be proper for Pound to employ Iseult full-time, for appearances' sake.[36]

Did she perhaps sense that her old friend, the husband of her best friend, was himself attracted by the near-perfect phase 14 beauty of Maud's daughter?

Back at Ballinamantane House, where they were waiting until the tower, or at least the cottage adjoining it, was made habitable, early in July George was able to give Yeats the news that "Martha" had failed to appear. ("Martha" was her word for menstruation.) The long-talked-of pregnancy was under way.

The news in no way slowed down Yeats's pursuit of the secrets of the cycles of history. "Thomas" urged the medium to read up on the fifth, eighth, ninth, sixteenth, and seventeenth centuries. Soon long tables of historical dates correlated with signs of the zodiac began appearing on George's pages. Again Yeats wanted more information. How did the cone through which an individual soul spiraled during its life fit in with the world cone through which whole civilizations passed? Not an easy question. George drew a sketch of overlapping cones with ten divisions and symbols down one side. Still unsatisfied, Yeats wanted to know the angle of intersection of the world cone by the personal cone, then about the movement of rise and fall. George obliged with a sketch of a cone with a spiral climbing from the narrow end to the top. This did not prevent two more days of questions along the same line. "Air stuffy," complained "Thomas" at one point, finally scolding Yeats for forgetting that the individual cones make up the world cone.[37] On July 7, after agreeing to take only one question and receiving five, "Thomas" laid down a basic equation, easily grasped: a cone equaled fate.

Yeats understandably wished for more details about the child they were to have. "Anne Hyde" reappeared, or rather, "Thomas" did on her behalf, saying that "Anne" would speak only through him, but that she was content. Yeats had much to ask about the son whom he and George were to reincarnate. Was there more historical material hidden away in libraries or letters? Had this son (an extremely hopeful suggestion) perhaps existed in another incarnation as an ancient

Arabic astronomer? Finally and crucially that day, "Why did you choose us not people of great station for your son's parents?"[38]

The Script's answer, as so often with the hardest questions, was blunt: "Anne" said she had no choice in the matter.

In late summer long breaks began to appear in the Script. Yeats was later to record that George remained sexually responsive and full of desire throughout much of the pregnancy.[39] As a mystical transmitter, however, she was getting increasingly irritable and bossy. She hardly bothered disguising her own voice, as when a stentorian new Control called "Erontius" appeared on August 28. This new voice said it didn't like the atmosphere of the house and ordered them to go through a ritual purification (a ceremony both knew from the Golden Dawn)— by burning a piece of wet blotting paper. This instruction was improved on the next day with the further order that they must "not just burn it but walk round room & burn in each quarter & then in middle." "Erontius" was snippy with Yeats, barking "unnecessary question" at him, giving him assignments for meditation, and declaring, "I am not here to give you geometry or definitions nor a grammarian."[40]

The Script was then interrupted by a trip to England, prompted by the news from Sean that Iseult was frightened of her flatmate, Iris Barry. Yeats and George checked into the De Vere Hotel in Kensington, then moved Iseult out of her troubled rooms and into Woburn Buildings. Yeats was proud of the way that George hired the removal van and helped carry out the furniture herself—a zeal he interpreted as a way to express her hatred of "Chelsea" (fashionably bohemian London).[41]

Yeats himself feared the influence of drugs and easy sex on Iseult, for whom, with her mother in jail, he felt more than ever responsible. He disapproved of Iris Barry, who was the mistress of Wyndham Lewis. Maud had brought up Iseult so anarchically, he fumed to Lady Gregory, that she simply did not notice behavior that would shock other girls of her age.

Yeats expressed his fears for Iseult's moral welfare in the poem "To a Young Beauty": "Dear fellow-artist, why so free / With every sort of company." In "Michael Robartes and the Dancer," he presents a dialogue between "He" and "She" in which "He" argues Yeats's belief, much strengthened by the sorry experience of Maud Gonne and Constance Markiewicz, that beautiful women should "banish every thought" and strive to please only their looking glass. But "She" gets the last word and dismisses her mentor with "They say such different things at school." All considered, George Yeats could hardly think that Iseult was no longer on her husband's mind.

They returned to Ireland, leaving Sean at Woburn Buildings with his sister and Maud's maid, Josephine, to try to get his mother out of prison. In spite of George's reservations, Iseult had gone to work for Ezra Pound after all and was doing his typing three days a week. Ezra told Yeats that he would not call her his secretary for "my poems are too Ithyphallic for any secretary of her years to be officially in my possession."[42]

"Thomas" resumed the Script when they returned to Ballinamantane House, ordering Yeats and the medium to rest regularly—particularly the medium—lying down, flat, for two hours a day. Not to do so was "bad for me bad for you bad for her bad for Anne."[43] The sense of double gestation—of a book and a baby—was accentuated by "Thomas's" ambiguous comment, "When the skeleton is complete another method will be adopted."[44]

On September 14, they moved at last into Thoor Ballylee, which even "Thomas" noticed was very cold.[45] Yeats wrote "A Prayer on Going into My House," in which he asked God's blessing on the tower, the cottage, and his heirs, and placed a curse on anyone who destroyed the view by cutting down a tree or (as if he foresaw the developmental blight that was to hit Ireland in later years) by "setting up a cottage planned in a government office." They then left.

Planning to return to Oxford for the winter, they went first north to Sligo, where Yeats showed his wife his childhood surroundings, Ben Bulben, Lough Gill, and Rosses Point. (This could well have been the occasion when, according to Sligo gossip, he rowed out onto the long lake dotted with small islands and could not find Innisfree.) "Thomas" followed them, ordering the medium not to move for two days. That command did not prevent difficult demands for descriptions and definitions until, back at Ballylee, the mask slipping, George wrote, "I am too tired to go on—why do you always begin this subject [analysis of the quantitive difference between anti- and primary selves] when we are tired—4 days I have had vigour & you did not ask."[46]

The news of their expectations was out. Lily was knitting little garments and dreaming. She poured out her thoughts to her father: how "Georgie," as she still called her, looked very pretty and would be furious if the boy did not have dark hair. Lily relayed a dream that surely portended the coming of John Butler Yeats's first grandchild. On top of a high stone tower a herald was blowing a trumpet; a voice then announced that the Yeatses were not dead. A good omen, surely? Warming to her theme, Lily recalled a vivid experience she had had seven years before. Walking through Hyde Park, just as she was thinking to herself how sad it was that her father had no grandchildren, she saw a very tall man, perhaps a diplomat, with prominent features and high color. Suddenly she was convinced that she was looking at Willie's son. Considering the man's great height, she could now appreciate that this waking vision had been a portent. Was not George's brother six foot four?[47]

Portents notwithstanding, Yeats kept up the barrage. His question "Can you explain relation between personal cycle and world cycle?" was followed by a command: "Give me a diagram of individual cycle showing one life influences another?" "Thomas" complained, "you mix me up," to no avail. There followed "Give me an individual cones place of PF [persona of fate], CG [creative genius] etc & show what they are related [to] in past lives."[48] The weeks rolled by, "Erontius" growing snappish at the ceaseless, legalistic questions, such as "Does soul suffer from having been excarnate at 27,"[49] to the point of answering on one occasion, "I am going to tell Thomas to come . . . it is all too scattered for me."[50] The Script nonetheless shows that during this time, George supplied a great deal of detail and definition from whatever sources she carried with her; there was no Bodleian in the Galway countryside.

✦   ✦   ✦

In September, the Yeatses gave up thoughts of Oxford and moved into Maud's house in Dublin for two pounds, ten shillings a week. With Lily's help, he bought a chest of drawers, tables, and washstands, and borrowed an armchair from her.[51] He wrote to the imprisoned Maud, "Should you be released & allowed to live in Ireland we will move out which strangers would not."[52]

Although Yeats regretted that from Ireland he would be able to do less to help Iseult, it seemed fitting that their baby should be born in Dublin. The Automatic Script had begun to consider the coming child as a savior for Ireland. The Yeatses were now using George Russell's word for it: avatar.[53] Russell had drawn on the archaism in 1896 to describe his vision of a new deity, a kingly ruler and magic sage, who would descend upon Ireland in bodily form as the nineteenth century approached its end. While it might seem that George Yeats, with her Home Counties accent, pure English pedigree, and Etonian father who had rowed for Wadham, was not the ideal bearer of the reincarnated god of old Erin, the Script promised no less. It dealt with any possible confusion in the persona of the coming child, who was still expected also to fulfill the aspirations of "Anne Hyde," by promising that the new avatar would have multiple identities.[54]

For about six weeks their joint labors flourished as at Oxford. There were almost daily writing sessions, combined with much calculating of the dates of the full moon. The familiar orders for the medium to rest and for Yeats to avoid talking to strangers were interspersed with long expositions of details crucial to the System. On November 1 Maud wrote joyfully that she had been released from Holloway and allowed to enter a nursing home under guard.

The warnings about her health had sunk in. With Maud's sister, Kathleen, dying of tuberculosis in a Swiss sanatarium, John Quinn had cabled an assistant of the press baron Lord Northcliffe to warn of the impact on American opinion if Maud Gonne were to die in a British jail. She was accordingly released, under the condition that she pay her own expenses at the Welbeck Street nursing home (ten pounds a week) and refrain from traveling to Ireland. Neither Switzerland nor France would agree to take her.

No one being sure whether she was a free woman or not, Maud simply walked out of the clinic and joined her children at Woburn Buildings. She was in a state of fury, however, at being forced to remain in England. All she longed for, she said, was to be in her own home in Dublin, with her Josephine to cook for her.[55]

The ban was unlikely to be lifted. On November 11 the Armistice was signed, and three days later a British general election was called for December 14. With Sinn Fein planning to field a great many candidates for the 103 Irish seats in Parliament (seats they once again swore not to take if elected), Maud's presence in Dublin was clearly not something the government would welcome. Ezra, as Iseult's part-time employer, was in a position to hear a great deal of the released Maud's political views. "Have *all* the Irish a monomania?" he asked Quinn in a letter four days after the Armistice.

> I notice with Yeats he will be quite sensible till some questions of ghosts or occultism comes up, then he is subject to a curious excitement, twists everything to his theory, usual quality of mind goes. So with M.G.[56]

For himself, Ezra said that he did not see how Ireland could demand self-determination for itself while refusing it to Ulster. For all he could see, Maud's only constructive idea was that

> *Ireland and the rest of the world should be free to be one large Donegal fair . . . The sum of it being that I am glad that she is out of gaol, and that I hope no one will be ass enough to let her get to Ireland.*[57]

He thought that Sean, who had had a promising mind, had been ruined by his months in Ireland. The boy was now burning to get arrested and started on his political career.

In Dublin husband and wife were increasingly at cross-purposes. Day after day, the Automatic Script plunged them into a curious mix of collaboration and conflict. Yeats was growing more and more public in outlook as he prepared to deliver a series of lectures on his System, while George was becoming more and more withdrawn and preoccupied with her pregnancy. A vast amount of the Script produced during this period was formless and unimaginative and must have taken a great deal out of them both.

"Restless all three of you," chided "Thomas."[58] "Shut out & isolate yourselves" was the command, and a complaint that "you have forgotten my incense."[59] The voices multiplied and issued direct orders for the medium's better care. "Erontius" advised bed rest and passivity extreme for a pregnant woman even of that day: "medium is not to go out tomorrow or walk or stand or exert."[60] "Thomas," calling a temporary halt for one day, signed off with a resounding scolding in mirror writing four times over: "the more you keep this medium emotionally and intellectually happy the more will the Script be possible now."[61]

On November 18 George took to her bed. They both attributed it to depression, as the day was the ninth anniversary of her father's death. But it was more than sadness; it was pneumonia, a form of the influenza epidemic that cruelly swept Europe and North America at the end of the war, taking millions more lives than were lost in battle. Yeats feared for her life: in one Oxford college five students living on the same staircase were found dead in a single day.[62] The crisis was compounded by a cable from New York: FATHER DANGEROUSLY ILL. John Butler Yeats was a victim of the same plague.

A knock on the door five days later, when the illness was at its worst and a day and a night nurse were in attendance, revealed Maud Gonne in the uniform of a Red Cross nurse. Yeats was appalled. Once the police heard that she had defied orders and made her way to Ireland, a raid on the house would surely follow. The scene was too easily imagined: the battered-down door, the shouts, the rush up the stairs, the armed men bursting into every room. He told Maud to go away. There is no greater measure of the finality of Yeats's switch of muse from Maud to his wife.

Maud was not one to go quietly. Lily, having helped her brother furnish the empty house, wrote Quinn contemptuously how "the patriot" was practically banging on the door the entire day and shrieking to be let into her own home, while Yeats reported ruefully to Lady Gregory that Maud was in a venomous state of paranoia, telling everybody in Dublin that he had persuaded the Ireland secretary to shut her up in a nursing home so that he could stay in her house.[63] He was not far wrong. The gorgeous gossip about the famous poet refusing his legendary love entry to her own house made the rounds of Dublin. Maud's political supporters, such as Cumann na mBan, the nationalist women's organization she had helped to found, were angered on her behalf.[64]

Iseult's reaction was ungenerous: they were both to blame, she told Ezra, and both needed keepers.[65] A casualty of the confusion was Sean MacBride; the boy now had, Yeats reported to Lady Gregory, no school and no fixed address.

If Sean wanted a revolutionary career, the prospects were bright. At the general election in December Sinn Fein candidates won an unexpectedly high number of seats—seventy-three—from Irish constituencies. As announced in advance, they refused to go to Westminister, promising instead to meet independently in Dublin in January as the parliament, or Dáil, of their self-proclaimed Irish Republic. Their victory, however, was less resounding than it seemed; much of Sinn Fein's support reflected rage against the British government and the Irish Parliamentary Party, rather than endorsement of the independence movement itself. Thus the seeds were sown for civil war.

As the first postwar year dawned, Yeats wrote to Lady Gregory on January 5, 1919, to ask if he might come to Coole: he was unwell because of the strain of George's illness; she would stay with his sisters.[66] Her illness, his father's, and the row with Maud, combined with anemia and eye trouble, had brought his general breakdown. His request seems to have been deferred, for he took George off to the country, to Lucan ("Thomas" and "Rose" accompanying them for more discussions of the coming avatar), and then, recovered, he wrote a denunciation (as he saw it) of the imprisoned Countess Markiewicz in the poem "On a Political Prisoner"—(for letting her mind become "a bitter, an abstract thing") and plunged into a "wild week of lecturing" in Dublin and in Belfast.[67]

⋆   ⋆   ⋆

Although he may have been working on it since the previous spring, along with "Phases of the Moon" and "The Double Vision of Michael Robartes," Yeats completed what is probably the best-known poem of his later years, "The Second Coming." Incorporating the symbols he had been receiving through the Script since his marriage, it could not have been more timely.

Europe was reeling from the physical and financial effects of the war. From Russia Bolshevism cast its shadow over the old patterns of work. War had broken out between the sexes. Not only had women learned during the war that they could do men's jobs, but millions of them would now never have husbands. They demanded equality. Ireland was on the brink of rebellion, and within Irish society the Protestant Ascendancy had lost its grip. The old order was dead. Yeats's poem encompassed it all:

> Turning and turning in the widening gyre
> The falcon cannot hear the falconer;
> Things fall apart; the centre cannot hold;
> Mere anarchy is loosed upon the world,
> The blood-dimmed tide is loosed, and everywhere
> The ceremony of innocence is drowned;
> The best lack all conviction, while the worst
> Are full of passionate intensity.

"The Second Coming" is strong enough to accommodate all the meanings that have been read into it: historical, political, religious, even scientific. "Things fall apart; the centre cannot hold" can be seen to describe the physical phenomenon of entropy, the natural increase of disorder.

But as no person lives entirely in the public or political sphere, least of all W. B. Yeats, his extraordinary poem can bear the weight of one more interpretation, the obstetrical. His personal life, with its newly established order, was menaced by the "shape with lion body and the head of a man" advancing toward him in George's expanding belly. Very soon, after a burst of water and blood, he would be "vexed to nightmare by a rocking cradle," deprived of the total attention of his wife on whom he had come to depend, torn by primitive jealousies he had long fought to bury, and disturbed by squalling noise when he needed absolute silence for writing poetry.

As the eldest child in his family, Yeats knew quite a lot about the impact of childbirth. His early life was troubled by the sight of a new arrival in the cradle almost every year. The hammer blows of his unforgettable phrases ring with the universal male terror of pregnancy. After the unstoppable beast's arrival, the one certain thing is that life will never be the same again.

> The Second Coming! Hardly are those words out
> When a vast image out of *Spiritus Mundi*
> Troubles my sight: somewhere in sands of the desert
> A shape with lion body and the head of a man,
> A gaze blank and pitiless as the sun,
> Is moving its slow thighs, while all about it
> Reel shadows of the indignant desert birds.
> The darkness drops again; but now I know
> That twenty centuries of stony sleep
> Were vexed to nightmare by a rocking cradle,
> And what rough beast, its hour come round at last,
> Slouches towards Bethlehem to be born?

Returning to Dublin from Lucan, Yeats threw himself into his public life. On platform after platform, he uttered the truths he had learned through his System. He spoke, for example, with a scientist from Glasgow University, who was also a medium, on the physical evidence for spirits. At the United Arts Club, he spoke on the influence on the human personality of the phases of the moon. The poet Douglas Goldring was one of those who jammed the club for the lecture to hear Yeats claim that the truths had "been revealed to him 'in a dream' by a Morrish initiate with whom he had made contact on the astral plane."[68] Goldring, as it happened, was one of Yeats's former tenants in the much-rented rooms in

Woburn Buildings and remembered seeing on its bookshelves an American treatise on the mystical significance of the phases of the moon. Hearing Yeats wax eloquent about astral transmission, Goldring realized he had an anecdote for retelling at the great man's expense.

In response perhaps to Yeats's busy schedule, George's Script took a new experimental form. She would lie in bed and speak the messages aloud for, as "Thomas" sensibly observed, the new method was less fatiguing for the medium. Improvement or not, resentment lay just below the surface. On January 30, the night of the new moon, after "Thomas" had obliged with a definition of "abstraction" ("that quality in every phase which impedes unity of being"), bitter words burst forth:

> I don't like you
> You neglect me
> You dont give me physical symbols to use . . .[69]

The Script began winding down for a long break. On February 3 "Thomas" announced that the link with other spirits must be broken (by burning incense). Then, on February 9, "I am far away & getting further—may return after 14th—Yes—will—all this time is abnormal."[70] The couple was ordered to do no more than reread what they had accumulated. Yet "he" slipped back for occasional comments, giving instructions for *Calvary*, the play begun at Oxford that Yeats was to work on over the next two months when there would be no Script. There was silence for a week, then "Rose" appeared to issue a valediction on February 16, not a word of which is comprehensible in conventional speech but which shows both partners still preoccupied with their emotional and sexual compatibility. George put a question herself. Were they perhaps too similar in temperament?

Yes, "Rose" conceded, they were both easily exhausted, and prone to excessive expenditure of mental and physical energy. Then, delphically:

> Desire rising from desire decreases power of mental image—
> desire rising from mental images decreases physical power—
> natural desire is balanced with mental Now goodbye[71]

The confinement date was approaching. George moved to Dundrum, to live with the sisters, where she could have her breakfast in bed and be cared for by Rose and Maria. She was nervous and frightened. The baby was not due for a week when, on February 25, Yeats and Lily persuaded her to go into the nursing home on Upper Fitzwilliam Street booked for her accouchement. George complained that they were just trying to get rid of her. How relieved they would all be, Lily wrote her father, when his grandchild was sleeping in his cradle.[72]

At ten o'clock the following morning, February 26, 1919, Anne Butler Yeats was born. Yeats wrote the news immediately to Lady Gregory. He recounted proudly how George had not cried at all through her pains. She had burst into tears only when told that it was a girl.[73]

Well she might have done. Nothing in her clairvoyance or her Script had prepared her or Yeats for the possibility that the avatar might be female. Harder still to bear was the knowledge that Yeats had married her precisely in order to produce an heir; she herself, through "Anne Hyde," had promised him a son.[74]

Yeats, however, accepted the unexpected with good humor. Apart from thwarted family hopes and disappointed relatives, he told Lady Gregory, he himself really preferred to have a daughter. He relayed to Coole the baby's horoscope as analyzed by George: good looks but no great talent.[75] It was just what he might have ordered.

If he had gained one daughter, however, he had lost another. In London Iseult surrendered the virginity Yeats had long thought might be his to her employer, the "Ithyphallic poet," Ezra Pound.[76]

Under the circumstances, "Thomas," "Rose," "Aymor," and Co. were unavailable for comment.

8

Only One More

(March 1919–May 1920)

ONE MORNING at breakfast two months later, in a suburban cottage rented near the sisters in Dundrum, Yeats complained that his tea was cold. George jumped up and shook him. He was playing the neglected husband, she said; only the night before, she reminded him, he had offered to write his own letters if she were busy with the baby. Yeats protested amiably. There had been no martyrdom in his offer; he simply recognized that George now had a lot more to do.[1]

Lily watched the scene with great happiness: Willie, a family man at last. Describing it for her father, she added poignantly that "Baby" was the happiest event she could recall in her whole life. She simply could not believe that there was a new little Yeats and that she was entrusted occasionally to be nursemaid—as Lolly never was. The forthcoming baptism at Saint Mary's Donnybrook would see a great family gathering, with tea for all at Aunt Fanny's. Only one thing could make her happier. Why would her father not come home? She missed him dreadfully, and she needed someone to talk to: Lolly was no use. She herself would meet him in Liverpool. Willie would give him the same living allowance as at present. Why, oh why, would he not grant her dearest wish?[2]

Late in March 1919, halfway between the birth and the christening, the new parents resumed their automatic writing. The first words to reappear on George's page after the long silence came from "Thomas." After an order that they must fumigate the new house (a purification ceremony, performed with incense), a defensive torrent of words poured out. "Thomas" seemed to know there was some explaining to do. No, they had not been tricked into expecting the reincarnated son of Anne Hyde:

> I knew it was not Annes son—it could never be—I did not say so . . .
> Physically we cannot create nor cause you to create—we cannot influence sex—your system is all we think of—only that matters
> It would be folly to command—such a son could not be willed—to will sterilises choice & chance . . .[3]

How could they have been so foolish as to think that spirits could determine the sex of an unborn child? "Thomas," speaking for the whole ghostly band—and undoubtedly for the new mother as well—demanded irritably, "We gave you Anne—is not that horary remarkable enough?????"[4]

There followed some clear family-planning advice. The Yeatses were to have another child, but only one more—a son. This directive included an escape clause; the spirits were not to be held to blame if the wrong sex emerged once again. "Thomas" was most insistent on the matter:

but only one choice more

> child is chosen but remember we have not complete control
> & only one more—more would destroy system

too domestic[5]

Yeats accepted this most personal command without question. In the private notes he kept for himself, he called it the spirits' way of explaining that a son and daughter were needed for the symbolism and symmetry of the System: "the son & daughter need[ed] by them as symbols are the only children we must have." "Luck evidently means 4," he added.[6] The calculation accorded with his own faith in the magic of the number four, already embedded in his System; his Principles, Faculties, and Critical Moments all came in fours. From then on, he never wavered in his conviction that the next, and final, child would be male. They planned to call it John Butler Yeats, and by March 21, scarcely a month from their daughter's birth, they were already referring to "J.B."[7]

The insistence on "only one *choice* more" had the additional virtue of safeguarding George from endless childbearing in pursuit of the desired male heir. Now she was guaranteed a sensible, modern, two-child family. Her Script soon came to associate this anticipated final addition with the Fourth Daimon (also called the Black Eagle).

Solicitous as he was about George's energies, Yeats in no way moderated his pursuit of personal revelation. The rigorous routine resumed as before: long sittings almost every evening after dinner. Once, when Yeats impatiently began at quarter to nine, "Thomas" scolded that Yeats knew he did not like to appear before nine o'clock and would have to wait.[8] As before, Yeats was not short of questions; he put up to fifty on some nights. The medium (who, "Thomas" said, was now to be referred to as the "Interpreter") continued to oblige with page after page of streams of words run together. The next six weeks saw voluminous output.

If George had thought that her endeavors of the past seventeen months had ended her husband's preoccupation with his past loves, she was sadly wrong. Despite marriage, parenthood, and miraculous revelation, Yeats continued to press the old points of pain: his trauma at Mabel Dickinson's supposed pregnancy, George's hurt at the arrival of Iseult's letter on their honeymoon. Indeed, he seemed far more interested in interrogating his spiritual advisers about his past love life than in putting their teachings to artistic use, and he still could not resist babbling around Dublin about his occult discoveries. "Thomas" finally exploded in wifely rage:

> For each public speech or lecture you give after tomorrow during the next 6 months I shall stop Script one month—For every occasion you talk system in private conversation one month—Yes you must begin writing[9]

The Script had never flourished at Woburn Buildings, and when in May Yeats and George returned briefly to London, it slowed down. "Thomas," however, appeared on May 21. Or, rather, a new Control did, "Eurectha," claiming to represent "Thomas" in a new, "prelife" state. Yeats's questions now became markedly sexual. He needed no justification. Schooled in the religious eroticism of William Blake, seeking to clarify the ideal that he called Unity of Being—harmony between bodily desire and spiritual quest—he saw it as quite appropriate to try to assess the balance of instinct and emotion in sexual intercourse. He put the question to "Eurectha": At what point during the sexual act was the pure energy of genius at its peak?

"The moment just after entering" came the ready reply, "Eurectha" adding cryptically, "wrong entrance produces erratic energy."[10]

The validity of the Script was confirmed when the Stage Society, a group dedicated to performing original drama, put on his new play, *The Player Queen,* with two performances at the King's Theatre, Covent Garden, on May 25 and 27. He had been working on it inconclusively since 1909, but not until his spiritual teachers had clarified for him the concept of the antithetical self (which he long called the Mask)[11] was he able to complete the play by turning what had been a tragedy into farce.

The Times liked the result. Its drama critic was amused by the plot, in which the young wife, Decima, in order to take revenge on her drunken poet-husband, changes places with the real Queen—"and serve him right, for he has been sadly unfaithful to her." The review welcomed "a new gift in Mr. Yeats . . . writing thoroughly enjoyable nonsense."[12]

The main purpose of the London visit was to move two decades' accumulation of books and furniture out of Woburn Buildings in anticipation of the autumn return to Oxford; a growing family had no use for shabby, walk-up rooms in Bloomsbury. Yeats, arriving alone, went at first to stay with his mother-in-law, Nelly Tucker, at her latest London address, 27 Royal Crescent, Holland Park, while George took the baby and went (to the astonishment of her sisters-in-law) without a nurse to primitive Ballylee for a week to plant the garden.[13] (The childnurse who had been engaged had proved unsatisfactory, but a replacement was soon found.)

While in London, they were drawn into a fresh crisis in the Amoun Temple of the Stella Matutina branch of the Second Order of the Golden Dawn. As Brother D.E.D.I. and Sister Nemo, they remained important members of the strife-torn temple—so much so that later that year Yeats was considered as a candidate for Ruling Chief. (He refused the offer but might have been turned down in any case because of reports that he talked too freely.)[14] George herself was far from being the "Noone" of her secret name, and her considerable correspondence on Order business filled a large, brown, alphabetized folder.

The cochief of the temple, Miss Christina Mary Stoddart, sought their guidance. She was troubled by astral suggestions that she participate in curious ceremonies, of which a Black Mass on Holy Thursday was just one.[15] She detected the influence of a dissident member and, beyond him, the temple's founder, Dr. Robert Felkin. Although Felkin was in New Zealand at the time, he was under suspicion for a number of reasons, including the attempt to rule the London branch by remote control, and the claim to be receiving teaching from a new source, a mythical Arab adept called Ara Ben Shemesh.

What Miss Stoddart asked from D.E.D.I and Nemo were rituals with which to purge the Amoun Temple of this psychic pollution.[16] Rituals in the Golden Dawn were formulas as specialized and guarded as computer software. Each stage of advance through the order required a distinct ceremony. Initiation to the 6 = 5 degree, for example, called for the ringing of thirty-six bells, the sprinkling of salt, the burning, in specified sequence, of brown, red, green, and violet candles, and the barring of the postulant's way by crossed swords.[17]

Designing new rites obviously required some inventiveness. The London temple was fortunate indeed to have as one of its guiding lights a major poet and dramatist whose new specialty was the Noh play. (Seen today, Yeats's Noh plays can seem stylized and amateurish until the electrifying moment when the supernatural breaks through and the hair stands on end.) In May 1919, when Miss Stoddart turned to the Yeatses for help, they were spending much of their time in private ceremonies of evocation. What she was asking from them on behalf of the Amoun Temple was no more than they were doing at home.

Both Yeatses wanted to discourage further splintering. Consulting "Thomas-Eurectha," they received (through George's hand) clear instructions to abolish and burn all "rosy cross rituals" and reconsecrate all concerned by giving each a bowl of clear water to be thrown at the troublesome forces.[18] This advice, passed on by Yeats to Miss Stoddart, was another of the many psychic occasions when George used her power over the Script to elbow her husband aside. For his part, Yeats optimistically suggested that good could come out of evil: the spirits had permitted the disturbance in order to enable the temple to be purified and only the truly earnest students left to carry on.[19]

"Thomas-Eurectha" had some stern advice for the Yeatses as well. The intensity of their private sessions was weakening; incense was needed to renew it, but, as they were about to go to Oxford to look for a house for the winter, they were ordered not to attempt more Script until back in Ireland. Yeats was specifically instructed to restrain himself; he was not to communicate too much with Miss Stoddart and not to try too hard to interpret the various mysterious odors that flooded their nostrils. He was to leave such matters to his wife: "the medium is quite safe but not you."[20]

Installed at Ballylee for the summer, Yeats drew an idyllic picture for his father: the trestle table covered with bouquets of wildflowers, George sewing, and the child asleep in a seventeenth-century cradle.[21] He might have added that the child lay under no ordinary blanket, but rather under a Cuala coverlet embroidered by Lily to a design by Sturge Moore. Moore, who was more accustomed to doing Yeats's book jackets, had been astonished to learn that Yeats had commissioned the quilt for a real baby. "The idea never entered my head," he wrote Yeats, "as you spoke so decidedly while at Oxford in a contrary sense."[22]

Conditions were primitive. The nearest shops were four and a half miles away. There was no plumbing. Water for washing had to be fetched from the river in a large galvanized water carrier on wheels, while drinking water came from another source farther away. Family life took place mainly in the cottage (where the single earth-closet was located); peat fires or oil stoves had to be kept lit to reduce the dampness seeping from the walls.[23] The roof and top floors of the tower were unfinished, and there was no possibility of sleeping there. Yeats estimated that the place needed another year's work before it was finished. But he was feeling pinched. He had sent £234 to New York toward his father's debts the previous month, selling his legacy from his Sligo relatives at a loss in order to do so. So strained were their finances that George had to realize £100 of her assets and to pay for her own confinement costs.[24]

Where the welfare of his father and his sisters was concerned, Yeats was generous, if protesting. He now wrote to New York, with remarkable lack of rancor, to say that he did not begrudge the money but hoped that his father would return to Ireland soon. He promised the old man an allowance in Dublin, as well as membership in the University Club (the club for which he himself was ineligible) and many new friends, thanks to the fine reception accorded the recently published essays and letters of John Butler Yeats.[25]

To raise funds for himself and his growing family, there seemed only one solution: an American lecture tour. And there was only one way to make the decision. "Do you object to my going to America next spring?" Yeats asked "Thomas."[26] "Thomas" kindly gave his blessing.

Thoughts of making Ballylee their permanent summer home were clouded by the growing guerrilla war of the Sinn Fein's military wing, the Irish Republican Army, against the British Army and the Royal Irish Constabulary. (The RIC, although composed of Irishmen, was unquestionably a Crown force.) Yeats could all too easily imagine his tower with its windows smashed and Sinn Fein arms stored inside the walls. Perhaps, he wrote to John Quinn, he would do better to abandon the project and stay away from Ireland until Home Rule was established. "But would one ever come back?"[27]

In April, telling her father about the baby, Lily had said, "Willy looks at her shyly but is writing a poem on her."[28] He finished "A Prayer for my Daughter" in June at Ballylee. Like the apocalyptic "Second Coming," written when the child was on the way, the later, more personal poem is full of foreboding.

> And for an hour I have walked and prayed
> Because of the great gloom that is in my mind.
> . . . .
> Imagining in excited reverie
> That the future years had come,
> Dancing to a frenzied drum,
> Out of the murderous innocence of the sea.

These lines can be read as a prediction of the anarchy let loose on the twentieth century by everything from the Russian Revolution and the Treaty of Versailles to the Irish rebellion and the enfranchisement of women.

By the end of the century in which it was written, "A Prayer for my Daughter" seemed to have been designed deliberately to offend women. By feminist standards, it *is* offensive. Yeats wishes upon his newborn daughter's head all the constraints of nineteenth-century womanhood. What she needs above all is a husband with a Big House and a private income:

> And may her bridegroom bring her to a house
> Where all's accustomed, ceremonious.

In 1983 the feminist critic Joyce Carol Oates led the case for the prosecution in an eloquent paper, "At Least I Have Made a Woman of Her," which examined English literature's patriarchal demand for women to be nothing more than the gentle, protected helpmeets of their spouses.[29] Oates singled out for contempt Yeats's wish that his daughter grow up to be courteous rather than clever, and beautiful, but not too beautiful:

> May she be granted beauty and yet not
> Beauty to make a stranger's eye distraught,
> Or hers before a looking-glass,
> . . . .
> In courtesy I'd have her chiefly learned;
> Hearts are not had as a gift but hearts are earned
> By those that are not entirely beautiful;

To Oates, the "crushingly conventional" Yeats, still smarting from his rejection by Maud Gonne, wants to deprive his daughter of the extravagances of sensuality ("It's certain that fine women eat / A crazy salad with their meat")—and to deny her cerebral passions as well:

> An intellectual hatred is the worst,
> So let her think opinions are accursed.
> Have I not seen the loveliest woman born
> Out of the mouth of Plenty's horn,
> Because of her opinionated mind
> Barter that horn and every good
> By quiet natures understood
> For an old bellows full of angry wind?

It is bad enough, in Oates's eyes, to use a poem dedicated to a child as a means of insulting an old love. Worse is the paralyzing ultimate goal Yeats sets for his daughter:

> May she become a flourishing hidden tree
> That all her thoughts may like the linnet be,
> . . . .
> O may she live like some green laurel
> Rooted in one dear perpetual place.

"This celebrated poet," Oates raged, "would have his daughter an object in nature for others'—which is to say male—delectation. She is not even an animal or a bird in his imagination, but a vegetable: immobile, unthinking, placid, 'hidden.'" The essence of Yeats's case, as Oates summed up, was simple: "Its starkness disguised by the mesmerizing power of his language: it is that written language belongs to men and that women's natural duty is to remain silent."

But time has moved on. The poem can now be seen to contain a wish for Anne's autonomy ("self-delighting, / Self-appeasing, self-affrighting . . ."). It holds also a quiet tribute to George Yeats, who earned his heart even though one of "those not entirely beautiful": the poet wants his daughter to become like her mother. Yet a darker meaning now also shows through the lines. The cause of "the great gloom" in the poet's mind could be the incestuous thoughts that a daughter can stir in a father (and that Iseult Gonne roused in Yeats and in her stepfather, John MacBride). Rather than guaranteeing him freedom from the father-son warfare that scarred his own youth, the arrival of a daughter suddenly raised the specter of his guilty lust for young women.

In this light, the laurel tree of the poem refers to the Greek myth of Daphne, who was turned into a laurel tree by her father, the river god Peneus, in answer to her prayer to be kept a virgin forever rather than be violated by the pursuing god Apollo. To Elizabeth Cullingford, who offered this interpretation in 1993, the patriarchal social order of which Yeats approved freed a daughter from the incestuous wishes of her father only when he publicly gave her away to another man during the marriage ritual. "Although formally he releases his daughter to the bridegroom," she said of the father in the poem, "covertly he invites her to return to him and to the imprisonment of the laurel tree."[31]

Yeats's richness both allows and demands that his poems be read in every light. Recent Yeats scholarship places paramount importance on the order in which Yeats arranged his poems for publication in his various books. Yeats, it is now accepted, wrote books, not poems—that he intended meaning to be read into his careful sequences. In *Michael Robartes and the Dancer,* to be published by the Cuala Press in 1921, the juxtaposition of "A Prayer for my Daughter" and "The Second Coming" was deliberate and meant to be noticed.

This uncontestable argument ignores the fact that many, perhaps most, people do not read Yeats's poems in sequence. They know them rather from anthologies, or even from just a few favorite lines, such as the stanza that captures the love mixed with fear that overwhelms the new parent:

Once more the storm is howling, and half hid
Under this cradle-hood and coverlid
My child sleeps on. There is no obstacle
But Gregory's wood and one bare hill
Whereby the haystack- and roof-levelling wind,
Bred on the Atlantic, can be stayed;

The very title of the poem captures the helpless wish to protect—the reason, surely, why "A Prayer for my Daughter" is so loved.

The summer of 1919 at Ballylee was notable quite apart from the great if confused poem it produced. The medium's new self-confidence was reflected in the Script. As soon as they arrived in mid-June, George stopped running the words together as she performed her daily magic. The content of her automatic writing was more straightforward and businesslike than before; there was less anguished repetition and fewer wavering sketches. She now wrote both questions and answers in the same book, rather than letting Yeats read his questions from his.

In keeping with the new mood, "Thomas" introduced a new Control called "Ameritus," whose name has the New World sound of the trip taking shape in their minds. In the ever-significant backward writing, "Thomas" described "Ameritus" as "interpreters daimon."[32] This role was soon evident, for "Ameritus" spoke more plainly than any of the predecessors for George herself. "Thomas" is referred to obliquely in several of the subsequent Scripts.

George was well acquainted with Yeats's concept of "the daimon." This ethereal figure (derived from the Emanations of Blake, the muse-goddesses of Keats and Shelley, and his own experience of "Leo") was defined in 1918, in *Per Amica Silentia Lunae* as Yeats's driving muse. He also understood the "daimon" as the "ultimate self," the individual's inner sense of what he or she might become by striving—what in today's parlance is called "potential." He did not confuse (although his readers well may) the "daimon" with the "antiself"; the former was supernatural, the latter a facet of the individual personality. In sum, his "daimon" was a personal ghost—not so much a guardian angel as a guiding and hovering taskmaster.[33]

Much effort that summer went into pressing "Ameritus" to distinguish the characteristics of the Fourth Daimon, the ghost associated with (and, before long, virtually interchangeable with) the longed-for son, from those of the Third Daimon, represented by their daughter. The picture of the daimonic nuclear family was completed by the Script's linkage of Yeats and George with the First and Second Daimons.

By August 1919, six months after Anne's birth, George had decided that the time had come to get pregnant again. But the old dilemma remained: there could be no conception without sex, no sex without desire or strength to act on it. Yeats's passion seemed to be going into the Script rather than the marriage bed, and "Ameritus" grew explicit, dirigiste, even coarse, as never before. Yeats was particularly anxious about the right frequency for someone of his age to perform the sexual act. "Ameritus" seemed to know all about it:

Sexual health unaccustomed for some time to twice—there-
fore, gradually try twice as always once will increase fatigue—
But you must accustom yourself to gradually declining power
& rest assured your power will always be amply sufficient[34]

Decades after his death, Yeats was accused by Conor Cruise O'Brien
of having pretended to be politically naive when in fact he was shrewd
and sophisticated.[35] That charge may very well be true. In the summer
of 1919, however, at the age of fifty-four, Yeats seems to have been still
a genuine Candide in his sex life. Why, for example, he humbly asked
"Ameritus," should he endeavor to repeat the sexual act rather than
doing it just once? The straight answer came back in language hardly
more subtle than "use it or lose it": "Because you cease to be able to do
more—it is like not taking enough exercise & a long walk exhausts
you."[36] Plain enough, one might think. Yeats nonetheless wanted the
explanation spelled out. "You mean by only doing it once I will lose
power of doing it twice?"

"Exactly," answered "Ameritus," adding darkly, "& then of doing it
once."

Yeats then ventured some calculations that suggest that his sexual
ambitions were modest and ran to intercourse only twice a month or
even just once every six weeks. This led to another blunt, if coded,
husband-and-wife exchange:

I have been under the impression that we have been too
irregular lately
   Yes certainly[37]

Yeats's reluctance to "try twice" or to perform more than twice a
month suggests that the habit of long abstinence had not been altered
by marriage. But the advice given him in the Script is strong evidence
that "Ameritus" had been studying Stopes's recently published *Married
Love*. In this marriage manual, Stopes prefaced her discussion of sexual
frequency with a warning about the appetite of the modern woman:

"In recent years some young women expect far more sex union than a husband's physique can stand." Accordingly, she recommended

> fortnightly unions; for this need not be confined to only a single union on such occasion. . . . The mutually best regulation of intercourse in marriage is to have three or four days of repeated unions, followed by about ten days without any unions at all, unless some strong external stimulus has stirred a mutual desire.[38]

The Script moved on, to more convoluted but hardly less sexual matters. It returned to "Anne Hyde," and renewed efforts to establish connections between their families. This mythical ancestor, apart from having provided the name for their child, had such a grip on their imaginations that they went for a few days' visit to Kilkenny where they believed Anne to be buried. (They searched in vain for the grave.) The Script then veered toward incestuous shoals. A new Guide called "Ontelos" preached confusingly at Yeats that he must try to understand the import of his having been first "Anne's" lover, then her father, as husband of her daughter who had turned into her mother.[39]

Meaning what, Yeats wanted to know? The vague explanation that came said, in effect, that the reason why Yeats was now married to the reincarnated daughter of Anne was because "Anne did not love her child."[40]

This verbiage contains a strong hint of George Yeats's unhappy relations with her own mother, Nelly Tucker. Mrs. Tucker had tried to stop the marriage to Yeats, she had not welcomed George's pregnancy, and now she was proving an awkward, indifferent grandmother.[41] She appears again in the Script, referred to as the "interpreters mother," who in a past life had been the victim of a drunken husband.[42] If so, that was bad luck, for Mrs. Tucker had suffered the same fate in her marriage to George's father, William Hyde-Lees.

Debris from past incarnations floated through the Script that summer. There was mention of an inclination toward sodomy in one of Yeats's past lives,[43] and of his marriage to a woman with a tendency to drink in another. The medium was described as having been unfaithful to a previous husband. Then, on August 26, Yeats burst out with the question that perhaps was the underlying motive for the entire Script: "Why had I that crazy passion for MG?"[44]

He never did get a clear answer. In spite of pushing on day after day, he was rewarded only with the date of meeting of the woman in a previous life who—he repeated the phrase—"gave me my craze for MG." The year was 1542, the woman beautiful, but not as beautiful as Maud Gonne—and she had hated his own wife and tried to destroy her.

Such tantalizing fragments only whetted the poet's appetite to know more about the previous selves that had led to his fruitless devotion to Maud. He was putting as many as fifty-seven questions a night to the hard-pressed interpreter as they prepared to leave the solitude of their castle. Yet George too was working to put the past to rest. She obviously knew of the affair with Olivia Shakespear, and her jealousy of Olivia surfaced—attributed to a past life. Incredibly, the Mabel Dickinson incident was revisited once more.

For Yeats, it was all grist to the mill. As he wrote in his introduction to *Michael Robartes and the Dancer*, "Souls that are once linked by emotion never cease till the last drop of that emotion is exhausted . . . to affect one another, remaining as it were in contact."[45]

Until a hovering past love was extinguished, in other words, there was no hope of fully loving anyone in the present. At times George must have wondered what all her labor had achieved. "Ameritus" was now orchestrating their sexual unions, apparently in tempo with the fertile and infertile periods of the interpreter's menstrual cycle. Occasionally sharp prohibitions issued forth: "No Touching for two days," as if obeying Stopes's instructions to abstain before indulgence.[46] That the couple was trying for a baby is clear from Yeats's notes. After a visit to Oliver St. John Gogarty's Galway home, "Renvyle," there was a hint that the new conception might have taken place. But the next day in the Script, Yeats regrets a "J. B. disaster."[47] "J. B." were his father's initials, and along with the Fourth Daimon and the Black Eagle, was one of their code names for the new child.

A curious feature of the Script from beginning to end, and particularly that summer, was its obsession with sleep. Over and over again the Controls and Guides insisted upon lots of sleep—ostensibly to encourage dreaming and to give the medium the strength for spiritual communion. This instruction accorded with George's personal inclination. In her ordinary life, she was a strong advocate not only of early bedtimes but of long naps after lunch; she called them "two-to-fours."[48] Accordingly, "Ameritus," in a discussion of ideal lovers, made the following observation to Yeats on September 11:

> You need more sleep
> sleep earlier—sleep in the dark is creative—sleep in the light only a stimulant[49]

By the second half of September, with the days drawing in and the time coming to return to Oxford, "Ameritus" changed the focus of the Script from sexual to physical health. Yeats was advised to see a doctor at once. He was to keep more regular hours, drink water morning and evening and milk at night, and have grapenuts or porridge for breakfast. "You eat too fast," said the words on the page.[50] Yeats asked in amazement: "Do you see our physical interiors?" He hardly needed to ask.

They left Ballylee late in September. The summer of intense, isolated collaboration had produced a great quantity of Script but had left them, just as they were the year before, at cross-purposes. Yeats wanted the sexual lessons from the spirit world to illuminate his system of philosophy, George wanted them to produce another baby. Yet together they were using the discourse of the Script to overcome the unhappiness of their separate pasts, and they were equally gripped by the fascination of the eerie game they were playing.

Returning to Oxford, they moved to 4 Broad Street, opposite Balliol. They took the house (long since pulled down) on a six-month lease, and George turned her hand to making it warm and beautiful, with pictures, dark bookcases, orange curtains, and a sitting room painted chemical red. As with her clothes, her home decoration was governed as much by occult symbolism as by aesthetics. Brilliant colors, according to "Ameritus," were, like incense, necessary to ward off "bad lunar neptunian influence."[51]

Back in the academic groves, Yeats pressed his spiritual tutors hard. He wanted to learn about the transference of thoughts and images from the dead to the living. In his engineer's frame of mind once more, he focused on the image of Keats's nightingale. Where had Keats gotten it? (Answer: "from a *previously existing transference.*")[52] And Keats's thoughts when composing the "Ode to a Nightingale": had these too been transferred to future generations? Told that they were, Yeats saw the exciting possibility of Keats's thoughts floating in what he was then calling the "general mind," available to be tapped. He pressed his line of questioning. If no one in Keats's lifetime had read the ode, would the image of the nightingale have had such an impact on thousands of readers in later generations?

When "Ameritus" said emphatically not, Yeats drew the conclusion (very reassuringly to a poet who had devoted much creative energy to public life) that a writer had to make an impact in his own time if his work was to mean anything to posterity.

The Script very soon circled back to sex. "Ameritus" was now blatantly dictatorial, specifying the days to make love or refrain: "Tonight no sun-in-moon" (sun-in-moon designated by their symbols), or, "No use tonight After next Martha without fail on these dates."[53] The dates were then written astrologically. On October 18 Yeats received a scolding—how many times did he have to be told?—that he should not ask the medium to perform automatic writing when she was menstruating. That was a time when she was open to "all influences" (a subtle warning of the Frustrators lurking about).[54]

"Ameritus" began to complain about a lack of "force." The words sound like a plea for more sex, as in the lament "I cant be left for so long again without force." There was also a strong statement about the interpreter's need for orgasm. Yeats, it appears, had already accepted the importance of "a long excited preliminary." Always willing to learn more, he asked "Ameritus" why, in sexual union, "the finish" (apparently his and George's code word for orgasm) was so necessary for the medium. He got in return a written lecture explaining that these things are very different for women than for men—that for a woman, the "fin-ish" was "a climax not a hollowing out." What was more, "Ameritus" continued, the Script was only possible *"between 2 who are connected."*[55]

Yeats was now truly bewildered. There were, he protested, three months before Anne's birth when sun-in-moon was impossible yet still the Script kept coming.[56] Why was sexual union so essential now? "Ameritus" was ready with the answer: sex was so central to the present subject matter that the medium's creative force was utterly dependent on it. If there was no desire in the medium, there was no mediumship.

George's motives in these exchanges are unclear. Was she pleading for more sex from genuine desire or from a conscious plan to com-plete her family before Yeats's potency disappeared entirely? Was she exhibiting the primitive fear of a traditional wife that if she fails to pro-duce the expected heir she will forfeit her right to hold her husband?

Of George's determination, there is no doubt. Under the name of "Ameritus," at bedtime on November 20, she wrote three times back-ward: "both the desire of the medium and her desire for your desire should be satisfied."[57]

Yeats knew that George was still worried about the other, more beautiful, women in his life. In November he wrote "Under Saturn," a poem that is almost an apology for neglect:

Do not because this day I have grown saturnine
Imagine that lost love, inseparable from my thought
Because I have no other youth, can make me pine;
For how should I forget the wisdom that you brought,
The comfort that you made?

These quiet lines fall somewhat short of the passionate sex begged for in the pages of the Script. As the poetry critic Marjorie Perloff has observed, "'Wisdom, comfort'" are "terms that no woman is likely to find very flattering, especially when 'A sweetheart from another life floats there.'"[58]

That worrying line had just appeared in another poem Yeats wrote that autumn, "An Image from a Past Life," a dialogue in which the female voice, clearly representing George, is frightened by her failure to dispel the ghost of her partner's past.

Yeats had been right to wonder if they would ever return to Ireland. The self-proclaimed Dáil had been formally suppressed by the British government, its headquarters and papers seized. News of raids and shootings shared space in family letters with domestic gossip. Lily, writing to her father that Iseult Gonne and Lennox Robinson had been to Dundrum to dinner and that Yeats and George hoped the two would marry, commented that the ruling military forces could not be making more mistakes.[59]

With the troubles in Ireland growing worse, Yeats was quite tempted by the offer of a two-year lectureship in Japan. He even told his father that he had accepted it subject to terms. In mid-November, however, "Ameritus" vetoed it absolutely, in the interests of his book of philosophy—"I said before no Japan next year"—and told Yeats to send a telegram staving off the invitation.[60]

Time was getting short before the trip to the United States, the interpreter was getting tired. The magical powers of sex and sleep were now combined. On December 10 "Ameritus" (writing four times backward) commanded Yeats to wait until his wife was asleep, then to put her into a "mesmeric sleep" (Yeats had some skill as a hypnotist) and, when she began to speak aloud, to make love to her.[61]

Shortly before Christmas, a new Control appeared, even more commanding. "Dionertes," edging "Ameritus" aside, reminded Yeats that the medium must be made "creatively active for script."[62] That is, as a hyponotist and a husband, Yeats had a responsibility to keep George in a state in which she could perform. Within days, "Dionertes" had halted the Script "because of monthly indisposition" and went on to declare that the medium was too exhausted for Script, that she would need an afternoon nap of at least an hour the next day, and that Yeats was at fault for not having put her "deeper."[63]

Yeats must at times have felt that he could not do anything right. He was ordered never to do hypnotism without permission. Yet he obviously was trying to play his part, for at Christmas he gave George a bracelet that the Script recognized as symbolizing "Daimonic concordance between two people." When "Dionertes" asked him as well to perform a "marriage invocation" over one of his wife's rings to break a link with the past, he probably obliged.[64]

Even as they packed for the United States, the Script poured out on most nights. The old themes whirled round with new anxious touches: deformed personalities, exhaustion, failure of desire, the need for getting to bed early. In the first week of January 1920, with the full moon approaching, there was a new reference to the arrival of the Irish avatar. A date was mentioned: the coming September 24.[65]

Was the avatar's conception being postponed until after the American journey?

As they left Oxford, Anne was dispatched with the servants to be looked after in Ireland. Yeats was sad to leave his first real home, one which so pleased his taste,[66] but George, looking forward to her first transatlantic trip, did a horary. Her stars foretold a warm, sunny crossing, with the occasional violent storm in which someone on the ship might break an arm or a rib.

Leaving a child of eight months runs contrary to current thinking on maternal deprivation. Yet it was then standard practice for the well-to-do to entrust their children to servants for long periods, just as it was considered a wife's duty to travel with her husband if required. Lady Gregory had left her young son, Robert, for nearly all of his first two years in order to accompany Sir William to India, Egypt, and Italy. Little Anne Yeats, with Lily as a virtual second mother, was well off in Dundrum where all marveled at her ruddy health and good disposition.[67]

For the parents, after months largely spent in seclusion in one another's company, a blast of fame and high living was not unwelcome. Sailing from Liverpool on January 13 on the *Carmania* and arriving in New York on January 24, Mr. and Mrs. W. B. Yeats were photographed as celebrities: he magisterial in soft hat and a massive, double-breasted fur coat that looks like the chinchilla mocked by George Moore six years earlier; she looking her most seerish, with a kind of bedouin headdress pulled low over her sharp brows and a voluminous and fashionably ethnic cape clutched around her shoulders.

They checked into the Algonquin Hotel. George was apprehensive that John Quinn and Yeats's father would not like her. Instantly upon arrival, she telephoned John Butler Yeats and introduced herself. Quinn then materialized and escorted them down to the boarding-house at 317 West 29th Street where the white-bearded patriarch was waiting to greet them, dressed, according to William Murphy's fine biography, in his best suit and dancing pumps. Like his daughters, the father gave George an artist's scrutiny and decided that she would be better looking if she did not have a certain drawn quality about the mouth. Her piercing gaze made him feel as if he were a specimen under observation, but he noticed too that she had a caustic tongue, a managerial flair, and a great capacity for taking care of Willie. "I like her, I think, very much," he wrote his brother Isaac.[68]

Quinn liked her too and thought that the couple seemed devoted to each other. He was surprised that Yeats had gone completely gray but was reminded, after the long wartime separation, not only of Yeats's brilliance ("the one man of absolute genius I have known personally and well") but of his affability ("one of the most pleasant companions I ever knew and one of my best friends)."[69] Quinn listened patiently while Yeats excitedly told him all his new theories about a new Renaissance based on the proven immortality of the soul.

Busy on a round of lectures and dinners, the couple had little time for automatic writing. Only once did the Script flicker into life: at the Algonquin, on Sunday, February 1, 1920. George recorded the encounter as "New York Time 3.40 Dionertes,"[70] as if the rest of their spirit masters were still on Greenwich Mean Time.

Their paranormal exercises, of course, had to be concealed from the rationalist John Butler Yeats, who had already scolded his son for his return to mysticism and saw all such activity as a self-indulgence by which the mystic sought to convince himself.[71]

The son was more alarmed by the self-indulgence of the father. Yeats quickly surmised that John Butler Yeats was disinclined to budge from Manhattan. He summarized the situation for Lady Gregory: his father feared sinking into his second childhood if he returned to Ireland, while in New York he was happy and as optimistic about the future as if he were a boy, convinced that if he stayed there he would paint a masterpiece.[72] (The masterpiece was to be his long-unfinished self-portrait.)

Personally, Yeats had none of Lily's longing to have their father back. Neither did Jack. For the sons, the oedipal war still raged. However, the stay in New York was consuming huge amounts of Yeats's own money. In addition to the £234 he had sent the previous summer, he had brought over with him a bundle of manuscripts for Quinn as yet another deposit into the bottomless pit. Furthermore, he had undertaken to guarantee his father's future debts, and these were unlikely to be small. The old bohemian, in spite of the occasional lucrative portrait commission, was as profligate in old age as in middle life and could be counted upon, once his bills were paid, to run them up to equal heights all over again.

(No evidence has ever emerged that any of the money was going on sexual favors or indeed that John Butler Yeats had any romantic involvement during his years in New York. He had, however, conducted a long epistolary romance with a woman in Dublin. Rosa Butt, the daughter of Isaac Butt, his Trinity College friend, founder of the Irish Home Government Association [forerunner of the Irish Home Rule movement], received hundreds of his passionate, confessional, and entertaining letters.[73] It is possible that he clung to New York in order to avoid facing this woman of his dreams.)

George Yeats and her father-in-law got to know one another well. While Yeats did short trips by himself for lectures in Toronto and Quebec, she remained in New York and trudged many times, even in the snow, down to visit the boardinghouse on West 29th Street. The portraitist did a fine pencil sketch of George, marred, like much of his work, by his usual fault of prettifying his subject. In the process, he surmised that she did not like Lolly and that she was the only woman he had ever met who was not afraid of Lady Gregory.[74]

As for George's reaction to the United States, she was her usual blend of disdain and docility. She liked Quinn, she liked the architecture; she disliked the social climbers she met in New York who were pursuing her (can she really have minded?) as "Mrs. W. B. Yeats."

Seated at the head table at the Hotel Astor at the Poetry Society's dinner in Yeats's honor, she wrote "ghastly bore" and "dreadful woman" against august socialite names in the program.[75]

Yeats was pleased to see his wife enjoying herself. In Pittsburgh late in February, he feared she would go home, as she missed the baby terribly and was worried by reports that the child was not gaining weight.[76] When better news arrived from Lily, she relented. Even so, when sending a book of poems to Wellesley College as a thank-you to the organizer of his visit, she enclosed a photograph of Anne, saying that the child was as precious to her as poetry was to her husband.[77]

The Yeatses crisscrossed the United States in the drawing room of a train, to a heavy timetable, designed by the J. B. Pond Lyceum Bureau. Yeats was a good platform performer. He spoke without a prepared text and unashamedly played the ladies' man. He would introduce "The Cap and Bells" as a poem "to win a lady" and "The Cloths of Heaven" as one "to lose a lady."[78] Lightly referring to the love for Maud Gonne that was on his audience's minds, he would announce that he absolutely refused to read any poem that could be construed as autobiographical. The readings usually began with his adolescent "Lake Isle of Innisfree," to get it over with, and were delivered in the throbbing, Homeric voice that told the audience, even as it made them squirm, that they were in the presence of a real poet.

Yet under the urbanity and the big fur coat was a man in constant battle with the spirits he felt were trying to invade his mind. The odor of violets seeped into their Pullman compartment, and other strange scents—incense, paraffin, feathers, new carpets, antiseptic, and candlewax—continued to haunt them. Yeats began to wonder if the souls of the dead were using his senses to think and feel through him.[79]

George also sensed a constant stream of signals from the other world. She reported these dramatically to Yeats, in tones of astonishment that his written accounts make it easy to imagine. While in Chicago she heard a voice say, "Fourth shelf from window third from floor, seventh book," and realized that at that very moment she was passing a bookshop.[80] She went in, located the specified volume, and bought it: Freud's *Totem and Taboo*. There she found the answer to the very question that had been plaguing her: why did she keep seeing the image of three birds? (If she had reread her earlier Script, she would not have needed Freud to tell her that the birds represented Maud, Iseult, and herself.)

In Chicago "Dionertes" offered an explanation of the barrage of mysterious aromas. It was that every sensation, sight, sound, or smell experienced by any living creature was caught and kept "in a strata between your world & ours." From that accumulated "general mind," or "record," spirits selected thoughts, feelings, and smells for transfer to particular individuals.[81] Yeats was growing clearer in his ideas of a universal memory bank.

Salt Lake City particularly impressed the traveling occultists, who recognized it as a spiritual center. Yeats lectured at two Mormon universities, and found the Mormons' claim of continuous miraculous inspiration very congenial.[82] Their own spirits, he noted, were so pleased with what they had learned during the visit that, when they were back in their Pullman car heading west, they were rewarded with the sensation of water being sprinkled on their foreheads.[83]

In Portland, Oregon, with a new flourish—upside-down writing—George wrote four times the equation "sword = birth," followed by another, "FISH = conception."[84] She wondered aloud whether she would soon have a son. Later in the day when the Japanese consul, Junzo Sato, had presented him with the gift of a ceremonial sword wrapped in embroidered silk, Yeats heard loud and clear the words: "quite right that is what I wanted."[85] The Script later confirmed that he had had a "direct voice" communication from the unseen world.

It was now March. They had been away three months. The Script appeared only fitfully, as the train carriages swayed too much for easy transcription. Such as it did, it dealt with the ways in which memory survives death. For much of the journey, the couple passed the time by shuffling and dealing out their pack, or packs, of tarot cards.

Arriving in Pasadena, Yeats saw a small picture begin shaking violently on its nail. More attuned to the tremors of the Golden Dawn than of the San Andreas Fault, he wrote in his notebook, "This has reminded me to make record of various supernormal events since we came to America."[86]

The most surprising supernormal event of the trip was about to come. In Pasadena, after more reflections on the universal record of sensations and thoughts, "Dionertes" abruptly called a halt to the automatic writing. George inscribed, under "Dionertes'" name, "I do not really want script here—I prefer to use other methods—sleeps. . . . always wait till she murmurs . . . "[87]

Yeats was dismayed. He wanted to know more about the universal record. Did it contain the sight of a tree, the sound of the human voice? Yes, "Dionertes" assured, all were there. Clearly flailing in the hope of keeping the line of communication open, Yeats tried one more question: "Does not touch also pass into record?"[88]

"Yes quite easily obvious goodnight," "Dionertes" replied, and vanished.

Yeats was not the only visitor from the British Isles to be touring the United States that spring. Edward, prince of Wales, was there, as was Eamon de Valera, the president-elect of the rebel-proclaimed Irish Republic, who had been in the United States for eight months drumming up support (after having escaped from Lincoln Jail and being smuggled across the Atlantic). The three men were covering much the same ground against a background of grim news from Ireland.

In April 1920 there was a general strike against the terrorizing methods of the Black and Tans. These were recruits, mainly ex-soldiers, hired for good pay (ten shillings a day) to bolster the police in the war against Sinn Fein and the IRA. The flippant nickname accorded these imports by the angry populace had a double source: the amateurishly assembled uniform of army khaki, worn with the dark belts and caps of the police, and a famous hunting pack of foxhounds in Scarteen, County Limerick.

The undisciplined Black and Tans swiftly made themselves hated as they swaggered about, smoking and drinking, fingering their revolvers, suspecting all young men of belonging to the IRA, and raiding and often destroying the homes of suspects.

American newspapers in cities with large Irish immigrant populations gave equal prominence to the news from Ireland (fires, cattle-driving, hunger strikes, and kidnappings), the Paris treaty negotiations, the American women's suffrage issue, and the Mexican Civil War. When Yeats reached Los Angeles, the headlines in the *Los Angeles Sunday Times* were MAKING READY FOR PRINCE and CLOSE WATCH ON SINN FEIN. On its inside page, at the end of an item on Yeats's coming lecture, "A Theater of the People" (tickets 50 cents, 75 cents, and $1), it added, "Mr. Yeats is not connected in any way with the Sinn Fein movement and is entirely removed from the political turmoil in Ireland."[89]

As their tour headed back east through the southern United States, the new method, "Sleeps"—George talking aloud while apparently asleep—got off to a florid start. There were stops at San Antonio, where the *Evening News* on April 15 recorded how Yeats, whom it described as "a native of Dublin and the son of the well-known artist J.B. Yeats," had captivated his audience with his talk on sincerity and realism in the Abbey Theatre: "If an actor was wanted to play a man from Cork, they got a man from Cork, brogue and all."[90] Then on to New Orleans, where de Valera had just made headlines, first with "IRISH REPUBLIC'S" HEAD WILL ARRIVE IN ORLEANS TODAY, and then by receiving an honorary doctorate of laws from Loyola University, where he declared there was no possibility of Ireland's compromising for anything less than full independence."[91]

After each city they were back on the train. For the Sleeps, Yeats was now the amanuensis, as he had not been allowed to be for the Script. He transcribed visions of George seeing herself dead, of many sleepers floating through the air—colorless, formless—shades in search of form, souls shifting between life and death. Many Sleeps went unrecorded as he struggled to catch her somnolent words over the screech of brakes and the shunting of carriages in the night.[92] At one point he received a warning from the speaking dreamer that if he did not talk to the medium about his System before beginning a session, "there is a danger of developing sleap into a secondary personality."[93] (Considering the number of personalities manifesting themselves through his wife, Yeats ought to have taken the warning to heart.)

The "Sleaps," as Yeats consistently misspelled the word in his notebooks, had an obvious advantage for the medium. They were less tiring and required less homework and heavy thinking.

Yet the end of the Script was a blow to the marriage. The intimacy and intensity of nearly daily question-and-answer sessions shared since the first awkward honeymoon days were gone. Gone too was George's power to deal with Yeats's considerable sexual difficulties, as well as the opportunity to make the case for her own satisfaction.

Back in New York the news from Ireland was grim. Hatred of the "B&Ts" in no way protected the public from fear of the IRA, which considered that anyone not supporting them was a traitor. As the IRA had no uniforms, its members were impossible to identify or avoid.

Yeats worried about bringing Anne back to Ballylee in the summer. With all the shootings, he wrote to Lady Gregory, was there a reliable milk supply?[94] But not to go made a nonsense of all the money he was pouring into the place.

There was other news from Ireland. Iseult Gonne was married. Her husband was a young writer about whom, Ezra Pound reported, the worst that could be said was that he was not yet a good poet.[95]

That was not true. The worst that could be said about the very tall, handsome, and gifted Francis Stuart, an Ulsterman educated at Rugby, was that he had only just turned eighteen. Iseult was twenty-five. The marriage had taken place against Maud's wishes, but, as young Stuart had converted to Rome for the purpose, she had consented to attend the Catholic wedding.[96] The event must have come as a relief to both Yeats and to George, for they firmly believed (as did Iseult and Francis Stuart, as things turned out) that marriage, no matter what happened, was for life.

In Manhattan, the Yeatses foresook the Algonquin for John Quinn's apartment at 58 Central Park West. The old breach between the two men over Quinn's mistress was a thing of the past, forgotten in the wake of Yeats's marriage and Quinn's ill health (he had bowel cancer).

Quinn escorted Yeats to a public meeting to hear (for the first time) Eamon de Valera. The occasion allowed Yeats to give his private verdict to Lady Gregory: he found de Valera patient, energetic, charmless, demanding, and lacking in human sympathy.[97]

On this visit Yeats also met Quinn's latest and most impressive mistress, the beautiful, calm, and intelligent Jeanne Robert Foster. She later told the story of the famous couple's arrival at Quinn's apartment. As Quinn had not yet introduced her, he pushed her into a closet, to be presented later when the Yeatses had freshened up and emerged from their room. From her involuntary hiding place, she claimed to have overheard the couple arguing whether or not to have a second child. Yeats, she said, was opposing the idea.[98]

She was not to know that "Thomas," "Ameritus," and "Dionertes" considered the matter settled. All she could have heard, if her ears or claustrophobia did not deceive her, were Yeats's residual doubts. Conceiving the son and heir was top of the agenda as the Yeatses sailed from Montreal for Liverpool aboard the *Megantic*.

John Butler Yeats was very sad to say goodbye to his son and daughter-in-law. When they invited him to come back with them (and Quinn had urged them to press the invitation hard), he had declined. But as soon as they were on the high seas, he wrote to George saying that the sight of them had released a great longing for Ireland in him.[99]

9

Waiting for J. B.

(May 1920–July 1922)

THERE WAS NO QUESTION of Ballylee upon their return. Workmen
were just beginning work on the tower they should have finished,[1] and
in the west of Ireland the Black and Tan war was in full swing. While
George went to Dublin to collect Anne from a heavy-hearted Lily
(who was ashamed of herself for being so reluctant to hand back the
baby),[2] Yeats waited in London. He dipped into his American earnings
to splurge on a green parrot and a medieval-looking set of pewter
dishes for the house in Oxford.

Once settled at 4 Broad Street, all was indeed "accustomed, ceremo-
nious." A Burmese gong sounded dinner. Irish maids scuttled about.
The parrot sat in a cage on the landing; Blake drawings hung from the
walls. Anne was, Yeats wrote Lady Gregory with pride, "staggering
about full of destructiveness."[3]

*   *   *

The "Sleeps," begun in California, gathered full force. George was good at them. She could fall asleep from one instant to the next, words streaming from her mouth almost immediately. Yeats, avid as ever, took advantage of this new method to be a more active partner. He now kept his own notebooks and amplified them with extensive comment in his card files. The alternative methods of spirit communication recommended by "Dionertes" suited him equally well: meditation, revelatory dreams, and visions summoned up in the state between sleep and waking—the kind of reverie that psychoanalysis knows as fantasy and of which Yeats was a world-master. With his book of philosophy in mind, he shaped his material as he went along. The resulting *Sleep and Dream Notebooks* have a freshness and coherence missing from the *Vision Papers,* made out of the erratic, obscure Script.

He and George meditated separately, then met to compare and discuss, happy when their visions harmonized as on the day when a golden boat appeared to them both. The synchronicity of their dreams was gratifying. When George reported a dream of a Greek mask suspended from a door handle, Yeats countered with his of a golden-haired, super-humanly handsome young man dressed in a seventeenth-century costume of purple velvet. Taken together, what did these mean? Conception, they hoped. Was it J. B.'s daimon? Yeats asked himself.[4]

Domestic life was shattered in late July by a letter from Maud, with the sorry tale of Iseult's marriage. Scarcely two months after her wedding, Iseult was estranged from her teenaged bridegroom, who had starved her, beaten her, burned her clothes, sold her engagement ring, but managed to get her pregnant nonetheless. In a subsequent letter Maud told Yeats he need not bother to come to Ireland, although she would be grateful for a chance to talk to him about Iseult's condition. ("*Except to George,* don't mention to anyone that I think there is a child on the way.")[5]

He arrived the next day. George did not accompany him, for two reasons: Lily was coming for a visit, and George thought that she too had a child on the way.[6]

Once in Ireland, Yeats found himself invigorated, even euphoric, wafted by the smell of violets as he swung himself into his role as guardian. Checking in at the Stephen's Green Club, he went down to Glenmalure to interview Iseult, who told him that when she had been alone with her husband in the remote house, she had heard the banshee[7]—an omen Yeats was never inclined to minimize. He interviewed various witnesses about Francis Stuart's behavior. All the charges were verified, with the additional information that Stuart refused to accept financial responsibility for his wife or child, although he had an allowance of over £350 a year from his mother.[8]

Yeats thought he might have some influence over the budding teenage poet, who, he knew, was full of admiration for him and eager for an introduction. Enlisting the help of Dublin's leading gynecologist, Bethel Solomons, he arranged for Iseult to go into a nursing home where Stuart was to be allowed to see her only once, under orders not to discuss any distressing matter with her, after which she was to disappear into the country without telling him her whereabouts. Stuart was then to be denied any further access to his wife until he agreed to a financial settlement.[9]

Iseult complied, but refused to consider separating from Stuart. If her husband were mad, she said, then he needed her all the more. Yeats was left to ponder the inexplicability of sexual selection. Writing all but the most graphic details of the case to Lady Gregory, he said he did not want anyone to know he had interfered in the matter.[10] Did he think that his presence in and around Dublin could go unremarked? At the Royal Hotel in Glendalough, where he and George had stayed on their honeymoon, someone had cut the celebrated name out of the guestbook.[11]

Out of touch with her husband, having received no letter for five days, George began to notice worrying symptoms. A long astrological calculation brought warnings of deception and entanglement in the Fifth House. Worse, even though a very English woman in a very English environment, she too heard the cry of the banshee. The conclusion was soon undeniable. She wrote to Yeats at the Stephen's Green Club to say that there was to be no baby.[12]

Yeats informed Solomons that his wife had suffered a six-weeks' miscarriage (*mishap* was their delicate word for it).[13] Solomons, a much-admired, rugby-playing Dublin medical man, master of the Rotunda—the maternity hospital—was a doctor in whom George placed great trust as he had delivered Anne. But she declined Yeats's suggestion that she come over to Dublin for a consultation.[14]

The "mishap" was accompanied by strange events at 4 Broad Street. George's excited letters to Yeats, with many exclamation points and bold underlinings, conveyed in essence that Lily *must have* picked up the vibrations of something's being wrong because every night she had felt a *hand* on her head, smoothing her hair or pulling it! Anne's nurse, what was more, had smelled incense outside of the nursery. Even more bizarre was the sudden appearance of a bill dated 1864 in an old bureau of George's father's—right on top of Anne's clothes. George knew for a certainty that the letter had not been there before. She had owned the bureau for a dozen years and knew its contents well, even during her father's lifetime. That was not all! Investigating the interstices of the bureau, she found a dozen more letters, equally old. How they came to be there was *totally* inexplicable. The stationery would need to be studied carefully, for one letter carried a crest with a stag or a *unicorn*. A portent clearly, but of *what*?[15]

Peace of mind, perhaps. Right after these incidents George suddenly felt serene and heard a voice saying, "Let the 3rd element begin its operation, for now Jupiter has no antagonists."[16]

Her letters to Yeats, like his to her during that period of separation, were effusive and loving; at this point in their marriage, they were still very close. When at last she received full details from him about Iseult (how she had been rationed to six cigarettes a day in the nursing home and examined by a "lunacy doctor"—Yeats's term for psychiatrist,[17] George wept with relief. She could not wait for his return and planned to meet him in London so that they could have dinner together without Lily around. She reminded him to label his luggage for Paddington so that it would not be sent through Crewe.[18]

Not surprisingly, Lily was not having a good time in Oxford, apart from seeing her cherished niece.[19] She was not told about the miscarriage and accepted the explanation that the indisposition was caused by "Martha." She thought that George's occultist friends—G. R. S. Mead, editor of two occult journals and cosecretary of the Esoteric Section of the Theosophical Society, and his wife—were cranks, and begged them to keep the conversation simple so that she could follow it[20]—a plea that infuriated George, who detested small talk, especially when theosophy was on offer.[21]

After a refreshing visit to Coole, Yeats returned home. Immediately the quest for conception resumed. "Dionertes" had indicated that August 13 would be a good date for an attempt—if they were not too tired; otherwise, two weeks later would be a good time to try, when the moon was full. By the end of the month George was once again counting the days. A new Control called "Thalassa" arrived, however, looked at the sleeping medium, and (as Yeats recorded the scene) diagnosed "conception has not taken place."[22] Events soon confirmed that "Thalassa" was correct.

The couple next turned to an astrological almanac, which showed that the prospects for "sun-in-moon" were good for the two nights after September 29 but bad for the ten days following. "Dionertes" volunteered a practical suggestion: that they should lie down every afternoon for five minutes between two and three o'clock and meditate on "The Heir." A new team of spirits, whose names Yeats recorded as the "Lunar group" or "the Poseidon," appeared and took up the cause. If there were no conception within a year, they promised to provide a ritual for using the Third Daimon to bring the Yeatses into contact with the Fourth.[23]

Spiritual instruction ran to the minutiae of daily life. On the Yeatses' drawing room mantelpiece was a small Indian boat. Any night when the couple did not wish "Dionertes" to appear, they were to cover the boat with a black cloth. If they did not wish images for meditation either, they were to hold an orange cloth over the boat before the black one.[24] Tigers and elephants were now appearing in George's Sleeps, as were cats (pets for which the Yeatses had a great fondness, domestically and psychically; they allowed their cat, Harry, to sleep between them.)

Yeats's meticulous description of George's talking dreams gives them a controlled, play-acting quality. If the question of fakery may arise in some minds once more, it never arose in Yeats's. One day, when he witnessed his sleeping wife making lapping movements like a cat drinking milk, he asked "Dionertes" what to do. The helpful suggestion was that he imitate a dog. Yeats obliged with a self-conscious "Bow Wow," at which the sleeping George pulled away from him in seeming panic.[25]

Another night, when apparently asleep, she moved her legs as if on a trotting horse, then threw her face in the pillow. Coming up for air, she blew with her mouth as if she were trying to expel something. At that point she awoke and told her watchful husband that, having dreamed that she had been thrown from a horse into some moss, she was trying to spit the moss out. "I did not know the meaning of the movements till she woke & told her dream," the poet wrote in his notes.[26]

He would address his comments to "Dionertes" directly, confident that George did not hear them. When her sleeping hands one night began to move over his ears, he scolded "Dionertes"—"I suggest you stop her feeling my ears"—whereupon George drew her hands away quickly and cowered back from him. "Dionertes" explained—through George's mouth—that she thought she was feeling the ears of a donkey and that the donkey had bitten her.[27]

Few hours can have passed in the Yeats household without a reference to an apparition, a transported object, a ringing bell, or mysterious whistling. One day when Yeats came in from his walk and said that he had been gone for an hour because, deep in thought over his philosophy, he had lost his way, George contradicted him: "O no for I saw you sitting in your chair in the study reading twenty minutes ago."[28] Yeats noted this as evidence that he had been in two places at once. Another day, after they searched in vain for George's code book of diagrams, she did a horary and was led instantly to the book, which had fallen behind a wardrobe in Yeats's room. The presence of odors with no apparent cause was almost too commonplace to record.

Astrology governed their every decision. In October 1920 Yeats, having been advised to have his tonsils removed, had gone to see a Harley Street specialist, even though George wanted him to have the operation in Dublin. When he got to London, he found he had the wrong address but then could not find the correct one in the telephone book. Going back to Oxford defeated, Yeats realized that he had not found the surgeon's double-barreled name because he had looked it up under the second half. George consulted the stars about Yeats's "mistake." "They said," Yeats reported to Quinn, "quite plainly that if I went to the London operator I would die, probably of hemorrhage." On the other hand, the omens for Dublin were "as favourable as possible—Venus, with all her ribbons floating, poised upon the mid-heaven!" Off he went to Dublin where Gogarty took out the offending tonsils with great aplomb and pronounced next day, looking into the poet's throat, "I have been *too* thorough."[29]

Tonsillectomy and traveling took a month out of spiritual pursuits. A visit from Ezra also took its toll: "The communicator likes him," Yeats noted, "but says communication impossible while he is in the house."[30]

Yeats cut a romantic figure in Oxford. Opening his home to undergraduates—by invitation only—on Monday evenings, he sat by the fire, looking distinguished and casual in the light-colored jackets and soft shirts he favored, while the students sat literally at his feet, drinking Italian vermouth from odd-shaped glasses and interrupting at their peril.[31] Always amusing and talkative, in private company he was given to telling ribald stories and otherwise playing the man of the world. One evening when he declared that a certain theory under discussion was as impossible as "making love to a bald woman," a young pedant declared that he could not see the impossibility of the example. Yeats retorted, "In that case, all further conversation between us is impossible."[32]

He made no effort at all to conceal his occult enthusiasms. The novelist L. A. G. Strong, an undergraduate at the time and source of these recollections, formed the impression of a shy, vastly intelligent man "far from dotty in his beliefs" who saw that the universe extended far beyond the range of human perception or scientific explanation and was, in his psychic experiments, endeavoring to find symbols to dramatize the reality outside space and time. As a visitor, Strong got no inkling of Mrs. Yeats's magical powers yet saw her on these pleasant social occasions as "often the catalyst, saying little, but filling the room with an aura of humorous perception."[33]

The secret life of Mr. and Mrs. Yeats could occasionally be glimpsed socially when they would classify various people by a phase of the moon. They would then explain to their uncomprehending listeners that the lunar code was a way of dividing personalities into subjective and objective. Such conversational pleasantries, of course, conveyed little of the intensity of the couple's private discourse the subject of classification. Yeats had decided that Francis Stuart must be a "14" and that an unwanted caller who dropped by one day in Oxford had irritated George because he was too much of a "22."

Yeats enjoyed the agreeable life of Oxford and its environs. He dined and gave talks in the colleges; he entertained and was entertained by writers and thinkers. Happily he allowed himself to be taken up by the flamboyant hostess Lady Ottoline Morrell and welcomed to her splendid Jacobean home, Garsington Manor. Far more courteous than a previous favored guest, D. H. Lawrence, who went on to caricature mercilessly his angular hostess and her house in *Women in Love,* Yeats honored Garsington and its "levelled lawns and gravelled ways" in the elegiac poem "Ancestral Houses."

Oxford, for Yeats, remained primarily a place of magic. "All Souls' Night," composed on or shortly after the first of November 1920, dramatizes a séance amid the dreaming spires. The strong *b*s and *l*s of the first stanza simultaneously invoke the sound of a bell and the bubbling of a witches' cauldron:

Midnight has come, and the great Christ Church Bell
And many a lesser bell sound through the room;
And it is All Souls' Night,
And two long glasses brimmed with muscatel
Bubble upon the table. A ghost may come.

Not one but three ghosts are summoned to the séance, three departed partners in spiritualism: William T. Horton, Florence Farr, and MacGregor

Mathers. The poet wants to tell his departed friends of his new learning: "I have mummy truths to tell / Whereat the living mock . . ."

Another of his former guests, the Oxford don C. Maurice Bowra, later called "All Souls' Night" the best poem ever written at Oxford.[34] Yeats placed it as epilogue to his philosophical book, *A Vision*. Its repeated references to wine suggest that incense was not the only essential ingredient in the evocations at 4 Broad Street.[35]

In September 1920 the re-elected coalition government led by the Liberal Lloyd George, keeping its prewar commitment to limited Home Rule, introduced a Government of Ireland Bill. The proposal was to grant Ireland the same status as Canada—that is, as a self-governing dominion within the British Empire. A parliament in Dublin would run the country, with the exclusion of six of the nine counties of Ulster, which were to be given the choice of opting out. If they so chose, they were to have a parliament of their own, in Belfast. To deal with matters concerning the whole island of Ireland, the two parliaments would meet jointly as a Council of Ireland.

The bill pleased nobody. While the Unionists accepted it, they were happy to continue to be ruled directly from London and unhappy about being cut off from Crown loyalists in the south. Both sides had supplied thousands of Irish troops to the Great War. In the rest of Ireland, nationalists were predictably angered, Sinn Fein and the IRA hardening in their resolve to use the force of arms to fight on for full independence for a thirty-two-county republic. The weary Irish people longed for peace and saw little prospect of it.

At this turbulent time, Yeats was looking inward. He worked almost entirely on composing his System, on poems, and on his autobiography. Trying to flesh out his theories of cycles of history, however, Yeats was hardly oblivious to events. For example, he borrowed the term "coven" from witchcraft to describe a group of minds held together by a single event or thought, and gave as an example Sir Edward Carson's Unionists.

It was a good illustration. If ever there was a group united by a single shared thought, it was the followers of the tall, grim Carson. His long determination, backed by the formation of the armed Ulster Volunteers Force, to fight to remain within the United Kingdom was about to be rewarded with a separate Ulster.

Besides, Yeats's life story was enmeshed in Irish politics. In late 1920 he was working on *Four Years,* the segment of his autobiography covering his early adult years in Bedford Park from 1887 to 1891. This was the very period when he began his championship of the national cause and recognized that Ireland and Irishness were to be his subject matter. When he put into his book his recollection of Oscar Wilde's saying over a London dinner table, "We Irish are too poetical to be poets; we are a nation of brilliant failures, but we are the greatest talkers since the Greeks," he intended it as no mere anecdote.

Yeats genuinely believed that his System could help Ireland. His ideal of Unity of Being held good for nations as well as for the individual. He envisaged that defining Ireland in terms of a national culture rather than political allegiance might unify its people and lead them through the current crisis. Yet as he wrote these ideas into *Four Years,* he feared, as he wrote his friend George Russell (AE) in March 1921, that his readers would simply say, "'O that is Yeats' and pass it by."[36]

And by and large they have. The book owes its brilliance to its captivating reminiscences of Wilde, Synge, Shaw, and the other giants of Yeats's youth, rather than to its political ruminations. Yeats would have been dismayed to know that what would be frequently quoted from the book in future years was his charming, Pre-Raphaelite, and heavily self-censored account of his first meeting with Maud Gonne:

> Her complexion was luminous, like that of apple-blossoms through which light falls and I remember her standing that first day by a great heap of such blossoms in the window.[37]

In spite of the political moves toward settlement, the savage Anglo-Irish war raged on, with murders and executions on both sides. In

October, in Brixton Prison in London, the jailed lord mayor of Cork, Terence MacSwiney, died on the seventy-fourth day of a hunger strike staged in protest against the actions of the Black and Tans against the Irish populace. His huge funeral in Cork was followed, on November 21, 1920, by Bloody Sunday, one the blackest of the many black days in Anglo-Irish relations before and since.

In Dublin at nine o'clock in the morning, the IRA carried out a dozen separate, carefully planned attacks on Englishmen living in various lodging houses and hotels in Dublin who were believed to be members of British secret intelligence. The men were shot in their beds or as they came down to breakfast. That same afternoon, the Black and Tans retaliated by opening fire on a Dublin crowd gathered for a Gaelic football match in Croke Park. Twelve spectators were killed.

For her father, Lily added local details to a week of horrors. Drunken Black and Tans were carousing in the streets of Dundrum and, with revolvers in their hands, riding around in trucks with REPRISALS GALORE written in large chalk letters on the side. She longed for the day when Ireland would be free and women could go about without fear of being shot or jeered at.[38]

Not long after, word reached Yeats and George that the Black and Tans had broken into Ballylee, smashed all the windows, and stolen all the locks.

In October Yeats wrote on one of his filing cards: "*Black Eagle* = Heir = 4th Daimon." Two months later, George had a vision of the Black Eagle. In mid-January she was able to give Yeats the news they had been waiting for: conception had occurred. "The nurse has begun to hear an occasional whistle," Yeats told his notes, "but is not afraid though she knows it is a ghost. We have of course told her nothing."[39]

They told Lolly nothing either. The awkward sister and Cuala Press business manager—who was about to bring out *Four Years* as well as *Michael Robartes and the Dancer*—came for a visit. Like Lily, she tried to be a tactful guest and not say everything that she thought—except in letters to New York. Lolly noticed that Willie's plates were dark, all one color, with no pattern. The cutlery was odd too: as Yeats and

George did not own any silver and disliked silverplate, they ate with utensils made of horn. Had her father, she asked, ever tried drinking soup from a spoon as flat as a knife? Or eating meat with a fork with only two or three prongs? But she saw that Willie was very proud of his home and was easily hurt if his things were not admired. She *could* admire the way that George had scattered brilliant cushions everywhere, and, as a thoughtful hostess, had placed notepaper *and* stamps in the guest bedroom.[40]

There was more open disagreement about the management of the Cuala Press. Lolly wanted the freedom to choose titles and authors herself in the interest of making some money; she felt she had the business sense to do it. Yeats insisted that as he was the man of letters, sole authority should remain with him.[41]

He had, in fact, helped his sisters considerably in their wobbly enterprise, and would continue to do so the rest of his life. Yet even he could not claim that the benefits flowed all in one direction. Within a few months of her visit Lolly sent him a check for five hundred pounds in royalties—a sum, he acknowledged gratefully, that would go a long way to help George balance their annual accounts.

With the second pregnancy established, and as they prayed fervently for a son, Yeats and George were more open to psychic stimuli than ever. When she felt unwell in late January, they went to the evocative, magical southwest of England. At Wells Cathedral George detected a sweet odor, perhaps of roses, emanating from Yeats; when they returned to their hotel, she could still smell it coming from his hands. Yeats ventured a thought. Was the fragrance possibly Glastonbury thorn? (As legend held that this bush had grown from the staff of Joseph of Arimathea who came to England shortly after Christ's death Yeats's suggestion carried more than a hint of the Second Coming.) He had no sooner uttered the words than

> there was a whistle, a signal of assent. I found presently that it [the smell] was being made in one of my pockets & that, when ever I put my hand in it, my hand came out scented with it.[42]

The happy bachelor.

The MacBrides: a rare moment in a short-lived marriage: Maud, Sean, and major John MacBride.

The lone parent: Maud, with infant Sean and Iseult,
her daughter by Lucien Millevoye.

Iseult in adolescence.

The house at Coole.

Lady Gregory.

The New Yorker: John Butler Yeats on the roof of 317 West Twenty-ninth Street, New York City, his happy home for the last fifteen years of his life. *(Courtesy of William M. Murphy)*

Lily Yeats, portrait by John Butler Yeats, now in
the National Gallery of Ireland.

"Lolly," Elizabeth Corbet years, and "Lily," Susan Butler May Yeats, in Dublin about 1904. *(Courtesy Cuala Archive Trinity College Dublin Library)*

Lolly (right) and fellow workers in the printing room of Dun Emer, the predecessor of her Cuala Press. *(Courtesy of Cuala Archive, Trinity College Dublin Library)*

John Quinn, New York lawyer and arts patron, 1917.

Ezra Pound in 1916. *(Courtesy of Humanities Research Center, University of Texas)*

Dorothy Pound in 1915: Olivia Shakespear's daughter,
Ezra Pound's wife, Georges' best friend and "dearest coz."

The new Mrs. William Butler Yeats in the garden at Dundrum. Georges' wool drop-waisted chemise dress, with a border panel across the knees, was deeply fashionable in 1918, the year the photograph was taken. *(Courtesy of Woodruff Library, Emory University)*

The first preserved page of George's Automatic Script, done on their honeymoon at Stone Cottage, November 5, 1917, introduces the important sun-in-moon symbolism.

The names or signs of five "Communicators"—Thomas, Fish, Aymore, Rose and AR—can be discerned in this Script of March 4, 1918, the last before the Yeatses left Oxford for Dublin on March 4, 1918. It warns Yeats against his habit of talking too freely about personal things.

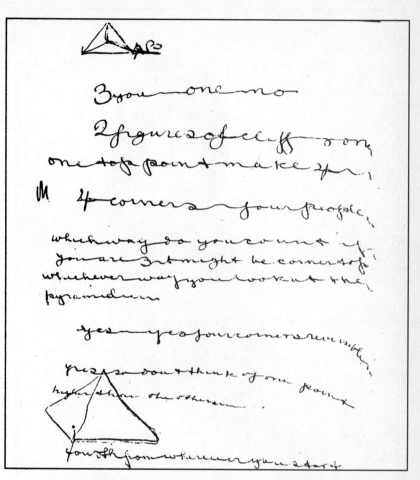

Automatic Script produced in the evening of November 5, 1917,
shows a pyramid representing Yeats and the three women on his mind:
Maud, Iseult, and George.

George Yeats in 1920: John Butler Yeats's pencil sketch shows
his skill at portraiture, and also his tendency to prettify his subjects.

The new father beaming at three-week-old Anne in March 1919.
His bitter lines written in 1914, "Although I have come close on forty-
nine, I have no child, I have nothing but a book," no longer apply.
(Courtesy of Woodruff Library, Emory University)

Eamon de Valera,
President of the rebel-
proclaimed Irish republic.

The poet and his wife on
their American tour in
early 1920, are each
well-dressed in an
anti-Establishment way,
her buttonless, waistless,
fur-trimmed coat as
eloquent as his bow ties
and light fedora. Spirit
communication through
"sleeps" began during
this journey.

From Wells and Glastonbury, they made their way to the first source of their revelations, Stone Cottage in Sussex. The portents at the honeymoon site were not without menace. When George fell asleep abruptly, Yeats was informed (by a new Communicator called "the Pulon," speaking, like the others, through George's mouth) that a Frustrator wanted to kill the Fourth Daimon.[43]

Back in Oxford, Yeats effortlessly changed gear from the supernatural to the political. On February 17, 1921, he appeared in a debate at the Oxford Union to denounce the British policy of terrorizing the Irish population. Orating dramatically, walking up and down the aisles as he spoke, declaring his heart torn between the tragedies in England and Ireland, he won the debate for his side: in favor of self-government for Ireland and against reprisals.

He had already decided that they would have to leave Oxford ahead of schedule that spring to economize. A new child would increase their expenses, and his father's bills hung over him. The large sum he had sent the year before, he told Lily, was now unlikely to be enough. His first plan—that they would move to Italy and live on a pound a week—had to be put off because of Nelly Tucker's illness; the second—to move to Cork, with occasional visits to Ballylee—was now impractical. George had overheard servants in the kitchen gossiping that the damage at Ballylee was worse than the Yeatses had been told, so rather than return to Ireland they moved only as far as Berkshire, where they took a small cottage in Shillingford, convenient to a Catholic church (for the sake of the maids, Yeats explained to Lady Gregory).[44] For the Broad Street house, they found tenants from April at five pounds ten shillings a week: "a pot of money," he gloated to Olivia Shakespear.[45]

From Berkshire he wrote to congratulate Iseult, who had had a daughter on March 9. Having cast the child's horoscope, he suggested that someday he and Iseult might arrange a marriage with his expected son. For Iseult's as for his own daughter, he wished a lucky marriage: "By that time I shall be very old and stern & with my authority to support yours, she will do in that matter what she is told to do."[46]

The entire Yeats family confidently awaited a son. Lolly wrote to her father, who had just turned eighty-two, that George was already referring to the baby as "John Michael."[47] The rest of the letter was a catalog of atrocities. Lolly wished that Willie and his family could live in Ireland but thought Galway too dangerous.

So it was. In May, Margaret Gregory was the only survivor of an ambush outside the gates of Coole; the three friends from the local garrison, with whom she had been playing tennis, died in the attack. Lolly could not imagine why Margaret had made herself such a mark by going about with British military people. The sisters were more shaken by what they saw close to home: old women whose houses had been raided repeatedly in search of absent sons who were in hiding, young men executed for "escaping arrest" ("really murder," said Lolly),[48] and the burning of a Dublin landmark, the beautiful eighteenth-century Customs House. The military curfew had ruined the theater and evening social life.

Irish patriots, the sisters tried to remain friends with both sides and invited Sinn Feiners and Unionists alike to their gatherings. But they were not neutral. As Lily observed, after three trucks of Black and Tans had raced through Dundrum one evening and their maid, Maria, had been forced to fall flat on the road to avoid being shot:

> If the present state of affairs goes on, England will have *no* friends left in Ireland. . . . some say the Crown forces were *very drunk*—drunk or sober they are ruffians—what will dear England do with them when the time comes—*it must come sometime* that they have to be disbanded?[49]

The expectant parents, meanwhile, were alert to every sign that the second pregnancy differed from the first. When George suddenly recoiled from physical and psychic contact, Yeats was full of wonder:

> When Ann was coming she was in all ways full of desire now she shrinks from touch. She has desire but shrinks from excita-

tion of touch. Further all psychic phenomena has ceased & this seems to me to suggest a withdrawal into the soul.[50]

Yeats accepted the burden of living with a gravid psychic. Any unexpected sight could trigger an extravagant reaction. Walking along the road in the country one night, he was talking of Persian history when George heard a hissing sound and knew it was a snake. Returning to their room, she was startled by a large black slug on the wall. Shuddering, she foresaw that a third frightening sight awaited her. The next morning a water rat slithered out the kitchen door before her very eyes. "She is much too sensitive to physical symbols," Yeats told his notebook, "but should get out of this as her spirits recover their positive capacity."[51] The odor of apples at bedtime was another sign, they agreed, that the "Communicators" (the pair they now knew as "the Pulons") were concerned about her.

Magic enveloped the household. The morning after Yeats dreamed that a rat bit his hand, he learned that at the same time Anne's nurse had been dreaming that mice were biting her throat and had woken to find the child seized with coughing. Of this conjunction, Yeats made a train of associations that led from rats to cats to mice to Anne, who, like a mouse, was small. He concluded, "The tendency of dreams & symbolism to complete themselves through any mind in a raport [sic] is a thing to study."[52] He added parenthetically that Anne had whooping cough.

The gestation of the Black Eagle was proving to be as demanding psychically as physically. They had long used Indian Tattwa cards of symbolic colors to induce visions by meditation. George now professed a strong need for blue; in her first pregnancy, she had been fixed on the color yellow. They each had an erotic dream of the god Hercules. George had nightmares that drove her to crawl into Yeats's bed (as a couple they kept separate rooms, although they frequently shared a bed). One night when she was alone, George saw a huge hand (large as a leg of mutton) seize a rabbit in the corner of her room and throw it out the window.[53]

In the name of the Fourth Daimon, "Dionertes" laid down a new ritual. A long, bright green ribbon was to be formed into a circle.

George was to sit in the center, facing south, while Yeats brandished a sword. Then he was to place symbolic objects—flowers, a stone, water, and incense—at specified points of the compass, invoking each element in turn, before standing in the middle himself. His notes for this rite concluded:

> I am to symbolize the Daimon as black eagle . . . I am to close with these words "Let the elements and the faculties be released, & all be as it was." . . . To be performed Sunday 29th of May.[54]

So tuned was Yeats to extrasensory perception that when a new gift from the Japanese consul in Portland, Oregon, arrived—a baby's quilt— he wondered how Sato knew they were planning another child. The truth dawned, and he entered in his card file, "He meant it for Anne."[55]

Grim news from Ireland—fifty thousand more troops had arrived there from England—was overshadowed by great news from New York: John Butler Yeats had finally agreed to come home. Early in June Quinn booked the passage for October. Yeats wrote to Quinn assuring him that his father would be quite safe in Dundrum, although privately he doubted whether the old man would be able to obey a curfew.[56]

Lest there be any doubt, Yeats sent his father an ultimatum, saying that Quinn was utterly out of patience and that he himself could not meet the New York expenses indefinitely with a new child coming. With satisfaction, Yeats then boasted to Lily that he had insisted on their father's return.[57]

The sisters were overjoyed. In what amounted to a letter of forgiveness for having deprived them of their youth and chance of happiness, Lolly assured her father that he would find them changed after thirteen years: not so irritable or overtired as before—and not old women either. They would be ready to sit and talk with him anytime he wished.[58] His room was freshly painted, and a new bed and new mattress were waiting.

That was before John Butler Yeats read the proofs of *Four Years*, soon to be published by the Cuala Press and printed in July 1921 in the American literary magazine *The Dial*. In this portion of autobiography, Yeats described his family as "enraged" by his brief absence from Bedford Park for a fortnight on a literary errand in Oxford.

The unfairness of the adjective turned the paterfamilias incandescent. He let fly in a letter. What right had the dreamer and aesthete to criticize the family that had supported him during his protracted adolescence?

> As to Lily and Lollie, they were too busy to be "enraged" about anything, Lily working all day at the Morrises, and Lollie dashing about giving lectures on picture painting and earning close on 300 pounds a year . . . while both gave all their earnings to the house. And besides all this work, of course, they did the housekeeping, and had to contrive things and see to things for their invalid mother.[59]

The tirade continued. If Yeats had remained with his father and not left him for Lady Gregory and her aristocratic friends, he might have written good strong plays in tune with the realities of life instead of wandering off into the Celtic fairyland. What was more, if the two of them had stayed together, painter and poet, they might even have collaborated in art. John Butler Yeats was now blaming his son for blighting his own painting career as well.

Yeats reacted coolly. He told Lolly to change the offending word in the Cuala proofs if it did not mean too much resetting,* and, incidentally, not to change a "that" to a "which" because he often used "that" where other people used *which*.[60] He then went on in a subsequent letter to remind his sister what his young manhood had really been like:

---

*The disputed sentence, as eventually published, in *Autobiographies*, 154, reads, "I spent a few days at Oxford copying out a seventeenth-century translation of Poggio's *Liber Facetarium* or the *Hypnerotomachio* of Philophio for a publisher—I forget which for I copied both—and returned very pale to my troubled family."

how during a row his father had smashed his head into the back of a picture, breaking the glass, and how the old man still had not stopped telling him how to write.[61]

With George's confinement approaching, Yeats was not inclined to move very far. He shifted his family to a larger house in the village of Thame near Oxford. There the doctor examining George took a look at the white-haired expectant father and asked him if he liked children. Without waiting for an answer, he warned the poet that not all children were like Anne: many were not in the least sunny and well behaved.

The omens had not been wrong. The expected male child was born at home in Thame on August 22. Yeats cabled the news to his father and Quinn, saying that all was well. Yeats relayed to Lily, recalling her old vision in Hyde Park, that the boy's horoscope was consistent with a diplomatic career.[62] He was in a jovial mood. He joked to Quinn that the baby was "better looking than a newborn canary," that his daughter was flirting with him, and that his children could finish his philosophy for him.[63] There was no hint of the baby's name.

All was *not* well. Two days after the birth, the baby started gushing blood from the rectum. George thought he would not live through the night—but she did not tell Yeats. Terrified, either of interrupting her august husband at his writing or of shaking his precarious equilibrium, she kept the crisis to herself. Swearing the servants to secrecy, she arranged for a doctor to be smuggled into the house in the guise of an electrician.[64]

The first emergency treatment seems to have been some form of transfusion (to judge from Lily's later fanciful reconstruction for her father's benefit): a "bacteriologist" took blood from George's arm and mixed it with "serum" to save the baby's life. The first Yeats learned of the procedure was when the boy was out of danger.

So successful was the conspiracy to shield him from the truth that as he carried telegrams of congratulations up to George's room, he never noticed that the maid's face was streaming with tears. Later, when the family was full of praise for George's self-restraint, Yeats declared that no one had needed to tell him that something was wrong for as he worked in his study "Dionertes" had caused a smell of burned feathers in the hallway.[65]

From New York the new grandfather sent particularly warm congratulations to George on her cleverness in getting through the crisis without Willie's even suspecting.[66] He also sent word that, owing to a bout of cold, ague, and indigestion, he had canceled his sailing.

It was almost more than Lolly could bear: "You *are* a heart-breaking father to have—fancy going back on your word *now* and saying you won't come home—of course you *will* come home."[67] He ought to want to see his daughters, she implored. She reiterated the attractions: his room was waiting, Lily was as lively as ever, except for having gray hair, and she, Lolly, truly believed she had improved over time: "*Not so irritable,*" she promised.

The news of the postponed return was waiting for Yeats and George at the end of September when they got back from Dublin. They had taken the baby to be operated on by Dr. Solomons. "This time astrology had nothing to do with it," Yeats assured Quinn.[68]

Son and patron then abandoned any pretense at politeness. Jointly they ordered the old man back to Dublin. Quinn sent a telegram, Yeats a stinging letter. His father's position was undignified; Quinn was angry and resented the responsibility, and he himself could not carry the expense any longer, what with the medical bills for the sick child. Finishing the self-portrait was no excuse for staying in New York; it could be completed in Dublin, where there was livelier talk than in New York. John Butler Yeats was to embark for Liverpool without delay.[69]

Quinn made a new booking for November 5 and paid the deposit.

In late October the baby, pale and waxlike, required a second operation, performed in London this time. Yeats remained in Oxford because he feared he would only add to his wife's worry if he were around.[70] He awaited news by letter.

Soon George was able to report complete success—two large ruptures and a "histocele" repaired in an hour and twenty-five minutes under chloroform. In her letter marked for his urgent attention (a sign of how little the telephone was used in 1921), she added that she would come back to Oxford in order to do his packing for his coming trip to Glasgow and then return to London to be with the child.[71]

Relieved that Michael—as he and George called the baby between themselves—was out of danger, Yeats went to Glasgow. At last enjoying his new role as father of a son, subtly boasting this manifestation of late virility, he wrote and urged Quinn to get married. Age should be no barrier, he said. In Glasgow he had met a relative of sixty, with a wife younger than his own; besides, the Mormon leader Brigham Young had had nineteen wives at the age of seventy-five. Describing himself as an orthodox Christian, Yeats added, however, that he could not recommend Quinn take more than one.[72]

When John Butler Yeats then exchanged the November booking for a sailing in December, Lolly raged. "You will make us a laughing stock if you don't come back," she wrote.[73] Lily tried a different tack. She and Lolly were not angry, she soothed, just desperately eager to see him. She was in bed with shingles when the letter arrived, dated December 5, the day that his ship was due to leave New York, saying that he was not on it.

At just after two o'clock the following morning, at No. 10 Downing Street, the exhausted Irish delegation signed the treaty presented them by Lloyd George and Winston Churchill, Secretary of State for the colonies. Faced with the alternative of all-out war or dominion status, the Irish team chose the second. They reluctantly accepted the required oath of allegiance to the Crown, signifying that Ireland remained within the British Commonwealth of Nations, of which the king was the head. They accepted also Ulster's right to opt out, as a (barely) tolerable price to pay for the creation of the Irish Free State. One of their leaders, Michael Collins, knowing that the treaty would be seen as a surrender by many in Ireland, famously and accurately predicted that he was signing his own death warrant. The president-in-waiting, Eamon de Valera, was absent; his critics have maintained over the years that he clearly avoided joining the delegation to London because he foresaw that the treaty would tear the country apart.

The birth of the Free State changed the direction of Yeats's life. He decided to return to Ireland; George encouraged him. Like many in Ireland, he grudgingly supported the treaty as the best solution available under the circumstances. He had no illusions about what lay ahead. He told Olivia Shakespear, with whom he was in regular, warm correspondence, that he expected the Dáil to ratify the treaty, but, "I see no hope of escape from bitterness, and the extreme party may carry the country."[74] Yet he could also see that the new nation-state would be in need of cultural institutions for which his System held the template.

A fortnight after the treaty, the baby, who had been referred to in family correspondence as "our little son" or "your grandchild," was christened Michael Butler Yeats. Since his birth, the possibility of "John" had not been mentioned. Plans to prefix the "Michael" with "William" were dropped at the last minute, so Yeats told Lolly. He said he had never liked his "soft, wish washy, moist day sort of name"[75] (which may have been his way of acknowledging the common use of "willy" as slang for "penis"). Three weeks later, he reported to Lolly that "JBY" now absolutely and finally refused to leave New York.[76]

To say that the new grandfather was taking his revenge because of the failure to name his grandson after him would be unwarranted. His health was declining; he genuinely thought he would finish his self-portrait in New York. But the snub hurt, and did nothing to overcome thirteen years' resistance to going home.

By the time the Dáil ratified the treaty on January 6, 1922, the ominously narrow margin of 64 to 57 as good as signaling the Civil War, Even so, George had gone to Dublin and, with her own money, bought a lease on a large Georgian house in Merrion Square.[77] The address, Yeats informed Olivia, was the equivalent of Berkeley Square in London.[78] The house was also, although he did not say so, the kind in which he himself might have grown up had his father remained a barrister. For one who so recently and bitterly had pleaded poverty, it was an extraordinary acquisition, but Yeats airily explained it by the depressed state of Dublin house prices and George's shrewdness in finding tenants for the top floors and stables.

John Butler Yeats was well aware of what Merrion Square represented. At the end of January he wrote a magnificent vituperative letter to Lily in which he lashed out at his late wife's family, the materialistic Pollexfens, whose only value was money and who had no use for "spiritual and artistic matters." They had never appreciated him, he felt, nor his eldest son either. The Pollexfens, he told Lily,

> all disliked Willie. In their eyes he was not only abnormal but
> he seemed to take after me. But however irritable . . . they
> were slothful and so let him alone. And therefore in Willie's
> eyes they appear something grand like the figures at
> Stonehenge seen by moonlight.[79]

Twenty-four hours after that rich paragraph, on February 3, 1922, John Butler Yeats died in his upstairs bedroom at 317 West 29th Street. The unfinished self-portrait looked down on his bed. According to the moving account in his biography, the final decline had begun with an afternoon journey to a gathering on 137th Street, when he had taken the wrong subway, ended up in the Bronx, and insisted on walking for two miles in the snow to reach his destination. In the days that followed he gradually succumbed to a malfunctioning heart, lungs, and the array of winter afflictions waiting for an old man just short of his eighty-third birthday. Jeanne Foster and John Quinn saw to his medical care and were with him within hours of the end.

Yeats wrote and thanked them both, Quinn especially. He also wrote each sister a moving personal letter of condolence. He told Lolly their father had died confident that he was completing his masterpiece and that her vivid letters over the years had given him great pleasure. For Lily, Yeats drew a picture of their father dying like an antarctic explorer in the midst of his work. In a more intimate tone, he recalled that the old man had written several times recently of dreaming of their mother—of waking so convinced of the presence of his late wife, Susan, that he searched the room for her.

The same thing had happened to him, Yeats informed his favorite sister. At a séance in London, their mother had appeared to him, to tell him that she would be much with him.

Father and son seem not to have been so very different in their views of the dead. Hardly was John Butler Yeats in his grave (in Jeanne Foster's family plot in the Adirondacks) than Yeats tried to reach him in the other world. On the advice of both "Dionertes" and George, before leaving England he went to a séance conducted by a trumpet medium at the College of Psychic Science in Wimbledon, and was rewarded when a voice came through the horn (although not very audibly) and identified itself by the initials J. B. and by the name of Susan.

The thought of his parents reunited in death was very much in Yeats's mind over the next few months of transition. In his notes interpreting various of George's Sleeps, he recorded that "when a spirit waits for some one, as my mother has perhaps waited for my father in the other world, they make themselves visible to that person."[80]

In midsummer, at Ballylee, the long psychic experiment was brought to an end. "We decided," Yeats recorded, "to give up sleap, automatic writing & all such means [of mediumship] & to get our further thought by 'positive means.'" "Dionertes" consented, adding, like a teacher or a therapist saying goodbye, that Yeats could always return for help if he needed it. He was to burn incense, and "I might not know it but help would be given—in work etc."[81] (George later told her cousin Grace that she had given up spirit work because it was bad for the children.)[82]

The time was right. The Script and the Sleeps had done their work. Yeats had his desired tetradic family. He had a hoard of raw material from which to draw philosophy and poetry for the rest of his life. He had seen the prophesied new age arrive, and the Black and Tans depart Dublin to a jeering crowd. The avatar was sleeping in his cradle.

Yeats had learned much from his "Instructors": the immortality of the soul, the universality of memory, and the existence of spirits, evil as well as good. The presence of lurking envious devils was acknowledged in "A Prayer for my Son," written about the time of Michael's christening:

> Some there are, for I avow
> Such devilish things exist,
> Who have planned his murder, for they know
> Of some most haughty deed or thought
> That waits upon his future days.

But "they," as he thought of them, had been for the most part benevolent and helpful, alerting him as he moved back to Ireland in January 1922 that he was about to receive an offer he should not refuse. When at the end of that year he was invited to become a senator in the Free State, he accepted the appointment, reasoning that "they want to keep me in active life."[83] In fact, Gogarty, who was becoming a senator himself, played an instrumental part in securing the honor for Yeats and told George that it was not a reward for services to the Abbey or to poetry but rather for her husband's youthful involvement with the Irish Republican Brotherhood (which, according to A. Norman Jeffares's biography, she had not even guessed at).[84]

As he prepared to assume a public role and prepared to write his book of philosophy, he did not hide from the knowledge that the main point of his ghostly instruction had been personal. "Summing up," he wrote in July 1922, "the sexual life . . . is a perpetual drama, which has for its real theme the nature of the unborn child, for whom the daimons have laid their plans."[85]

But what plans had his daimons laid for him? Five years of ghostly conjugal communion had left him no wiser as to why he had had "that crazy passion" for Maud Gonne. It had not solved the mystery of sexual attraction. Nor had it alerted him to the banked fires of physical desire ready to break loose and ravage his old age.

Part 3

10

The Silent Woman

(1863–1900)

> How much of the best I have done and still do is but the attempt to
> explain myself to her?
> — Yeats, "Journal," 1909, *Memoirs,* 142

THE SECRET OF YEATS is that his mother did not love him—at least not in any way that warmed him in recollection or that a child needs for confidence in life. "Whatever else is uncertain in this stinking dunghill of a world," says Cranly in *A Portrait of the Artist as a Young Man,* "a mother's love is not."[1] Susan Yeats's was.

Unlike James Joyce, who drew his supreme cockiness from his mother's faith in him, Yeats grew up without this endorsement. Unlike Joyce, being the eldest by no means made him the favorite. With Lily born fourteen months after his own birth in 1865 and with four more babies arriving by the time he was nine, Yeats was edged to the periphery of the attention of a cold, despondent, overburdened young woman. Maud Gonne's should not be the first name to spring to mind when reading Yeats's lines

> The folly that man does
> or must suffer, if he woos
> A proud woman not kindred of his soul.[2]

Susan Pollexfen Yeats, born in Sligo in 1841, died in Bedford Park, London, in 1900, was silent, undemonstrative, expressionless. Yet she was at least as great a force in shaping the imagination of her impressionable son as was his well-publicized and self-publicizing father, and probably the greater. When George Yeats told Richard Ellmann in 1946 that "the mother's influence has been under-estimated," she was referring to Susan Yeats's store of Irish folktales, her narrative gift, and her keen sense of the supernatural.[3] That there was a darker side to the maternal legacy was acknowledged when George told Ellmann that Mrs. Yeats was a timid and frightened woman and that Yeats suffered from a strong need to justify himself.

His celebrated poem "Among School Children" is powerful evidence. In 1926, when visiting a Montessori school in Waterford as an Irish Free State senator and a Nobel laureate (he won the prize for literature in 1923), the "smiling public man" seemed to feel that his mother would not think that he had amounted to much:

> What youthful mother, a shape upon her lap
> . . . .
> Would think her son, did she but see that shape
> With sixty or more winters on its head,
> A compensation for the pang of his birth,
> Or the uncertainty of his setting forth?[4]

This poem, arguably his greatest, was not the first use Yeats made of his terrible sense of unworthiness in his mother's eyes. At the start of his first Noh play, *At the Hawk's Well,* written in 1916, the masked First Musician sings:

> A mother that saw her son
> Doubled over a speckled shin,
> Cross-grained with ninety years,
> Would cry, "How little worth
> Were all my hopes and fears
> And the hard pain of his birth!"

This cry from a disappointed mother's heart rose straight out of bitter memory. John Butler Yeats once told Lily what it was like to come home to his wife when the children were small:

> I was no sooner in the house than I had to listen to dreadful complaints of everybody and everything—especially of Willy it was always Willy—sometimes I would beg of her to wait till after supper—I always hoped she was not as unhappy as she seemed.[5]

It was hard to tell how unhappy Susan Yeats was, for if she had nothing bad to say about anybody, she said nothing at all[6]—unless she was telling stories or talking of Sligo. There was good reason why all the Yeats children loved this seaport town in the northwest of Ireland, quite apart from its scenic contrast with London. Their austere and remote mother was happier there. Listening to her speak of her birthplace, loving it, and absorbing its rich lore were the only ways they could get through to her. As Yeats told his friend and confidante, the Irish poet and novelist Katharine Tynan, "I remember when we were children how intense our devotion was to all things in Sligo & still see in my mother the old feeling."[7]

Yeats bears the main responsibility for underplaying his mother's part in his life. He blamed her lengthy illness and paralysis (which extended from 1887 to 1900). As he told Mabel Dickinson, "My mother was so long ill, so long fading out of life that the last fading of all made no noticeable change in our lives."[8] In the autobiography on which he lavished so much attention after 1914, he gave his mother short shrift. The omission glares. When Maud Gonne read the book, she scolded Yeats for blanking out his early years: "It does not tell of the things that were really vital to you *as a child,* from it I could not tell what sort of child you were . . . Once you get to the part where your father's influence played on you . . . it became very real & living."[9]

In *Reveries over Childhood and Youth,* the first book of what is now *Autobiographies,* Susan Yeats's presence can be felt from her absence, from the lack of any sense of "the comfort you gave"—the gift for which Yeats later thanked his wife.[10] Instead, he wrote the chilling line "I remember little of childhood but its pain." He confessed also that as a boy he had prayed that he would die, even though "there was no reason for my unhappiness."[11]

The first faint sketch of his mother that does appear well into "Reveries over Childhood" shows her not in any conventional maternal pose of feeding, soothing, or scolding, but rather in the act of narration:

> When I think of her, I always see her talking over a cup of tea
> in the kitchen with our servant, the fisherman's wife, on the
> only themes outside our house that seemed of interest—the
> fishing-people of Howth, or the pilots and fishing-people of
> Rosses Point. She read no books, but she and the fisherman's
> wife would tell each other stories that Homer might have told,
> pleased with any moment of sudden intensity and laughing
> together over any point of satire.[12]

In another glimpse:

> She would spend hours listening to stories or telling stories . . .
> of her own Sligo girlhood; and it was always assumed between
> her and us that Sligo was more beautiful than other places. I
> can see now that she had great depth of feeling.[13]

If "Sligo" can be translated as "Mother," Yeats's longing for it becomes a hunger for something more tactile than rural tranquillity, as in this reminiscence from the same *Autobiographies*:

> I remember when I was nine or ten years old walking along Kensington High Street so full of love for the fields and roads of Sligo that I longed—a strange sentiment for a child—for earth from a road there that I might kiss it.[14]

Or in this infantile image from *Memoirs* of a return to the womb or breast:

> I was going along the Strand and, passing a shop window where there was a little ball kept dancing by a jet of water, I remembered waters about Sligo and was moved to a sudden emotion that shaped itself into "The Lake Isle of Innisfree."[15]

His parents' marriage had seemed to be a love match. In 1862 John Butler Yeats, finished at Trinity College, Dublin, and studying for the Irish bar at the King's Inns, went to Sligo to visit his school and college friend George Pollexfen. Even though he himself had abandoned his religious faith for rational skepticism, he was captivated by George, a strange personality and a storyteller, who at their boarding school on the Isle of Man, would keep the other boys awake with astonishingly inventive stories.[16]

During the visit the tall, handsome, eloquent Johnnie Yeats fell in love with George Pollexfen's eldest sister, Susan. He was of an age to marry. A Sligo connection made sense. His grandfather (the Reverend John Yeats) had been rector at Drumcliffe, a village a few miles north of Sligo. The girl was pretty and well off. The Pollexfens, and her mother's family, the Middletons, jointly owned a Sligo milling and shipping business. His proposal, coming from a member of the Dublin Protestant bourgeoisie, whose family had an aristocratic if tenuous "Butler" association, was accepted and the wedding set for the following summer or autumn.

During their betrothal, when she remained in Sligo while he in Dublin, they exchanged letters. His are full of desire: "when we are alone our kisses shall be as our love is hot and passionate and which never can be satisfied."[17] At the same time, they reveal a curious kind of sexual taunt, a feigned male fear of the anger of the woman over whose life he will have complete power. The theme persisted through the year:

> I do firmly believe you when you say you are more easily made angry because you so terribly love me. . . .
>
> It is always to me a delicious joy that I can make you unhappy—It shows what value you put on me. . . .
>
> I hope you won't henpeck me or make me withdraw from the intimacy of all people who are not acceptable to your lady-ship . . . how cross you'll be with your head thrown back and your utterance short and abrupt—your dress rustling angrily—what a tyrant you'll be thought.[18]

The letters show that, up to a point, John Butler Yeats and Susan Pollexfen knew what they were getting into. He told her not to change her faults, which he recognized to be petulance, sulkiness, and silence, because otherwise she would not be herself. She, for her part, knew how he could infuriate her even though she loved him. He worried that she was going to be lonely in the long hours when he would be away at court. His suggested cure was that she make herself interested in his work so that he could talk to her about it when he came home at the end of the day.[19]

Where the suitor totally misled the bride-to-be, and, apparently, himself, was over their financial prospects. He gave her to understand that they would enjoy both his good earnings as a barrister and a substantial income from the Yeats family holdings of 560 acres in County Kildare and a house in Dublin. Indeed, he foresaw their being so prosperous that she would hold a commanding position among his Yeats relatives in Dublin. He joked again that he hoped she would not use her power to usurp his place as man of the house.[20] A warning sign that she would not have noticed lay in the sketches that covered his letters. The budding barrister had a compulsion to draw faces with his pen.

Married in September 1863 and moved to Dublin, the new Mrs. John Butler Yeats was very lonely. She had never lived in a city before, never been away from her large family, never been without a staff of servants, never had to think about money. Their living quarters were more modest than she had been led to expect.

Willie, a handsome, well-formed child, was born in June 1865. But he was not a barrister's son for long. Quickly bored once called to the Irish bar in January 1866, John Butler Yeats spent his time in court, like a naughty schoolboy, sketching the faces around him, and, like a naughty schoolboy, was caught and scolded. On the strength of an interest shown by a London magazine in one of his drawings, he decided to throw over the law. He would become a portrait painter in London, going there first to study in order to perfect his technique. Depositing his wife and by then two children in Sligo (where Lily was born in 1866), he left for London, enrolled in Heatherley's Art School, took a long lease on a terraced house in Fitzroy Road, Primrose Hill, and grew a beard.

For a country girl, north London, with its maze of tracks bringing trains from the North into the big stations of King's Cross, Euston, and St. Pancras, must have been urban hell. Susan Yeats hated it. She also disliked her husband's friends even more than he had foreseen. She took no interest in his painting, never went to his studio, and was bitter at their lack of money. The intention had been to subsidize these apprentice years with a new mortgage (the third) taken out on the Irish properties. But the rents from the troublesome tenants (when they bothered to hand them over) did not cover the payments due. John Butler Yeats, moreover, soon demonstrated that he was as incapable in art as in law of turning his formidable gifts into income. Although he made progress, few paintings came up to his standard of what constituted finished.

The pregnancies continued apace. Lolly arrived in 1867; Robert, or Bobby, followed in 1870; and Jack (formally, John Butler), in 1871, all three born at Fitzroy Road. Summer holidays were spent in Sligo and for two years, from 1872 to 1874, in the interests of economy Susan Yeats and the five children remained there the entire time.

Of the many ways Yeats split his identity—between the fictional Michael Robartes and Owen Aherne or Hic and Ille, or between England and Ireland—the Sligo-London divide may have been the sharpest. The fact is that he was in many ways a London boy. He spent the years from the ages of two to seven, then from nine to sixteen, in the teeming capital, and was fully acquainted with its streets, museums, shops, and underground railway.

For the children, Sligo was a haven of relief from want. The change of status began at Liverpool where they boarded, free of charge, a ship of the family-owned Sligo Steam Navigation Company for the thirty-hour journey around the north coast of Ireland, then along the west coast, past County Donegal and down into Sligo's harbor. The Pollexfens lived not far away from the quays, in a large, square, gray limestone house called Merville. Set on the edge of town, in sixty acres with a view across the harbor to the rocky head of Ben Bulben, it was not a Big House by Anglo-Irish standards—it had no long avenue—and it certainly did not qualify the mercantile Pollexfens for invitations to Lissadell, Hazelwood, and other great houses of the local gentry. Merville was a child's paradise, however, apart from the people inside it. "The crossest family I ever met," said John Butler Yeats.[21] But by then the Pollexfens had a good deal to be cross about.

The clan was angry at the way he had thrown over professional security in Dublin for bohemian scattiness in London and relied on their support to see that his children did not go hungry. They would have been less angered by the swift succession of babies. William and Elizabeth Pollexfen had produced twelve; John Butler Yeats himself was one of eleven. Considering that three decades later, Sigmund Freud was reluctant to use contraception to limit his own family,[22] it is clear that childbirth in the mid-nineteenth century was accepted as an inescapable consequence of marriage. In any event, Susan Yeats's long stays in Sligo served as an effective form of birth control.

Her family was alert to any signs that Willie was taking after his father. As merchants and manufacturers, they distrusted artists and dreaminess, of which they detected a worrying symptom in the inability of Willie, large for his age at seven, to learn to read. Aunts and a governess labored at the seemingly impossible. After multiple attempts failed, they decided that his faculties were deficient.[23] Overall, the Pollexfens far preferred little Bobby, more robust, active, and amiable.

John Butler Yeats hated the way the Pollexfens disparaged his eldest child, but he himself was infuriated by the boy's illiteracy. He finally succeeded in teaching Willie himself, with rigorous methods that included throwing a hymnbook at his head.[24]

Is dyslexia the right diagnosis? Probably not, even though Yeats's life-long inability to spell simple words is as remarkable as the lateness of his literacy. On the other hand, once he learned, Yeats became, and remained, a voracious reader. He began his literary career in his teens and was seeing work published before he was twenty. Later, as an editor, as Lolly had reason to complain, he was an uncompromising perfectionist, never tolerating single quotation marks where he wanted double. None of these is the sign of a dyslexic. In the end, the Pollexfens seem to have accepted that he was just a late starter, and to agree with his old nurse, "Master Willie's not the fool he looks."[25]

John Butler Yeats's unconventional attitude toward schooling contributed to his son's slowness. Having himself been caned at school, the paterfamilias distrusted educational institutions and kept his children away from them, preferring to give them a governess at home and sporadically to teach them himself, with the additional satisfaction of being able to impart his own ideas uninterrupted.

Yeats's persistent and often comic spelling mistakes, however, are intriguing. His spelling was by no means consistently incorrect; rather, he seemed to stumble over particular words and sounds. The *Vision Papers*, like his letters, show a chronic difficulty with the vowel combination *ea*. He inserted it where it did not belong and often substituted *ee* where it did. All his life he was liable to spell *sleep* as *sleap*, *feaver* for *fever*, *hear* for *here*, *deel* for *deal*. In one letter, he stumbled over *measels*, then gave up: "how do you spell it?"[26] As the *ea* combination appears in his own surname, the quirk clearly touched the root of his identity.

As a boy, Yeats liked Merville because "the house was big and the grounds ample, so that one could enjoy nature and had room to get away from human nature." He was allowed a lot of freedom, to roam and ride, to swim and skate. But it was not only his mother's family from whom he had need to escape. There was trouble with his brothers and sisters too. Lily, to whom he was always closest, recalled a governess saying, "Everything is all right in the nursery until Willie comes home and then the fighting begins immediately."[27]

Yeats was not as oblivious to his siblings as he made himself out to be. He fought with Lolly constantly. In his unpublished autobiographical novel, *The Speckled Bird* he saw himself as, the odd one out. He took the title from the Book of Jeremiah, 12:9: "Mine heritage is unto me as a speckled bird, the birds round about are against her." In the autobiographical novel that he did publish, the eponymous hero, John Sherman, is also an only child, a young man who lives in a town exactly like Sligo with his devoted widowed mother. But Yeats was very far from being an only child. His savage poem, "The Dolls" gives some idea of his childish thoughts about the near-annual refill of the cradle. The "oldest doll of all the dolls . . . Out-screams the whole shelf" to protest the "noisy and filthy" new arrival.

The "doll-maker's wife" then apologizes to her husband for the outburst of "the wretch." Could the vivid allusions to the trauma of childbirth in this and other poems mean that as the oldest (and wretchedest) child in the family, Yeats witnessed or overheard some of his mother's many accouchements? He wrote the fierce poem, appropriately enough, in the year of Mabel Dickinson's pregnancy scare.

Any hope of displacing the Pollexfens' favorite child vanished when at Merville during the summer of 1873 three-year-old Bobby died suddenly of croup. Yeats's memoirs candidly acknowledge a sense of happiness:

> I was in the Library when I heard feet running past and heard
> somebody say in the passage that my younger brother, Robert,
> had died. . . . A little later, my sister and I sat at the table, very
> happy, drawing ships with their flags half-mast high. . . . Next
> day at breakfast I heard people telling how my mother and the
> servant had heard the banshee crying the night before he
> died.[28]

If Mrs. Yeats had no favorite before, she did now. Letters poured in
to console her for the loss of her little angel. Lines such as "The dar-
ling little fellow is dead" can only have plunged the grieving mother
deeper into her depression.[29] The family told the seven-year-old Willie
that God had taken Robert.

Thirteen years later, in what was to become one of his best-loved
poems, "The Stolen Child," Yeats made not God but the fairies per-
form the lightning kidnapping:

> *Come away, O human child!*
> *To the waters and the wild*
> *With a faery, hand in hand,*
> *For the world's more full of weeping than you can understand.*

Being snatched away by the fairies was a common myth in the west
of Ireland, where not the least of the attractions for the young Yeatses
were the servants' tales of haunted houses, the "little people," and
other forms of the supernatural that might be met any day coming
down the road. The fantasy of being somewhere else, transported
through the air to a distant (and better) place, is universal and tempt-
ing, especially to those who see themselves as the odd one out.

A corollary of this primitive belief, as Deirdre Toomey has pointed
out in her perceptive paper, "Away," is that a dead, mad, or deformed
person is simply a decoy for the real person who has gone to another
world.[30] Yeats, who had collected such stories with Lady Gregory,[31]
uses this myth in *The Only Jealousy of Emer,* where the false Cuchulain

slips into the real Cuchulain's place. Indeed, his concepts of the Mask and the antithetical self may have been inspired by this ancient dream of substitution.

In the event, it was the youngest brother, Jack Yeats, who had a better claim on the title of the stolen child. For eight years Jack was left behind in Sligo, to live with his grandparents to lighten the load for his mother in London. As things turned out, Jack bore no hard feelings. Of all the Yeats children, he was the one genuinely devoted to his mother.

Tales of fairies, leprechauns, and sights in the sky were not just a backstairs phenomenon, confined to the servants with pagan beliefs underlying their Catholicism. The dour Protestant Pollexfens and Middletons were full of the same superstitions and visions. Finding a black lamb in the middle of a flock of sheep, they took it as a warning from the fairies never again to cut down a fairy bush.

Magic was part of the magic of Sligo. It was at Merville that Yeats saw his first fairy, sliding down a moonbeam. The place names of the town and its surrounding features themselves held supernatural significance for him. He filled his poems with incantatory geographic references, such as Rosses Point (a sandy beach resort north of Sligo), even though these could mean nothing to most of his readers, while other names, such as Sleuth Wood, were unpronounceable by anyone who had not heard them spoken aloud. (*Sleuth,* from *slios,* meaning "sloped," sounds like "Slooh," or, in local pronunciation, as echoed by Yeats in his *Reveries,* "Slish.")[32]

The scenery around Sligo warrants iconization. The pregnant bump on top the great hill of Knocknarea may very well, as alleged, contain the tomb of Ireland's ancient Queen Maeve. The massive brooding outcrop of Ben Bulben deserves to be ranked as one of the world's magic mountains; like Popocatepetl, Fuji, and Vesuvius, it casts its spell over the human settlements beneath.

When the family returned to London in 1874, with no improvement in their finances, they lived at Edith Villas, a dreary street in West Kensington, where another child, Jane Grace, was born, and died ten months later of pneumonia. The loss of the second child in three years did nothing to lift the spirits of a naturally depressed woman. There were no more children after that.

After the summer holiday of 1876, Susan Yeats remained with the younger children in Sligo while Yeats (now eleven) was isolated yet again by being sent back to England with his father. The pair settled temporarily in Berkshire, where John Butler Yeats determined to learn to paint landscapes and where Willie, still unenrolled in any school, roamed free, indulged his botanical interests, and noticed that his father seemed unable to complete a picture.[33] When the rest of the family joined them, they returned to London, and the unconfident Yeats became a pupil at the Godolphin School, Hammersmith.

In 1879 John Butler Yeats moved the family farther west in London, to the salubrious artists' colony of Bedford Park. But food was always short—not that Susan Yeats could cook ("could not have boiled an egg," in her husband's judgment)[34] and not that she needed to. The Yeatses were middle-class poor—that is, they were never without at least one servant and occasionally a governess.

Schoolmates at Godolphin later recalled a familiar classroom type: an odd-looking boy, unusually tall, with black hair falling over a pale, thin face, and luminous eyes staring off into space; scolded by the masters without ever seeming to mind, talking to the school pariahs without noticing that they were scorned by the other boys. He was mocked for his Irish accent, for his unwillingness to fight (although he did, not unsuccessfully, when challenged), and for having no clear answer to the question of what his father "did." He was a poor student; in one term he was near the bottom in every subject, and when he did do moderately well (rising to sixth out of thirty-one), it was in classics. Nothing in his grades for English—poor—suggested the place he would hold in the textbooks of the future.

It was in this uncertain dreamy state in his midteens that he began writing poetry. It was then too that he discovered masturbation. In

Reveries over Childhood and Youth, published in 1916, he gives the age of sexual awakening at "nearly seventeen." His original version (referred to in chapter 2) places the event somewhat earlier:

> I was tortured by sexual desire and had been for many years. I have often said to myself that some day I would put it all down in a book that some young man of talent might not think as I did that my shame was mine alone. It began when I was fifteen years old. I had been bathing, and lay down in the sun on the sand on the Third Rosses and covered my body with sand. Presently the weight of the sand began to affect the organ of sex, though at first I did not know what the strange, growing sensation was. It was only at the orgasm that I knew, remembering some boy's description or the description in my grandfather's encyclopedia. It was many days before I discovered how to renew that wonderful sensation. From that on it was a continual struggle against an experience that almost invariably left me with exhausted nerves. . . . It filled me with loathing of myself.[35]

Yeats's next educational stop was Erasmus Smith High School in Dublin, where the desperate John Butler Yeats next took his family, settling them in the peninsula suburb of Howth. His influence on his adolescent son's thought was then at its height. As they traveled together into Dublin on the train every morning, father lectured son on beauty, poetry, style, Keats, Shelley, and his pet hate (because of his sensual private life), Raphael.[36] Then, Trinity College being out of the question, Yeats began at the Metropolitan School of Art on Kildare Street. Lily and Lolly were already studying there. At last he became his own man.

He developed a wide circle of friends, including George Russell, who saw visions and called himself "AE" (for the Greek word *aeron*), and John O'Leary, the fierce Irish republican recently returned from exile in Paris. He had his first poem published, "The Song of the Faeries." In 1885, when merely twenty, he presided over the founding meeting of the Dublin Hermetic Society.

A Pollexfen launched his interest in the occult. Once his aunt Isabella (Mrs. John Varley) had given him a copy of A. P. Sinnett's *Esoteric Buddhism,* Yeats never looked back. Hindu mysticism, theosophy, the search for the hidden secrets of the universe, astral traveling—the ideas that were to fuel his later psychic experiments—seized his imagination at this fertile time. He was in good company. Magic, fantasy, and the supernatural held great allure in the late nineteenth century for those unable to follow the paths of scientific rationalism or Rome. Fortified by his growing inclination to rebel against his didactic father, Yeats was an inevitable and eager convert.

As R. F. Foster has shown in *Protestant Magic: W. B. Yeats and the Spell of Irish History,* the Anglo-Irish were especially susceptible to the otherworldly: Sheridan Le Fanu's vampire tale *Carmilla,* and its successor, Bram Stoker's *Dracula,* are eloquent proof. Whether isolated in the Chekhovian silence of its decaying country houses and or watching its power shift to the rising Catholic bourgeoisie in the cities, the Ascendancy—the former ruling class—was losing its grip, psychologically and socially. To Foster, the Yeats family, "with their clerical connections and declining fortunes," epitomized this increasing Irish Protestant sense of displacement.[37]

But few of the Irish Protestant enthusiasts were to match Yeats in practical experimentation or organizational zeal.

Immersed as he was in his own writing, with intense activities very far from his father's ideas, Yeats remained with the family troop as it relocated once again in London in 1887. The young adults were reminded that they could not afford to leave home. Number 58 Eardley Crescent, Earl's Court, was the darkest and ugliest of their many London residences, with a small, dark concrete garden at the back and a glimpse of the giant exhibition hall of Earl's Court at the front.

In the summer of 1887, in that ill-favored house (which still exists, at the end of a treeless terrace), Susan Yeats suffered her first seizure. The following December she had another, tumbling down a flight of stairs as it struck. With these attacks, she passed beyond emotional reach forever. Lily believed that their mother never even knew that Willie wrote poetry.

Two months later, in January 1888, at a Dublin séance, Yeats suffered the nervous disturbance that frightened him off further séances for years. In the following months, in spite of prodigious work and the family's move back to pleasant Bedford Park, he was dogged by gloom and despair. In June he was so worried about money, his mother's health, and the pressure of work that he wrote his friend Katharine Tynan (who witnessed the convulsion at his first séance) that all he could do was "bury my head in books as the ostridge does in the sand."[38] He began his novel about the bachelor living alone with his mother. He finished his first long narrative poem, "The Wanderings of Oisin," which brought together his fears of death and fantasies of islands. He began fighting fiercely with his father (who nonetheless encouraged him to avoid regular employment because of its threat to creativity).

In November he suffered an attack by "lunar influences," which was followed in December by "another of my collapses." Even so, he was able to complete the first draft of the poem then beginning, "I will arise and go now and go to the island of Innis free," based, he said, on "an old day dream of my own."[39] A month later, on January 30, 1889, as if on cue, Maud Gonne arrived at their house at 3 Blenheim Road (in a hansom cab, which she kept waiting), and the whole load of longing for an unattainable love—"the troubling of my life"—transferred to her.[40]

The next day he wrote Katharine Tynan, "I see you ask about my Mother. She is as usual, that is to say feable and unable to go out of doors, or move about much."[41]

A visitor to the family home, Ernest Rhys, a Welsh poet and Celtic folklorist, caught the situation in a glance. Invited to supper, he saw "the opinionated talkative father, delightful sisters and in the corner the silent, dark-eyed mother whom Willie seemed to resemble more than any of the rest."[42]

Did he resemble her? Physically, in a sense; mother and son shared a curious asymmetry of the eyes, hers from color—Susan Yeats had disconcertingly one brown eye and one blue—Yeats from what he called a "conical cornea," which spoiled the sight in his left eye and gave him a myopic, wall-eyed look. They shared the same facial structure—full mouth, slightly protruding jaw and chin, full flat lips—as did the two Yeats sisters. But something more was wrong with Susan Yeats than the after-effects of a stroke, and had been wrong for a long time.

In retrospect Lily described her mother's affliction as "mental": "She used to fall asleep as a young woman any time she sat quiet for a while or read out to us children."[43] John Butler Yeats for his part, captured this quality in a revealing pencil sketch of his wife six weeks before Bobby's birth; it shows her with eyes downcast, hand covering her mouth, seated with a shawl over her lap, utterly oblivious to her young daughter (Lily) smiling at her side.

The conventional explanation for Susan Yeats's depression blames her husband for plunging her swiftly into a life entirely different from that she had enjoyed as a girl and had been led to expect upon her marriage. But English literature is full of examples of women let down by their men—the mothers of D. H. Lawrence, James Joyce, and Anthony Trollope spring to mind—who used their strength and resourcefulness not only to feed their children but to turn their sons into great writers.

In later life (when it was too late), John Butler Yeats also blamed himself. He told John Quinn how painful it was for him to think back to the way his daughters had to work to support the family: "and behind all was my poor wife. *I knew perfectly well* that it was this terrible struggle with *want of means that had upset her* mind."[44]

But he knew it was not the whole story. Three of the eleven Pollexfen children had been in mental institutions. William was "put away" for life when a fairly young man.[45] Excitable Agnes, after marrying a man not accepted by her family, spent years in asylums. One day she escaped and turned up on the Yeatses' Bedford Park doorstep, forcing them eventually, from sheer exhaustion, to call attendants to take her away again. Agnes's daughter was also afflicted with a multiple-personality. Another married sister, Elizabeth Orr, had a mental collapse characterized by nonstop talking. She too had to be put in a secure hospital for a time. The precipitating factor in her case was the death of the Pollexfen parents a few months apart in 1892. (At that point Yeats wrote Lily, "I am afraid that Grandpapas death will make Mamma worse. Please let me know how she is every now & then.")[46] Even Yeats's captivating uncle George Pollexfen, for all his Freemason's rank and high standing in the business community, was held in Sligo to be "very odd"; he too had spent time in an asylum because of depression. John Butler Yeats caught the family's peculiar blend of silence and combustibility when he said (and said more than once) that by marrying a Pollexfen, "I have given a tongue to the sea cliffs."[47] The implication was that the Pollexfens were stony and unpleasant until they started to talk of fairies. Another way of putting it might be manic depression. In this light, Yeats's preoccupation in the last decade of his life with eugenics and bad blood looks less like a product of snobbery or fascism, and more like a realistic and long-standing fear of the alarming biological inheritance from his mother's side of the family. The fear of the Pollexfen madness hung over the Yeats children all their lives, as when Jack had a severe breakdown in 1915–16.[48]

It was therefore not entirely a tribute to Susan Yeats when Yeats wrote in 1903, in the *All Ireland Review,* "Has it not been said that a man of genius takes the most after his mother?" He expressed his anxiety more openly to his journal in early 1909 (when he was forty-three):

> I begin to wonder whether I have and always have had some nervous weakness inherited from my mother. I have noticed my own form of excitability in my sister Lolly, exaggerated in her by fits of prolonged gloom . . . In Paris I felt that if the strain were but a little more I would hit the woman who irritated me, and I often have long periods during which Irish things—it is always Irish things and people that vex . . . —make life nearly unendurable. . . . It often alarms me: is it the root of madness? . . . There was a time when [my writings] were threatened by it. . . . I escaped from it all as a writer through my sense of style. Is not one's art made out of a struggle in one's soul?[49]

The case for writing to preserve sanity has seldom been better put.

At writing he pushed himself hard, to the exclusion of all else: "My life has been in my poems . . . I have buried my youth and raised over it a cairn—of clouds."[50] In July 1888 he complained to Katharine Tynan of severe depression, of having "one of my dreadful despondent moods on—particularly fatigue. To keep happy seems like walking on stilts. When one is tired, one falls off."[51]

Part of his workload that year was the book of folklore of the Irish peasantry that he was editing for Camelot Classics. According to his classification (and his spelling), it was to be divided into Fairies, Changlings, Leprehauns, Banshee, Ghosts, Headless horsemen, etc.; Tir-nan-oge (Land of the Young, Childhood), Witches, Fairy docters, Saints, The devil.

As Toomey shrewdly observes, Yeats had reason to "sacramental-ize" these beliefs about stolen lives, for they gave some degree of protection for sufferers: "The paralysed figure in the corner of the kitchen was regarded with awe rather than embarrassment."[52] A contemporary version of this humane superstition is seen in Christy Brown's *My Left Foot*, where the inarticulate cripple is trundled round Dublin and indulged by his large family. (This true story is a perfect illustration of the myth of substitution, for the babbling, twisted man turned out to have a writer inside him.)

A benign vision of Susan Yeats as simply "away" in a world of her own is how Yeats leaves her in *Reveries over Childhood and Youth:* "her mind had gone in a stroke of paralysis and she had found, liberated at last from financial worry, perfect happiness feeding the birds at a London window."[53]

As his mother passed out of reach, a succession of surrogates presented themselves, capped by Lady Gregory, whom he met in 1896. An earlier refuge and important protector was his occultist uncle George Pollexfen; a keen astrologer who spent hours working his charts,[54] and who had followed him into the Golden Dawn and the attempt to found a Celtic counterpart. After the Pollexfen grandparents died, George's big, bleak house high on a hill overlooking the harbor became Yeats's Sligo home. At Thornhill, the bachelor George kept a witch-mother of his own, in the form of his housekeeper, Mary Battle, a second-sighted old widow from Mayo, whose wondrous visions—a flying hearse (when it touched the ground someone died), Queen

Maeve traveling over Knocknarea with a sword by her side and a dagger in her hand—gave Yeats, notebook at the ready, a mine of fairy lore. Lily saw Mary Battle as "half-mad."[55]

George was game for magical adventures. One October night in Sligo in 1892, Yeats took him, "a hard-headed man of 47," and his cousin Lucy Middleton, "the only witch in the family," out to a supposed fairy locality at Rosses Point where he drew a magic circle in the sand and invoked the fairies. Called, they came. After a rush of noises and distant music, "the queen of the troop . . . —I could see her," appeared, held a long conversation with them and wrote in the sand "be careful & do not seek to know too much about us."[56]

Like the occultists, the fairy-seekers were on a popular trail. Fairyland flooded the Victorian imagination and Victorian painting. In imps, elves, bosky dells, and gossamer wings, artists found a happy refuge from science and industrialization, their flight often assisted by laudanum. Gilbert and Sullivan took a wry look at this craze in *Iolanthe*.

George's confidence in his nephew's magical powers was rewarded when Yeats helped him through an illness following a smallpox vaccination that had gone wrong. In his fevered delirium, George reported seeing "red dancing figures," whereupon Yeats invoked the symbol of water and some cabalistic names, and the dancers vanished. Should they return, Yeats, breaking the rules of the Golden Dawn (not for the last time), prescribed a secret phrase, one that George, at his lower degree in the order, was not entitled to know. (The magic words were "The Archangel Gabriel," and when George needed them, they worked.)[57]

Susan Yeats died on January 3, 1900, at Blenheim Road. Excusing his lateness in sending a poem to an editor, Yeats reported the death only as "an unexpected family trouble."[58] He gave the news more directly to Lady Gregory, saying that the event was inevitable, that his mother had been unconscious and without pain, and unable to recognize any of them for a long time. "I think that my sister Lilly & myself feal it most through our father. . . . It will be a great blow to Jack [who was away at the time] . . . he was devoted to his mother."[59]

That much was evident. Jack (who got on badly with his father) paid for the plaque in Saint John's Church, Sligo, just as with his first earnings as a cartoonist and illustrator he had hired a medical specialist to see his mother. He had continued to write newsy, amusing letters to her until the very end, as if she were still of sound mind. For six months following her death he abandoned his sketchbooks.[60]

Yeats's grief was more attenuated. To the two women with whom he had had satisfactory sexual relationships, he wrote when their own mothers died—movingly and enviously. To Olivia Shakespear:

> I sympathise with you very deeply, for I know that you cared for nobody else as for your mother, & when a mother is near ones heart her loss must be the greatest of all losses.[61]

That was in May 1900. On the black-bordered paper he was still using five months after his own mother's death, he passed on the faith to which he was to cling:

> The Irish poor hardly think of a mothers death as dividing her very far from her children & I have heard them say that when a mother dies all things often go better with her children for she has gone where she can serve them better than she can here.[62]

In 1911, during his affair with Mabel Dickinson, her mother became mortally ill. Perhaps struck by the difference between her feelings and his own in the same circumstance, he suggested that he could only imagine how he would feel. She must be under a terrible strain, he said. If he were sitting by the deathbed of someone he loved, he thought he would feel isolated from life.[63]

A stronger outburst of buried grief came when, in 1909, Robert Gregory informed him that his mother was ill and not expected to live. Yeats's mind suddenly clouded over, and he found he could not think straight. He told his journal:

> I thought my mother was ill and that my sister was asking me to come at once: then I remembered that my mother died years

ago and that more than kin was at stake. She [Lady Gregory] has been to me mother, friend, sister and brother. I cannot realize the world without her.[64]

Yeats's images—the severed head, the topless tower, the winding stair, the broken wall, the hunger for the apple on the bough most out of reach, the disdainful dome, the swords, scepters, and unicorns—would fill a textbook on the Freudian symbol. In a long psychoanalytic study of his work in 1973, the American scholar Brenda Webster took the symbolism beyond the phallus, breast, and vagina to a representation of the damaged woman herself. The obvious way for Yeats to cure the sense of being abandoned by his mother, she suggested, was to identify with her: ergo, the feeling of worthlessness and the use in his work of symbols like the ship with a broken mast and "a long scratch in the stern," sailing away from shore.[65]

In this Freudian light, Yeats's work becomes full of oral deprivation and a longing for a return to the passivity of the infant as a refuge from conflict with the father. His first play, *The Countess Cathleen,* can be read as substituting physical hunger for the need for love (the beautiful queen gives all she has to feed her hungry children). His many approximations of parental intercourse, as in *The Player Queen* (where the Queen mates with a unicorn) and *Purgatory,* are clear and classic illustrations of the primal scene. And if Sligo can be read as Mother, the hated London easily becomes Father. In sum, Webster found, the weak self-image in Yeats produced by his unreachable and damaged mother accounts for the themes of masochism and disembodiment in his work, as well as for the devastation of his relations with women.

Months after John Butler Yeats's death in Manhattan in 1922, three boxes of his papers and letters arrived in Dublin. The material was eminently publishable: Yeats swiftly edited the long-prepared rough draft of the old man's autobiography into *Early Memories,* brought out by the Cuala Press in September 1923. Perhaps then, if not before, Yeats may have come across the dozen letters later filed among his papers as "Papa's Letters to Mama Before Their Marriage."

These letters carried, like a whiff from a time capsule, the spirit of his parents as young lovers, sensually expectant, stealing away from the family to kiss, planning their future, blind to the hints of incompatibilities and broken promises that were to blight their own and their children's lives.

The impression that the love letters, with their sadomasochist undertones, would have made upon Yeats can be imagined. Rape fantasies float through his work, supremely in "Leda and the Swan":

> A sudden blow: the great wings beating still
> Above the staggering girl, her thighs caressed
> By the dark webs, her nape caught in his bill,
> He holds her helpless breast upon his breast.
>
> How can those terrified vague fingers push
> The feathered glory from her loosening thighs?

This poem, written in 1923, is now a feminist target; it has been called sexist and pornographic.[66] In that light, the "great wings" and the "loosening thighs" do not seem a million miles removed from the godlike young Dublin barrister swooping down on the helpless girl from Sligo.

At some point Yeats seems to have been shocked to realize that his mother hid bodily appetites under her scowl. His new female persona, "Crazy Jane," which emerged in 1926, may owe as much to Susan Yeats as to Mary Battle or any other Irish eccentric now thought to be the model for the well-used crone:

> Though like a road
> That men pass over
> My body makes no moan[67]

Yeats's long communion with spirits, from the early experiments in magic writing to the Sleeps and the séances he continued to attend all his life, was thus doubly determined. It was both a return to his mother and the ultimate revenge against his father. "If John Butler Yeats had lived to read *A Vision*," says his biographer, William Murphy, "the shock would surely have killed him."[68]

That, one might say, was the point. Killing the father is a theme that runs straight through Yeats's plays, from *On Baile's Strand*, written in 1904, to *Purgatory*, written in 1938, not to mention through *The Playboy of the Western World*, Synge's oedipal satire of which Yeats was the most ardent champion. Personal history was to doom Yeats to end life as he began: dreaming of murdering his father to gain the favor of his unhappy mother.

Part 4

11

Politics and Potency

(1922–1928)

IN THE SIX YEARS following his return to Ireland in 1922, in spite of much illness, Yeats interwove public life and poetry with astonishing success—a heroic marshaling of waning energies to get done what he wanted to get done. As a senator from December 1922 to September 1928, he oversaw the design of a handsome national coinage and led the fight against the Free State's swerve down a repressive clerical path. He continued the campaign to retrieve the Lane pictures for Dublin. At the Abbey Theatre, he introduced the work of Sean O'Casey and championed O'Casey's *The Plough and the Stars* against rioting audiences who took the play as mocking Patrick Pearse and Ireland's decade of blood sacrifice. He published *A Vision,* his cryptic personal analysis, drawn from the Automatic Script, of the historical causes of political upheaval.

During these same years he wrote, in addition to three plays, his finest volume of poetry. With the appearance of *The Tower* in 1928, it was clear that he was becoming, like Verdi and Milton, one of the rare artists to achieve his prime in old age. In congratulating him for winning the Nobel Prize for Literature in 1923, Standish James O'Grady, the father of the Irish literary revival, recalled that Sophocles had written *Antigone* at eighty, and said, "I think your powers are growing still."[1]

The greatness of Yeats's late poetry is recognized. The extent of his public service and sheer management of complexity is not, his achievement obscured by the permanent cloud of his foray into 1930s fascist politics. Would that surprise him? His poem called "The Choice" says, "The intellect of man is forced to choose / Perfection of the life, or of the work." As he entered the years beyond sixty, although very far from perfection in his life, he made an impressive attempt to have both.

One casualty was his political reputation: the fascist label, however inappropriate, has stuck. The other was his family life. His marriage, a compromise even at the start, deteriorated into a custodial and administrative partnership. Letters to his wife, which once opened with "my beloved," now began "Dear Dobbs" (the childhood name her brother called her).[2] He was a distant, often absent father. The long-awaited children were sent off to boarding school in Switzerland when Anne was eight and Michael only six.

With the easy chauvinism of his time, he used his wife as business manager, nurse, real estate agent, hostess, editor, literary agent, and proofreader while allowing his sexual interests to drift elsewhere. One of his first affairs was with Dolly (Dorothy) Travers-Smith, an artist and scene-painter for the Abbey and the daughter of the automatic-writing medium Hester Travers-Smith.[3] Yeats found Dolly "slim and red-lipped."[4] Friends were amused to watch him one day at a party at Lennox Robinson's cottage try to put her in a trance.

George played her part well. For a time she housed his sisters' Cuala Industries in the basement. She made their home at 82 Merrion Square an elegant setting from which he reigned over the Dublin literary and political scene; visitors saw her as highly intelligent and were amused by the way she saw through Yeats's posturing and teased him.[5]

For male company, she turned to suitable escorts nearer her own age, Lennox Robinson, playwright and director of the Abbey, and Thomas MacGreevy, poet, scholar, curator (and later friend of Samuel Beckett). Both were bachelors, Robinson until 1931. They took her out to dinner, films, and the theater, and served as confidants to whom she poured out her woes. When she traveled, she deluged them with long affectionate letters, in which they were "Dearest Lennox" and "Dearest Tom" (using a term of endearment not seen in her surviving letters to her husband) and she was "Dearest George."[6] Lennox had his own latchkey to let himself into 82 Merrion Square. If he was bored by the conversation when guests were there, he would say, "Georgie, let's take a walk, just once round the square," and the two of them would go out.[7] The relationship seems to have been platonic. She had confided, years before, to MacGreevy that she hoped that Lennox would marry and put an end to the rumors that he had "Wildish" tendencies.[8] (Dublin did not entertain similar rumors about Tom MacGreevy who, unlike Lennox, never took a wife. In Ireland MacGreevy was accepted as a pious, Mass-going celibate; at the École Normale in Paris, however, it was assumed, from his circle of friends, that he was homosexual.)[9]

She also developed interests of her own. She served, for example, as secretary of the Dublin Drama League (1918–1928), a group founded by Yeats and Lennox to bring world drama to Dublin because the Abbey seemed too parochial.[10] She also attempted some play-writing herself. But with servants to care for the children when they were not away at school, time hung heavy. If she had no evening engagements, she went to bed early and got up late. Increasingly she turned to the solace of drink.[11] (Alcohol, according to Alex Owen's study, *The Darkened Room: Women, Power, and Spiritualism in Late Victorian England*, was a frequent recourse of mediums who lost their spiritualist powers.) Yet she never weakened in her conviction that her duty was to help a great poet continue to write great poetry. Her mother thanked Yeats for giving her daughter a great and splendid life. If only that were true, he reproached himself.[12]

Yeats was once more living at the Savile Club in London, working on *A Vision,* when George wrote to remind him that Michael had just passed his third birthday. One of the servants had given the boy a clockwork train. Seeing his fascination with it, she suggested that Yeats buy him a mechanical toy.[13]

Yeats did as he was told. He took himself to Harrod's; the ensuing scene—the large great poet trying out the toys, perhaps lifting his pince-nez to peer more closely—would be worth retrieving from the Anima Mundi. For his small son, he selected a mechanical duck that waved its wings and chimed when pulled along on a string.[14]

Two years later he was to write:

Once out of nature I shall never take
My bodily form from any natural thing,
But such a form as Grecian goldsmiths make
Of hammered gold and gold enamelling
To keep a drowsy Emperor awake;
Or set upon a golden bough to sing
To lords and ladies of Byzantium
Of what is past, or passing, or to come.[15]

Did what may be the best-known bird in English-language poetry after Keats's nightingale come from Harrod's toy department?

Yeats's children, far from keeping him young, made him feel old. Like many fathers, he saw them as rivals and threats. They had first claim on his wife's attention. They were little bundles of noise and infection; in Dublin he tended to move to his club (the Kildare Street) when they were ill (to save George the burden of looking after him as well).[16] As Michael grew rapidly and was tall for his age, Yeats joked that he would soon be equaling the boy in growing out of his clothes. How curious it was, he wrote his wife, that old age and childhood should so resemble each other.[17] But his growth was all in his waistline. He had the body of an old man, and he hated it.

"Sailing to Byzantium," the first poem in *The Tower,* is among the

world's favorite Yeats poems. But is it loved for expressing the endur-
ing beauty of art? Or for venting age's envy of youth? The artificial
songbird at the poem's end comes as a grudging substitute for the
mating creatures of the famous opening lines:

> That is no country for old men. The young
> In one another's arms, birds in the trees,
> . . . .
> Caught in that sensual music all neglect
> Monuments of unageing intellect.

Much the same sadness can be found in "The Tower," the second
poem. The elderly narrator contrasts his loathsome body with his
youthful spirit:

> What shall I do with this absurdity—
> O heart, O troubled heart—this caricature,
> Decrepit age that has been tied to me
> As to a dog's tail?
> > Never had I more
> Excited, passionate, fantastical
> Imagination

As a simile for age as a gratuitous attachment, "to a dog's tail" could
hardly be bettered, unless by the image at the end of the same stanza:
"A sort of battered kettle at the heel."

Yet why complain about a long life, considering the alternative? The
speaker in "The Tower" sees the absurdity. Why should he be any
angrier than any one else at growing old? With an autobiographical
frankness that must have dismayed his wife, "The Tower," composed
the year Yeats turned sixty, supplies the answer. The poet envies Red
Hanrahan, the character he himself created as a boy to be everything
that he was not: "Old lecher with a love on every wind." He goes on,
with coruscating self-analysis, to look back on a youth wasted in soli-
tary longing for a woman who was in someone else's arms.

The splendor of "The Tower" comes both from its humanism—

And I declare my faith:
I mock Plotinus' thought
And cry in Plato's teeth,
Death and life were not
Till man made up the whole

—and from its acceptance of mortality. Yet in this as in his other valedictory poems on the transitoriness of life, Yeats's rhetoric is more impressive than his argument, his sound more convincing than his sense. There is little evidence, poetic or biographical, that he ever cured his regret for his onanistic youth.

What he dreaded was not death but impotence. The poems of these years flaunt codes for a flaccidity—not only the battered kettle and the drooping dog's tail, but "a tattered coat upon a stick." More straightforwardly, his intimate letters to Olivia Shakespear, from whom he seems to have had few secrets, convey a sense of being cheated of what other men have had. He shuddered when he looked at the portrait his father had done of him at twenty: "looking very desirable— alas no woman noticed it at the time—with dreamy eyes and a great mass of black hair . . . a pathetic memory of a really dreadful time."[18]

Even as he received his Nobel Prize in Stockholm, he raised the question of his desirability. Looking at the design on his medal, a young man listening to a muse, he thought to himself, "I was good-looking once like that young man . . . now I am old and rheumatic, and nothing to look at, but my Muse is young."[19]

Self-doubt in private, but not in public. He was still a fine-looking, if somewhat stout, man. He had a full head of white hair that fell boyishly over brownish skin whose color could be described as liverish or leathery (some Indians thought him Indian) but which could also pass for a healthy suntan.

Dublin counted on him to make a beeline for a pretty girl at a party. With his charm, his international reputation as the Great Irish Poet, and undimmed powers of conversation—G. K. Chesterton said, "W.B. is the best talker I ever met, except his old father who alas will talk no more"—he had little trouble attracting female company. Any woman was flattered by his attention as he bent down with theatrical courtesy and intoned in his melodious voice, "Who have I?" The Nobel Prize did not hurt.

His first term as senator began at a dangerous time. By the end of 1922 the Irish Civil War was at its height. The country had begun to slide into it in January following the Dáil's narrow ratification of the treaty with Britain. Although the majority of the people supported the treaty out of a desperate hope for peace, de Valera and his supporters in Sinn Fein immediately determined to battle on for a fully independent republic. They repudiated the Dáil and declared themselves a provisional government. Considering their own forces to be the real Irish Republican Army, they set up an executive to issue orders to the IRA all around the country. Thus former Volunteers, who had fought against the British, found themselves split into pro- and anti-treaty factions (known respectively as the Free Staters and the Irregulars). Both factions moved into military installations vacated by the British; whether a particular barracks was pro- or anti-treaty depended on the personal stance of its commanding officer. In consequence, the civilian population was left in a nightmare world of arson, bank raids, derailments, kidnappings, and murders. Lily Yeats described for John Quinn how the body of a young Irregular had been left in a coffin in the church in Dundrum before his family even knew he was dead. "The Village is Free State," she explained.[20]

The Free State government, under Arthur Griffith as president and Michael Collins as chairman of the Executive Council, was still provisional, awaiting a general election. Yet it commanded the heavy artillery and the armored cars of official power. With British support, it began to move against the IRA guerrillas with a ruthlessness that outdid that of its old imperial masters. Full-scale civil war exploded in June 1922 when, under pressure from Britain to retaliate for the assassination in London of a leading Unionist, and with the loan of two 18-pound guns by the British Army, the Free State sent its forces to bombard the republican stronghold, the imposing Four Courts on the Liffey. At Easter, the Irregulars, in an echo of 1916, had seized the symbolic public building and dug in, declaring themselves an alternative government.

As in 1916, the well-equipped official forces easily shelled the insurrectionists into surrender. However, this time the victory was of Irishmen over Irishmen. Part of the price paid was the destruction of the fine neo-classical domed structure and, with it, centuries of Ireland's public archives. Four hundred prisoners were taken, among them the archrepublican Sean MacBride. This successful military operation may have won the new Free State the approval of the British government, but not of the British public. For many, the spectacle of the Irish destroying their heritage in order to kill each other simply proved that the natives of Britain's oldest colony were unfit for independence.

In June 1922 the provisional government won the general election, but its majority was narrow, with minor parties such as Labour and Farmers splitting the large pro-treaty vote, and the civil war raged on. In August, Griffith collapsed and died. Ten days later, Collins, being driven (foolhardily) through anti-treaty, pro-de Valera territory in Cork, was caught in an ambush and killed by a sniper's bullet. The new state thus had to get on its feet without the leaders who had bargained it into being. The new president, William Cosgrave, colorless but competent, managed to exert some restraint over his troops.

During the summer of 1922, Yeats, with his wife, small daughter, and baby son, remained secluded at Ballylee. Cut off from newspapers and letters, he often did not know how the war was going. Himself wholeheartedly pro-treaty, he nonetheless presented a neutral face to the random Free Stater or Irregular who came to the door. He remained calm even when the Irregulars blew up their bridge (having given a courteous warning that the children should be moved to the upper floors).[21] The ground floor of the castle was left flooded with two feet of water. Yeats told Quinn that Anne enjoyed the sound of the blast.[22]

The contrast between the violence of men and the peacefulness of nature went into his long and wonderful poem "Meditations in Time of Civil War." After watching the starlings (the birds he called "stares") build their nests in the masonry, Yeats wrote the segment called "The Stare's Nest by my Window," which ends:

> We had fed the heart on fantasies,
> The heart's grown brutal from the fare;
> More substance in our enmities
> Than in our love; O honey-bees,
> Come build in the empty house of the stare.

Yeats was in England in November when the news circulated in Dublin that he was being considered for an appointment to the Senate. It was no sinecure. To the Irregulars, all the members of the Free State government—and their homes—were legitimate targets. Maud was already spreading a rumor among republican women to the effect that Yeats was not only pro-treaty but that he wanted a restoration of British rule.[23]

George knew what might lie in store. She had been alone in the house in Merrion Square with the children and servants during the week when Erskine Childers was tried and sentenced to death. Childers, the English-born author of *The Riddle of the Sands,* Irish patriot and gun-runner for supporters of the Home Rule movement, had been one of the heroes of the war against the British. A member of the treaty delegation to London in 1921, he had opposed the treaty and had subsequently joined the IRA to work for the Free State's overthrow. Hunted by the Free State authorities (and referred to as a "damned Englishman"), he was captured in his childhood home at Glendalough, charged with unauthorized possession of a pistol and condemned to death. Jack Yeats (also anti-treaty) appealed to Cosgrave, "I urge you to hold your hand and not to execute Erskine Childers. I write to you in the name of humanity and sober judgement."[24] His words fell on deaf ears. One night during the unrest that preceded the Childers execution, explosions rocked the Yeats home, causing the lighted candles that the cook had left in the windows to set the curtains on fire. George put out the blaze, then went down to the nursery, where she found the maids weeping and saying their rosaries. Crossly, she told them to stop being imbeciles and gave them some sweets. These, and her pagan spirit, she reported to Yeats, cheered the girls up.[25]

At the time Yeats was visiting Lady Ottoline Morrell at Garsington. George told him to stay where he was. Having anticipated that the rebels might blockade the roads into Dublin, she had laid in stocks of food. There was no need for him to worry.[26]

That was not quite true. After Childers was put to death the next morning (November 24, his dying words to his executioners passing instantly into Irish martyrology: "Take a step or two forwards, lads, it will be easier that way"),[27] the republicans were out for revenge. As soon as the Free State formally came into existence, on December 6, two members of the Dáil were shot, one of them killed.

Tit for tat. The Free State's stern young minister of justice, Kevin O'Higgins, ordered the summary execution of four of the Four Courts prisoners. The four included Rory O'Connor, who had been best man at O'Higgins's wedding the year before. In retaliation the Irregulars shot dead O'Higgins's father, at just about the time that Yeats was sworn in to the Senate.

Maud wrote Yeats that if he did not denounce the government's actions, their friendship was over. She herself was arrested next day. (Initially a supporter of the treaty, in the hope of peace, she was now passionately back in the republican camp.) Yeats could do nothing but try to send blankets.[28] Iseult too was picked up in the government's general sweep of republican sympathizers. Her husband, who had joined the Irregulars, was also in prison, arrested while helping to capture a train carrying Free State ammunition at Amiens Street Station in Dublin. Francis Stuart welcomed prison, he said later, as an escape from the pressures of his marriage.[29]

In January 1923, although he had made two speeches in the Senate, Yeats took himself back to the tranquillity of the Savile Club (where, as a "country" member, he was allowed a fire in his room).[30] He was not a coward. He was committed to a search for reality—in his philosophy, in his poetry, and, as he saw it, in his politics. In the Civil War, he saw unreality all round: in Britain's insistence on the meaningless oath to the king, in the republicans' determination to fight on for the goal of complete independence. (The partition of Northern Ireland was not then the issue it would become.) Reading an interview with de Valera in the *Daily Mail*, Yeats judged that the republican leader was a theologian at heart, a man willing to sacrifice lives for principle.[31]

Yeats felt he could best help the search for peace from London, talking, with the authority of his new senatorial status, with old friends in high places, notably Winston Churchill and Churchill's secretary, Edward Marsh. Conceivably, he thought, he might persuade them to soften the terms of the treaty by dropping the despised oath.[32] His own view on the oath remained constant over the next decade. As he was to say in a press statement in London in 1932:

> Ireland will not be a pennyworth more loyal because Ireland has taken the Oath. . . . Personally I have no objection to the Oath. I have taken it myself, but a considerable part of our population objects to it, and it is very difficult for us to keep the peace in Ireland until everybody feels that he can safely enter the Dail and agitate there for his rights. As long as we have the Oath we shall have little revolutionary bodies disturbing the peace. It is as much, therefore, in the interests of Great Britain as of Ireland that we be rid of the Oath or modify it.[33]

That said, he was determined to attend to his primary duty, writing poetry. The strain of Dublin, he feared, would drive the verse out of his head. So he lingered on in London. Without question, however, he enjoyed the quieter life. He renewed contacts with the Order of the Golden Dawn, and he went to some interesting séances.[34] With the assistance of the typist who had helped him in his Woburn Buildings days, he had reached phase 23 of the phases of the moon in his book of philosophy. He visited the College of Psychic Science. To George he wrote wistfully that he wished she might come over to London, to get a look at the new trumpet medium, but he knew that she was held in Dublin. Anne was recovering from scarlet fever.

Every day he rushed for the papers. The news of January 31 was as bad as could be imagined. IRISH REBEL OUTRAGES. MANY HOUSES BURNED. KIDNAPPED SENATOR, said headlines in *The Times*.[35] The paper carried a vivid account of the destruction of the home of the Free State's chief solicitor. The official being away at the time, the band of armed young men had ushered his wife and children out into the street in their nightclothes before planting a landmine in the house and blowing it to bits.

Over a London dinner, Yeats sought advice from his friend, the writer and surgeon Oliver Saint John Gogarty. Gogarty was worth listening to. He had already paid the price of joining the Free State Senate, having been kidnapped, seized naked in his bath, by republican forces. That he was comfortably dining out in London a few weeks later was owed to ingenuity and physical strength: he had outwitted his captors by plunging into the Liffey and swimming to his escape under a hail of bullets. (His Galway home, Renvyle, was burned to the ground a month later.) Speaking strictly as a medical man, Gogarty recommended that Yeats take his family out of Ireland. The noise and shock of the explosions, he said, might be bad for Anne's kidneys.

Yeats took the point and conceived of a plan: if he moved his family to Holyhead, the ferry port in North Wales, he could easily cross over to Dublin when he needed to attend the Senate. George's grandmother had been suggesting to him a move even farther inland, to what she saw as the civilized town of Chester. He put the idea to George. Did she want him to go to Holyhead to make inquiries about lodgings?

Indeed she did not. She believed that the Civil War was at its climax and would soon subside. In a letter written on February 1, 1923, she as good as shamed Yeats into coming home if he were serious about doing something for his country. To be seen to move away, she said, would be a serious error. Anne, far from being troubled by the bombs, had slept right through. For her part, she was not afraid at all. Indeed, her very lack of fear was a sign that her instinctive trust in her husband was justified.

Her brave and, in its brisk way, loving letter moved Yeats deeply. He wrote back immediately, full of humility and gratitude: he knew she was not one to show her emotions in a letter; he accepted the truth of what she said.

There was no more talk of leaving. George's insistence that Yeats brave the fire and come home to be seen to live in Ireland during its time of greatest danger—a decision for which he was later praised—is probably her least-recognized contribution to Yeats's life and work.

The Civil War fizzled out three months later, in May 1923. The outnumbered republicans had no prospect of wresting power from the Free State government, which now held the full military apparatus of state plus the approval of the war-weary public. De Valera issued a proclamation telling his followers that it was hopeless to fight on. As they did not, however, surrender their arms, a coup d'état remained a constant threat.

With the restoration of law and order, on August 23, 1923, new elections were held. De Valera (who had been arrested once again and was campaigning from Kilmainham Jail) had the satisfaction of seeing Sinn Fein win the second largest number of seats. Their seats, of course, remained empty because of the required loyalty oath to the king. Thus the Free State was exposed at its start to the dangers of one-party rule.

The party in power, President Cosgrave's Cumann na nGaedheal (later Fine Gael), could do little to heal the scars of the terrible year in which brother fought brother with appalling savagery, creating political divisions that survive to this day. The legacy was similar to that left by the American Civil War, all the bitterer for having been fought in such a small space by men often known to each other. As Yeats was to write, "Great hatred, little room / Maimed us at the start."[36]

Among the families split by the Irish Civil War were the Yeatses. Jack was a passionately pro–de Valera republican who, years before his elder brother, had made the decision to move from England to Ireland permanently. He could take little pleasure from his brother's high position in a government that executed seventy-seven of its opponents during its first year in office, allowed hunger strikers to starve to death, and held twelve thousand prisoners for months after the war was over.

Yeats did not protest at the government's harsh regime, and did not wish to. He and George became personal friends of the government's strongman, O'Higgins, and his pretty young wife. Yeats valued order above all; he accepted the possibility that at any time the republicans might pick up their arms again and declare a republic.[37] Like other public men, he now lived with an armed guard in front of his door. When, in spite of the guard, two bullets were fired through the front door on Christmas Eve 1923, Yeats wrote Olivia, "Only isolated shots now at night but one is sure of nothing."[38]

Yeats swiftly came to enjoy the Senate. "We are a fairly distinguished body," he wrote Edmund Dulac, "much more so than the lower house."[39] That was another way of saying that a good proportion of the senators was Ascendancy Protestant, sympathetic to the interests of southern unionists and not hostile to Britain. It was in order to placate this substantial minority that the Senate had been designed to have half of its sixty members appointed rather than elected. The form of proportional representation adopted gave a number of smaller parties seats as well. Yeats sat with one of these, the Independents (effectively southern unionists). Mainly, however, he spoke for himself and was a shrewder politician than he pretended, as he prefaced political comments with the disclaimer that he was really a man of letters.

Being a senator was the first job Yeats had ever had, and it was an ideal one: £360 a year, tax free, flexible hours, great status, and influence on cultural matters dear to his heart. The Senate's timetable left his mornings free for writing verse and philosophy. A short walk from his fine house on Merrion Square took him to Leinster House, the splendid neoclassical mansion built by the duke of Leinster in 1745, where the Dáil Éireann (Assembly of Ireland) and the Seanad (Senate) now met. He was given, and welcomed, the chairmanship of committees on coinage, Irish manuscripts, and the arts.

His prominence in a new nation put Yeats in line for the Nobel Prize for literature. The Nobel committee, then as now, placed a strong emphasis on the nationality of its beneficiaries. Desmond FitzGerald, the new minister for defense, visited James Joyce in Paris and suggested that the Free State government might put forward his name for the prize, but Joyce replied that the suggestion was more likely to do FitzGerald harm than himself any good.[40] (Joyce was the first to send a telegram of congratulations to Yeats when the award was announced.) Yeats himself acknowledged that the Nobel recognition was as much for his country as for himself. His remark on receiving the news over the telephone from the editor of the *Irish Times*—"How much, Smyllie, how much is it?"—is famous.[41] It was also appropriate.*

Since July of that year, Lily had been a patient in a nursing home in north London. She had collapsed with what was thought to be consumption. Yeats and George had agreed to cover the expenses of her treatment, and their promise was made easier by the bounty of Sweden.[42] Lily was profoundly grateful. Early in 1924, she set down on paper how much she hated Lolly:

> Life with her the past twenty years has been a torture. . . . it is impossible ever to think of living with her again. . . . And now there is hope. I want to thank Willy and George for this ease of body and mind they have given me. . . . Whether I recover or not while lying in bed I will get great happiness out of thinking that there can be a life for me of the freedom that I have all my life longed for.[43]

Life *was* unkind to Lily Yeats. The actual cause of the chronic fatigue, poor breathing, and "nerves" that she suffered from since birth

---

*Yeats received 115,000 Swedish kroner from the Royal Academy of Sweden, or £6,678 at the prevailing exchange rate of 17.22 kroner to £1. By the Bank of England's calculations that £1 in 1923 was worth £26.11 in October 1998, Yeats's prize was worth approximately £174,370 in 1998—a much smaller windfall than enjoyed by later recipients. In 1995 Seamus Heaney received 7.2 million kroner as the Nobel Prize for literature in 1995. At the then-exchange rate of 11.26 kroner to £1, Heaney's prize amounted to £639,437—more than three and a half times the value of Yeats's.

was not to be diagnosed for another six years: an abnormally large thyroid gland pressing on her chest and throat.[44] And her release from Lolly never came. She was to return to Dundrum, to live with her short-tempered sister for the next fifteen years. Only Lolly's death, in 1939, released her.

For George too, Lolly was a cross she had to bear. George tried to minimize her encounters with her difficult sister-in-law, while at the same time taking a more direct hand in Cuala affairs—enlivening the design colors, opening her elegant drawing room for exhibitions and sales, taking Cuala goods (with no great enthusiasm) to London and displaying them for sale there.[45] In 1924 George managed to move both the printing and the weaving out of the basement of her home into new premises in Dublin on Lower Baggot Street. Even so, the little company never stood on its feet.

John Quinn, as soon as he heard the news from Sweden, told Yeats not to waste the Nobel money on Ballylee but to invest it. Yeats needed little persuading. Hardly back from Stockholm, he told Lady Gregory that he had bought £6,000 worth of stocks, as well as the finishing touches for his home, such as silverware, staircarpet, and a set of the *Encyclopedia Britannica*. He kept the residue for Lily's bills and the outstanding debt on the house.[46]

The sound advice was the last he was to receive from his friend in New York. Quinn died of cancer in the summer of 1924, another blow for the sisters. Letters to Quinn, as to their late father, had been the main outlet for their literary talents as well as for their thoughts about their family and Ireland.

From his position as senator, Nobel laureate, and holder (since December 1922) of an honorary doctorate from Trinity College, as well as long-time director of the Abbey Theatre, Yeats enjoyed the rare privilege of being both an artist and a patron of the arts. He wrote to Olivia of "the slow exciting work of creating the institutions of a new nation."[47]

He was not partisan in his favors. He used O'Higgins's revival of an ancient Irish sporting festival (the Tailteann Games) as an opportunity to celebrate Irish literature as well. In the summer of 1924 he invited Joyce, by now notorious for *Ulysses,* to return home for the event. (Joyce, who knew something of Irish public opinion, politely declined.) He made no attempt to deny recognition to writers who had been on the republican side in the war. Now persuaded that Francis Stuart was not a mad sadist but rather one of Ireland's most promising young writers,[48] Yeats assisted him in starting a new magazine called *To-morrow* in August 1924. His own yearnings were obvious: the magazine was to be "a wild paper of the young which will make enemies everywhere and suffer suppression,"[49] and he contributed his startling new poem "Leda and the Swan" for the first issue.[50] The poem had a somewhat longer life than the magazine. *To-morrow* lasted for only two issues before being suppressed for blasphemy because of a Lennox Robinson story about a raped Irish girl who thought she had had a virgin birth. Yeats further honored Stuart, who had now reached twenty-two and who had only been released from prison at Christmas 1923 under a general amnesty for republican prisoners, by crowning him with a laurel wreath at the Tailteann ceremony, thus placing him, with Gogarty, James Stephens, and G. K. Chesterton, among men who had conveyed honor and dignity upon Ireland. (Yeats, as he would later demonstrate as editor of *The Oxford Book of Modern Verse,* could be overenthusiastic to the point of misjudgment toward the work of writers he admired.)

He put to good use his chairmanship of the committee on the new coinage. The task was to replace the discarded likeness of the British monarch with emblems of Irish significance. With his good aesthetic eye and deep belief in the importance of symbols, Yeats engineered the choice of fish, flesh, and fowl as representations of Ireland and of its main industry, agriculture.

Like every other aspect of the new country, the coinage was fraught with controversy. The Department of Agriculture wanted the emblazoned bull and stallion to depict the finest anatomical features of breeding stock; others feared that overexplicit detail might cause public embarrassment. There was concern that the symbols were impious and also that the designer, Percy Metcalf, was English—but in the end his fine designs prevailed.˙

In his wish to costume the Irish judiciary in the style of the Gaelic past, Yeats was less successful. Michelangelo, Yeats pointed out, had designed the uniforms for the Papal Guard, so there was a precedent for treating them as works of art. A commission to the English artist and theatrical designer Charles Shannon, who, Yeats knew, was, like William Morris, a lover of the Middle Ages, resulted in an operatic range of bright, color-coded tunics (red for criminal trials), cloaks, and caps. However, the judges were not tempted. To Yeats's dismay, the higher levels of the judiciary insisted upon the black gowns and white wigs of the pre-1921 era.

Amid all this public activity in 1924, and perhaps because of it, his health began to falter. Diagnosed with high blood pressure, he took to his bed. Not that this in itself was unusual. Bed, for Yeats, as for his wife, was a place of refuge. He would remain there all morning, and in the afternoon as well, if he had an evening of engagements ahead. Visitors found him well wrapped, propped by pillows, on occasion with a half bottle of champagne at his elbow. Appearances were deceiving; like John Maynard Keynes, he got through a great deal of work by not rising and getting dressed before lunchtime.

George complained to Tom MacGreevy that public life was consuming too much of Yeats's time to the detriment of the verse that filled his head. She thought he ought to give up the Senate.[51] MacGreevy, then in London (where he escorted Olivia Shakespear to parties and the ballet), joked that the ideal government job for Yeats would be to be Irish high commissioner in London; he would love to be there to watch George introducing people to the queen. However, he ventured that Yeats enjoyed the Senate.[52]

˙Today, in spite of the change in coins with decimalization, some of the original designs remain. The bull of the old shilling is now on the five-pence coin, the salmon on the tenpence (the old two-shilling piece); the stallion from the old half-crown now graces the twenty-pence piece, while the new fifty-pence piece bears the woodcock of the obsolete farthing. From 1980 to 1992 Yeats's own face gazed out from the twenty-pound note.

And so he did, racking up an above-average attendance record, speaking with wit, dry humor, and the occasional quotation of poetry, and involving himself closely in issues such as welfare, hydroelectric power on the Shannon, and education.

For his first real holiday since their marriage, George got him to Italy in the early months of 1925. After a week in Capri, where Yeats finished *A Vision*, the couple joined Ezra and Dorothy Pound in Sicily, then went on to Rome, where Yeats had his first look at the achievements of Mussolini.

Mussolini in the mid-1920s was admired by many outside his own country. He and his black-shirted fascists had marched into Rome in October 1922 and in a bloodless coup d'état taken power from King Victor Emmanuel III. His boldness seemed to have saved Italy from both Bolshevism and civil war; his reforms, seen from abroad, were not the butt of jokes about making the trains run on time, but were rather the model for the modernization of an anarchic country through discipline and education.

Even before his Italian holiday, Yeats was an admirer. At a public banquet in August 1924, he had declaimed on the virtues of authoritarian government and quoted with approval Mussolini's phrase "We will trample upon the decomposing body of the Goddess of Liberty." Future generations, he said, would "have for their task, not the widening of liberty but the recovery from its errors."[53]

Yeats's enthusiasm for the fascist leader with the funny name added to the mountain of Dublin stories about his indifference to facts. Cruise O'Brien, the father of Conor Cruise O'Brien (whose essay "Passion and Cunning" takes a harsh and unforgiving look at Yeats's flirtation with fascism), parodied Yeats speaking warmly about "that very great man, Missolonghi" and, when corrected, saying magisterially, "I am told the name is not Missolonghi but Mussolini—but, does . . . it . . . really . . . matter?"[54]

What excited Yeats about the success of the Mussolini regime was its apparent illustration of the truth of his own just-completed System: that history moved in alternating cycles (or gyres). Mussolini represented the return of autocratic government—one man surrounded by selected, able assistants—a reversal of the trend toward greater and greater democracy. (*Democracy,* to Yeats, was a bad word; it meant mob rule, as in Russia.) He expressed this, as so much of his inner thought, to Olivia, "History is very simple—the rule of the many, then the rule of the few, day and night, night and day for ever."[55]

Yeats had already detected the philosophy behind fascism in Benedetto Croce's *Philosophy of Giambattista Vico.* As he read it, Vico's cycles of history gratifyingly corresponded to his own. (Joyce, from a rather different perspective, was also a Viconian. *Finnegans Wake* opens with the end of the sentence in the middle of which the book ends, thus bringing the end round to the beginning in "a commodius vicus of recirculation.")

For Yeats personally, the Mussolini regime held a role model in the form of its minister of public instruction, the idealist philosopher Giovanni Gentile. In Rome that spring Yeats had his wife scour the bookshops for Gentile's book *The Reform of Education,* and for any other explanation of the Italian revolution that he might take home.

Yeats still approached Great Books as a plunderer. He took what he wanted and rushed on. In the case of Gentile, what he wanted were the ideas on the essential unity of soul and body. He hoped that some Italian scholars might translate the entire three volumes of Gentile's work. From George he asked merely a summary, relying on her knowledge of Italian. Indeed, he relied on her to travel with him anywhere on the Continent. In all his foreign trips, except those to North America, he clung close to his female protectors: Lady Gregory in Italy in 1907, Maud Gonne over many years in France. For a man so reliant on eloquence in his mother tongue and so hopeless at foreign languages, he was in dread of being alone, even on a train, in a country where he could not make himself understood.

For a poet, nothing is wasted. Just as Yeats's scraps of Gentile were to metamorphose into "the great-rooted blossomer" and "the best modern way" of the Montessori method in "Among School Children," the mosaics of Palermo reappeared in the Byzantium poems, as did paintings of dolphins in the Castel San Angelo, and the Sistine Chapel ceiling provided ammunition against the Irish censors. He brought home photographs to prove that popes were not averse to the nude figure, a point he made in "a Long-legged Fly" as well:

> That girls at puberty may find
> The first Adam in their thought,
> Shut the door of the Pope's chapel,
> Keep those children out.

Yeats returned to Ireland to give the ringing speech on divorce that, the beautiful coinage apart, may be the main legacy of his Senate years. The issue was whether the Irish legislature wished the Free State to allow civil divorce with the right of remarriage (as had been allowed in England and Wales since the Matrimonial Causes Act of 1857). Yeats, as his support for executions and floggings showed, was no natural liberal. On the other hand, on matters of free speech, tolerance of dissent, and particularly on artistic freedom, he was consistently outspoken against state intervention: "I think you can leave the arts, superior or inferior, to the general conscience of mankind," he said on proposed film censorship.[56]

Yet he knew his strength. He was so august—known as Dr. Yeats since his Trinity degree—that he could speak out as very few could against the narrow Jansenist form of Catholicism gaining hold in the Free State. Just why sexual repression, preached with little success by a celibate clergy across the rest of Catholic Europe, should have been so readily adopted by the Irish people has been the subject of much sociological analysis. The Great Famine itself is part, but by no means, the whole explanation. It reduced the population of Ireland by half, lowered marriage rates, and sent emigration soaring. Even as the population recovered, the acreage of many family farms was scarcely enough for subsistence, with the consequence that any subdividing of land among sons virtually stopped after 1852.[57] Only one son (usually the oldest) could inherit, and only when his father agreed to retire. This rigid stem-family pattern and the struggle for land contributed to the exodus.

But not until 1880 did remaining in Ireland, unmarried, become a conspicuous alternative to emigration. The rate of celibacy began to rise markedly. Ireland, by the 1930s, had the highest incidence of bachelorhood and latest age (and lowest rate) of marriage in Europe, and the highest percentage of unmarried adults. The percentage of the mature unmarried was very high. For the other children, the alternatives were emigration or celibacy, or, in the case of daughters, marriage. For parents desperate to have girls taken off their hands, loss of virginity was an economic disaster. The situation grew worse when the American escape route was effectively closed in the 1920s by stringent new U.S. imigration laws. Accordingly, the notorious severity of the Irish Catholic Church—the snooping priest beating the hedges with his blackthorn stick to rout out lovers—was more effect than cause. It was, concludes F. S. L. Lyons in *Culture and Anarchy in Ireland,* a response to a social necessity, an attempt "to preserve or to assist what in effect amounted to perpetual celibacy for many men and women."[58]

In the same light, the Free State's imposition of strict censorship and compulsory Gaelic can be seen as a defense against the sexual temptation presented by the easily imported English newspapers, magazines, books, and films.

This was the background against which Yeats rose to his feet on June 11, 1925, two days short of his sixtieth birthday. He began by predicting (accurately, as subsequent unhappy history has shown) the long-term consequences of catholicizing Irish civil law:

> It is perhaps the deepest political passion with this nation that North and South be united into one nation. If it ever comes that North and South unite, the North will not give up any liberty which she already possesses under her constitution. . . . If you show that this country, southern Ireland, is going to be governed by Catholic ideas and by Catholic ideas alone, you will never get the North. . . . You will put a wedge into the midst of this nation.[59]

The right to divorce, he pointed out, had been won in the seventeenth century by great men such as John Milton and was part of the tradition of Protestantism. He then breached custom by referring to members of the Catholic hierarchy by name, particularly an Archbishop O'Donnell, who had argued against divorce on the grounds that no power on earth could break the marriage bond created by God. Yeats rebutted the argument:

> **That is to say that you are to legislate on purely theological grounds and you are to force your theology upon persons who are not of your religion. . . . Once you attempt legislation on religious grounds you open the way for every kind of intolerance and for every kind of religious persecution.**[60]

The gospels, he declared, were devotional not historical texts. Mischievously he alluded to Ireland's three great heroes—O'Connell, Parnell, and Nelson—and recalled that none of these had been models of marital propriety. Should their monuments in Dublin be torn down? At this point he was interrupted:

> *An Cathaoirleach [the Speaker]:* **Do you not think we might leave the dead alone?**
> *Dr. Yeats:* **I am passing on. I would hate to leave the dead alone.**[61]

By this point he was being heckled and senators were walking out of the chamber. He continued:

> **I think it is tragic that within three years of this country gaining its independence we should be discussing a measure which a minority of this nation considers to be grossly oppressive. I am proud to consider myself a typical man of that minority.**

Then came the majestic, musical, and, undeniably, snobbish peroration in praise of the Anglo-Irish:

We against whom you have done this thing are no petty people. We are one of the great stocks of Europe. We are the people of Burke; we are the people of Grattan; we are the people of Swift, the people of Emmet, the people of Parnell. We have created the most of the modern literature of this country. We have created the best of its political intelligence.[62]

The speech, his finest hour as a poet-politician, did him no good. The *Irish Times* regretted his tone. Legislatively, it made no difference; the Senate had only delaying powers over new legislation; anyway, the initial effort to ban divorce bills fizzled out. In the end, however, Ireland chose to be a land without civil divorce, and remained so long after Irish couples were receiving annulments from a liberalized Catholic Church on social and psychological grounds. Not until 1997, after a fierce court battle following a controversial referendum passed by a fraction of a percentage point, were Irish citizens allowed a civil liberty available in all other countries of the European Union.

Yeats's condescension toward Ireland's Catholic majority is undeniable. So too is the fact that many of the greatest names of Irish culture—Swift, Wilde, Burke, Shaw, Synge, Parnell, even the working-class trade union organizer O'Casey—were Protestant.[63] Yet Yeats knew very well that the Penal Laws had denied Catholics education until the nineteenth century, and mentioned in an American speech that there had been in effect no university for Catholics until 1908 and that achieved only after a century of fierce political and religious controversy.

Historical understanding, however, did not save him from snobbery. Certainly there was more than a whiff of Ascendancy condescension to Catholic rabble when, the following February, Yeats mounted the Abbey stage during the fourth night of uproar over O'Casey's *The Plough and the Stars* (prompted by the play's irreverent treatment of the words of the sacred 1916 martyr Patrick Pearse) and, de haut en bas, scolded the audience (after sending for the police): "You have disgraced yourself again. Is this to be an ever-recurring celebration of the arrival of Irish genius?"[64]

In fact, the booing was so loud that nobody could hear him. However, as with his divorce speech, Yeats had shrewdly gotten a copy of his remarks to the *Irish Times* in advance, to make sure his well-honed words were accurately reported.

For his pains, Yeats acquired a reputation as a Freemason and a snob; the riots were seen as no more than he deserved for the divorce speech.

He did not want a divorce. Yeats was a grateful, dependent husband. George had made Ballylee, he had told Quinn, "a fourteenth century picture."[65] She was a warm hostess to whom young Irish writers, such as Frank O'Connor, Francis Stuart, and Sean O'Faolain, were grateful for easing their approach to the great man. She was bringing up his children to be well spoken, well mannered, and well read. She nursed him and them through many illnesses. Without her, he told her, he could get no peace or order in his life. On his trips away from home he was followed by a steady stream of things he needed or had left behind, from tax demands to his shaving brush.

Sun-in-moon seems to have faded entirely from the marriage.[66] When Yeats and George were together in London, she might join him at a séance. But she would stay at a hotel while he remained at his club. Her role in the genesis of *A Vision* remained hidden when it was published in 1926.

Yeats had paid a profound, if coded, tribute, however, to her prodigious contribution, sexual and psychic, to the transformation of his life in a long poem published in January 1924, "The Gift of Harun Al-Rashid." An aged scholar has been presented by the Caliph with the gift of a young bride who has the power of speaking in her sleep, "sitting upright on the bed," speaking such long-sought mystical truths that "she seemed the learned man and I the child." Sleepwalking, she also traces geometrical emblems in the sand. He shudders to think what would happen if she ceased to love him. As the long, colorful narrative poem ends, Yeats manages to face both Araby and Freud:

> All, all those gyres and cubes and midnight things
> Are but a new expression of her body
> Drunk with the bitter sweetness of her youth.
> And now my utmost mystery is out.

Even more playfully, Yeats hid his own role too. The subtitle to this first edition of *A Vision* proclaimed it as *An Explanation of Life Founded Upon the Writings of Giraldus and Upon Certain Doctrines Attributed to Kusta Ben Luka.* What followed was a puzzle, a secret whose origin lay buried within a succession of framed tales.

The opening dedication, by Yeats, in his own voice, is followed by a bewildering first-person "Introduction" in which two fictional characters from Yeat's past work, Michael Robartes and Owen Aherne, meet by chance in London's National Gallery in the spring of 1917 and discuss a "Mr. Yeats." The real Yeats or another fictional concoction? The reader is left to decide.

Robartes and Aherne both claim to have a grudge against the man they know as Yeats because he has given their names to fictitious characters. Robartes wants to find Yeats, to show him a dilapidated calf-bound book that he (Robartes) discovered propping up a bedpost in a tumbledown boardinghouse in Cracow. The book, written by one Giraldus in 1594, contained allegorical diagrams of gyres and circles. With this mysterious book, Robartes says, he headed for the Holy Land. On the way he came across a tribe of Judwalis who possessed a similar book, with "desert geometry" describing the mathematical laws of history and the adventures of the soul after death.

After Robartes has thus enlightened Aherne, the two men seek out Yeats and present him with the diagrams, which he agrees to write up. The main text of *A Vision* then follows, with the Great Wheel of history and the Phases of the Moon. "The Gift of Harun Al-Rashid" concludes the book, paying homage not only to George, but, as Warwick Gould has shown, also to the *Arabian Nights* and the link between love and wisdom which it celebrates.[67]

The illustrations compound the deliberate obfuscation. The designer collaborating with his old friend once again. Dulac made them appear as ancient woodcuts, including one said to be a portrait of Giraldus—yet the face is that of Senator W. B. Yeats of Dublin, Ireland. A good joke, but upon whom? There was nothing frivolous about Yeats's intent. *A Vision* was his blueprint for a new world, much as D. H. Lawrence's gaudy Mexican novel, *The Plumed Serpent*, published in 1925, was Lawrence's model for an ideal society. Yeats believed that a disintegrating world needed the truths that he and George had privately discovered.

What did readers make of *A Vision,* so tortuously derived and so long in preparation? Not much. They were too few. The first edition, issued by T. Werner Laurie on January 15, 1926, was of only six hundred copies, privately printed for subscribers only. There was only one review, by Yeats's old friend "AE." Olivia confessed that she could not fathom it. Yeats himself acknowledged in a manuscript draft that, in spite of the great effort he had put into it, he had not fulfilled his intention, "for I have said little of sexual love nothing of the soul's reality." Almost immediately he began to rewrite it.

More of his philosophical message may have reached the intended hearts and minds through the cover of *The Tower.* Designed by Sturge Moore in green stamped with gold leaf, the cover subordinates all the lettering, the title, the name of the author and the publisher (Macmillan) to a double image of Thoor Ballylee. One tower stands upright, the other upside down, mirroring the first in the stream, with a barely perceptible line between. The design proclaims the Golden Dawn's concept of a mirrored universe—"as above, so below"—and in its beauty justifies all the discomfort and expense of reconstructing Thoor Ballylee.

Many of the poems within *The Tower* derive from Yeats's System—references to the Primum Mobile and Magnus Annus, for example. Few readers notice. A partial list of contents shows why the book was Yeats's first best-seller. "Sailing to Byzantium," "The Tower," "Meditations in Time of Civil War," "Nineteen Hundred and Nineteen," "Leda and the Swan," and "Among School Children" are among the peaks of his achievement.

In the summer of 1926 Yeats, with George and without the children, went to Ballylee, taking only two books with him, Baudelaire and Plotinus, the latter to help him answer questions from one of the rare readers of *A Vision.* The tower had an unusual effect on him: he was flooded with sexual dreams, one stimulated, he wrote Olivia, by a drawing at Coole of "two charming young persons in the full stream of their Saphoistic enthusiasm."[68] More strongly than ever, he told her, he was convinced that mystic vision and sexual experience were essentially the same and that the way to the first lay through the second.

He forwarded to Olivia his copy of *My Life and Loves,* by Frank Harris, with its graphic descriptions of cunnilingus and other sexual variations. She found it pornographic and begged him not to send any more. He also began writing love poetry. First he wrote as an old man—full, he said, of "wild regrets, for youth and love."[69] Then, in a striking change of direction, he began writing in a woman's voice.

Yeats did not embarrass easily. If he wanted to play a female part, he would do so. He had long equated poetry with femininity, Ireland too. Moreover, his young daughter was developing before his eyes. He used one of her shrewd female observations as the basis for the first poem in his new series, "A Woman Young and Old." (When George had rebuked Anne for liking a little boy she herself found uncouth, Anne, then six or seven, retorted, "But he has lovely hair and his eyes are cold as any March wind.")[70]

Other poems were openly sexual. From the woman's position, he dared to be explicit as never before, about the act and about female desire. The speaker in "A Last Confession" asks, "What lively lad most pleasured me / Of all that with me lay?" In "Parting," a dialogue between "He" and "She," the woman has the last word, with the bold declaration: "I offer to love's play / My dark declivities."

All his life Yeats had been afraid of the great labyrinth, the burning hair, the foul ditch, the broken ship with the long scratch—the many images he invented for the terrifying Medusa of female genitalia. To move, as he did in the late 1920s, from "the tower" to "the winding stair" as a dominant image marked a great psychological shift.[71] To write and publish, in a misogynist, puritanical country where women were revered as nuns or mothers but not as lovers, lines such as "I offer to love's play / My dark declivities," was an act of political defiance.

All that sex was very far from his wife's mood. George, claiming to be worn out from nursing Anne through yet another illness (pneumonia), was rejoicing in a month without the children. While Yeats was writing his great verse, she was writing to Tom MacGreevy. She too was thinking back to the convent school in Waterford they had visited together in February, and she too was left with thoughts of the difference between nuns and mothers. The nuns, she confessed to MacGreevy, left her "ashamed, ashamed of life and drinking and smoking And caring for nothing not even husband and children or relations (*who* really does?)."[72]

The curious personality that George brought to the marriage—responsible, capable, detached—was probably necessary to survive life with Yeats. In spite of her flippancy when speaking of him to her friends, she was nonetheless in awe of him. In nearly ten years of marriage she never dared tell him that she had creative ambitions of her own. But one day—so she related to MacGreevy—she fortified herself with four "gins and its" (dry martinis) and got up the courage to read him a play she had written. He listened, and was kind. There might be a play in the first two scenes, he ventured—but the third scene was worthless.[73]

In this verdict, she maintained to MacGreevy, she found encouragement. Although she nourished no illusion of ever writing anything worthy of being acted, she at least now had something to do instead of merely struggling to get through the day. She set to work on another play, and also on book reviews for "AE."

Yeats's Senate career was curtailed by ill health. Measles (or was it "measels—how do you spell it?" he asked in a letter to Olivia)[74] gave way to a rupture, caused by strenuous performance of his Swedish exercises; then came arthritis, influenza, and congestion of the lungs. In the waning months of 1927 George persuaded him to take a trip to Spain, the south of France, and Italy.

His eagerness to get away from Dublin was accentuated by the assassination of his friend Kevin O'Higgins in July. O'Higgins, vice president as well as minister of justice of the Free State, was shot outside his home on his way to Mass. Brought indoors, the dying man joked to his wife that he was soon going to be sitting "on a damp cloud with Mick" ("Mick" was Michael Collins).[75] Later Yeats sadly recalled

O'Higgins saying, "Nobody can expect to live who has done what I have done."[76] He and George were deeply shaken and wondered if they had had psychic forewarning.[77]

De Valera (who had left Sinn Fein in 1926 to found a new nationalist party, Fianna Fáil—the Warriors of Destiny) quickly disclaimed the responsibility of any republican organization. In the search for the killers, Sean MacBride, as an IRA stalwart, was arrested yet again, but later released. A drastic new Public Safety Act followed, increasing the number of crimes carrying the death penalty. Yeats wholeheartedly approved, and traveled from Ballylee to Dublin to cast his vote in the Senate.

His stand led to an emotional correspondence with Maud. Although Yeats assured her that he had tried to secure Sean's release and that anyway the heads of the Free State were unlikely to be unjust to the son of their hero, John MacBride, he declared himself personally in favor of the new draconian measures. "One does not vote for 'treason bills' and the like, out of hatred for anyone, but because one believes they are necessary to protect many harmless people against anxiety, danger, poverty & perhaps death," he said.[78] He told Maud that his reading of Balzac in 1903 and 1904 had cured him of his youthful unflinching republicanism; he now favored authoritarian government as a bulwark against the chaos of human nature.[79] Her church, he reminded Maud, was not opposed to capital punishment.

Maud accepted none of his argument. To his claim that he hated nothing, she accused him of hating the Catholic Church. She was worried, even so, to hear that he had been very ill. As he was about to leave Ireland, she relented with a final sermon:

> Go away into the Sun & reflect on it [the Public Safety Act],
> write poetry & pray to God to send men who understand what
> *love of Ireland & of their fellows* means to undo this mischief
> you—unwillingly perhaps have helped to do. For your poetry
> you will be forgiven, but sin no more.

But what kind of sin? Before leaving he wrote to Olivia about a Blake plate of Dante entering Purgatory which summed up his own state: "between spiritual excitement and sexual torture and the knowledge that they are somehow inseparable."

Yeats does not look ill in the footage from a home movie shot by a fellow tourist in Algeciras in November 1927.[80] With his big confident head and cigarette holder, he looks as jaunty as Roosevelt. Laughing, smoking, well dressed, he bends to light George's cigarette; she too is laughing. He sounded cheerful too in letters; he reported to Maud that he was now in excellent health, although his lung was not quite healed; to Olivia that he had not had a moment's depression.

George's letters to Lennox Robinson tell a different story. It had been a nightmare trip. In Seville she went sight-seeing on her own while "W." or "William," as she called him, remained in bed at the Grand Hotel. In Madrid he had managed only a half hour in the Prado. Barcelona was worse. Spitting blood, he was so weak she dared not leave him alone in the hotel. When they moved from place to place, they had to travel expensively by sleeper at night so that he would not have to sit up. When they arrived, he went straight to bed. Local doctors were giving him injections. She had written his doctor in Dublin for advice.[81]

William hated Spain, she told Lennox. His poem "At Algeciras—A Meditation upon Death" suggests that she was right. In it the poet imagines himself facing "the Great Questioner" and asks himself, "what if questioned I / Can with a fitting confidence reply."

The Spanish trip was a turning point. In an astonishing about-face (which each, in correspondence, attributed to the other), they decided to reorganize their life. Yeats would leave the Senate. They would sell the house in Merrion Square, and give up Ballylee too, put the children into boarding school, take a flat in Dublin and find another somewhere in the sun.

Yeats made this domestic revolution sound quite cheery in a letter to Olivia: George was planning winters abroad and other arrangements "which will make it possible for me to give up everything I really don't like and keep everything that I like."[82]

He was amazed at the way innate gaiety leaped up when things went wrong. He gave no hint that it was a wrench to think of parting with the tower, even though he had rebuilt it as a personal monument and legacy for his "bodily heirs," and two poems, "My House" and "My Descendants," had just been published, declaring that "whatever flourish and decline / These stones remain their monument and mine."

Now moved on to Cannes where George thought the doctors more trustworthy, he put a bright face on his mood. George did not. She sent a torrent of letters to Lennox, thanking him for being a perfect listener. (That he was a fellow psychic probably helped.) William was so depressed, she said, that he was resigning from everything he could resign from. For her at least, giving up Ballylee would be a relief. Running the place with its massive inconveniences just added to her burdens.[83]

These now included the immediate task of getting the children from Dublin to Cannes for Christmas. The plan was for "Nurse," as they called her, to bring the children over to London, where George would collect them. How pleasant a day by herself in London would be![84]

There is little doubt that George herself was depressed. When she heard from "Nurse" that Michael had a bad cold, she grumbled that she would rather not know. What did she matter to the family anyway? All they needed in the way of housekeepers and the rest could be hired. They would get on better without her. She had felt for a long time that she was completely dispensable.[85]

When, after that outburst, she got to London and found her son sicker than his father—Michael, grown painfully thin, was now feverish and unable to travel on—she spluttered because she had to put him into a nursing home. When the doctor there listed all that was wrong with Michael, she burst into tears. She begged Lennox to come out to Cannes to ginger Willie up by talking to him about the Abbey.[86] Lennox was to come first class at their expense; a little more bankruptcy in a year didn't matter. Adding insult to injury was a wire from the doctor in Cannes, advising her that her husband was reading too much.

Husband and wife continued on separate tracks. In January 1928 George reported to MacGreevy that Yeats was heading for despair after the doctor told him he could never expect to recover his former strength. The visit from Lennox had helped, but now Lennox was gone.

Yeats described himself to his correspondents as free from care. Relieved of the burdens of his public life, he was sleeping and lazing about. Under the orders of a new doctor, he strove to relax and avoid work so as not to excite himself. He read nothing but detective stories or "wild Wests," as he called the cheap American fiction he loved. He watched the seaplanes take off and land. He watched his children play on the sandy beach that reminded him of Rosses Point. He was amused when a Communist couple decided that he was tubercular and asked the manager to force him to leave the hotel. He offered to oblige; the Russians left instead.[87]

At the end of January 1928, they moved from the French to the Italian Riviera, joining the Pounds at Rapallo. Ezra asked George—or "Jarge," as he addressed her—to assure "the estimable W." that the place was *warm*, with an oil stove for emergencies.[88]

After a quick glance, they agreed. Rapallo would be their winter base from now on. George was delighted; for her everything nice had always been in Italy. She welcomed the freedom of a smaller household and dining out most of the time.

Rapallo is a small port south of Genoa, on a stretch of the Ligurian coast long popular with the English. Ezra and Dorothy had been installed there since 1925, fortified with money from the sale of Olivia's London house following the death of her husband. Ezra now considered that living anywhere north of the Alps was an error he hoped not to repeat.

Ezra and Dorothy did not want a divorce either. Theirs was an open marriage. In 1925 Pound's mistress, the beautiful American violinist Olga Rudge, bore him a daughter, who was promptly fostered out with a couple in the Italian Tyrol. The following year, Dorothy, thirty-nine and childless after fourteen years of marriage, returned pregnant from a holiday in Egypt. Ezra accompanied his wife to Paris in September 1926 for the birth of a son, registered in his name. She proceeded then to London where she presented the child, Omar, to her mother, now living in a large Kensington flat. Two weeks after Yeats had congratulated Olivia on her expectations of becoming a grandmother, he wrote, "I divine that you have already adopted the grandchild." As, in effect, she had. When Dorothy returned to Rapallo the following autumn, Omar remained with Olivia in London.

By spring 1928, still living at the Albergo Rapallo, George looked back on a harrowing time. To MacGreevy she wrote bitterly that if she had known that "W." was going to collapse—she slangily referred to it as "crocking up"—she would never have had the children. By "crocking up," she meant having a nervous breakdown. To her the trouble seemed psychological. She could not accept that the alleged "lung" could explain the total exhaustion of four months. Her husband could put away huge meals. When he was interested in something, she noticed, he forgot he was supposed to be tired.

Exhaustion? The record of poems reads otherwise. Between July and December 1927, following the deaths of Constance Markiewicz in September and her sister, Eva Gore-Booth, the previous year, Yeats wrote "In Memory of Eva Gore-Booth and Con Markiewicz," bestowing beauty on a brute of a stately home, with the liquid lines, "The light of evening, Lissadell, / Great windows open to the south." The poem immortalized the Gore-Booth sisters as well: "Two girls in silk kimonos, both / Beautiful one a gazelle."

He also found the strength to write a profound acceptance of the pain of life in "A Dialogue of Self and Soul." "A living man is blind and drinks his drop. / What matter if the ditches are impure?"

The poet says he would willingly relive "The ignominy of boyhood; the distress / Of boyhood changing into man" and the suffering of loving "a proud woman not kindred of his soul."

In the dialogue, which is really a debate, the mortal "Self" wins out over lofty "Soul":

I am content to follow to its source,
Every event in action or in thought;

Measure the lot; forgive myself the lot!
When such as I cast out remorse
So great a sweetness flows into the breast
We must laugh and we must sing,
We are blest by everything,
Everything we look upon is blest.

Words to live by; indeed, inspirational. He had mastered the art of the moralistic aphorism quite to the standards of his beloved Plotinus and Nietzsche. As a personal declaration of the achievement of peace of mind, however, the words were not entirely true. He had not cast out remorse for his lost youth. Upon his return to Dublin in April, he reread the just published *The Tower* and was astonished at its bitterness.

Dolly Travers-Smith was a guest at Merrion Square in the summer of 1928 as preparations were under way to pack up and move into a flat on Fitzwilliam Square. Now that the sale was irreversible, George was heartbroken at giving up their beautiful home. She was also worn out; the elderly Lady Gregory had been a guest for a month. ("Christ, how she repeats herself now," George later commented to Dorothy.)[89] And there was Yeats to deal with, on the one hand pleading fatigue, on the other dealing with the rumpus caused by the Abbey's rejection, on his recommendation, of Sean O'Casey's new play, *The Silver Tassie;* George was hard-pressed to keep him calm. With the same selflessness with which she had invited Iseult to join their honeymoon, she suggested that Dolly entertain Yeats by trying some automatic writing.

The trick that had worked for George as a bride worked for their young lodger. And who should appear in Dolly's magic script but "Thomas" from Stone Cottage days? Yeats recognized an old friend, especially when "Thomas" characteristically delivered an important truth: "Have no fear. You have time." This news was, of course, just what Yeats, with his intimations of mortality, wanted to hear. It was, he said, a "psychic event." He passed it on to Olivia: "This message has cheered me greatly—so much so that to-day being tired I have been content to do nothing."[90]

*   *   *

Yeats left the Senate in September 1928, not sorry to go. Irish politics were becoming more conventionally party-political, with the decision of the republicans in 1927 at last to take their seats. His legislative career, such as it was, left him more than ever predisposed to a form of government that chose its leaders by ability and not by ballot. All the same, his record overall was a liberal one. He had opposed compulsory Gaelic, as well as the restriction of university degrees to those fluent in the ancient language. He had favored admitting women to the civil service and to juries on equal terms with men. He defended women's right to work after marriage. He had fought censorship in the many forms proposed, including the denial of copyright to any Irish writer not published in Ireland and the ban on children under sixteen from attending films unless accompanied by an adult. He lost most of these battles, just as he had lost on divorce. Shortly after he left office, the Dáil passed the Censorship of Publications Bill, which prohibited the sale and publication of "unwholesome" literature and set up a five-man board to censor books.

But he had done the best he could. He was delighted to be declared an enemy by the Catholic press. He could not wait to get back to Rapallo, to his new life in the sun, where he looked forward to renewing his strength and rewriting *Vision,* this time revealing its true origin. He would also find a coarse new register for his woman's voice.

Politics and Potency, Cont'd.

(1928–1934)

GEORGE WAS NOT the only one to wonder what was really wrong with Yeats. No aspect of the past is more susceptible to the distortion of hindsight than its illnesses. The diagnoses of yesteryear are meaningless today: the thought is inescapable that they made no sense to the medical profession at the time either, that fuzzy labels like "neurasthenia" or "a chest" were simply covers for hypochondria or ignorance.

The medical procedures of the 1920s were brutal. When Yeats began to fall seriously ill, Gogarty chattily told him about removing a pint of blood to ease a patient's heart.[1] A Paris clinic applied leeches to the purblind James Joyce's eyeball. There were surgical fixes for everything, from tuberculosis to epilepsy.[2] Dentistry was licensed torture: a tooth extracted from Yeats's unhealthy mouth (in a lifelong history of dental pain) came out in four pieces; Olivia Shakespear spent two weeks in the hospital having several teeth out and a cyst taken from her lower jaw.

Diagnosis was an exercise in imagination. When at Cannes Yeats asked his doctor why he was so exhausted, the professional answer was "the overwork of years."[3] For his assorted afflictions, from a sore lung to high blood pressure, he was advised variously: to go to the casino and gamble, live like an animal, get "soused"; alternatively, to do nothing, not even to read—certainly nothing that taxed the brain, not to move his head too fast. He was spitting blood in 1927 and 1928, yet the word "tuberculosis" seems not to have been mentioned, nor is there evidence that an X ray was suggested.

Hindsight also obscures the fact that the generations before antibiotics were sicker than ours. Scarlet fever and diphtheria were common. Ordinary infections such as influenza or tonsillitis took weeks to pass and were treated with bedrest prolonged to a degree now unthinkable. High fevers lingered for days, with a consequent weakness of the legs that confined the patient to bed for longer still.

The smoky fog and unheated rooms of London and Dublin were cruel to chests and sinuses. For any sufferer who had the means, the routine prescription was to go to Italy or the south of France for the winter. Thus, when at the end of his first visit to Rapallo, Yeats told a friend that he must always winter abroad,[4] he was not relaying the fatuous advice of a society doctor but what passed for common sense. It was because of a weak chest that little Michael Yeats was sent to a Swiss boarding school at a high altitude in 1928, his parents confident that they were doing the right thing for him.[5] (The hazards of maternal deprivation remained to be recognized.) For Michael's father, on the other hand, as George explained to MacGreevy, high mountains were judged the worst possible environment. She and Yeats, therefore, dutifully sought the sun.

The first of the two full winters spent in Rapallo was a great success. Their flat consisted of nine rooms on the fourth floor of 12 Via Americhe (now the Corso Cristoforo Colombo), a new building near the port, with an elevator and modern electrical fittings. Yeats had a bedroom and an adjoining study with French doors opening onto a balcony. George had her own room (shared with Michael when he was there) and a study. The plan was to have a nurse come and look after the children during the holidays, but otherwise to have no live-in help. George gloried in the freedom from responsibility.

Ezra Pound, as the high priest of modernism, the man who had excavated T. S. Eliot's "The Waste Land" from the mountain of original manuscript, was the center of a lively circle at Rapallo. He introduced Yeats to the German dramatic poet and Nobel laureate Gerhart Hauptmann, and to George Antheil, the young American composer whose "Ballet Mechanique" had caused a sensation in Paris. Also on the scene were the writers Max Beerbohm, Richard Aldington, and Brigit Patmore, and the young English poet, pacificist, and Pound's protégé, Basil Bunting. Literary friends from London and Dublin, such as Lennox Robinson and Siegfried Sassoon, passed through.[6] Ezra himself, then writing his idiosyncratic *Cantos*, remained a constant stimulant and mentor for Yeats. (He later said Yeats was always pestering him to be "a 4th at table-rapping").[7] All in all, "Rap," as George called the place, offered a pleasant life of cafés and conversation, mainly along the fashionable seafront where the stenciled images of Mussolini and his Nietzschean slogan, *"Viva pericolosamente!"* (Live Dangerously!), were not too conspicuous.

Yeats was the star of any occasion. The wealthy Hauptmann invited him and George to dinner and enviously admired the youthful appearance of the poet who was only a few years younger than himself. George in turn admired Hauptmann's insistence on serving them lashings of ice-cold champagne.

More than ever George's breezy letters to Lennox Robinson are those of the minder of a doddering, not particularly self-aware geriatric. She relayed an account of a lunch with the Antheils when Willie, having overslept, arrived late with tie undone and coat buttoned wrong. Even so, Antheil was charmed, and launched into long anecdotes that Yeats could not follow—because, he claimed later, he could not understand the accent. (Antheil was born in Trenton, New Jersey.) The accent barrier was not unsuperable, however. Soon Antheil began setting to music some of Yeats's plays, notably "Breaking the Waves," a dance drama adapted from *The Only Jealousy of Emer.*

Yeats's view of his mental state was much more cheerful than his wife's. "I am writing more easily than I ever wrote and I am happy," he reported to Olivia and mentioned twelve short poems that might be set to music.[8] When the poems were published as *Words for Music Perhaps,* he said in the accompanying notes, "In the spring of 1929 life returned to me as an impression of uncontrollable energy and daring of the great creators."

The poems show what he meant by "daring." That spring saw the first appearance of "Crazy Jane," a raucous hag who mocks Catholic teaching on sex. Yeats modeled the character, he said, on an old woman in Gort, known as "Cracked Mary," who had an awesome capacity for what he called "audacious speech."[9]

This Galway local character seems to have had unique powers of narration; she may also have suffered from the form of dementia—Tourette's syndrome—that releases obscene talk. Either way, she cannot have been any more audacious than Yeats's crone, who curses the bishop for telling her that she and her lover, Jack the Journeyman, had "lived like beast and beast."

In "Three Things," written in March 1929, Yeats used another aged female voice. Identified only as "a bone on the shore," an old woman laments the lost joys of two forms of physical love: "A child found all a child can lack . . . / Upon the abundance of my breast" and "A man if I but held him so / When my body was alive / Found all the pleasure that life gave."

While he wrote, Yeats gazed out from his balcony across the Bay of Tigullio to the hills and villages beyond. The lovely view provided the opening for "A Packet for Ezra Pound."

> Mountains that shelter the bay from all but the south wind,
> bare brown branches of low vines and of tall trees blurring
> their outline as though with a soft mist; houses mirrored in an
> almost motionless sea; a verandahed gable a couple of miles
> away bringing to mind some Chinese painting.[10]

Yeats liked to think that the cluster of buildings high on the hillside in the distance was the village described in Keats's "Ode on a Grecian Urn." This notion undoubtedly came from Ezra, who believed (incorrectly) that Keats had passed through Rapallo on his fatal journey to Rome.

The following winter in Rapallo was a disaster. Yeats arrived late in November 1929 after two weeks in London. There he saw Olivia, a cabalist or two, and all his usual crowd, which including Edmund Dulac, Sturge Moore, the American-born beauty Lady Lavery, and Charles Ricketts. George then joining him, he continued a round of lunches and dinners that left him back in bed, tired out, coughing up blood. To protect himself on the train journey to Italy, he wrapped himself from waist to toe in a fur bag, over which he placed a rug and four blankets.[11] Even so, he arrived with a cold. This soon turned into a fever that mysteriously soared every evening. In that unsteady state, he wrote (working from a prose draft and thinking back to the quiet evenings he had just spent with Olivia) the beautiful eight-line lyric "After Long Silence."

> Speech after long silence; it is right,
> All other lovers being estranged or dead,
> Unfriendly lamplight hid under its shade,
> The curtains drawn upon unfriendly night,
> That we descant and yet again descant
> Upon the supreme theme of Art and Song:
> Bodily decreptitude is wisdom; young
> We loved each other and were ignorant.

It was a love poem, sent to his dearest friend and first lover, the woman he probably should have married.

His hope that his illness was another "nervous collapse"[12] was now belied by the thermometer reading of 104.9 degrees. The Scottish doctor in charge of his case decreed that until the results of laboratory tests could be known in two weeks' time the disease was to be treated as typhoid. By Christmas Eve Yeats thought he was going to die.

Conscious enough to fear he might not live through the night, he wrote his will and summoned Ezra and Bunting (whom he had pronounced "one of Ezra's more savage disciples")[13] to witness it.

By the time 1930 arrived, George called in a specialist from Genoa who dismissed the typhoid diagnosis in favor of Malta fever (a form of undulant fever, transmitted through milk).[14] Yeats would recover, but he would have to remain in bed for ten days after his temperature had stayed at normal for forty-eight hours. He was allowed custard, jellied consommé, and three spoons of brandy a day. (The children hovered in the background. Basil Bunting had fetched them from their school in Switzerland as George could not leave the bedside.)

Never was Yeats's dependence on George greater, or more pathetic. When told he needed a night nurse so that his wife could get some relief, he wept. When the nurse arrived, he refused to let her wash him. His wife washed him, he snapped. She was sleeping? Then he would wait until she woke.

Never had George needed her letters to Lennox more; one day she wrote two. She vented her anger. She felt that Yeats had concealed his symptoms when he arrived in Rapallo, compounding the infection carried from London. She resented having to find nurses who could speak English (an essential, as Yeats had mastered no more Italian than *pronto, brutto,* and *bagno*—which he pronounced "bag-no").[15] As he got better, she had to watch him all the time to stop him from getting out of bed and prancing about the flat. One night he had dictated a letter resigning his directorship of the Abbey. George burned it, believing that he was too ill to be responsible.

As soon as a nurse arrived to do the day shift, she promised herself she would run down to the café and have three quick Luigis, one after the other. She gave Lennox the recipe: gin and orange juice, with a few drops of curaçao.[16] (Cocktails were the rage at the time; Mussolini favored the dry martini.) The loneliness and her psychic inclinations led her at one point to believe that Lennox was in telepathic communion with her; his voice came through to her telling her that everything would be all right.

At the age of thirty-five, George was facing up to the reality of having married a man twenty-seven years older than herself. That Yeats would predecease her was virtually certain. But she desperately hoped he would not die in a foreign country; the responsibility and the isolation would be terrible. Eight days without going farther outside than the balcony of their flat was almost more than she could bear. Her consolation was visits from Dorothy, who did her shopping, and from Bunting, who took the children out on expeditions. Ezra, on the other hand, a hypochondriac by the standards of any age, was terrified of the infectious Yeats and stayed away.

After six weeks in bed, Yeats was allowed at last to sit up half an hour a day. From that he progressed to being pushed in a borrowed wheelchair into his study. He could not walk or stand, George told Lady Gregory, but was delighted to feel better.[17] By March he was still feeble, running a fever every night; he had to pause several times even while dictating a letter. Ezra stayed away so long that he was rehearsing the phrases he would say when Ezra did come.

By May the crisis was forgotten. Yeats bounced back once again, with a fresh burst of vitality and a raffish white beard. He was as pleased with himself as if he knew that the decade ahead was going to be the most productive of a productive life.

After a spell in the mountains—where Ezra at last consented to visit him—he went back to Rapallo and basked in the great heat. He loved sitting in the sun, either at the Caffè Aurum or on his balcony, where he oiled himself and grew even more leathery brown than usual: "We colour like an old meerschaum pipe," he boasted to Olivia.[18] He lounged about the flat in a dressing gown. He sometimes got dressed in the afternoon to go for a swim, displaying in the water his old Rosses Point skills—backstroke, underwater swimming. Otherwise, he did not bother until it was time for the evening sortie.

The Rapallo flat was now a bright and lively place, filled with canaries, paintings by Burne-Jones and Rossetti, and, in early summer, Anne and Michael, returned from their Swiss schools. Yeats was equable about living with children of eleven and nine. To Olivia he wrote with amusement about a sibling squabble over a game of chess that ended with hair pulling and chair toppling. He coupled it with a story of the day when Anne could not be found at lunchtime, and her brother explained, "She's run away." As she had. She had packed the classic knapsack of biscuits, promising—according to Michael—to be home by dark. In the event, she was home somewhat earlier, having been spotted by a family friend walking out of town. "What a lot Dorothy is missing," he observed drily to Olivia.[19]

He was pleased with his children. Lady Gregory complimented him on their good manners. He was proud that they were learning French and German, "and with the impulse that should come from their parents should have enough intellectual curiousity to create minds for themselves."[20]

Stories of Yeats as a parent are legion and emphasize his distance from his children. There is no mention of his being angry or irritable with them, merely remote and preoccupied. One anecdote, variously told, has little Michael, out of sorts with his father, asking his mother, "Who is that man?" Another tells of Yeats, when the boy was older, passing his son on the street without a sign of recognition. Anne Yeats, later in life, laughed at the famous photograph of Yeats the paterfamilias seated on the grass with a book at his feet and his two young children looking over his shoulder. To her, it showed a man impatient to get back to his book. Frank O'Connor recorded a rare view of Yeats as disciplinarian. One day when George could not stop the children from fighting, she summoned their father. The old poet came into the room, sank slowly into an armchair, intoned, "Let dogs delight to bark and bite," then stalked out again.[21]

The Rapallo retreat was not to last. In the spring of 1930, just as life was getting back to normal, Yeats startled George by letting drop in conversation with a friend that he thought that the following year they would experiment with a winter in Dublin. Any support he needed was soon supplied by Gogarty. Yeats did not need the sun, wrote the medical man: "All that is necessary for you to Winter unharmed in Ireland is central-heating to 69% or 70%."[22]

The family left for Dublin in July. Before they left, he followed another piece of professional advice from Gogarty. The beard had to come off at once; it made him look old and would prevent him from forgetting his illness.

The "packet" Yeats prepared for Ezra Pound (which now appears as the start of *A Vision* in the 1937 edition, the only one now generally available) is deceptively simple; Yeats had learned his modernist lessons well. It consists of three sections, but only the third is labeled "To Ezra Pound." The first, called "Rapallo," contains his tribute to the beauty of the place and its stimulus to his imagination. The second is startling. Confusingly called "Introduction," it was undoubtedly the cause of the row that George later claimed was the only serious one of their married life.[23]

This pseudo-introduction opens with Yeats's reporting a compliment from Lady Gregory: that he is a better-educated man than he was ten years before. Very true, he says, and he owes it all "to an incredible experience": "four days after my marriage, my wife surprised me by attempting automatic writing."[24]

Thereupon he pours out everything he had promised his "Communicators" to keep secret: how the automatic writing began in the Ashdown Forest in 1917; how it shifted toward "speech during sleep" in a compartment of a train in southern California, how George dreamed that she was a cat lapping up milk, how he smelled burned feathers when newly born Michael was ill. He lists the inexplicable phenomena such as mysterious whistlings and smells that marked their married life. He refers to his fifty copy books and card index of accumulated material. He describes his wife as someone who still sees visions and walks in her sleep. All of this personal revelation is offered as a preliminary to what he acknowledges might seem "an arbitrary, harsh, difficult symbolism."[25] He then anticipates the obvious: "Some will ask whether I believe all that this book contains":

> To such a question I can but answer that if sometimes, over-
> whelmed by miracle as well men must be when in the midst of
> it, I have taken such periods literally, my reason has soon

recovered; and now that the system stands out clearly in my imagination I regard them as stylistic arrangements of experience comparable to the cubes in the drawing of Wyndham Lewis and to the ovoids in the sculpture of Brancusi. They have helped me to hold in a single thought reality and justice.

It was the perfect answer and no answer. His suggestion that "reality and justice" are polar opposites recalls his poem of 1915, "Ego Dominus Tuus," in which Dante is said to have "found the unpersuadable justice, he found / The most exalted lady loved by a man."

The reiteration of the pursuit of justice makes one wonder. Was the enormous effort Yeats poured into *A Vision*—seven or more rewritings of what he must have known would be his least-read book—the consequence of a lifelong struggle to reconcile the love he felt he deserved with what he got?

In spilling the beans about the System's origin, Yeats gave George enormous credit for her wide reading, her grasp of Plotinus and Pico della Mirandola, and her visionary powers. But that cannot have made up for the hurt he caused her. Small wonder that she called him "William Tell."[26] His candor about how his wife and not an Arabian traveler was the source of his received wisdom had the virtue at least of confirming Dublin rumor. As a friend wrote him after the first version of *A Vision*, "I have been told that in reality it's [*sic*] source is not from the East transmitted as you tell in the preface by a traveler returning from there whom you had previously known." Rather, it was "a romantic way of introducing a system of philosophy evolved not entirely by yourself but conjointly with one of your household."[27]

What was in the packet for Ezra? The advice in the section addressed to him—"Do not be elected to the Senate of your country"[28]—was ironic. Ezra was even then in the grip of the eccentric economic theories that would keep him in Italy and land him in a U.S. Army cage at the end of World War II.

Ezra was probably even more amused by Yeats's declaration that his book proclaimed a new divinity. It was then that he pronounced Yeats's theories "very, very bughouse."[29]

In designing his divine book, Yeats had yet another trick up his sleeve. Before plunging into the serious exposition of the System, he inserted another framing device: "Stories of Michael Robartes and His Friends." These stories contain much of the invention of the first edition—the meeting of Robartes and Aherne, the discovery of the ancient book by Giraldus in the Cracow boardinghouse, and the rest. Yeats apologizes for repeating this fanciful material, but he was forced to do so, he explains, because he was "fool enough" to have made some of his poems incomprehensible without them.[30]

This extra layer of tales made room for the sexual ingredient Yeats felt he had left out of his original *Vision*.[*] A curious preface to a book of revelation, perhaps. But art comes from low haunts, Yeats was persuaded. He would not apologize for his unconscious. "Muses," he wrote in the packet for Ezra, "resemble women who creep out at night and give themselves to unknown sailors and return to talk of Chinese porcelain."[31] His hard-won artistic creed told him that the spunk and shit of human existence are the wellsprings of creativity and that, for him, they were more easily approached through the female voice.

A man who would not censor himself was ribald in his conversation. To his wife he referred to "Crazy Jane" as "that slut."[32] Mocking the Church's teaching on coitus interruptus, he told Gogarty, a nominal Roman Catholic, "Gogarty, the trouble about the Church is that it won't let you put it in, and it won't let you take it out!"[33]

He embarrassed Iseult Stuart with dirty stories, Lady Gregory too, and, according to his later pamphlet, *On the Boiler*, his fellow senators as well.[34] Others found his anecdotes amusing. On one of his visits to London, the *Daily Mail*'s gossip column observed of W. B. Yeats, "His head is not always in the clouds. His worldly talk is very racy and very pungent."[35] (The *Mail* also noted that his figure had grown "comfortable.")

In his late sixties, Yeats liked the company of young women. His

---

[*]In a tale added in July 1936, a free-thinking modern young woman tells of an unusual cure for impotence: an Oxford undergraduate who found that he could make love to her only if a friend lay with her first.

thoughts cannot have been merely avuncular when he wrote "For Anne Gregory" at Coole in September 1930. The pretty nineteen-year-old detected nothing untoward in his manner when he summoned her to his room and read aloud, "'Only God, my dear, / Could love you for yourself alone / And not your yellow hair.'" Anne Gregory was more concerned that she did not understand it and asked him to read it again. Not long after, Francis Stuart introduced him to Mercedes Gleitz, a young German swimmer, but feared that Yeats would be bored. Far from it. When Gleitz described the various protective oils that were tried on her body before she swam the English Channel, Yeats listened raptly, according to Stuart, "taking her in as if she were the draught that he had long thirsted for."[36]

Yeats had little need any longer for George's psychic talents. For dictating the final version of his System, he used a typist sent over from Paris by Tom MacGreevy (still at the École Normale and a close friend of Joyce and Samuel Beckett). "If I dictate to George," he confided to Olivia, "it would almost certainly put her nerves all wrong. I don't want any more mediumship."[37] But he never forgot the profound difference her spiritualistic intervention had made in his life. As 1930 drew to its close, he told Olivia, "I have a great sense of abundance—more than I have had for years. George's ghosts have educated me."[38]

If George's ghosts are responsible for "Byzantium," they should not be mocked. This nocturne was first sketched in the hills above Rapallo in the spring of 1930 just after Yeats's return from death's door. His notes are helpful: "A walking mummy. Flames at the street corners . . . birds of hammered gold singing in the golden trees, in the harbour [dolphins] offering their backs to the wailing dead that they may carry them to Paradise."[39] The poem, like his System, rests on the belief that the great shifts in the world's cultural history coincided conveniently with the millennial dates on the Christian calendar.

He explains in his notes that he had selected Byzantium (a.k.a. Constantinople, or Istanbul) in the year A.D. 500 as the time and place he would most like to have lived—that is, halfway between East and

West and halfway between Christ and the first millennium, "a little before Justinian opened Saint Sophia and closed the Academy of Plato." There, he thought, "I could find in some little wine-shop some philosophical worker in mosaic who could answer all my questions."[40]

Scholarly interpretations of the meaning of "Byzantium" are not in short supply. Ellmann explained the poem as the attainment of re-incarnation through the purgative process of creating a work of art.[41] But the decipherable theme, the flux of life turning into the permanence of art, is secondary to the rich *son et lumière* that unreels from the first stanza to the last:

> The unpurged images of day recede;
> The Emperor's drunken soldiery are abed;
> Night resonance recedes, night-walkers' song
> After great cathedral gong;
> A starlit or a moonlit dome disdains
> All that man is,
> All mere complexities,
> The fury and the mire of human veins.
> . . . .
>
> Astraddle on the dolphin's mire and blood,
> Spirit after spirit! The smithies break the flood,
> The golden smithies of the Emperor!
> Marbles of the dancing floor
> Break bitter furies of complexity,
> Those images that yet
> Fresh images beget,
> That dolphin-torn, that gong-tormented sea.

The sonorous repetition of *o* sounds burns the lines into the brain: Yeats, the Celtic aural magician, showing off at his best. Robert Graves later criticized Yeats for building his poems on obscure references that not a reader in a million could understand. But Richard Ellmann countered, interpreting Yeats's lyric "I saw a staring virgin stand / Where holy Dionysus died" as an example of a Yeats poem achieving an extraordinary effect "even when imperfectly understood."

The poem may have been a rehearsal for his next journey toward death, yet Yeats was healthy enough when he completed it in September 1930. They had not tried to spend that summer at Ballylee. Both he and George agreed now that the tower was too damp and remote for family life. (Ezra referred to the tower as "Ballyphallus or whatever he calls it with the river on the first floor."[42] The offer of a year in Japan tempted Yeats, but George vetoed it, on the grounds of Michael's health.

The winter season of 1930–31 was brightened by the success of Yeats's new play, *The Words Upon the Window-Pane,* performed at the Abbey in November 1930. He was surprised at its popularity. He should not have been. Rather than his usual Noh mixture of masks, dancers, and drums, the play was an occult thriller, set in a 1930s Dublin boardinghouse, with a medium who finds herself possessed by the ghost of Jonathan Swift, then by a child speaking for Vanessa and Stella, the two women in Swift's life. Yeats, with his eighteenth-century enthusiasms, identified with the bitter and isolated dean of Saint Patrick's, the national Protestant cathedral. Swift's fears of sex and madness touched even deeper chords. And no one knew better than Yeats the dramatic power of the séance.

In February he and George gave up the flat in Fitzwilliam Square and took a rented house at South Hill in Killiney, on the sea to the south of Dublin. There Yeats rewrote *A Vision* yet again, as well as another play, *Resurrection.* He began preparing an "Edition de Luxe" of his collected poems, under the guidance of his publisher, Harold Macmillan. "Months of re-writing," he wrote Olivia. "What happiness!"[43]

An honorary degree from Oxford that spring added more letters to follow the name of the man who had not attended university. His sense of well-being vanished with news of Lady Gregory's illness. Nearing eighty, she had had a recurrence of breast cancer (referred to as "a tumour"), and the outcome was not in doubt. He did not spare himself the pain of watching a loved one slowly die. At the same time, responding to what he said was the family's request, he installed himself at Coole. He knew it would be the last visit. Margaret Gregory having remarried, the house had been sold to the Forestry Department, and Lady Gregory had rented it back for her lifetime.[44]

He remained there, even though it meant new wrangles with Margaret (about Lady Gregory's medication)[45] all through the autumn and winter of 1931. At Lady Gregory's request, he wrote two elegiac poems about the house: "Coole Park, 1929" and "Coole and Ballylee, 1931." Michael's school reports were sent to him for perusal, and he was amused to see that his son (now at school in Ireland) got a star in Composition.[46]

From Killiney, George nobly denied that she was feeling neglected. The evenings when she had no social engagements, she went to bed at 8:30 or 9:00 P.M. with a crime novel. She was busy with the children, their schools, their friends, and the constant correspondence relating to Yeats's work, from Abbey productions to broadcasts over the BBC. There were also the administrative chores connected with rescuing Cuala, which involved closing down the embroidery half of the sisters' joint enterprise.[47]

Lennox Robinson was no longer available for escort duty. He had married Dolly Travers-Smith and was away on honeymoon in Florence. George cannot have been too unhappy at this turn of events, considering her earlier concern about his reputation.

Christmas 1931 was bleak. Anne was in bed with suspected diphtheria, and Yeats, with a cold, stayed at Coole. By the end of February 1932, with him still at Coole, George felt such a desperate need to talk to him about the recent election results that she offered to come overnight to Galway so that they could meet.[48] As if she did not entirely trust the household at Coole, George marked this letter to her husband PRIVATE.

The Irish general election of February 1932 was worth talking about. It presented Ireland with the greatest test of a new democracy—the orderly transfer of power from a sitting government to its political opponents. Eamon de Valera's party, Fianna Fáil, founded in 1926, defeated the Cosgrave government, which had ruled the Free State since 1922. Fianna Fáil won with the combined support of the Labour Party, the IRA, and popular approval of its promise to get rid of the oath to the king.

After years of waiting and a fair time in jail (six separate stretches between 1916 and 1929), de Valera was his country's leader at last; his official title was president of the Executive Council of the Irish Free State. The tall, thin, and dour "Dev," also known as "The Long Fellow," was a devout and strict Catholic who had once considered becoming a priest. Trailing the glory of his 1916 record, he was a hero among Irish Americans; his tours of the United States raised millions of dollars for his pursuit of a fully independent Irish republic, and allowed him to be much photographed with members of the American Catholic hierarchy. From George Yeats's point of view, the immediate concern was what de Valera's victory would mean for censorship and the Abbey.

Yeats had briefly left Coole at the time of the election to cast his vote in Dublin for the Cosgrave party. Shrewdly, however, he wrote an article in the *Spectator* in which he brushed off the threat to order from the imminent Fianna Fáil victory. In it he promised that the wild nationalist rhetoric would fade once republicans learned they were asking the impossible: "Then they in their turn will govern. An Irishman is wild in speech, the result of centuries of irresponsible opposition, but he casts it off in the grip of fact."[49]

He was soon to change his mind.

Lady Gregory died in May. There was no doubt about the depth of Yeats's grief over the loss of the woman who had been his "mother, friend, sister and brother" and also his theatrical tutor. In spite of near-constant residence at Coole for a year, he was in Dublin when death came. He returned to Coole the next morning. Lady Gregory's granddaughter Catherine collected him at the station and was startled to see him weeping. It was the first time she had ever seen a man cry.[50]

Not long after, Yeats moved with his family to a new, larger house in the country. The move and the death were not unrelated. "Riversdale," at Rathfarnham, south of Dundrum, was to be his new Coole, a restorative for his health. After searching all spring, George had found a house with tennis courts, croquet lawn, and garden, suitable for the children and far enough out of Dublin to insulate Yeats from the excitement of theater and politics. He loved the place. After his first inspection, he said that if they didn't get it, he would never take another house.[51]

"Riversdale" was decorated and furnished before Yeats moved in. He was, as ever, appreciative. "George's fine taste has made the inside almost as beautiful as the garden," he informed Olivia.[52] Even so, he was away from home a good deal of the time. Acquiring two kittens on one of his trips to London, he was worried whether or not he would need a permit to import them into the Irish Free State. (He was informed that both cats and dogs were allowed as "free trade" between Britain and Ireland.[53])

The lease ran for thirteen years. In 1932 George was firmly rooted in Ireland and would make it her home for the rest of her life. Nonetheless, she remained resolutely English. She was pleased when Ireland failed to win the triple crown in rugby. She found the Irish loquacity tedious at times; she would use a very English "quite" to close off conversation.[54]

Since the passage of the Censorship of Publications Act, Yeats had braced himself for the transformation of Ireland into a repressive clerical state with laws that, he joked to Olivia, "will enable Holy Church to put us all down at any moment." His own opinion of the prevailing Catholic opinion was "ignorance organized under its priests."[55]

The slide toward theocracy was assisted in June when the Church held its International Eucharistic Congress in Dublin. De Valera, as clever as he was pious, was delighted to welcome cardinals and bishops from around the world. He contrived to make the location of the conference seem as if the pope was on the Warriors of Destiny's side. "Pope Pius XI has turned his august regard to our country," he declared at a reception for the papal legate at Dublin Castle.[56]

Yeats struck back. In September 1932 he carried out his long-held wish to found an Irish Academy of Letters. He hoped writers would unite to protest against the censorship that was putting the work of many Irish writers out of bounds in their own country, not to mention excluding as "unwholesome" everything from William Faulkner's *Sanctuary* to pamphlets on birth control.

A man wanting to avoid unnecessary strain would not have bothered. He took upon himself an enormous administrative labor and guaranteed that he would make himself an even more tempting target for the Catholic press. He cannot have anticipated, however, how much criticism he would draw from those he considered friends. Lord Dunsany was furious at being asked to become a mere associate member as if he had done less for Irish literature than a newcomer like Francis Stuart, who was accorded full membership. James Joyce declined, saying that his case "being as it was and probably will be, I see no reason why my name should have arisen at all."[57] The apostate Catholic whose *Ulysses* described Ireland as a "priestridden land" surrounded by a "snotgreen, scrotumtightening sea" had no reason to seek honor in his native land. He would not even risk a visit to see his dying father; his mortified sisters who lived in Dublin tried desperately to conceal that they were related to *that* Joyce.

Another refusal came from George Bernard Shaw, long settled in London. When Yeats asked him to become the academy's president, Shaw wrote back, "You need a Resident."[58] His wife weighed in to remind Yeats that T. E. Lawrence, one of those awarded associate membership on the basis of a supposed Irish ancestor, had been born in Wales and never lived in Ireland.

George Russell saw no point in joining: "Your Academy of Letters will not have the slightest effect in a country where all the papers are united in fears of clerical denunciation."[59] Yeats's old adversary George Moore did not even answer the invitation.

The academy became a reality, nonetheless. In October Yeats sailed once more for the United States to raise money for its support. For a man who had less than two years before been under a nurse's care and wheeled about by his wife, he showed no sign of invalidism, although he did take along a (male) secretary. As on previous American tours, he did not stint himself. He went to Cincinnati, Chicago, Detroit, and Toronto, as well as New York and Boston. After diverting himself with séances in Boston where he saw objects move and heard voices from the air, he went to the wilds of Maine in winter to speak at Bowdoin College. The tour kept him away from home for Christmas yet again.

At Bowdoin, in November 1932, a large crowd turned out for his lecture on "the Irish Renaissance." They were treated to a *tour d'horizon:* the death of Parnell had revived Irish literature by turning Ireland away from politics; the first writers were Protestant because no universities were open to Catholics; Lady Gregory began writing plays at the age of fifty because she felt it her duty to Ireland; she had just died and the speaker had been with her during her last months; the name of James Joyce should be added to the roster of great writers Ireland had given to the world.

So much was recorded in the local newspapers.[60] Private recollections of his visit were less literary. The poet seems to have gone to bed, leaving his boots outside his door to be shined; as there was no one to do it, the college president, Kenneth Charles Morton Sills, took them to the kitchen and polished them himself. When a small faculty dinner party for twelve was arranged in Yeats's honor, he was said to have requested in advance that no one should speak to him unless spoken to first.

The trip, however, succeeded in its objective. Yeats raised the required funds—not to de Valera levels, but in an amount sufficient to put the academy on its feet, with enough left over to give his wife seven hundred pounds for the new house.

His personal money worries were less than his letters suggest. Through the death of an aunt, George had inherited a third of her father's money and now enjoyed an income of £350 a year, virtually replacing what Yeats had given up by leaving the Senate. On the other hand, Cuala was still a financial drain, and Lily was now a dependant. The Cuala Press was still vigorous, however, and when he returned to Ireland in the new year, Yeats had the pleasure of seeing its finished copies of *Words for Music Perhaps*, published in his absence.

*　　　*　　　*

The politician in him was irrepressible. He liked de Valera much better than he expected when the two met for the first time, yet he saw the new leader as, in his pejorative word, democratic—that is, a man put in power by "the ignorant."[61] He accepted that his Academy of Letters was being reviled by the Jesuits and the Catholic press, but dismissed their influence, saying—in an echo of George's scorn for her Catholic maids—"fortunately in this country they can merely make a row in the kitchen."[62]

For Yeats Irish politics was becoming a matter of class: the educated (mainly Protestant) versus the uneducated (Catholic) masses. The Anglo-Irish eighteenth century glowed even more brightly in his mind when a bookish military friend, Captain Dermot MacManus, started him reading George Berkeley, the philosopher-bishop of Cloyne, born in County Kilkenny in 1685. Yeats liked to think that Berkeley's philosophy of the world as an idea in the mind and Edmund Burke's comparison of the state to a tree were two great Anglo-Irish gifts to the understanding of reality.

His own *Vision,* when completed and published, would be a third. By the midsummer of 1933 he believed he had found a way to translate his vision into action.

From Manhattan on the first of January 1933, in a letter to Olivia, Yeats had sent a vivid picture of his mental state: "My mind is like an hotel lobby—endless movement seemingly nowhither."[63] The hotel lobbies with which he was acquainted were the very best, the Copley Plaza in Boston, the Waldorf Astoria in New York, but his restlessness was no more comfortable for that. Ireland had an election pending the following day which would vitally affect his academy and his next five years.

De Valera had called the snap new election for January 2, 1933, less than a year after the one that had put him in power. Alarmed at the signs of formation of a new conservative political party and determined to consolidate his hold, he appealed, says his biographer, "to poor, pocket and Pope."[64] Fianna Fáil won easily, with IRA support. In exchange, de Valera let all IRA prisoners out of jail and put appointees lenient toward the IRA in charge of the civil service and the police. He went further. He withdrew the armed protection that had been given to the ex-ministers of the Cosgrave government, and he sacked Eoin O'Duffy, the commissioner of police.

Making an enemy of the head of the police is a risky move in any country. So it was in Ireland in February 1933. O'Duffy had headed the Gárdai since its beginning in the Free State and enjoyed a wide popular following.

Yeats returned to Ireland on January 29. It took five months for him and O'Duffy to get together. In the interval, Hitler came to power in Germany. To those in England and Ireland who admired Mussolini and feared Communism, the Hitler of 1933 was no bad thing. The *Irish Times* welcomed him as "Europe's standard bearer against Muscovite terrorism."[65] To those in Ireland who feared de Valera's ambitions, a counterforce to de Valera seemed necessary. Already an Army Comrades Association had formed, in the belief that de Valera was letting the IRA run riot.

By summer Yeats was exhilarated. From the tranquillity of his new country house, admiring his rose garden and lily pond, he wrote Olivia in July,

> **Politics are growing heroic . . . A Fascist opposition is forming behind the scenes to be ready should some tragic situation develop. I find myself constantly urging the despotic rule of the educated classes as the only end to our troubles. (Let all this sleep in your ear.)**[66]

One week later the opposition was no longer behind the scenes. O'Duffy was named leader of the Army Comrades, with the name changed to National Guard, and he adopted a distinctive blue shirt as its uniform. Not that there were many colors to choose from. Green indisputably belonged to the republicans; orange to the Ulstermen, red to the Communists; Mussolini's supporters (and Oswald Mosley's British imitators) wore black shirts, Hitler's, brown. The Blueshirts, as they were instantly dubbed, however, borrowed another distinctive mark of Hitler's supporters, the straight-armed salute.

These so-called shirted movements were part of a wave of patriotic organizations springing up as far away as Australia, where ex-servicemen from the Great War were uniting against the Communist threat perceived in the trade unions and Irish immigrants. D. H. Lawrence's *Kangaroo* describes the gathering in Sydney of such disgruntled veterans banding together in a secret army against the day "the balloon goes up."

Captain MacManus, the military friend who shared his political ideas, brought Yeats and O'Duffy together. MacManus thought that Yeats might serve as philosopher of the Blueshirt movement. Yeats was ready. Fresh from revising proofs of *A Vision*, he launched into an eloquent lecture on the need to abolish parliamentary government. Throwing in references to the Italian philosopher Gentile whose (surprisingly) nonauthoritarian educational reforms he had so admired, he outlined his scheme for a hierarchical state, ruled by the educated classes, each district to be in the hands of its ablest men.[67]

It was not a meeting of minds. O'Duffy did not understand a word Yeats was saying. Yeats, for his part, long worried by the colorlessness of Ireland's post-Collins leaders, found himself looking into the short, puffy face and blank, spectacled eyes of a hard-drinking, devout bachelor cop.

But he did not give up hope. He tried to think that, with experience of leadership, O'Duffy might improve. For his own part, he set about writing songs for the movement. An unmusical, unmilitary man, however, he was not well equipped. The lines he wrote, such as "But good strong blows are his Captain," were fairly unsingable and unmarchable, not in the "Giovinezza" or "Internationale" class.

The Blueshirt march that might have used them never took place. O'Duffy set Sunday, August 13, 1933, as the date for a mass parade, when a column of Blueshirts would pass Leinster House and lay a wreath in honor of the fallen Free State heroes, Collins, O'Higgins, and Griffith. Special trains were laid on to bring marchers in from the rest of Ireland. The country braced itself. Would O'Duffy do a Mussolini and lead his band straight into government buildings and take over? De Valera did not wait to find out. He banned the march, instituted martial law, created a special police force, and declared the Blueshirts an illegal organization. But would O'Duffy obey?

His tactics worked. At the eleventh hour O'Duffy called off the march. Shortly after he led his supporters instead into a safer political channel, a new party formed from the old Cumann na nGaedheal, with the more manageable name of Fine Gael. O'Duffy became party leader, while Cosgrave, who, unlike O'Duffy, held an elected seat in the Dáil, became parliamentary leader.

By September Yeats had already begun to back away from the Blueshirts when he referred to "our political comedy" to Olivia.[68] In his letter, he was defensive—but not about his politics, rather about his erotic Crazy Jane poems: "Sexual abstinence fed their fire—I was ill and yet full of desire."[69]

That these extraordinary frank words about his own sexuality should have been written six days after de Valera's master stroke against the Blueshirts shows his priorities.

The heart of Yeats's disagreement with democratic government was artistic. He believed that only a leadership drawn from an educated minority could tolerate creative freedom. He saw the quivering hand of the censor undermining everything that he, Synge, Lady Gregory, and others in the literary revival had been trying to do for more than thirty years.

In "Crazy Jane talks with the Bishop," first published in November 1932, and then as part of the longer and widely praised collection *The Winding Stair and Other Poems* in 1933, Yeats in effect tells the Church that its theology is wrong. He allows the bishop to state his case:

> 'Those breasts are flat and fallen now,
> Those veins must soon be dry;
> Live in a heavenly mansion,
> Not in some foul sty.'

But Jane's rejoinder is unanswerable:

> 'Fair and foul are near of kin,

And fair needs foul,' I cried.
. . . .
'A woman can be proud and stiff
When on love intent;
But Love has pitched his mansion in
The place of excrement;
For nothing can be sole or whole
That has not been rent.'

That he should have braved an excremental reference shows how eager Yeats was to join the modernist tide. He knew he was late to jump in. While he had been designing beautiful euphemisms such as "the blood and mire of human veins," Joyce had given the world Leopold Bloom sitting in his privy, and Lawrence his gamekeeper in a forest shed rooting out the shameful places of Lady Chatterley's body. Both *Ulysses* and *Lady Chatterley's Lover* were banned books in England and the United States. The essence of the battle against the censor was the insistence upon the right to reproduce in print the ordinary words and actions of everyday life. Why should a writer be left out just because he lived in Ireland? As Yeats said defiantly to Olivia, "Say what you think of Crazy Jane (I approve of her)."[70]

It is is tempting to read the entire exchange between "Crazy Jane" and "the Bishop" as Yeats versus de Valera.

Yeats's fascist flirtation was a summer romance. During it, he got no support from his wife, who hated O'Duffy. By the time that his "Three Marching Songs to the Same Tune" was published in February 1934, he was apologizing as if for a past folly. The songs had been written, he said, in the fear that "our growing disorder . . . was about to turn our noble history into an ignoble farce. For the first time in my life I wanted to write what some crowd in the street might understand and sing."[71] But, finding that the party "wherewith I had once some loose associations" neither could nor would achieve his ideals of a disciplined, cultured way of life, he increased his songs' fantasy and obscurity "that no party might sing them."[72]

The Blueshirts faded fast. Another of their constituent parts, the Young Ireland Association, was outlawed in December 1933; the movement itself was split and crushed by 1934, although it flickered briefly in 1936 when O'Duffy raised an Irish brigade to fight for Franco in the Spanish Civil War. As Maurice Manning has pointed out in *The Blueshirts,* the organization never espoused the basic features of fascism, violence and the cult of the leader, and may not really deserve the fascist label. A safer designation might be "the only shirted movement in Irish politics."[73] Its subsequent notoriety outweighs the actual numbers involved, estimated to have been no more than twenty thousand at its height.

Be that as it may, Yeats never abandoned his belief in the desirability of a ruling class. In his public pronouncements he never called for violence, nor did he personally relish it in any form. On the other hand, he did call the violence of 1916 "a terrible beauty," did write boisterous things about the joys of being shot, and did believe that states were built upon strength, military might, and the right to take life. In other words, in his politics, he was a conservative.

What makes it so hard to detoxify Yeats's flirtation with fascism is his much longer held, more deeply felt passion for eugenics. His growing concern in the 1930s for the danger of breeding inferior stock produced some ugly, phrases, such as "the unintelligent classes."[74] Genetic arrogance is difficult to reconcile with the "Everything we look upon is blessed" Yeats.[75]

Yet perhaps a rough justice has been at work. If subsequent opinion has been unforgiving about Yeats's flirtation with fascism—Conor Cruise O'Brien, one of the harshest critics, says that Yeats left the Blueshirts only when he saw the fiasco of O'Duffy's march[76]—it may have been too kind on another score: the mad pursuit of virility that was to mark Yeats's final years.

Yeats's lurch to the extreme right was linked, with embarrassing literalness, to the search for potency. In early 1933, comparing his new Irish movement with Hitler's, he saw it as puny: "There is so little in our stocking . . . how can we not feel emulous when we see Hitler juggling with his sausage of stocking."[77]

Even more anatomical was his admiration for his fascist friend Captain MacManus. MacManus was lame, crippled from wounds suffered in service with the British Army. But he had another affliction as well, and he confided it to Yeats: impotence. He had cured himself, he said, by oriental meditations performed standing in front of a mirror. Two years later Yeats passed this information to a young actress with whom he had fallen in love: "His wound had given him my inhibition and several others."[78] Yeats went on to give the proof of cure: MacManus, with his renewed manhood, rode down an opponent who got in his way during a hunt.

Yeats did not crave any such demonstration of machismo, but he did want to be able to act on his physical desires. His Crazy Jane poems proclaimed publicly that he would if he could. He said the same, more openly, to Olivia: "I shall be a sinful man to the end, and think upon my death-bed of all the nights I wasted in my youth."[79]

The rest of his days would be spent trying to make up for lost time.

13

"This Is Baghdad"

(April 1934 – December 1935)

> Who can know the year, my dear,
> When an old man's blood grows cold?
> —W. B. Yeats, "The Wild Old Wicked Man," 1937

"I HAD IT DONE."[1] When a delighted Yeats made this announcement to a Dublin friend in the early summer of 1934, the friend had no doubt what "it" was: the genital operation devised by Professor Eugen Steinach of the University of Vienna Institute of Biological Research for the "rejuvenation by experimental revitalization of the aging puberty gland."[2] The news swiftly went around that Yeats had undergone a transplant of monkey glands. Gogarty said that it had made Yeats "sex mad."[3] Frank O'Connor's joke was the best: he said it was like putting a Cadillac engine into a Ford car.[4] The laughter continues.

In 1997 a book review in *The Scotsman* referred to Yeats as "The Gland Old Man."[5]

Of all the bizarre procedures Yeats used over the years to stimulate his muse, the Steinach operation was the least dubious. It was an off-shoot of medical research into sex hormones that began in the late nineteenth century when a French scientist, Brown-Séquard, injected himself with extracts of guinea pig and dog testicles.[6] It led by the 1950s to the development of the oral contraceptive pill and on to the hormone replacement therapies of the present day. Steinach's operation, developed in the 1910s, was simply a vasectomy, performed on the then-plausible theory that ligature of the spermatic duct would increase production of male hormones and thereby generally mobilize the body's resources. One of the supposed side benefits was a reduction in high blood pressure—a condition from which Yeats suffered. Sigmund Freud underwent a Steinach operation in 1923 with the primary objective of preventing a recurrence of his cancer, but also with the hope of increasing his sexuality and capacity for work.[7] That a vasectomy was hormonally meaningless was not recognized at the time; the male hormone, testosterone, was not isolated and synthesized until 1934.

If Yeats did not want to be laughed at, he should not have told his Dublin friends what he had done—especially not Gogarty, the reigning medical wit. One of the classic comic characters of the human race is the vain old (and, in Yeats's case, large: he now weighed about 225 pounds) geezer preening himself for younger women. In Yeats's time, what is more, any mention of surgical rejuvenation called up thoughts of the goat-gland transplants of Dr. John R. Brinkley of Kansas. Brinkley achieved such fame by packing goat glands into the testicles of sixteen thousand impotent men that he set up his own radio station and ran for governor of the state before his medical license was revoked and he was forced to flee to Mexico, to continue his lucrative practice there.[8]

For his Steinach operation, performed on April 6, Yeats had put himself in the hands of a reputable Harley Street specialist in gynecology and urology. He probably was as much rejuvenated by the surgeon as by the surgery. Norman Haire, who held the degrees of Master of Surgery and Bachelor of Medicine from the University of London, was an Australian Jew, a giant of a man, an intellectual, a collector of oriental art, a homosexual, a gourmand, a eugenicist, and a friend of the sexologist Havelock Ellis (who had introduced Yeats to mescal four decades earlier). Haire's conversation was as racy as his cable address: Sexology, London. He was president of the Sexual Reform Society, which attracted such *bien-pensants* of the day as Naomi Mitchison, A. H. L.-F. Pitt-Rivers, Marie Stopes, and Bertrand Russell; he was also secretary of the World League for Sexual Reform, chairman of the Rationalist Press Association, a member of the Men's Dress Reform Society, which endorsed "rational" dress (sandals, knickerbockers, no ties), and editor in 1934 of the *Encyclopedia of Sexual Knowledge*. Haire preached the importance of sexual fulfillment, in his silk-draped consulting room at 127 Harley Street and also in his clinic for the poor in London's East End. As a gynecologist, he was a pioneer in contraception and was one of the first to introduce the intrauterine ring.[9]

Eight years after Yeats's death, helping Richard Ellmann prepare his short life of the poet, George said that while the Steinach operation had immensely increased her husband's sense of well-being, it had failed to restore his capacity to have erections.[10] But she may not have been the best judge.

Yeats had at least four serious sexual liaisons in the years following the Steinach operation. Whether he achieved full intercourse in any of them is the subject of continued speculation in Yeats scholarship. It seems clear that he gazed on the naked bodies of the women who offered him, in his own phrase, "the bed's friendship,"[11] and that, at least occasionally, he was surprised and pleased to find himself (again in his words) "a man full of desire."[12] After one encounter, he wrote and thanked his partner: "The knowledge that I am not unfit for love has brought me sanity and peace."[13]

This gratitude suggests that if he did not achieve penetration, he was at least capable of trying. For the first time in his sexual career, what is more, he was free of the worry of making a woman pregnant.

The primary and unquestionable effect of the Steinach operation was sterilization—a useful side effect that cannot have escaped Yeats's notice.

In Britain there was considerable debate about the legality of voluntary sterilization. Norman Haire argued vehemently that the procedure was not against the law. However, as a highly sophisticated medical man, he was well aware that "rejuvenation" was a bright, benign label for a minor operation that, to many people of the time, was as unethical as abortion.[14]

Interestingly, even as a young man Yeats nurtured the idea of a shameless old man trying to recapture his vigor. In his autobiographical novel, *The Speckled Bird*, written between 1894 and 1902, a young occultist visits a venerable mystic to find him lying naked in a long box with a lid of orange glass. The old seer explains to his visitor, "I always like a sun-bath; when I am ill I vary the colours of the glass according to the illness, but orange is the only colour that increases the vitality."[15]

The fact is that increasingly as he grew older, Yeats feared that excessive masturbation was responsible not only for his sexual decline but for his overall ill-health. As he confided sadly and defiantly, in one of his revealing letters to Olivia Shakespear, "I repent of nothing but sickness. I ask myself perpetually what acts of my youth have weakened me."[16]

The period of recuperation that Yeats required was lengthy. Five weeks after the event, back in Rathfarnham, he still clung to his bed all morning and worked quietly at a table in the garden in the afternoon, stirring himself occasionally to play croquet with his daughter. George delayed their planned journey to Italy for several weeks. Yet Yeats was optimistic about the benefit of the operation. His blood pressure seemed to be down; so, he reported to Olivia, was his irritability. As for other details, he needed to talk to her in person, he had "so much quaint information."[17]

All considered, it is perhaps not surprising that in the months just before and after submitting his private parts to the knife, Yeats should write two plays about a severed head. They are variations on the same theme: a queen demanding that her suitor's head be cut off. In *A Full Moon in March,* the man who would wed her is a swineherd; in *The King of the Great Clock Tower,* written in the spring of 1934, he is "the Stroller." In both versions, the queen dances around and kisses the amputated body part. In the second play, her dance is accompanied by the blunt lyric, "Clip and lip and long for more."

After *The King of the Great Clock Tower* was performed at the Abbey at the end of June, Yeats explained why it was bolder than Oscar Wilde's *Salomé:*

> Wilde's dancer never danced with the head in her hands—her dance came before the decapitation of the saint and is a mere uncovering of nakedness. My dance is a long expression of horror and fascination. She first bows before the head (it is on a seat,) then in her dance lays it on the ground and dances before it, then holds it in her hands.[18]

Continuing to tinker with these plays, Yeats was mystified as to why "this blood symbolism has laid hold of me." But, he wrote to Edmund Dulac, "I must work it out."[19]

The Steinach operation was just one maneuver by a man who was in constant negotiation with his body about what he might and might not do. This was not pure hypochondria. Yeats's body, like a singer's, was the instrument of his art. Ideas gripped him viscerally; he was easily overwhelmed. If he read a bad play, an alternative version began forming in his mind. In the throes of excitement over a project or a new idea, he could not sleep; illness often followed. While working on *A Full Moon in March,* he became so overwrought that he felt he had to sit in a chair for two days without even reading. As always, however, the resolve to conserve every scrap of energy was accompanied by the determination to push himself through an enormous volume of work.

Raking over the past is hardly a tranquillizing exercise. But for Yeats autobiography was well paid.[20] In the spring of 1934 he completed the third volume of his autobiography, covering the years from 1896 to

1902, reliving the move into Woburn Buildings, the early years of friendship with Lady Gregory and refuge at Coole, and the jousting with George Moore. In *Dramatis Personae,* published in 1935, he indulged in a gossipy and indiscreet analysis of the character of his old enemy. His labor was all the more arduous because, as he wrote Olivia, "alas, the most significant image of those years must be left out."[21] Their old affair was a warm memory for them both.

One way to save strength was to jettison public service. He gave up the presidency of the Ireland branch of the international writers' organization, PEN. "How the devil I became president I don't know," he wrote Sean O'Faolain. "I never consented, never knew anything about it, never went to a meeting. Consider me as resigned."[22]

Frailty did not mean a retreat from the running battle with de Valera over censorship of the Abbey Theatre. The Abbey's tour of the United States in 1932 had drawn protests from Irish American Catholic groups and Fianna Fáil supporters; certain plays, notably Synge's *The Playboy of the Western World* and O'Casey's *Juno and the Paycock,* were felt to hold Irish Catholics up to ridicule as superstitious drunken oafs. Powerful Irish American voices were calling upon de Valera to withdraw the Abbey's subsidy in the name of Irish honor.

Yeats was the Abbey's public defender—a role he played so well as to secure a place in Irish history as one of the very few successfully to stand up to de Valera during the leader's decade of unbroken triumph. The two were a formidable pair of adversaries. "Yeats," says de Valera's biographer, Tim Pat Coogan, "was also possessed of remarkable political skills . . . and was tenacious in defence of artistic freedom."[23]

As the row boiled on, Yeats yielded to none of de Valera's demands. He categorically refused to withdraw the Synge and O'Casey plays, arguing that they were mainstays of the Abbey's repertoire, and increasingly of American curricula. He rejected de Valera's choice of a clerically sympathetic government representative to sit on the Abbey's board. He did not obey the request to send in advance a list of the plays that the Abbey planned for its next American tour. (He had Lennox Robinson send it instead.) And he cleverly wielded the press to his advantage. On April 7, 1934 (as it happened, the day after the Steinach operation), the *Irish Independent* carried a fierce and laudatory account of Yeats's defiance of de Valera. It quoted Yeats as saying in an interview that he "had fought the political societies before and was prepared to do so again . . . the Abbey Theatre was not to be regarded as a minor branch of the civil service."[24]

The extent of Yeats's political shrewdness was shown by his next move. Having won his battle with the government by refusing to change the Abbey's tour repertoire, he wrote a letter to the de Valera–controlled *Irish Press* in which he declared that newspaper reports had exaggerated the dispute between himself and the country's leader:

> Mr. de Valera has not "demanded" the withdrawal of any play by Synge or by O'Casey, nor have I "insisted" upon their presence there. We are on friendly terms with the Irish Government.[25]

Norman Haire was not Yeats's only new guru. In 1932, while living at Coole, Yeats read a book of poems by "an Indian saint" who had the gift of encapsulating mystical truths about the universe in the self with homely precision. As luck would have it, the saint, Shri Purohit Swami, lived in Bayswater. Olivia invited him to tea at Yeats's request. Yeats was soon introduced to the handsome, pink-robed, strong-faced Swami, who had drawn a circle of admirers to his Institute of Indian Mysticism. Yeats fell for the wise man of the East with a characteristic lack of reserve. He was astounded to find that the Swami (as they referred to him) "suddenly makes all wisdom if you ask him the right questions."[26] He was moved by the little poems the Swami sang in his strange tongue, and by the "little mound" on his forehead. Yeats believed it was the Indian stigmata despite Frank Sturm's assurance that the bump was a cyst or a wen.[27] He read the Swami's autobiography, *An Indian Monk: His Life and Adventures,* and found it "one of the world's fundamental books."[28] He wrote an introduction for a new edition, and another for *The Holy Mountain,* the Swami's translation of an account by his master, Bhagwan Shri Hamsa, of travels in the Himalayas.

The Swami did not come unaccompanied. He had a hanger-on, or mistress, a writer in her fifties. Mrs. Gwyneth Foden lived almost next door to the Swami in Bayswater and was a fantasist and devotee of the kind that both the Swami and Yeats attracted.[29] She claimed to have had an illegitimate child by the Swami, although no one had ever seen it. Her one book was a competently written light novel, *A Wife's Secret*. It had a moral—two, in fact—spelled out in an "Author's Foreword": that love will triumph even in a cruelly hypocritical age, and that a wife may safely lie about her past "with the knowledge that a woman *need not tell*."[30]

Yeats is said to have become briefly infatuated with her. She asked him to try to find an American lecture agent for the Swami.[31] Olivia, who liked the jovial Swami very much (as did her little grandson, Omar), disliked Mrs. Foden intensely and, perhaps trying politely to warn Yeats of trouble ahead, pronounced her "twittery."[32]

Reading the proofs of *The Holy Mountain*, Yeats was stirred anew. He drew up a new table of correspondences between the self and the universe; in it he equated the four elements, earth, water, air, and fire, with four quarters of the body (bowels, blood and genitalia, lungs and mind, and soul) and four periods in history. This schema appeared, fuzzily, in a letter to Olivia, then in a terse, controlled short poem about the human struggle with body, heart, mind, and God. He called it "The Four Ages of Man."

When George judged Yeats at last well enough to travel, they went to Italy, to move their things out of the flat they were turning over to Ezra Pound's parents. Homer and Isobel Pound, from Jenkintown, Pennsylvania, were making Rapallo their retirement home in order to be near their only child, whom they referred to as "our boy." The very American ways of the "old Pounds," as Yeats dubbed them,[33] were a source of constant amusement to their boy's European friends, but the couple took a big worry off the Yeats's minds; the arrangement on the flat was mutually convenient. Back to Dublin went the Pre-Raphaelite paintings, the books, and the Genovese-designed modern furniture; in came Ezra's own homemade furniture and the doting parents' photographs of him as a child. During this transition, Yeats, still respectful of Ezra's sharp editorial eye, gave him *The King of the Great Clock Tower* to read, and waited.

The verdict came within a day: "Putrid."[34] Nothing crueler could have been said to the man who equated poetic and sexual potency and who was even more afraid that he was too old for poetry than for love. Ezra did not spare the scorn. He told Yeats that the play was written in "nobody" language.[35] At least he had the grace not to tell Yeats what he really thought—that he could not read "the buzzard" anymore and that he hoped his friends would chloroform him "before I get to THAT state."[36]

Yeats knew, without being told, what THAT state was, and he embraced it. Angry and defiant, he wrote "A Prayer for Old Age" in answer to Ezra, in which he asked for what he had indeed already achieved: "That I may seem, though I die old, / A foolish, passionate man."

The verse written in that post-Steinach summer was far from putrid. "Supernatural Songs," completed by late August, commandingly restates Yeats's main themes. The manifest resurgence of creative vitality stands as evidence that the psychological effects of the Steinach operation were genuine.

Four of the songs pit an imaginary hermit, Ribh (pronounced Reeve), against Saint Patrick. If the verses were not so obscure, the Censorship of Publications Board could have banned them for blasphemy. In "Ribh Denounces Patrick," Yeats dismisses one of Ireland's cherished beliefs—that Saint Patrick had used the shamrock to teach the people the doctrine of the Holy Trinity. The poem mocks the Trinity as "an abstract Greek absurdity." Its original title, "Ribh Prefers an Older Theology," makes Yeats's political point even more clearly— that the Irish should turn to their pre-Patrick past and rediscover an earlier, Eastern religion in which soul and body are not enemies.

Like Yeats's plays after *The Words Upon the Window-Pane*, the poems called "Supernatural Songs" are preoccupied with sexual intercourse—

ostensibly as a metaphor for the union of opposing principles: divine and human, universal and personal. Ribh sings:

Natural and supernatural with the self-same ring are wed,
As man, as beast, as an ephemeral fly begets, Godhead begets
  Godhead,
For things below are copies, the Great Smaragdine Tablet
  said.

The Smaragdine Tablet was the kind of gorgeous image from the teaching of the Golden Dawn that Yeats loved: it referred to a medieval Latin work on alchemy alleged to have been drawn from the work of the Egyptian Hermes Trismegistus and was thus a bridge between Christianity and the supposed lost wisdom of Egypt and the ancient Orient.

Yet his personal sexual dilemma was never far from Yeats's meaning. "The point of this particular poem," Yeats wrote, giving Olivia the benefit of an explicit lesson, is "that we beget and bear because of the incompleteness of our love. Strange that I should write these things in my old age, when if I were to offer myself for new love I could only expect to be accepted by the very young wearied by the passive embraces of the bolster."[37]

The picture of himself as a solitary masturbator had not vanished. Indeed, he referred to the result of his operation as a "second puberty."[38]

Early in September, back in Ireland, Yeats received a letter from a young English actress, telling him how much she admired his work and that she would like to meet him when he was next in London. He wrote back politely saying that he would try not to lose her letter and, although very busy whenever in London, he might possibly have a spare hour for a fellow artist if business or fatigue did not otherwise occupy him.

Like a true fan, his correspondent took this brush-off as encouragement, and wrote again. This time she got through to the inner man; Yeats liked the way she praised the "trueness" of his poems. If she had used the word *veracity*, he told her, instead of *trueness*, he would not have been interested. Now he wanted to meet her.

She was Margot Ruddock, a twenty-seven-year-old actress who performed under the name of Margot Collis and lived in Notting Hill. She had large, expressive eyes, full, curving lips and the marcel-waved elegance of beauties of her day. That she had also a husband and a small daughter did not seem to trouble either her or Yeats. Within a month of her first approach to him, she had become "Dear Margot" and had directed Yeats to a lodging house at 45 Seymour Street near Marble Arch, which offered bed and breakfast for two pounds a week. Although the nearby Savile Club (which had moved from Piccadilly to 69 Brook Street) was undoubtedly more comfortable, it was not a place where a member might take a young and beautiful actress up to his bedroom. Women, in fact, were not admitted into the club at all. (By the late 1990s the Savile had relaxed its ban to the extent of admitting women to the dining room on Friday evenings.)

Yeats, about to return to Italy for an international congress on the state of the theater, wrote back, grateful that he had taken a room for a week from October 17: "I have long wanted such a place. You are bound to nothing, not even to come and look at me."[39]

George and he then went to Rome, as guests of the Royal Academy of Italy. Invited by Luigi Pirandello to take the chair, he had some trouble following the proceedings as he did not understand the language—nor the Latin contempt for brevity. Knowing that each speaker was limited to ten minutes, Yeats shocked everyone by rapping his gavel loudly when the eminent futurist Filippo Marinetti exceeded his time. When another speaker droned on, Yeats was heard to ask loudly, "But is he keeping to the point?"[40] The festivities required him to attend an opera performance in the presence of Mussolini. However, he did nothing to tailor his own conference speech to suit the regime. According to the report sent back to London by the Rome correspondent of *The Times*, he condemned "the theory that the stage should be made a medium for any form of propaganda and expressed hope that the fight for intellectual and artistic freedom still being waged on the stage would end in triumph."[41] For this ringing declaration, he was warmly applauded. The conference then adopted (against expectations) a resolution opposing state interference into the life of the theater.

But his mind was back in London. He wrote a letter to Margot Ruddock in the careful language of a man trying to outwit his wife without open discourtesy. He would reach London on October 17. His wife would not be with him, but would go straight on to Dublin. He would ring her, his "dear Margot," the morning after he got in, and she was to keep the day for him. He added, what she surely was delighted to hear, that he was rewriting *The King of the Great Clock Tower* so as to give the queen a speaking part that she might play. (In the original Abbey production of the dance-play, the silent queen was played by Ninette de Valois.)

The affair moved fast. By October 30 he was writing excited notes to say that if he were slightly late meeting her after a scheduled lunch, she was to wait (presumably in his room), because "I cannot bear the thought of a half-hour lost."[42] Upon his return to Dublin, she became "My dearest" and was assured that he was hard at work on her behalf. He would write two poems for her as soon as he had finished revising the play, which now opened with a song "partly addressed to you." The song (which he enclosed) tells of "old Pythagoras" who falls in love and pleads, "Open wide those gleaming eyes / That can make the loutish wise."[43]

In the same letter, however, a more prosaic phrase jumps out: "I must not meet you again a tired man." Another embarrassing sexual failure? Another letter, written two weeks later from his Dublin club declares that he is in "utter black gloom" because of a fear that "'this nervous inhibition has not left me'—I pictured Margot unsatisfied and lost."[44]

Yeats ought to have known that his young lover was more concerned with professional than with sexual satisfaction. What Margot Ruddock wanted from him was to be turned into a great poet: to put on his knowledge with his power. She showered him with examples of her work and eagerly awaited the comments that he gave with the rigor and consideration of a schoolmaster. He balanced criticism with praise and held out the possibility that her genius might emerge if she learned to curb her faults, such as confused metaphors and irrelevant detail.

Of her willingness to sleep with the man who was now "My darling Yeats" there is no doubt. Later in their relationship, she wrote complainingly that her first husband did not suggest going to bed after they had lunched together: "What's the use of having a nice body and wanting to give people happiness if they will not take it?"[45]

Yeats knew that Margot Ruddock was vulnerable; she complained of depression and boasted of cheering herself up by getting drunk at the pub. Oddly enough, he did not seem to notice that, as their affair began, she was a very new mother. She had given birth to a daughter (her second child) in February in Barcelona. Although the son from her first marriage remained with his father, the new baby was with her and her second husband, Raymond Lovell, an actor, in their Notting Hill flat.

So smitten was he that, doing something he had never done before, Yeats addressed a love poem to a woman by name. He had not abandoned his care for appearances. "Margot" was not published in his lifetime (nor in his wife's; it remained unseen until 1970).[46] But he worked exceedingly hard on the poem, and its directness, poignancy, even desperation, show that in November 1934, old Pythagoras really was in love:

I Margot

All famine struck sat I, and then
Those generous eyes on mine were cast,
Sat like other agèd men
Dumfoundered, gazing on a past
That appeared constructed of
Lost opportunities to love.

II

O how can I that interest hold?
What offer to attentive eyes?
Mind grows young and body old;

When half closed her eye-lid lies
A sort of hidden glory shall
About these stooping shoulders fall.

III

The Age of Miracles renew,
Let me be loved as though still young

Or let me fancy that it's true,
When my brief final years are gone
You shall have time to turn away
And cram those open eyes with day.[47]

Writing it made him so excited that he could not sleep and had to take a sleeping powder. He told his beloved not to be shy of writing to him at his home in Rathfarnham, for his wife knew they had theatrical business together. As for his and her friends in London, if they thought the two of them were having an affair, so much the better. To Dulac, Yeats wrote as a couple: "Margot and I will dine with you to-morrow."[48]

Olivia, with the detachment of a seventy-year-old beauty, followed the unfolding tale with wry sympathy. "Your renewed activities," she wrote, "are most interesting—I should not say perhaps 'renewed' but 'accelerated'—don't you feel rather as though you had been wound up again?"[49]

Accelerated he certainly was. In December he sent Olivia the giddy announcement: "Wonderful things have happened. This is Baghdad. This is not London."[50]

Did Yeats now have himself a harem? That month he began a friendship with another young, beautiful free-thinker whose habits, like Margot Ruddock's, were well beyond the stage of the "passive embraces of the bolster." Ethel Mannin had large generous eyes too, but hers, like her center-parted, smoothly drawn-back hair, suggested cool composure rather than dramatic excitability. She was English too, although proud of her father's Irish roots, thirty-four years old, left-wing, and highly successful as a writer. A friend of Norman Haire's and a member of the Sexual Reform League, she believed, and wrote, the doctrine that Haire taught: "There is more unhappiness in human life caused by sexual problems than by anything else, not excluding money problems."[51]

Her novel *Crescendo* had been greeted as "a saga of sex." Her frank and witty autobiography, *Confessions and Impressions,* published in 1930, went into fifteen printings during its first year, with its account of London life in the 1920s. By the time Yeats met her in 1934, the book was into its twenty-ninth printing, thanks to such bold assertions as that Haire's description of the voice of Paul Robeson was the best she had ever heard but "unfortunately it is unprintable, since sexual imagery in this country is *verboten* in spite of the fact that sex is life, and all art sexual."[52]

Such words were music to the ears of the creator of Crazy Jane. But there was a huge philosophical gap between them. Ethel Mannin was rationalist and skeptical, he mystical and credulous. Politics divided them too. She was left-wing, just short of being a Marxist, and had recently returned starry-eyed from the Soviet Union; his leanings were firmly the other way. But that hardly mattered when, as a companion, she was brilliant, fun, and full of the salty talk that Yeats adored. She was not worried by his cultural baggage: "Yeats full of Burgundy and racy reminiscence was Yeats released from the Celtic Twilight and treading the antic hay with abundant zest."[53]

When their relationship became actively sexual is not known. Haire had enlisted Ethel specifically to reassure Yeats about the success of the Steinach operation, and she had obeyed his orders, when going to dinner to meet the poet, to dress as seductively as possible.[54] She was an independent woman, with other lovers, an estranged husband (J. A. Porteus), and a teenage daughter. Although she left for Monte Carlo for the winter not long after they met, there is little question that he enjoyed the benefit of her practice of what she preached.

The arrival of another exciting young woman in his life, was a heady experience for a man who had declared the year before that "all my personal experiences have come to an end." That December he did not return to Dublin for the holidays. At Christmas he thanked George and the children for their telegram of greetings and wired his to them.[55] Every day he visited Norman Haire for injections, to get his body back to "normal."

One of the best bits of evidence that he achieved his ambition appears in the letter he wrote to Ethel Mannin on December 30, thanking her for their reassuring encounter; he said he came away from her with a feeling that he had been blessed. He made a date to take her to lunch at The Ivy—late, at 1:30 P.M.—because he would go for an injection from Haire first. Would his pleasure have been spoiled if he knew that his sex therapist was reporting back to Norman Haire?

Baghdad took its toll. By mid-January 1935 he was back in Rathfarnham with a congested left lung, coughing and spitting blood. He sent Ethel Mannin and Margot Ruddock vivid descriptions of his frailty: how he had collapsed, shivering and exhausted, how he had been able to sit by the fire for a few minutes a day, how he was bullied by his doctors, how he had to rely on his daughter or his gardener even to put a stamp on a letter.

Eager as he was, as his poem "Margot" claimed, to be loved "as though still young," he wanted at the same time to be loved as one who is very old—that is, one who expects that his every symptom is a subject of surpassing interest to others. Bedridden, with a head full of seraglio thoughts, he found that his favorite reading was the *Arabian Nights*. He savored a passage where Scheherazade tells the king there is no need to send her little sister out of the room while she tells him licentious tales: "There is nothing shameful in speaking of those things that lie below our waists."[56] So impressed was Yeats by these wise words that he wrote them to Margot Ruddock as something that might be a motto for an educational book for children—"a very advanced book." Indeed, he liked them so much that he sent them also to Ethel Mannin, changing "below our waists" to "beneath our belts."[57]

To her too he suggested that the motto might do for a children's book such as she had written. (Her published work included a paper for the Sexual Reform Society on "Sex and the Child.")

George, however, saw the effect the *Arabian Nights* was having on him, and took the book away; it fell into the category of serious literature, as did Balzac—a threat to his health. She put a "wild West" in his hands in its place.

A striking theme in his letters to both young women and also to Olivia is his stress on his need for salacious anecdotes and scandalous gossip. He told Margot Ruddock that "wild stories" were to him what the public house and glass of ale were to her: "without them I should go mad."[58] Iseult Stuart told Ellmann that Yeats's fondness for telling dirty stories increased with age and that "it wasn't pretty."[59] Ethel Mannin, on the other hand, enjoyed them, and the poet F. R. Higgins shamelessly indulged him by making up fantastic anecdotes about his own love life (and then joking about it around Dublin later). This prurience seems to have been a carry-over from the uncertain days when he had to read love poetry to Olivia Shakespear to work himself into the mood for sex.

Spring saw resurrection as before. Yeats convalesced from his collapse by correcting the proofs for *Dramatis Personae* and also by contracting for a monumental project that any busy person might shy away from. He agreed to edit *The Oxford Book of Modern Verse,* to be an anthology of his own choice of the best poetry written between 1892 and 1935. He expected it to make him a lot of money. That settled, he dashed over to London to discuss the performance of his plays with a small company called the Group Theatre. He checked into his Seymour Street lodging, only to collapse once more with a violent cold. George had to come from Dublin to collect him.

At the point when he was in a black gloom over the difficulty of finishing the "Margot" poem, George responded by arranging to cheer him up; she set up a dinner, for example, with the ever-amusing Gogarty. Yeats appreciated her gesture, although he believed she did not know the cause of his misery.

He underestimated her. By now George Yeats understood her husband very well. She was used to his affairs. When George Russell died in the summer of 1935, she remarked to Yeats that "AE" was as near a saint as they were ever likely to know. She added, "You are a better poet, but no saint."[60]

That Yeats was no saint was obvious to the sharp-eyed writers around him. Gogarty said that all Yeats needed was a mistress.[61] Sean O'Faolain later recalled that George had become Yeats's "procuress"— pleased when her difficult husband found young women to make him happy, concerned to ensure him a steady supply. "He likes her! He likes her!" she said to O'Faolain when Yeats was captivated by Elizabeth Bowen, whom O'Faolain had brought to meet him.[62]

Now past forty, George gave her adolescent children priority, Michael particularly; with his frail health, fast growth (he reached nearly six feet before he was fourteen), and excellent progress at school (first in Latin and in history in December 1934), he required care and attention. The children's busy social life required organization, and their developing interests supervision. Anne, who had become involved in theater work, encouraged her brother to help her build a theater in the nursery at home, using dyed sheets and tent poles. Amid so much activity, the demanding Yeats could be an obstruction; George sometimes asked Yeats to defer his return home or to stay at his club until the household was ready to receive him. From her fixed base, she was able to report to him when he was away about the children's progress and also about affairs at the Abbey, the size of the audiences, and the state of the latest of its endemic woes. (In 1935 Lennox Robinson was causing difficulty by drinking heavily and squabbling with his wife, Dolly.)

Even so, after eighteen years, George still felt at a distance from the complex, contradictory creature she had abruptly married. So timid was she of invading his privacy that when, from London, he instructed her, to help a would-be biographer, to search his papers for the date of his move into Woburn Buildings, she dared not open the packet of late-1890s memoirs marked "Private." Yeats laughed when she told him of her hesitation. He assured her she would have found nothing to disturb her.[63]

The long-suffering wife is as much a stock character as the self-deluding old lecher. But the stereotype does not sum up George Yeats. There were discordant elements in the woman who so captivated Ellmann. While she was undoubtedly a person of intelligence, dignity, independent aesthetic judgment, and managerial ability, she was odd, or had become so in the years following the move to Ireland. She felt at times so solitary that she became timid, almost afraid to go out.[64] The young woman who had dressed in the very height of fashion had become, certain female acquaintances noticed (perhaps because they saw her at Ballylee, where conditions were difficult), someone with a strong body odor, suggesting unwashed underclothes and self-neglect.[65] She was also, Francis Stuart noticed, drinking heavily; at one of the Yeatses' garden parties she was wearing one shoe and one carpet slipper. When he asked, "Have you hurt your foot, Georgie?" she glanced down and said, "No, I just forgot to put the other shoe on."[66]

If Yeats noticed his wife's strangeness, he would never have put it in a letter. However, in 1935, he confided to Iseult Stuart, the woman he had tried so hard to marry in 1917, that at home "everything was terrible": he and his wife had become alienated from one another, she had become a mother rather than a wife, and she humiliated him in public.[67] (This was possibly a reference to George's collapse from drinking at a public dinner in the late 1920s.) When Iseult countered to Yeats that George must have had to put up with a lot, the poet said to her, "Ah, if only we had married." Iseult's response was swift: "We wouldn't have stayed together a year."[68]

From this interview, Ellmann put only the last sentence into his *Yeats: The Man and the Masks*. For such self-censoring omissions, he has been accused of giving a false picture of the happy Yeats marriage because of his admiration for George. This may well have been the case. Ellmann, although a great biographer, tended to be protective of the family member (in his biography of Joyce, Joyce's brother Stanislaus) who was his main source of information. However, writing in 1948, he was constrained by the publishing conventions of his time; not until Michael Holroyd's *Lytton Strachey* in 1967 was full disclosure of a writer's sexual life considered appropriate, or even relevant in a biography.[69] Ellmann also must have been impressed, as were so many others, with Yeats's fundamental loyalty and attachment to his wife and children; many of the letters written during his absences speak of a longing for hearth and home.[70]

Another American academic who met Mrs. Yeats during the early postwar years formed quite a different judgment of her character, one that deserves to be set beside Ellmann's. Curtis Bradford, who went to her home many times to work on the Yeats papers, was impressed with George's encyclopedic knowledge of her husband's work. Yet he recorded later that there was *"something in her personality beyond good and evil, something mocking, irresponsible. I was never certain what she would do or say next."*[71]

The strains in the Yeats marriage, it seems fair to conclude, were not caused by one partner only.

In late May 1935 Yeats's mercurial affections changed yet again, when Lady Ottoline Morrell took him to meet Lady Dorothy Wellesley, a poet whose work he had admired while reading for his anthology. Dorothy Wellesley held her title as the wife of the son of a duke (of Wellington). An estranged wife with two grown children, she now lived apart from her husband, Lord Gerald Wellesley, a diplomat, who was homosexual, as was she. In the early years of their marriage, she had traveled with him to many of the places of Yeats's imagination: Greece, Egypt, Persia, Russia.

The rapport between the two poets was instant. Dorothy Wellesley had not only seen camels and the desert; she had seen ghosts in her bedroom. Two minutes after they met, Yeats was giving her the advice that she should sacrifice everything and everyone to her poetry. She retorted that she was a mother and could not.

Lady Dorothy's splendid country seat, Penns in the Rocks, in Sussex, was named after William Penn, the English Quaker and founder of Pennsylvania, who had married the heiress of the property. The William-and-Mary house had been improved with Victorian additions and Bloomsbury touches (wall paintings by Vanessa Bell and Duncan Grant in the dining room). In that setting she lived the life of a country gentlewoman with passions for gardening, the arts, weekend entertaining, and a dog as big as herself.

Her appearance was vividly described for the *Dictionary of National Biography* by her former lover Vita Sackville-West: "Slight of build, almost fragile, with blazing blue eyes, fair hair, transparently white skin." As for her character, the same source said (citing "Private information; personal knowledge") that she was a natural rebel who fancied herself something of a philosopher, with a sense of history and a smattering of archaeology, and who "often imposed upon a verse a weight it should never have been asked to carry."[72] Apart from the fact that Yeats's verse certainly could carry the weight of the pseudo-history and eclectic myth that he piled upon it, the same character sketch could have applied to him.

Ottoline Morrell soon joked that Yeats had abandoned her for Dorothy: "It's not that he is interested in her poetry, but he likes her chef."[73] That was not fair. He did like the Wellesley poetry very much. It was more like his own, rather than the "Ezra, Eliot, Auden" school through which he was plowing with great difficulty.[74]

But he also liked her genes. In Dorothy Wellesley and her house, Yeats saw aristocratic lineage in its proper setting. By the mid-1930s, eugenics was the rage among Fabians and fascists alike; both groups were alarmed by the disparity between the reproduction rates of the educated classes and the teeming masses. Yeats still had his old fear of inherited madness. He told Dorothy,

> We all have something within ourselves to batter down and get our power from this fighting. I have never "produced" a play in verse without showing the actors that the passion of the verse comes from the fact that the speakers are holding down violence or madness.[75]

Yet long before he fell under the influence of eugenicists such as Haire, he had transmuted his family fears into societal terms. In an essay published in 1919 he had argued that "a single wrong choice may destroy a family."[76] In his old age, he was more concerned than ever with the survival of ancient bloodlines and the leisured classes.

They certainly looked after him well. At Penns in the Rocks, he had found himself a new Coole. There was a room he could call his own. He was always welcome, and the house was always full of stimulating guests: he much enjoyed the company of W. J. Turner, an Australian poet and music critic of the *New Statesman,* who was a frequent visitor. He also very much liked Hilda Matheson, Dorothy Wellesley's partner, who lived in a small house on the grounds. Hilda Matheson, who was lovely to look at, trim, intelligent, deft, was another of Vita Sackville-West's cast-offs. She worked for the BBC and had formerly been employed by military intelligence. Neither she, according to her biographer, Michael Carney, nor Dorothy could be categorized as strong or masculine in demeanor.[77]

For the phallically challenged Yeats, the company of two sophisticated lesbians was exhilarating. The sexual frisson between him and his hostess, later to intensify, was present from the start. Less than a month after meeting Dorothy, he wrote with great candor, "I find my present weakness made worse by the strange second puberty the operation has given me, the ferment that has come upon my imagination."[78]

His seventieth birthday in June 1935 brought him face to face with the need for choices. What did he wish to do with the rest of his life? How could he best get through the coming winter? He was now complaining that he could not climb the stairs without panting; the heavy reading necessary for his anthology was exhausting him. He needed a week, he said, for each poet.[79]

His decision was clarified by an offer from Harvard and by an unusual birthday gift. Harvard's president, James Bryant Conant, hoped that he would come to Cambridge, Massachusetts, in February 1936 to be the Charles Eliot Norton Professor of poetry. The requirement was that he be in residence, although not continuously, and give six lectures. For this he would be paid $4,500, plus $500 for travel. He had already turned down Harvard's offer of an honorary degree, as he was unwilling to meet the university's requirement that such degrees be received in person.[80] However, the dollars were a lure; perhaps he ought to be turning his fame into money for the sake of his family.

As he pondered, he gazed at the gift presented him by his friend Harry Clifton, a poet and artist in stained glass. It was a large chunk of lapis lazuli stone on which a Chinese sculptor had carved the design of a mountain with temple, trees, paths, and two figures who, in Yeats's eyes, were "an ascetic and pupil about to climb the mountain."[81]

The scene brought home with new force the wisdom to be gained from the East. Yeats glimpsed, as he wrote Ethel Mannin, the chance of plunging himself into "impersonal poetry," expunging all the bitterness that his recent struggles in Ireland had stirred in his soul, and to "make a last song, sweet and exultant, a sort of European *geeta,* or rather my *geeta,* not doctrine, but song."[82] With the sexual frankness he used with Ethel, he told her that a young and overincisive doctor in Dublin had ordered him to observe strict celibacy until his health improved, but he assured her that he expected to surprise the doctor with the speed of his recovery.[83]

With George's agreement, he turned down Harvard and decided to spend the winter in Majorca with the Swami, translating and putting into Yeatsian English the Upanishads (the Sanskrit spiritual treatises dealing with the Deity, creation, and existence). Yeats thought the experience would enable him once again to be "reborn in existence."[84] Nevertheless, he liked to insist that he was making the trip under doctor's orders. He declined Mrs. Foden's generous offer to pay all his expenses herself. He would have no difficulty in paying two pounds a week, and even three, to help out Swami.[85]

Harvard's loss was poetry's gain. The great poem "Lapis Lazuli," written the following year, was another result of his decision in the summer of 1935 to face East, not West.

Every discoloration of the stone,
Every accidental crack or dent
Seems a water-course or an avalanche,
Or lofty slope where it still snows
Though doubtless plum or cherry-branch
Sweetens the little half-way house
Those Chinamen climb towards, and I

Delight to imagine them seated there;
There, on the mountain and the sky,
On all the tragic scene they stare.
One asks for mournful melodies;
Accomplished fingers begin to play.
Their eyes mid many wrinkles, their eyes,
Their ancient, glittering eyes, are gay.

His seventieth birthday brought many tributes, a full page of articles on his work in the *Irish Times,* a PEN dinner, and so many letters and telegrams of congratulation that it was like getting the Nobel Prize all over again. The tributes were more than a counterbalance to the Yeats stories of which Dublin now had a goodly store, most of them making fun of his "But . . . does . . . it . . . really . . . matter?" approach to reality.

One anecdote, by Professor W. B. Stanford, had Yeats declaiming that one good thing about the Reformation was that it had led to the Renaissance. When a colleague protested that he had reversed the order of history, "the poet, with a magnificent gesture of his hand, proclaimed: 'Just look at O'Brien here: he's the kind of man who would bring down the Archangel Gabriel in full flight with a brickbat of *fact*'—and he put a wealth of scorn, it is said, into the word 'fact.'"[86]

The very way Yeats dressed invited mockery, but that now was tinged with admiration for his achievement. Frank O'Connor remembered his entering a room with a sideways glance:

He wore a pale, beautifully-cut, soft suit, a full silk shirt, and a huge ring. His speech was suave and mannered, he held his hand out very high, raised his brows and looking down his nose at you;. . . Everything about him was expensive and beautiful . . . the touch of dandyism in the lofty, ecclesiastical stare, the ritual motion of the hands, the unction of the voice that caressed the slightly oratorical cadences, the occasional elaborate mispronunciation like "weld" for "world" or "midder" for "murder."[87]

All his life one of Yeats's most consistently useful qualities was the willingness to make a fool of himself. Poetry came out of personal conflict and self-exposure; all that mattered to him was to get the words right and to know when he did. As he told Dorothy in a famous phrase, "A poem comes right with a click like a closing box."[88]

Once he had met Dorothy Wellesley, Yeats's passion for Margot Ruddock cooled entirely. By August, contemplating a visit to England, he told her he would stay at the Savile "where I may be looked after" and politely declined her offer to meet him at the boat as he would have his daughter with him.[89] His letters to the actress with the generous eyes no longer opened with "My dearest" but used instead "My dear Margot," and were signed "Yours, W. B. Yeats," rather than "Yours always." No longer was there any mention of physical desire; instead there was sound advice about revisions to her poetry, combined with a recital of his symptoms. Even so, her letters to him continued heated: "My darling Yeats."

As an aspiring poet, Margot Ruddock had more reason than ever to pursue the great man. He was considering putting her work in his *Oxford Book of Modern Verse.* Cruelly, perhaps, he kept her on tenterhooks all through the summer of 1935, saying he had not made up his mind: he was weighing her work against that of far more famous poets whom he was leaving out.

Preparing for his winter with the Swami, Yeats went over to London in October for a revival of *The Player Queen.* Margot played the queen even though Yeats thought she should have been cast as Decima, the substitute queen, a richer part. Dorothy Wellesley invited him to a supper at the Café Royal after the opening night and asked him to bring a friend (who she as good as said must not be Margot). "I like most men better than most women," she wrote.[90] Yeats promised not to invite anyone without consulting her.

Margot now began to pile her personal problems on Yeats's shoulders. She feared that her little daughter was being sacrificed to her acting career. She began to think of the child as dead. She thought she ought to give up the stage.[91] Yeats countered with a problem of his own—he had had a lump cut out of his tongue and feared it might be cancer. (It was not.) He told her, he said, because he thought the worry might serve as a stimulus for her acting. She poured her troubles onto the Swami as well; he urged her to meditate.[92]

Ethel Mannin was less impressed by the Swami. She was struck by the ascetic's remarkably well-nourished and well-groomed appearance. The trousers emerging from his ample robes were sharply creased, the brown shoes were highly polished, and the wristwatch was gold. When she pointed out to Yeats that these accessories were remarkable in a man who lived by the begging bowl, his reply was that, naturally, the Swami accepted what was given him.[93]

At the end of November, the anthology finished, Yeats was ready for Majorca. George crossed with him to Liverpool to see him off. At his side on deck were the Swami and Mrs. Foden; she was going along, Yeats said, to save them from bad cooking. The Swami's passage was assisted by a gift of one hundred pounds from Margot Ruddock and fifty pounds from himself.[94]

It was a cold, blowy day. George left the Liverpool dock without waiting to see the ship sail. She felt sorry for herself, but shrugged it off, reminding herself how much she had to do back in Dublin.[95] Yeats, having met his publisher's deadline for the verse anthology, declared, "The rest, the business arrangements, are my wife's task."[96] Another task, which she completed, was to make an index of the first lines of his poems.

The sea journey was marred by storms in the Bay of Biscay violent enough to be reported in the newspapers. Yeats reached the Mediterranean haven of white walls and blue sea shaken. Waiting for him were more poems from Margot, and a letter: "Darling I love you so much, I wish I was with you in Majorca."[97]

He had been warned.

Yeats's depressed mother: this photograph of Susan Pollexfen was taken in 1863, before her marriage to John Butler Yeats.

Susan Pollexfen Yeats, a sketch done by her husband, with Lily at her side, in February 1870, several months before the birth of her second son, Robert.

Thoor Ballylee, County Galway. *(Courtesy of the Irish Tourist Board)*

Brother against brother: the Free State shelling of Dublin's Four Courts,
the republican stronghold, in May 1922.

Maud Gonne's house at 73 Stephen's Green after a raid in 1923 by
authorities looking for the escaped Sean MacBride. This is exactly
what Yeats feared in 1918 when he refused to let Maud in because
George was pregnant and ill. *(Courtesy of Geoffrey Elborn)*

Olivia Shakespear, passport
photograph, 1921.
(Courtesy of Omar Pound)

Edmund Dulac's etching of
"Girldus," the supposed author of
part of *A Vision*.

Yeats with Michael and Anne and the book waited to be picked up as soon as the photographer has finished. *(Rex Roberts photo)*

Coinage of Saorstat Eireann 1928–1937: the Free State coinage adopted by committee led by Yeats replacing the British monarch's head with a noble Irish bestiary. *(Courtesy of the Central Bank of Ireland)*

Francis Stuart, the fiery young Irish writer who married Iseult Gonne in 1920. *(Courtesy of Geoffrey Elborn)*

T. Sturge Moore's jacket design for Yeats's volume of poetry, The Tower, published in 1928. The tower mirrored the stream illustrates the neoplatonist concept of a mirrored universe: "As above, so below."

The four "Daimons" as promised by the Automatic Script.
(Courtesy of Rex Roberts)

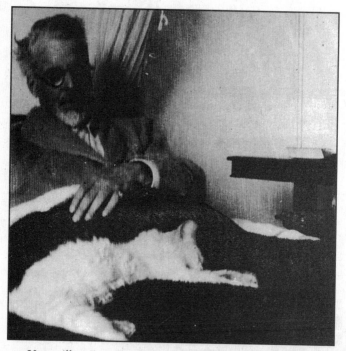

Yeats, ill at Rapallo, found a cat, like his fur-body rug,
a great comfort.

Recovery at Rapallo: Gogarty told Yeats "that beard will only prevent you forgetting illness, so shave it off at once." But Yeats obviously liked it.

At Majorca in 1936: Yeats towers over his stately peacemaker,
Swami Shri Purohit.

Jack and W. B. Yeats outside their sisters' home at Dundrum.
(Courtesy of R.A. Garfield)

Congress of Irish Blueshirts, August 1934.

Patriarch of the Abbey: Yeats and a group from the Abbey Theater
c. 1930: Lennox Robinson, playwright and escort of George Yeats, is
back row, second from left; the Irish actor Barry Fitzgerald is in the
second row on the right. *(Courtesy of the National Library of Ireland)*

Norman Haire, the larger-than-life
Harley street surgeon and crusader
for sexual liberation who performed
Yeats's Steinach operation, shown
wearing the "rational" garb favored
by the Men's Dress Reform Society.

Ethel Mannin, novelist, one of
Yeats's lovers and confidantes.

Lady Dorothy Wellesley, poet, later
Duchess of Wellington, one of the
principal female protectors of
Yeats's last years. *(Photograph by
Harold Coster)*

MARGOT LOVELL, wife of Raymond Lovell, the actor, who is lying in a grave condition at a Barcelona hospital following a fall from the window of a friend's house.

POETESS FALLS FROM WINDOW

After Interview With Mr. W. B. Yeats

CONSULTED HIM ABOUT BOOK

Barcelona, Wednesday.

MARGOT LOVELL, the 27-year-old wife of Mr. Raymond Lovell, the actor, of Westbourne Gardens, London, is lying in hospital here in a condition stated to be "grave." She is suffering from a broken knee cap, serious bruises and slight concussion following a fall last night from a first floor window of a friend's house.

She was picked up in the street and taken to hospital at once.

Mrs. Lovell had been in Barcelona for two days, having come from Majorca where she had gone to see W. B. Yeats, the Irish poet. She wished to interest him in a book of poems she had written under the name Margot Collis, before having it published.

The "Barcelona incident" when the beautiful actress, Margot Ruddock, threw herself out of a window after visiting Yeats in May 1936 made juicy gossip for the London and Dublin press. *(British Newspaper Library, Colindale)*

Hilda Mathseson, founder of the BBC's "Talks," partner of Dorothy Wellesley, and one of the last visitors to the dying Yeats in Menton in 1939. *(Courtesy of Nigel Nicolson)*

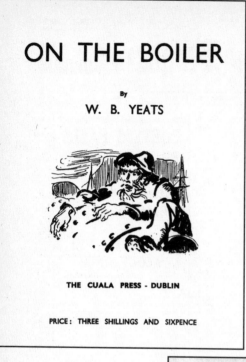

ON THE BOILER

By
W. B. YEATS

THE CUALA PRESS - DUBLIN

PRICE: THREE SHILLINGS AND SIXPENCE

A family enterprise: On the Boiler was published in 1938 by the Yeats sisters' Cuala Press, with a design by Jack Yeats showing an old Sligo captain climbing onto a ship's boiler top. *(Courtesy of Cuala Archive, Trinity College Dublin Library)*

Lolly Yeats, printer and publisher, 1932. *(Courtesy of Cuala Archive, Trinity College Dublin Library)*

The Hotel Ideal-Sejour at Menton where Yeats died in the upstairs room shown with shutters closed. *(Courtesy of Princess Grace Irish Library)*

The grave at Roquebrune, beside that of A. G. Hollis. (to the right)

Yeats in the 1930s telling a joke.

Yeats and Edith Shackleton Heald in the garden at The Chantry House. According to Rowley Marriott, a neighbor, "Edith worshipped him, fetched and carried for him and treated him as if he were a god." *(Courtesy of the Huntington Library)*

The Chantry House, Styning, Sussex. "Yeats's Room," where he composed many of his great last poem, is on the first floor to the left of the entrance as seen from the house.

Edith, bare to the waist, suns herself in her garden, to Yeats's obvious delight.

Yeats's grave at Drumcliffe, the famous inscription and
Ben Bulben's head in the distance captured in the same shot by
photographer Dan Harper.

14

O My Dears

(January 1936–March 1937)

POETICALLY, YEATS'S REJUVENATION WORKED. The three years that began in Majorca in January 1936 were the most productive of his life. He wrote fifty poems, whereas he had written only seventy in the entire 1920s. The late surge, in which he continued to grow in mastery of theme and craft, was all the more remarkable because two strains in his personality—the scatty and the splendid—diverged more widely than ever.

The poems reflect an unquiet mind. "Why should not old Men be Mad?" written in the first weeks in Majorca, answers its own question; old men are mad because they know "that no better can be had." Another self-questioning poem, "What Then?" was described by Yeats himself as melancholy and biographical.[1]

All his happier dreams came true—
A small old house, wife, daughter, son,
Grounds where plum and cabbage grew,
Poets and Wits about him drew;
'*What then?' sang Plato's ghost, 'what then?'*

For a man whose life gave every appearance of discipline—he had a stable marriage, raised fine children, shaped his country, knocked an unruly theater company into order, kept his publishers happy, and his sisters' business alive—Yeats had a knack for surrounding himself with out-of-control women.

Yeats seemed not to notice as long as he was looked after. If Mrs. Gwyneth Foden came along on the Majorcan trip as the Swami's mistress, it was the least of her functions. She saw her role as that of hostess, tour leader, and nurse. Onboard ship she informed the crew that she was there to care for Dr. Yeats who suffered from heart attacks.[2]

Yeats was most anxious that Olivia Shakespear not let his mother-in-law (her sister-in-law) know of his unorthodox traveling arrangements.[3] Olivia had no illusions about Mrs. Foden's stability. As the Swami's permanent companion for four years, the woman was well-known to all those involved with the Indian Institute of Mysticism in Bayswater. She claimed that her child by the Swami had died and used this sad story to explain her fits of wild weeping and threats of suicide. She said also that she was suffering from cancer.[4] Both claims were unproved, and more alarming if false than true.

On shipboard Mrs. Foden took charge. She argued with the purser about changes of cabin. She volunteered to perform an Indian temple dance at the ship's gala, and got herself up in a sacred sari she had brought to wear at Majorca's pre-Lent carnival. Reporting back to George, Yeats described the Hindu stewards as so impressed that they lined up, with the head steward prostrating himself on the deck, to salute the holy garment.[5]

Once the travelers were installed in Palma, at the Hotel Terramar ("Own sea beach. All comforts. Central heating"), Mrs. Foden busied herself with aggressively looking after her two charges and telling them how lost they would be without her. When Yeats and the Swami, immersed in translating the Upanishads, pointed out that they had warned her she would be alone much of the time, and bored, she angrily decided they were denigrating her intellect. Things grew worse when she overheard Yeats, his tongue loosened by a strong cocktail, disparaging her book on Russia to the local British consul. She retreated to her room in a sulk and would not come out. Yeats thought of her as a troublemaker but worth having around for her social skills.

It is not clear what her value was—money apart. Mrs. Foden seems to have paid for at least some of the Swami's trip; plans were that she would accompany him back to India in June and perhaps endow an ashram. However, Yeats did like feminine company, and he is acknowledged to have had at least a brief infatuation with the lady.[6] She was also skilled, when she was in a good mood, at organizing social life. She arranged motor trips and visits to the cinema. When she discovered, for example, a very aged member of the London County Council, she invited him to lunch. Her self-imposed duties included writing gushing reports back to George about the state of health of the great poet. George cringed at the language, but felt that the letters had to be endured as the price of chaperonage.

Yet Mrs. Foden has had a bad press in Yeatsiana. The Swami, on the other hand, has got off lightly, protected by the penumbra of the holy man. He certainly could do no wrong in Yeats's eyes: "The Swami is always profound and unexpected"; "He thinks about the gods as Homer thought."[7] There was enough in his tales "to restore the poetry of the world."[8] His aphorisms were full of wisdom—"There cannot be two swords in one scabbard"[9]—and even of dietary advice—"Give an ageing man food and he turns it into poison."[10] Yeats could laugh at the way the short but massive Indian in bright pink robes preceded him slowly up and down the stairs to prevent him from walking too fast; he also welcomed the stately pacemaker. Soon he moved his room to the ground floor in accordance with the lesson to save straining his heart.

Yet Shri Purohit Swami was scarcely unworldly. He took a great deal of money from his admirers; there is no reason to think of him as any less devious or manipulative than Mrs. Foden was. The Majorcan venture clearly suited him very well. As one who also suffered from the London climate, thanks to Yeats he had the benefit of wintering in the sun in distinguished company. He had, furthermore, the prospect of joint authorship of a second book with the world-famous poet.

In truth, the delicate, passive Yeats had, in early 1936, placed himself completely in the hands of two dubious characters who might have come from a Marx Brothers comedy. And for the first time he was abroad without his wife or sophisticated friends like the Pounds to safeguard his welfare.

But there was work to be done, work that Yeats believed in. As he wrote in his introduction to the book that emerged, "Upanishad is doctrine or wisdom"; "when we turn to the east . . . [we] discover in that East something ancestral in ourselves." The task was to get into strong, simple English such truths appealing to Yeats as "Sun is the Gate of Heaven, where the wise can pass." He was pleased when he could talk the Swami out of a flowery phrase and change "maiden of surpassing loveliness" into "a pretty girl." Their book, he was sure, was going to be the classic translation of the ancient Hindu treatise. Meanwhile, he had his mornings to himself, during which he worked on his new play, *The Herne's Egg*. This required intense concentration, as he saw it as "the strangest wildest thing I have ever written."

The verse play is loosely based on the long poem "Congal," written by Samuel Ferguson in 1872, filtered through the Swami's Indian philosophy and Yeats's long-simmering thoughts on the legend that one of Leda's eggs had remained unhatched. In his play, the virginal priestess Attracta wishes to be the bride of the Great Herne, a bird representing divinity or artistic muse. However, she is dragged down to earth, literally, when raped by seven men, including the play's hero, Congal, King of Connacht. For Yeats the dramatic challenge was to differentiate all seven rapists and to present Attracta as serene and enlightened by the recognition that to have her body entered by many mortal men is a way of experiencing the divine.

*   *   *

Yeats was delighted with his new life among the palm trees. Liberated from the demands of the Abbey, the Irish Academy, and his family, and feeling as if he had passed through a doorway into a different world, he kept up an exuberant exchange of letters with the three women currently close to his heart, Margot Ruddock, Dorothy Wellesley, and Ethel Mannin. Always frank with Ethel, he revealed that Norman Haire had pronounced him "well enough for work and pleasure."

From London Margot wrote that she too was writing a play. If only she could find better help to look after her little girl, she could throw herself entirely into her exciting project; her play, she assured Yeats, was being written *"because* of you." Yeats sent back the sensible advice to continue with acting, rather than concentrating solely on writing; that way she might earn enough to hire a proper nurse.

Margot, it seems, was not entirely out of funds. That spring she sent the Swami a further twenty pounds in addition to the one hundred she had already given him.

The inevitable illness struck in the third week of January. Suddenly Yeats could not take a breath without pain and could not lie down. He slept as best he could, sitting up. A new country meant a new doctor, but the diagnosis had a familiar ring: "the overwork of years." The prescribed remedy was also as before: Yeats was to give up creative work; it was too exciting for him. He was allowed, however, to continue with the Upanishads, and the translation was soon completed. Recovered, Yeats sent Margot a detailed account of his symptoms and his suffering, saying that he did not want her to worry.

He wrote too soon. An attack of breathlessness followed, so acute that the Swami thought Yeats was going to die. The news traveled swiftly around the English colony in Palma and then to the London newspapers. The *Evening News* of January 31, 1936, carried the Reuter's flash W. B. YEATS GRAVELY ILL on its front page and reported him suffering from a heart attack. The *Evening Standard*'s front page had him "seriously ill."

In London when Raymond Lovell (Margot's husband) brought the paper home to their flat, she went into a frenzy. All that day a vision of

Yeats had been before her; she now recognized this to have been a sig-nal that he needed her. Difficult and expensive as international calls were at the time, she telephoned to Palma; the following day she sent a telegram announcing that she was flying to Yeats's side. The Swami immediately wired back to say that her presence was not required; Mrs. Yeats was on her way.

Indeed she was. Yeats had dictated a letter to the Swami, asking George if she would care to come out and and look after him. It was a polite, reasoned, and respectful letter. He knew that she would have to arrange alternative accommodation for Anne. He was aware too of the expense. However, she should consider that the money saved on hiring nurses would cover the cost of her ticket. The only other solu-tion—for him to go into a nursing home—was out of the question because of the language barrier.

Ill as he was, Yeats still had his wits about him and took the precau-tion of burning some of the highly personal correspondence he had been receiving.

Torn once again between her children and her elderly husband, George accepted where her duty now lay. She arrived in Palma by plane on the second of February. The scene she found was not pretty: Yeats gasping for breath, the Swami struggling to cope, and Mrs. Foden, for some reason, in a state of high anger at both men. And the hotel was noisy and crowded.

George took charge. Consultation with the doctor revealed that Yeats had nephritis, or kidney trouble, with residual heart and lung problems, but no congestion. He was not dying; the newspaper stories had been monstrous exaggerations. Even so, there was no question of leaving Majorca for at least three months. She felt angry; the Swami, she believed, had overworked her husband, and Mrs. Foden had been spying on both men. The solution arranged through the doctor was to rent a pleasant hillside villa nearby where Yeats could be moved, with a nurse. Anne would join them toward the end of March. The move would be cheaper than staying at the hotel, so the ever-economical George, explained in a letter to Lily and Lolly—even considering the extra cost of Anne's food.[11]

Matters were not settled so quickly, however. Mrs. Foden confronted George in front of the Hotel Terramar and demanded to know if George had ever received the many gifts that she had given Yeats in London to bring home to his wife. The very question implied that Mrs. Foden knew very well that Yeats was an unfaithful husband who had neglectfully left the various presents behind in London or possibly even given them to someone else. George found herself in the awkward position of having to admit that, apart from one green-and-gold sari, she had not seen the articles in question.[12]

What was really going on may never be known. Yeats later described it to Olivia as a "witches cauldron."[13] It is clear that George's arrival was the catalyst for the breakup not only of the traveling trio, but of the Swami's relationship with Mrs. Foden. She stormed back to London soon afterward, cursing the Swami as "a prince of evil darkness,"[14] and Yeats as a man who behaved badly and talked too much. Yeats warned Olivia to expect some "mad, threatening letters."[15] Meanwhile, he added, "Swami stays while we stay."

Yeats still liked to believe himself the center of a concerned circle of protectors. In April he wrote to Ethel, "My family have come out to look after me."[16] But his teenage children had come out to Majorca that spring to be looked after themselves.

The predicament of Anne Yeats reflects the protected status of girls of the time. Now seventeen, stage-struck, and gifted at theater design, she was expected to live at home, dependent on her parents, with no thought of higher education. Her brother, in contrast, was being formally educated at Saint Columba's School, a distinguished Protestant public school in Rathfarnham where he studied Virgil and the rest of the classical curriculum, and then would go on to Trinity College.

In their travel arrangements as in their schooling, the children were treated differently. As a girl, Anne was thought to need the protection and safety of the ship direct from Liverpool. But fifteen-year-old Michael, on the other hand, was expected to find his way to Majorca by the cheaper combination of train and ferry.

Yeats's aspirations for Anne were precisely in accord with his "Prayer for my Daughter": "In courtesy I'd have her chiefly learned." As her career progressed, he fought hard against her spending too much time hanging about the Abbey and also opposed her wish (finally granted) to go to Paris to study. As he boasted to Ernest Rhys, with no concern for how it might sound to later generations, "Her sole education is languages, the Academy Art School and my conversation."[17]

George's determined presence put a damper on Yeats's flirtatious correspondence. Not until April, living at their villa, the Casa Pastor, was he strong enough to write his own letters and thus escape the wifely censor. He wrote as one long starved. To Ethel, he reported that his potency had survived—sort of: "Only twice for months, some days ago and then last night," he said, "have I known that I was a man full of desire."

To Olivia too he was indiscreet, if less explicit. He said he was now thin and elegant and hoped to stay that way. But his liberty was in jeopardy.

> George means to look after me for the rest of my life—"You must never go away again without Anne or me"—and that will suit me not at all. . . . And O my dear—as age increases my chains, my need for freedom grows. I have no consciousness of age, no sense of declining energy, no conscious need of rest. I am unbroken.[18]

Self-preoccupied, he did not give close attention to the increasing incoherence of the Ruddock letters. These were full of non sequiturs, rambling thoughts, and protestations of not being mad in spite of what others might think. Margot was hearing voices criticizing her work: "Halve that which is done and it won't do," said one. She began to make sick jokes—how she would cut her throat from ear to ear if she were not afraid of knives, how no matter how much she drank she could not get drunk anymore. All in all, she did not sound like a person to whom one ought to write:

I do not like your recent poems. You do not work at your tec-
nic (I cannot spell the most familiar words because of my ill-
ness—this is my first real letter) you take the easiest course—
leave out the rhymes or choose the most hackeneyd rhymes,
because—damn you—you are lazy.[19]

Yeats had courted trouble, and early one wet morning in mid-May it
arrived. At 6:30 A.M., George Yeats, looking through the open window
of the Casa Pastor, found herself staring into the face of Margot
Ruddock. The young woman, distraught because Yeats had said her
poetry was getting worse, had come to Majorca to find out if he really
meant it. She said she ought to die. If her work was good, perhaps she
should die anyway, because her poems could live after her.

The Yeatses solicitously invited her in and gave her breakfast. Yeats
calmed her down, saying—as he believed—that some of her lines had tragic
magnificence. Soothed, she left and wandered out to the beach, where she
could be seen from the villa, dancing in the rain and chanting verse to her-
self. Her next stop was the pension where the Swami was staying. Seeing
that she was soaking wet, he gave her a change of clothes and some money,
and arranged a room for the night. The next day she was gone, off on the
nightboat for Barcelona, a city where she had lived and had friends.

Almost immediately the Swami left for India. Yeats went to the dock
to see him off. A photograph of them together shows a well-matched
pair, two smooth-faced, broad-fronted men, the shorter with a turban,
the taller with thick white locks, both smiling and looking immensely
pleased with themselves.

The next thing the Yeatses heard of Margot Ruddock was a message
from the British consul in Barcelona. She had been picked up by the
police after falling, or jumping, from an upper-story window, crashing
through the glass roof of a barber's shop and breaking her kneecap.
She was now in the Enfermería Evangélica, under restraint.

His own health worries put aside, Yeats, with his wife, went to
Barcelona to see what they could do for "the girl." (He always referred
to Margot as a girl, even though she was a twenty-eight-year-old twice-

married mother of two.) They found her in the hospital, seemingly recovered except for her bandaged knee. She was sane in her speech and sitting up in bed, writing the story of her recent days of hallucination and vagrancy. The couple bought her some wine; then, setting aside their usual concern for economy, accepted financial responsibility for transporting her, with a nurse, back to London. (Yeats joked to Olivia that he would not now be able to afford new clothes for a year.)

Did they believe their generosity would spare them publicity? If so, they were mistaken. The incident was tailor-made for an expatriate colony—and one where Yeats had a significant adversary. The poet Robert Graves lived in Majorca, with his partner, Laura Riding, also a poet; both had refused permission for their work to be included in Yeats's anthology because he had rejected the poetry of James Reeves, a young poet they had just published, as too realistic. Graves saw the Margot scandal as a tragi-comic sequel to Yeats's sexual operation and knew it would furnish café gossip for the island for months.[20] It was fodder for the English and Irish papers too. Yeats blamed Margot's publicity-seeking actor-husband for alerting the press.

The story, carried on the Reuter's newswire, appeared on the front pages of at least three London papers, as well as in the *Manchester Guardian* and the *Dublin Evening News.* Several of the reports coupled the actress's fall with her visit to W. B. Yeats. Margot was referred to by her married name, Margot Lovell. The inference was obvious: Reuter's flash, which appeared in the prominent Late News box in the *News Chronicle,* reported, on May 13, 1937:

> **Barcelona, Tuesday. Margot Lovell (27), of Westbourne Gardens, London, W., fell from a window here tonight and was injured. She had come from Majorca, where she went with a view to the poet Yeats reading poetry she had written.**

By Saturday, May 16, a few days after the story had changed to BRITISH POETESS "GREATLY IMPROVED," there was an item in the *Dublin Evening Mail,* under "Fashion and Gossip in Dublin Today," by "Maeve."

Headed "W. B. YEATS," it sounds like a plant to counteract any suggestion in the earlier stories that there might have been an improper relationship between Yeats and Margot. "Maeve" drew a picture of happy family life *chez* Yeats:

> W. B. Yeats, who is in Mallorca, is better, but he will not be home this summer. He is now bound to remain there, for he and Mrs. Yeats have rented a home for three months and are very happy out there. They have their children, Michael and Anne, with them. The house, I am told, is a unique one, of which both Mr and Mrs Yeats are very proud. It is the only one in Mallorca without steps at the entrance. They spent a long time looking for it and are pleased with their choice. The weather is beautiful and ought to set W. B. Yeats on his feet again.[21]

In June, returned to Dublin, with Anne and three hundredweight of luggage, George received a registered letter from Mrs. Foden. There was no one, said the excited woman, for whom she felt sorrier than George Yeats: "Your illustrious husband cannot claim that his visit to Palma was a flaming success, can he?" The ghastly episode had caused wounds that would never heal. Only a superhuman effort had saved her in Palma from being driven to a similar fate by those two disreputable men. Her only hope was that Yeats, an old man, would make peace with his Maker and also make every restitution in his power, not least to his wife and children, before he left this world. For herself, she would never be able to resolve the contradictions in his character between genius and immorality.[22]

Yeats was in London, by himself at last. Wisely he determined not to see Margot. In no other way, however, did he turn his back on her or her work. He believed that madness was a form of spiritual ecstasy.[23] All he asked from her was to refrain from immediate publication of her account of the incident for both their sakes.[24] Yet at the same time, he wrote an introduction to accompany a selection of her poems to appear in the July issue of the *London Mercury*—hardly a way to dissociate their names. Also, before May was out, he wrote the touching poem "At Barcelona," which would later accompany her story when it was made into a small book, *The Lemon Tree,* published the following year.

"A Crazed Girl," the title under which "At Barcelona" appears among Yeats's *Last Poems,* captures the beauty of madness; it pays Margot the further tribute of using a line from her ranting beach song: "O sea-starved, hungry sea." Yeats did more. Some months later he wrote "Sweet Dancer," which ends:

> If strange men come from the house
> To lead her away, do not say
> That she is happy being crazy;
> Lead them gently astray;
> Let her finish her dance,
> Let her finish her dance.
> *Ah, dancer, ah, sweet dancer!*

By 1938 when this poem (almost a preview of the final scene in Tennessee Williams's *A Streetcar Named Desire*) was published, Margot Ruddock was locked away in a mental institution, where she remained until her death in 1951 at the age of forty-four.

Recovery from the Barcelona episode took a surprising form: Yeats fell more deeply in love with Dorothy Wellesley. Even before the drama, he had invited himself for a long stay at Penns in the Rocks when he returned from Spain. He explained to Dorothy, as he had to Olivia, that he was facing a long period in Dublin, "for months being looked after which I shall not like."[25]

The stage was set for a new degree of intimacy. In their frequent letters, Yeats and Dorothy had moved, with much seeking of the other's permission, to a first-name basis, or close to it. She became "My dear Dorothy," and he "My dear W. B.," the latter agreed upon because, as he still believed, "I have a detestable Christian name."[26] After Margot, Dorothy was a cool and intelligent delight, skilled as a poet, racy in talk, in tune with his own ideas on poetry, and opposed to the bleak mundanities of the Auden-Eliot camp. Her house remained the finest refuge he had found since Coole.

Over the previous months, he had introduced the occasional ribald reference into his letters. The modernists, he told Dorothy, knowing that she would agree with him, failed to appreciate that poets must be good liars and must never forget that the muses are women who like "the embrace of gay warty lads."[27]

When they met, they were reminded how much they liked one another's looks. Dorothy's pale, fine-boned face seemed to Yeats "the most beautiful of Chinese lanthorns [lanterns]."[28] She admired his thick white hair, his expressive brown hands, his excited, darting eyes. As for his clothes, she was dazzled: "the most elegant Bohemian sort that our generation has seen. He was always immaculately clean, always precisely shaved ... His suits were of soft corn or brown tweeds, with bright blue shirt or dark green, and always with handkerchief to match."[29]

During that summer, they evolved a form of sexual congress unique to their requirements. That Yeats had difficulties was no secret. All his friends knew of the Steinach operation and the condition it was intended to remedy. Virginia Woolf did a good imitation of Yeats describing his cure. One night, he told her, he had seen a coat hanger emerge from his cupboard and travel across the foot of his bed; the next night the hanger emerged again, wearing one of his jackets; the third night, a hand protruded from one of the cuffs, and the fourth night ... "Ah! Mrs. Woolf, that would be a long story; enough to say, I finally recovered my potency."[30]

Dorothy, although in an apparently stable relationship with Hilda Matheson, had her own problems, which were to climax in two breakdowns the following year, and in severe alcoholism.

That summer she and Yeats began sending back and forth versions of a ribald ballad in which a high-born woman who wishes to make love to a nobleman has her chambermaid do it for her under cover of darkness. In version after version, the two poets tossed bodily images back and forth, climbing on each other's words, with much coy flirtation and challenge.

That this communal composition was a sexual exercise Yeats left no doubt: "Ah my dear how it added to my excitement when I remade that poem of yours to know it was your poem. I remade you and myself into a single being."[31] In writing to her, he repeatedly used the refrain from his ballad, "*O my dear, O my dear.*"

This code of three little words appears increasingly in Yeats's intimate correspondence with other women too. "O my dear" or "my dear" invariably signals love and sexual longing, with a touch of the naughty old man–young girl frisson that he found exciting. In one of his versions of the chambermaid ballads, the nobleman commands, "Lie down again dear child."

Playing this game was an ingenious way for the impotent poet to make love to the lesbian lady. For Yeats it had the further advantage of allowing him to indulge once again one of his favorite fantasies, from Villiers de l'Isle-Adam's *Axël:* "As for living, our servants will do that for us." It also allowed them to exchange gender roles. In one much-quoted letter to Dorothy, he said of her poetry, "Your lines have the magnificent swing of your boyish body."[32] In another:

> My dear, my dear—when you crossed the room with that boy-
> ish movement, it was no man who looked at you, it was the
> woman in me. It seems that I can make a woman express her-
> self as never before, I have looked out of her eyes. I have
> shared her desire.[33]

For Yeats the titillating exercise resulted in a sequence of seven poems, beginning with the long ballad "The Three Bushes," in which the lady gives her instructions to her maid:

> 'So you must lie beside him
> And let him think me there
> . . . .
> And maybe we are all the same
> That strip the body bare.'
> *O my dear, O my dear.*

The sequence grows coarser as the story progresses and descends the social scale. It ends with the six lines of "The Chambermaid's Second Song":

From pleasure of the bed,
Dull as a worm,
His rod and its butting head
Limp as a worm,
His spirit that has fled
Blind as a worm.

This "worm-poem" was too much for Dorothy. "Otherwise there are lovely things my dear; but like all women I dislike worms . . . Can you think of something to take the place of the worms?"[34]

Back in the security of his household at Rathfarnham, although he stayed in bed and in his room until noon, Yeats woke at four in the morning and was hard at work soon after. He wrote to Dorothy, "A mass of new subjects (not now on sex) are crowding upon me."[35] He finished "Lapis Lazuli" and added the tale of the impotent Oxford lover to his revised introduction for the not-yet-reissued *A Vision*. He was pleased with this tale of the young man who could make love to a woman only if his friend bedded her first. Not only did it mimic the poems he had just written but it was drawn from real life—or at least from what had been told to him as true by an American woman student in Oxford.

He arrived back in Ireland bearing a medical report from his Spanish doctor; he gave it unopened to Gogarty, who tried to conceal the contents. He insisted on being told. When Gogarty obliged and read out, "We have here an antique cardiosclerotic of advanced years," he was delighted. "You know, Gogarty," he said, "I'd rather be called cardiosclerotic, than Lord of Lower Egypt."[36]

He was extremely pleased when he finished the "Lapis Lazuli" poem and pronounced it one of the best he had ever written. A few days later he wrote "To D.W." (first printed under the title "To a

Friend" and later as "To Dorothy Wellesley"). After sending it to Dorothy and following it with corrections, he signed himself, "Yours in love, W. B. Yeats."[37]

The Wellesley poem has aged. The lines, "What climbs the stair? / Nothing that common women ponder on / If you are worth my hope!" can sound snobbish if "common" is understood in terms of class rather than ability. In contrast, "Lapis Lazuli" remains fresh, with its joyous epigram, "All things fall and are built again / And those that build them are gay."

How deeply did Yeats feel the tragic joy that runs through his last poems? The eminent American scholar Harold Bloom was skeptical in his critical study *Yeats*. He disputed "Lapis Lazuli's" assertion that "Hamlet and Lear are gay; / Gaiety transfiguring all that dread."

But Lear is not, by any reading, gay, Bloom declares. To him, this line, when set alongside Yeats's dismissal of Wilfred Owen as "all blood, dirt & sucked sugar stick," cast grave doubts on Yeats's gifts as critic or as philosopher. So did his unwarranted praise for Dorothy Wellesley's poetry. "Perhaps we might be a little wary of the message of affirmation that Yeats brings us," Bloom said.[38] On the other hand, he greatly admired "To Dorothy Wellesley," calling it an enduring monument to a friendship—evidence that Yeats's pre-eminence lay in the love lyric.

George Yeats was well aware that Yeats had formed an attachment to his titled hostess. In the summer of 1936 Lady Ottoline Morrell, visiting them in Dublin, had taken George aside and told her that her husband was safe in Dorothy's hands; Dorothy, Ottoline said (with an obvious dig at Margot), was "no minx."[39]

As before, George seemed not to mind as long as Yeats stayed healthy. When the BBC that summer invited him to give its annual National Lecture in the autumn, she would not let him accept until he had done a trial reading at home, out loud, with suitable expression, for three-quarters of an hour, to see if he could stand the strain. Yeats tried and passed the test, to his great pleasure. The BBC was offering to pay him one hundred pounds; he had been chosen over fourteen others, and he would be allowed to speak on modern poetry.[40]

In the BBC invitation Yeats saw the chance for another long visit to Penns in the Rocks. He now wrote of it to Dorothy as "the perfect country house" where there was "lettered peace" in beautiful countryside. "O my dear, let me stay longer than a week," he implored. He calculated that as the lecture was scheduled for October 11, he could go to her as early as the end of September.

George consented, and sent Dorothy a typed slip of instructions on Yeats's diet, and, as if he were a hyperactive child, on his required hours of rest. He was to be made to lie down (or sit by himself) for one hour between lunch and tea and for another two hours between tea and dinner. She knew how obstinate he was; sometimes the only way to force him to rest was to "plant him in a room by himself with a detective story and leave him sternly alone."[41] George concluded, pointedly, that this visit was very likely going to be his last trip to England—certainly the last that he would make unaccompanied.

In the event, Yeats managed two trips to Penns, before and after the BBC lecture. In it, he managed to pay several fulsome tributes to the work of Dorothy Wellesley, as well as to cast a nice dig at T. S. Eliot for whom "poetry must resemble prose . . . Tristram and Isoult were not a more suitable theme than Paddington Railway Station."[42] He sent so few letters home that George feared he had caught another cold and begged him to send for her before he became too ill.[43]

He was not ill; the time with Dorothy was all he hoped for. They parted with "an intimate understanding between them," he wrote in gratitude, and more:

> O my dear I thank you for that spectacle of personified sunlight. I can never while I live forget your movement across the room just before I left, the movement made to draw attention to the boy in yourself.[44]

Back in his Rathfarnham bedroom, he wrote Dorothy a description of his surroundings: the windows looking out onto the gardens, the walls hung with paintings, drawings, and photographs, the desk covered with letters to be answered and proofs to be corrected. The discordant note was the image he saw every morning in his dressing table mirror: an old man. "'O my dear, O my dear.'"[45]

Not long after writing his love poem to one who was superior to "common women," Yeats sent off a guinea to the Eugenics Society for a year's membership. The wonder is that it took him so long. Considering his friendship with Haire, his own careful family planning, and his deep belief in ancient blood lines, he was late climbing on the bandwagon. So late that the movement, under the influence of the biologist Julian Huxley, one of its vice presidents, was moving away from its fixation on breeding stock and toward a recognition of the importance of nurture as well as nature in human development. In his Galton lecture in 1936, Huxley claimed that until all groups and classes enjoyed similar nutrition, it was meaningless to attribute constitutional inferiority to any group or class; social programs, therefore, were the way to improve the human race.[46] Yeats, however, reading his first complimentary copy of the *Eugenics Review,* is likely to have been more interested in the main article: "Is National Intelligence Declining?"

November 1936 saw the publication of his *Oxford Book of Modern Verse, 1892–1935.* He had invited ridicule with his eccentric and self-indulgent selection, and now he got it. His friends and cronies were conspicuously overrepresented at the expense of far better poets. W. J. Turner had twelve entries.[47] Margot Ruddock was rewarded with seven, W. H. Auden with a mere three; Dorothy Wellesley had eight to T. S. Eliot's seven. Ezra Pound got only three but would have had more had he not charged too much. (Yeats anyway had doubts about the quality of Ezra's poetry, with its uncontrolled ranting and self-interrupting, and cut his number of selections way down when Ezra demanded five guineas per poem; his own fee for anthologies was two.) His scholarly friend Frank Sturm made the grade. Wilfred Owen was left out entirely. In general, England's war poets got short shrift.

The war always had been a blind spot for Yeats. About Wilfred

---

*Sir Francis Galton (1822–1911), cousin of Darwin, was the founder of eugenics and one of the first to apply mathematics to biological problems.

Owen and the rest, he was frank: "I have a distaste for certain poems written in the midst of the great war." Catastrophic events that were someone else's responsibility were "passive suffering," "not a theme for poetry . . . some blunderer has driven his car on to the wrong side of the road—that is all."

He also justified including poems by nineteenth-century figures such as Walter Pater and Oscar Wilde in his modern anthology, saying that "even a long-lived man has the right to call his own contemporaries modern."[48]

That did not save him. He was roundly scored, not only for ignoring the century's greatest trauma but for self-indulgence and excessive loyalty to his friends, particularly to Dorothy Wellesley and "the Irish brigade," as it was called by H. A. Mason, writing in *Scrutiny*. Mason said, "It seems a counsel of despair to entrust the selection to one whose taste is merely eccentric. . . . It seems probable that the greater part of what has been written between 1892 and 1935 just hasn't interested him at all."

To John Sparrow, on the other hand, writing (anonymously) in the *Times Literary Supplement,* "The personal character of this selection, however, does not upset its balance; it provides a fair, if not a full, conspectus of the poetry of the last half-century." The reviewer in *The Times* also refused to cavil at Yeats's principles of selection: "Greatness, even where it is wilful, is given us to learn from, not to teach."[49] Over the years, the criticism continued. W. H. Auden held up *The Oxford Book of Modern Verse* as prime evidence for the prosecution of the case against Yeats. The sorry collection showed, Auden charged, how little Yeats understood his own age.[50] Whatever its failings, however, this controversial anthology is remembered best for its introduction, with its light-hearted dismissal of fin de siècle millenarianism:

> Then in 1900 everybody got down off his stilts; henceforth nobody drank absinthe with his black coffee; nobody went mad; nobody committed suicide; nobody joined the Catholic church; or if they did I have forgotten.[51]

Yeats's publisher, the Clarendon Press, was delighted with the reception; the anthology was an instant best-seller, with fifteen thousand copies sold in three months. They thanked him for being so controversial and gave him a further advance on royalties.

"Here," Yeats wrote to Dorothy Wellesley on December 9, 1936, "is my final apology." It was a new poem, "The Spur," directly addressed to readers shocked by the unseemly exhibition of geriatric lasciviousness:

> **You think it horrible that lust and rage**
> **Should dance attendance upon my old age;**
> **They were not such a plague when I was young;**
> **What else have I to spur me into song?**

Rage spurred a number of political poems that autumn and winter. Adopting once more the rollicking ballad form favored by his crony Higgins and highly suited to Cuala's new series of monthly *Broadsides,* Yeats wrote "Come Gather Round Me, Parnellites," based on what had been told him about how the Protestant Parnell had been tricked by the Catholic O'Shea, the husband of his lover, Mrs. Kitty O'Shea. He wrote also two ballads in praise of Sir Roger Casement. Casement, a British consular officer turned Irish republican, was executed by the British in 1916 as a traitor for attempting to organize German aid for an Irish rebellion, and was stripped of his knighthood before being hanged.

Yeats's anger was roused in December 1936 when he read *The Forged Casement Diaries,* a new book claiming that the notorious diaries of homosexual encounters, texts circulated by British authorities before and after Casement's trial and death sentence, had been fabricated.[52] His impassioned ballad named Spring-Rice, the former British ambassador to the United States, as having been one of the culprits who "turned a trick by forgery / And blackened his good name." "Roger Casement" went off to what Yeats called "de Valera's newspaper"—the *Irish Press,* established by de Valera with his American funds.

He sent a copy too to Ethel Mannin, the most politically minded of his confidantes. In doing so, he knew he had to justify himself. Months earlier Ethel, with the playwright Ernst Toller, had implored Yeats to use his influence as a Nobel laureate to nominate the German pacifist, poet, and editor Karl von Ossietsky for the Nobel Peace Prize. Ossietsky, in a Nazi concentration camp since 1933, was known to be suffering from tuberculosis; winning the prize might get him released and save his life.

In an awkward meeting in London at Claridge's Hotel, Yeats had sat distressed and uncomfortable while the two writers pleaded Ossietsky's case. When they finished, he refused sorrowfully to lend his name. He was not familiar with Ossietsky's work; more important, he saw it as no part of a poet's business to become involved in politics. Such interest as he had, he said, was confined entirely to Irish affairs; Ireland had nothing to do with Europe politically.*

Once in Majorca, however, Yeats felt the need to justify himself all over again. In a moving letter to Ethel that shows how very far he was from his protestation to have given up remorse, he wrote, "If I did what you want, I would seem to hold one form of government more responsible than any other, and that would betray my convictions." All forms of government and religion were guilty, he said, according to the number of their victims. "I have not been silent; I have used the only vehicle I possess—verse." He suggested she read "The Second Coming." The poem would show that he had foreseen the gathering storm: "I am not callous, every nerve trembles with horror at what is happening in Europe." He begged her not to cast him out of her affections.[53]

This nerve-trembling was hardly the ringing denunciation of Hitler that some wish Yeats had made. He had not condemned Nazi Germany as many other writers had done once the book burnings had started in 1933, and had accepted (but not in person) in February 1934 the Goethe Prize from the city of Frankfurt.

---

*Ossietsky won the Nobel Peace Prize in 1936 anyway. Although the Nazis did not allow him to collect it in person, they released him (under police supervision) two years later. He died shortly after in a Berlin hospital from the effects of his imprisonment.

Yeats's neutrality, however, must be set in context. That he was never interested in any but Irish politics was the truth. Ireland itself was to remain neutral in World War II, while in World War I, Ulster apart, it had been cool to the call to defeat Germany. James Joyce sat out the 1915–18 years in neutral Zurich, writing *Ulysses*. He said at the time that he did not care which side won.

But on Casement, Yeats *was* willing to fight. The facts of Casement's private behavior did not concern Yeats. "If Casement were a homo-sexual, what matter?" he wrote Dorothy, restating a position that had been clear since his support for Oscar Wilde.[54] As far as Yeats was con-cerned, if Dorothy Wellesley was a lesbian, what matter? He approved of love in all forms. When he looked at her boyish body, he told Dorothy, he wished that he "could be a girl of nineteen for certain hours."[55] It was the thought of forgery that had enraged him, reviving his Irish bitterness at the injustice inflicted on his country by gold braid and ermine.

When Ethel Mannin, with her own Irish sympathies, received "Roger Casement," she took Yeats to task for inconsistency. The ballad pro-claimed a deep hatred of England. Yet was Yeats not still drawing an annual pension from the British Crown?

Touché!—or it should have been. Yeats would not concede that he had been wounded. Of course he did not hate the people of England: "considering all I owe to Shakespeare, Blake, Morris—they are the one people I cannot hate."[56] Their government and its policies were another matter. As for the Civil List pension of £150 a year, yes, he still received it. He rehearsed the conditions under which it had been offered to him twice, for "intellectual services," and, on the second occasion, accepted:

It was given at a time when Ireland was represented in parlia-ment and voted out of the taxes of both countries. It is not voted annually, my surrender of it would not leave a vacancy for anybody else. . . . The second time it was offered it was explained to me that it implied no political bargain. . . .

I consider that I have earned that pension by services done to the people.[57]

The letter went on to describe himself and Ethel as revolutionaries who had found a way to fight yet keep their independence. He concluded, after discoursing on his dislike of the bigoted form of Catholicism gaining strength in Ireland, that he could not recall ever having written so much in self-defense.

Ethel's good opinion meant a great deal to him. He had already sent her the "worm-poem," copying it out by hand because he had no typist; he sent her "The Spur" too, to explain his lust and rage. He addressed her effusively, "Mother goddess, I put your hand to my lips"; if at times he sounded distant, he was, he said, merely afraid of quarreling with her about politics: "my dear, though bold in public speech and public writing, I am a timid man."[58]

This tender correspondence was carried on in tandem with his involvement with Dorothy Wellesley, to whom he often was sending not only the same poems but the same words, such as "How can I hate England, owing what I do to Shakespeare, Blake & Morris. England is the only country I cannot hate."[59]

He was careful not to name Ethel to Dorothy, but rather described her dismissively as "an Irishwoman in England" and an "extreme revolutionist." He did not mention that the "Irishwoman" was a former lover, one of his dearest friends, and one of England's best-known writers. "Limp as a worm" he may have been; he still enjoyed the power of keeping his women in ignorance of one another.

Late 1936 was a time for Irish reassessment of attitudes to things English. On December 10, King Edward VIII abdicated his throne for love of Mrs. Wallis Simpson. Supporting the king was a way of defying Britain. Yeats took the ex-king's side easily, consistent with his belief in divorce;[60] he admired, moreover, the quiet restraint of the abdication speech. He sensed that the Irish young generally were siding with Edward. Ethel Mannin certainly did; she said she drank to the king for the first time in her life. In contrast, the very English Olivia Shakespear recoiled from the thought of

Mrs. Simpson near the throne: "The female isn't even properly divorced
... She is evidently a rowdy & common sort of woman."[61]

For the Irish government, the abdication crisis provided a perfect
opportunity to act on the hallowed Wolfe Tone principle, "England's
difficulty is Ireland's opportunity." While Britain's attention was other-
wise engaged, de Valera moved, as he had long wished, to undo the
terms of the 1921 treaty. He abolished the oath of allegiance to the
king, and the post of British governor-general in Ireland as well. He
prepared a new constitution, making Ireland a republic in all but
name. He redesigned the Senate to give it fewer nonelected members.
He changed the name of the country too: the "Irish Free State"
became simply "Ireland," or, in Irish, "Eire."

Early in 1937 Yeats, complaining of the exhaustion the Casement bal-
lads had cost him, dreamed of going to India and rejoining the Swami;
he would "hide myself there for a time." He went so far as to write to
his friend Lady Elizabeth Pelham, a member of the Swami's London
institute, to ask her if she would join him on the trip. But Lady
Elizabeth, replying that she had given up all personal friendships in
pursuance of her belief in Alma-vidya, the science of self, suggested
that Yeats consider going to India alone. However, if the "Master" (the
Swami's guru) wished her to go, she said loyally, she would go.

Hearing of Yeats's inclination, both holy men urged him to come to
India and lecture. But Yeats changed his mind, giving a highly original
excuse. The operation that had revived his creative power had also
revived his sexual desire in a way that would last the rest of his life: "I
believe that if I repressed this for any long period I would break down
under the strain as did the great Ruskin."[62]

Yeats said much the same for public consumption. "The Wild Old
Wicked Man," written just after the rejection of the Indian trip, is as
coarse and nakedly confessional as he was ever to get. In this bouncing
ballad (full of "my dear"s), the crude old lecher, "his stout stick under
his hand," propositions a religious young woman to make love to him
even though he is of the age to die:

'Because I am mad about women
I am mad about the hills,'
Said that wild old wicked man
Who travels where God wills.
'Not to die on the straw at home,
Those hands to close these eyes,
That is all I ask, my dear,
From the old man in the skies.'
Daybreak and a candle-end.

'Kind are all your words, my dear,
Do not the rest withhold.
Who can know the year, my dear,
When an old man's blood grows cold?'

The rest of this stanza addresses the question that cannot help but form in the mind of the reader facing the evidence of the doddery Yeats snaring woman after woman:

'I have what no young man can have
Because he loves too much.
Words I have that can pierce the heart,
But what can he do but touch?'
Daybreak and a candle-end

If the old poet is no match in performance with a younger man, he has superior ways of seduction. At the same time he is pretending nothing. The refrain after each bawdy stanza is a repetitive confession of burnt-out power: *"Daybreak and a candle-end."* This unrepentant poem shows Yeats, as he had told Ethel, regretting nothing. Far from being another "final apology," it is a final defiance of Catholic Ireland and, one suspects, of his wife:

'But a coarse old man am I,
I choose the second-best,

I forget it all awhile
Upon a woman's breast.'
Daybreak and a candle-end

This poem, first published in *The Atlantic Monthly* in April 1938, shows how true Yeats was to his creed that poetry was his politics and that a poet's war is the war with himself. His conscience required him at the end of his life to reveal himself as he was, as a confused, vulgar, sometimes generous, but often selfish old lecher.

His flagrant self-exposure stands in stark contrast to his widow's wish to cover him up. George Yeats told Richard Ellmann of having promised Yeats that when he was gone and she was asked about his love affairs, "I shall say nothing because I will remember how proud you were."[63] Her understandable reticence ignores the pride he had in flaunting the affairs.

How could he hate England, being a member of the Athenaeum? On February 16, 1937, the distinguished club offered him membership, under its Rule 2, which allows men of literary, artistic, scientific, or ecclesiastical distinction to be admitted without an entrance fee. (Rule 4 gives honorary membership to the prime minister.)

In the two decades since Lady Gregory advised him to join a London club, Yeats had progressed from the respectability of the Royal Societies to the sophistication of the Savile to the splendor of the Athenaeum. Was this last a wise move? His fellow new members were the permanent secretary to the Treasury and a Cambridge University professor of applied mathematics.[64] When H. G. Wells made the same move, he regretted it and eventually returned to the Savile, saying, "Thank God. This is the Athenaeum for the living."[65] But Yeats did not want to go back. A decided advantage to him was that, unlike the Savile, the Athenaeum had (and has still) a ladies' annex in which female guests could be entertained to lunch. More than that, he confessed to Dorothy Wellesley, he had always had "a childish desire to walk up those steps & under that classical facade—it seems to belong to folk lore like 'London Bridge' & that is my subject."[66]

This was strange talk from an "Irish revolutionist"—even one belonging in Dublin to the landowning bastion, the Kildare Street Club. Yeats maintained that he was more comfortable working in Ireland "because I am not afraid of anybody and most people are afraid of me. It is the reverse in London."[67] Actually, the reverse was true—at least when he was not working. In Ireland he was a public figure regarded with some animosity and suspicion by militant Catholics, who were more alert than ever to the moral threat emanating from remnants of the Anglo-Irish intelligentsia. With alarm Yeats learned that a priest had warned that the Catholics of Ireland would not always be patient; Yeats took this as a threat of mob violence. "An ignorant form of Catholicism is my enemy," he told Ethel.[68] He feared the possibility that General Eoin O'Duffy and his seven hundred Blueshirt volunteers, then fighting for Franco, might return from Spain as heroes. If that happened, "my 'pagan' institutions, the Theatre, the Academy, will be fighting for their lives against Catholic or Gaelic bigotry."[69]

All considered, it was not the best time to offer the Abbey a verse play about a virgin goddess raped by seven men. The Abbey board, always respectful to its founder's work, reacted with shock to *The Herne's Egg*, even though one member generously interpreted the seven rapists as the seven sacraments. Yeats withdrew the play. He was just as glad, he said; he was too old for riots; although the work would not be performed, Macmillan would publish the play anyway. He himself did not know what *The Herne's Egg* meant except that it was Rabelaisian.[70]

In the spring of 1937, Yeats was in many ways more English than ever. (Hugh Kenner has estimated that over his lifetime Yeats spent less time in Ireland than James Joyce, "the professional exile," had done.)[71] If politically, artistically, and domestically he was committed to Ireland, England remained for him a haven of tolerance, urbanity, and freedom. He could not have carried on his romantic intrigues in Ireland; he enjoyed being a star of the BBC. Now he was about to find, through an Englishwoman, something that through a long life had largely eluded him: happiness.

15

Such Friends

(April 1937–January 1938)

YEATS OFFERS an easy ride to English-language journalists and politicians. His rich phrases make anybody's prose sound better; his lapidary epigrams provide a sharp start or finish for the unfocused editorial and rambling speech. In the London *Sunday Express,* on October 17, 1926, Edith Shackleton, the First Lady of Fleet Street, drew on reliable Yeats to open her weekly article:

> Some years ago the poet Yeats wrote in his diary: "My father says, 'A man does not love a woman because he thinks her clever or because he admires her, but because he likes the way she has of scratching her head.'"[1]

The wry essay that followed, "Wives—And the Other Woman: The Indefinable Mysteries of Charm," mocked the lawsuits that were being brought by angry wives against other women "on the grounds that they have enticed their husbands away." The writer took the idea a step further.

> If wives are actually going to sink to the ignominy of prosecuting other women for being more attractive than themselves, it ought to be made possible for other women to prosecute wives for allowing their husbands' affections to run so to waste that they become a public nuisance.

In April 1937 Edith Shackleton Heald (her full name) became the other woman in Yeats's life. She was unmarried, and proud of it. The vantage point from which she wrote her well-regarded contributions to the press was that of a spinster (as she called herself) and a feminist: an amusing, forthright, shrewd defender of equal rights and equal pay. She defended a woman's choice to remain single, "to Be Forty and Not Think It Ghastly,"[2] and to claim to understand children without having any.

A pioneer in women's journalism, she made herself an acerbic reporter on the sex war and shifting gender roles. She defended "bachelor women" and ridiculed the folly of trying to please men. "If there is anything in feminism, women must surely now cease to regard themselves as lumps of turkish delight to be bought, sold and rewarded according to their fascination."[3] Women, she preached, must give up the idea that "to lose love is as humiliating as to lose respect or friendship."[4]

Edith Shackleton Heald, like Olivia Shakespear, has been undervalued as a love of Yeats's life. This is largely her own doing. When in the early 1950s Allan Wade was preparing *The Letters of W.B. Yeats* for publication, with George still alive, Edith expertly edited out all the highly personal passages from the poet's letters to her before handing them over. However, she kept the originals, which show clearly that she was the light of his last years. He wrote her genuine love letters, brimming with "O my dears," with happiness, gratitude, and longing. Unlike his experience with his other mistresses, his feeling for her grew stronger as the months went by.

There is little doubt that it was a physical affair, consummated as far as was possible with his myriad infirmities. He spent weeks at a time at Edith's house in Sussex. They holidayed together. He signed himself in his letters to her as her lover. There was nothing furtive about their affair. On one summer's day, he was photographed sitting in a deck-chair in the garden of The Chantry House, gazing delightedly at Edith sunning herself on a mat, bare to the waist.

At fifty-three, Edith was the oldest of his late loves, and the most girlish. Tiny ("I am taller than Queen Victoria"),[5] dwarfed by his massive bulk, she was past her youthful prettiness but pleasantly pert, with a wide, curved mouth, turned-up nose, and merry eyes. Yeats's good friend Edmund Dulac, and his partner, Helen Beauclerk, who had introduced them, called her "Kokosha," Russian for "little kitten."[6] Conversationally, Edith was more cat than kitten. Highly intelligent and witty, she was adept at the unanswerable sharp remark: a kinder, gentler Dorothy Parker. The *Times* obituary in 1976 which praised her serenity and wisdom also acknowledged the centrality of the Yeats relationship in her life; its opening sentence defined her as "essayist, critic and friend of W. B. Yeats."[7]

Edith, born in Manchester, lived with her sister, Nora Heald, also unmarried, also a woman journalist of repute (as editor of the weekly magazine *The Lady*). Their mother, to whom the sisters were devoted, had lived with them until her death in 1934. Their father had departed during their adolescence under a cloud of drink and scandal and was never spoken of. A beloved brother, Ivan Heald, who was for a time Fleet Street's most acclaimed humorous writer and who had introduced Edith to journalism, was killed during the war while serving with the Royal Flying Corps.

In 1934 the Heald sisters, having decided to make their lives together, bought The Chantry House, a Queen Anne enlargement of a sixteenth-century priests' home in the small west Sussex village of Steyning, below the downs and about five miles from the sea. Once the enormous labor of renovating the house and sheds was done, and the garden re-created, they settled in with their books, paintings, gramophone records, and period furniture. The house was within a few hours' motoring of Yeats's other country home-away-from-home, Penns in the Rocks, in Withyham. Although not as grand, it was well appointed, with servants, wine cellar, motorcar, dog, gravel drive, walled gardens, and orchard.

Once The Chantry House was finished, Edith gave up active journalism and retreated to the country and to book reviewing, an art at which she was, in the opinion of the novelist Arnold Bennett, brilliant. On his recommendation she succeeded him (briefly) as literary editor of the London *Evening Standard* in 1931. Like Yeats's other highly successful woman friend, Ethel Mannin, she had an Irish connection, which she fostered by owning a cottage in Donegal. Her mother, Mary Shackleton, had been born in Ulster; a distant cousin, the famous antarctic explorer Sir Ernest Shackleton, also Irish, had made Shackleton a household name.

All his life Yeats fell in love easily, and in April 1937 when Dulac brought him down to Steyning, he did so again. The amusing, serene, well-read, and amiable Edith was not an improbable choice for a man of nearly seventy-two, while she for her part was not ill-disposed to being taken up by a man old enough to be her father, whose towering, nonthreatening presence suggested comfort and a need of comforting. Nora Heald liked him too. Again, his great fame must not be forgotten; the gregarious Nobel laureate was a trophy for a household that prided itself on good conversation and interesting guests.

Edith had fallen under Yeats's formidable platform spell as a young woman. In 1910 he had visited Manchester where she was starting out as a journalist. Subsequent acquaintance must have followed, for in 1929 in the *Daily Express* she listed among the small number of men who interested her "Yeats whose grave manners and melodious conversation seem to take one back to a more spacious ancient world, who can be as practical as any other Irishman (which is saying a lot) and yet sees the fairies and has dealings with spirits."[8] He was in good company. The others on her published list were "Shaw, Wells, Dulac, Einstein and the King."

★　　　★　　　★

Yeats arrived in London early in March 1937 to prepare for the first two of four programs for the BBC. *The Ten Principal Upanishads* was also about to be published.

Yeats and radio were made for each other. His voice was beautiful, his poems popular, his ear phenomenal. In the many rehearsals for the broadcasts (such was the formality of radio's early days), his BBC producer, George Barnes, remarked to himself how strange it was that Yeats was utterly tone-deaf to music, yet his ear for sound was sensitive beyond belief and picked up nuances of intonation that others could hardly hear.[9] Yeats enjoyed broadcasting. A BBC photograph of "Yeats at the Microphone" shows him looking relaxed and mischievous, in his characteristic light-colored, rough-textured three-piece suit, with soft, darkish shirt and carelessly knotted matching bow tie—the poet dressed as his unseen audience would want him to be.

Yeats was, for once, in excellent health, but in a curious state of mind. The self-inventing machine had not stopped. "Myself I must remake," he wrote in a new poem, "An Acre of Grass." Yet he had just emerged from a period of, in his own words, "a particularly black attack," hardly welcome even though he knew, he said, that despair was the source of his poetry.[10] There was much to disturb him. The infernal Mrs. Foden was badgering George as well as a number of their friends with unpleasant letters insinuating blackmail, while he found on reaching London that his good friend Ottoline Morrell now refused to see him. He had irredeemably offended her by singling out for praise, in the widely read introduction to his poetry anthology, a novel that caricatured her—*The Aesthetes,* by W. J. Turner.

"I still cannot understand what induced you to write as you did," Ottoline wrote him on March 10. "The book after all was not poetry. There was no need for you to mention it at all."[11]

Perhaps this was the violent emotional upset to which he referred when he wrote to Ethel Mannin saying that something terrible had happened about which he urgently needed to see her alone. They should meet for dinner and talk afterward, without the rattle of plates. Staying at the Athenaeum for the first time, he suggested dining at the club's ladies' annex, or, if she did not want to dress, at his old favorite haunt, The Ivy.[12]

Their affair was finished, but he and Ethel remained confidants, especially on matters extramarital. The request to see her alone meant without the presence of Reginald Reynolds, a fellow member of her Independent Labour Party, a Quaker, and the secretary of the No More War Movement. Ethel was now deeply in love; her long-estranged husband would soon sue for divorce. Yeats told her that he would be happy to meet "Reggie" provided they could have a quiet hour by themselves first. He needed her advice.

He was unsettled too by the rush of adrenalin that comes when the subject of a deep personal concern becomes a matter of public contro-versy. Since at least 1909 Yeats had worried about the eclipse of the Anglo-Irish gentry by the rising Irish Catholic bourgeoisie and even then had seen the development in biological rather than sociological terms. In 1909 he wrote of his fears of "the new ill-breeding of Ireland, which may in a few years destroy all that has given Ireland a distin-guished name in the world"; he pictured his native land growing "ster-ile, because power has passed to men who lacked the training."[13]

By the late 1930s the temptation to see social change in genetic terms was almost irresistible. Eugenicists of both left and right were growing louder in their call for measures to protect human breeding stock from degeneracy. In March 1937, not long after Yeats joined the Eugenics Society, a sensational book raised the threat of the over-breeding masses to the status of an invasion by the imbecile. In *The Fight for Our National Intelligence,* Raymond B. Cattell portrayed the human race as being at a crossroads, with civilized countries menaced by the "continual rapid replacement of the constitutionally bright by innately dull and limited types." International politics would be affected. The country that found a way to encourage the breeding of those with higher mental ability, Cattell declared, thereby protecting itself against the rise of the unfit and uneducable, had "every prospect of inheriting the earth."[14]

A country trying to do just that lay not far away. Germany had passed a eugenic sterilization law "for the Protection of Hereditary

Health" in July 1933. In his book Cattell applauded this "positive emphasis on racial improvement" and contrasted it with Huxley's woolly ideas about improvement through social reform, which he dismissed as bad Christianity and bad science.[15] (It must be said that Cattell, even in his stridency, stopped short of endorsing the German program of compulsory sterilization and that the London Eugenics Society's general secretary, C. P. Blacker, took steps to distance the group from the ugly authoritarianism of the Nazis.)

The Cattell book caused a great stir. Reviewers were generally hostile toward its militaristic and simplistic tone. In the socialist *Daily Herald,* the respected science writer Ritchie Calder called *The Fight for National Intelligence* one of the most reactionary books on psychology and eugenics that he had ever read.[16] But Yeats loved it. Whether he read it immediately or initially just in the long summary carried by the *Daily Telegraph* (a conservative newspaper unlikely to be scarce at his club), Cattell's argument accorded with his own fears as a member of "one of the great stocks of Europe."[17] He wrote to compliment the author, while thoughts of a prose work setting out his own ideas on race took root in his mind.

Exciting as London was, after a month he was homesick. He wrote to George in Rathfarnham to list the things he most missed. They were (in the following order): the cat, the dog, her, Anne, F. R. Higgins, and the local gossip. He wished he had come home sooner.[18] A week later, however, he was writing to say that complications had arisen that forced him to postpone his return. Could she send his sleeping pills?[19]

The "complications" were Edith Shackleton Heald. The first letter to her was written on May 4 by a smitten man. Back in Rathfarnham, he sent her a copy of one of his lectures. She did not have to read it: "It is a tribute—that is all."[20] To Dorothy Wellesley the same day, he wrote, without mentioning a cause, "I never felt so acutely the presence of a spiritual virtue and that is accompanied by intensified desire."[21] Coming from a man who had worked so hard to intensify his desire, this was no small tribute. As always, sexual and poetic inspiration went as one in his mind. Edith and her peaceful home opened new vistas for achievement; he was astonished at the amount of successful work he had produced in his brief, happy time at The Chantry House.

He was counting the days until he could see her again. Until he returned to London in about a month to rehearse his next BBC broadcast, he was stuck in Ireland, selecting poems to go into the series of *Broadsides* (a sporadic but well-produced series of illustrated broadsheets with which he and his brother, Jack, made work to keep the Cuala Press busy). Edith grew in his imagination; her age was an advantage: "Were you younger a true intimacy would be impossible . . . the finest bond is possible when we have outlived our first rough silver."[22] But there were things she might not like about him. His letters were full of self-effacement. He apologized for not having written sooner to ask her for "a friendship from which I hope so much. You seem to have that kind of understanding or sympathy which is peace."[23] He apologized too for his wishy-washy first name: she was to call him "W.B." or whatever she liked—anything except his Christian name. Then, brushing aside nearly twenty years' effort, he asked to be forgiven for *A Vision,* of which he was correcting the proofs. This book was not to be confused, he said, with the first edition written years before. It was the skeleton in his cupboard; his friends might think him "a crazed fanatic."[24] He did not know whether or not he wanted them to read it.

Whatever he wanted from Edith, it clearly was not further illumination of the unseen world.

In June Dulac, continuing his role as go-between, found a room for Yeats, at 52 Holland Park in familiar west London territory. Dulac's description—"modern bathroom off it . . . Quite self-contained"—make the place sound like another love nest.[25]

Reunited, Yeats and Edith saw each other many times a week. He took her to dinner at the restaurant next to the Coronet Theatre in Notting Hill one night and met her the following day for lunch at L'Escargot, a Soho restaurant he chose as being more intimate than The Ivy. On June 13 he spent his seventy-second birthday with her and afterward wrote guardedly and gratefully of their union on that significant day.[26]

The following week, writing from 52 Holland Park, in an impassioned and unguarded outburst, he pledged (echoing his pledge to the ghosts who had brought him metaphors for his poetry) to devote to her what remained to him of life.[27]

Yeats took great care to keep in the good graces of the women in his life—in order, it seems, to retain what he needed from each. The friend who got short shrift was Olivia Shakespear: his long, intense, and self-examining correspondence with her had dried up. With Dorothy Wellesley too there was a change: the bantering flirtatiousness was gone. Although he was in regular contact with her and still enjoyed staying at Penns in the Rocks, their letters now were businesslike, poet-to-poet affairs, much concerned with the verse she was contributing for a new edition of *Broadsides*.

His relationship with his wife is the most puzzling. He was utterly dependent upon George—but not upon her presence. His wife "wound him up," he told Gogarty.[28] On one of his many long stays in England that year he wrote her—as if it were a compliment—that in his sleep he had seen her as a large, cold, cooked chicken.[29]

George knew about Edith. At least, she knew that there was someone new to take the load off her shoulders. When Yeats left for London in June, she wrote drily that she hoped he was enjoying his birthday with the Dulacs and Miss Shackleton.[30] She then went on to discuss various editorial matters, signing herself "Georgie" and asking him to tell her if there were anything else she could do.

Unquestionably the couple shared the intimacy of husband-wife jokes and gossip. Yeats confided in George (if "confide" is the right verb for the chatter of a man who could not keep a secret) the details of the nervous breakdown that Dorothy was suffering that July. Dorothy had not lost her mind, he explained, but rather succumbed to depression brought on by the strain of seeing her daughter through the Season; the London summer social round represented a world she had rejected.[31] (The Season was more exhausting than ever that year because of the coronation of George VI). George was privy too to a ribald lyric he had written for Dorothy which displayed the strain of sadomasochism that Yeats occasionally indulged in his poetry. "The

Poem of Lancelot Switchback" sings of the joys of flagellation as part of the art of love (with breaks for wine):

> A beating on the buttocks
> Will warm your heart and mine
> My lash is all good leathers
> Yours a penny worth of twine
> Yet maybe half a dozen strokes
> Will do the trick for me[32]

That "half a dozen strokes," much like the "nine bean-rows" of "The Lake Isle of Innisfree," is jarringly specific. George herself thought the poem funny and was amused that it had succeeded in its intention of shocking the aristocratic lady.

Dorothy Wellesley seems to have been less equable about Yeats's new attachment. She soon saw that Penns in the Rocks took a poor second place to The Chantry House, although her "collapse," as Yeats called it, did not stop him from being a frequent visitor that summer. Guests continued to arrive at Penns, and the good conversation flowed on. With Hilda Matheson, he had much to talk about. At the BBC she had raised the radio "talk" to a separate art form,[33] and his current appearances were the direct result of her initiative with her former colleagues.

Dorothy's long-term problem was drink. The cocktail hour played its part in the hospitality of Penns in the Rocks and The Chantry House; heavy drinking, like smoking, was unremarkable at the time. However, in July 1937 Dorothy's manifest symptoms were tantrums, depression, and endless reiteration of what she had said and what others had said to her.[34] Her son, like Hilda and Yeats, found it all a great strain.[35]

Even so, Yeats took care not to arouse her jealousy. References to Edith, which appear in his letters to Ethel Mannin, are conspicuous by their absence in those to Dorothy. He does not seem to have told her of his new little flat in Holland Park. Writing to her from there, rather than using the address or that of his club, he headed his letters simply

"London." And on the first day that Edith drove him to Penns from Steyning, he did not invite her in. His excuse was that Dorothy was confined to her room with an unfortunate injury: at a court ball a man wearing a spur had trod on her foot. However, when Dorothy found out that the famed feminist journalist Edith Shackleton had been at her door, she scolded Yeats for not having brought her in to see the house. She would have come downstairs; Edith was just the kind of woman she wanted to meet.[36]

Did Yeats consider Edith lesbian when he fell in love with her? Was, as with Dorothy, an indifference to the potent male part of her attraction? Edith's journalism made a forceful case for the dispensability and iniquity of the male sex. Under headlines such as "MANNISH" WOMAN THE PRODUCT OF PRUDERY and DAY OF "SURPLUS" MEN, she argued the case for "women who do not like men" and, with what now seems an echo of her wastrel father, for a self-supporting single woman's ability to be domestic and home-loving: "It is commonly known that women sometimes marry for a home. It is much less commonly known how many women stay single for one."[37] Seven years later, Edith found a permanent partner, the handsome, cross-dressing painter who called herself Gluck. However, when Edith took up with Yeats in the spring of 1937, there was no visible rival, female or male, for her affections, and she was clearly enchanted with Yeats's company.

Preoccupied with his new affair, Yeats saw little of his eighteen-year-old daughter, who was living in a room in Sussex Gardens near Paddington Station while following up introductions in the theater world and going to plays every night. Father and daughter had lunch together one day; that was all. He did notice that she was experimenting with makeup, and he approved of the results.[38]

His English summer idyll flew by. He acquired his own room, at the front of The Chantry House: a large bedroom on the second floor above the entrance, with two paned windows overlooking the small green. Time spent with Edith was a joy. She somehow seemed to understand that an artist had to give in to his sexual fantasies; he told her, "We who create have to cultivate our wild beasts; most people have to subdue them."[39] They were his raw material. By the time his Holland Park lease was up and he was preparing to return to Ireland, the lovers had agreed to spend part of the winter together in Monte Carlo.

Back in Rathfarnham in August, he was in high spirits and full of energy. He finished six poems, which seem to have included (although precise dates of composition are hard to pin down) "Those Images," "The Spirit Medium," and "The Old Stone Cross." This last bore eugenic markings, with its references to the careless modern generations that "engender in the ditch" and blur the social classes: "If Folly link with Elegance / No man knows which is which."

He reported proudly to Edith how much he had accomplished. However, he was looking forward, not back. "When do you and I (or you and I and your sister) go abroad? I live for that."[40]

Tender loving care from another quarter was waiting in Ireland. Fifty well-to-do Irish Americans, under the banner of the Testimonial Committee for W. B. Yeats and the chairmanship of James A. Farrell, president of U. S. Steel, had collected three thousand dollars and sent it, converted into a bank draft for six hundred pounds sterling, to Dublin. One of the contributors, sending in his hundred dollars to the committee, said his wish was not to defend "old Ireland" against the charge of being a country of peasants, but rather to express a genuine admiration for Yeats and to prove that "we Irish can clothe our dreams in reality and be as practical as the best."[41]

Yeats, who was open and straightforward about money, accepted the gift on the understanding that the committee knew that he and his wife had enough for their own and their children's needs. He also insisted that he be allowed to make news of the gift public.

The question arises, although the Testimonial Committee does not seem to have asked it, why the winner of a Nobel Prize should have needed any further financial assistance in life. The answer seems to be that, although Yeats invested his Nobel money as soon as he received it, the value of his investments was no better protected than anyone else's from the Great Depression. A large chunk of his capital, moreover, had gone to help his sisters.

On August 17 in Dublin the Irish Academy of Letters gave a celebration banquet to thank the two representative members of the committee who had come to Dublin. The centerpiece of a carefully prepared evening of Irish song and ballad was Yeats's speech. In an expansive vein, he spoke of Ireland as "that great pictured song" and of the far-flung Irish millions around the world as "held together by songs."[42] He then described how just the week before he had visited the Municipal Gallery of Modern Art in Parnell Square and was so moved by the pictures and work of many intimate friends, now dead, that he had had to sit down. As an aside, he raised once again the matter of the controversial Hugh Lane pictures, which should have been in the gallery but hung still in London.` He revealed, as if from special knowledge, that the late King George V had been reluctant to open the Duveen wing of the Tate Gallery until the Lane collection had been returned to Dublin. But, he continued, the king had been prevailed upon to withdraw his opposition and open the wing anyway.[43]

He then thanked the visitors for giving him "that something more which is precious to an old man," something that would give his declining years "dignity and ease."[44] He promised to thank the rest when he had all their names with a poem that had begun forming in his head.

When Yeats called a poem "one of my best," he was usually right. By September, a copy of "The Municipal Gallery Revisited" was on its way to each of his fifty American benefactors in a pamphlet comprising his speech that evening and a few poems. Written in August and September 1937, it was dedicated, as its second verse says, not to the "dead Ireland of my youth, but an Ireland / The poets have imagined."

`The pictures remained at the Tate until 1959 when the British and Irish governments agreed that the two capitals would share them.

In it he expressed the poignant sense of communion with dead friends who had done so much for modern Ireland and who lived on as subjects of portraits on the walls of the gallery. What has also lived on is the poem's much-quoted concluding couplet: "Think where man's glory most begins and ends, / And say my glory was I had such friends."

Thanks to the generosity of his Irish American friends, when he revisited the Municipal Gallery to check details for the poem, he was able to travel from Rathfarnham to Dublin by taxi.

His view of the Irish as a scattered race of twenty (as he had told his audience) or thirty (as he had written to Dorothy) million "held together by songs,"[45] has much in common with the vision of Mary Robinson, president of Ireland from to 1990 to 1997, who argued that the diaspora of millions of Irish emigrants around the world had made Irishness a state of mind, rather than of territory.[46] The Ireland of 1937, however, was not concerned with universality. It had embarked on a course that would lead it to become, for several more decades, a narrow, inward-looking, theocratic and censorious state. If Yeats had won his battles with Eamon de Valera, he had lost the war.

Article 41 of the new Constitution, ratified by the electorate in June, was worded almost as an answer to Yeats's divorce speech: "No law shall be enacted providing for the grant of dissolution of marriage." The same article opened the way to excluding married women from the workforce: "In particular, the State recognises that by her life within the home, woman gives to the State a support without which the common good cannot be achieved."

As if in rejoinder to Yeats's long battles against censorship, Article 40 declared that Ireland's citizens had the right to have their morals protected by the State, which would "endeavour to ensure that organs of public opinion, such as the radio, the press, the cinema . . . not be used to undermine public order or morality or the authority of the State."

Articles 2 and 3, far from attempting to repair the breach with the North and with Britain, widened it by defining the Irish nation as the "whole island of Ireland, its islands and the territorial seas" and claiming jurisdiction over the whole island "pending the re-integration of the national territory."

The new independent state was to be headed by a president (not, as the Free State had been, by a leader of the executive council). Personally dismaying to Yeats was the reduction by more than half of the number of nominated senators—the nonelected elite group whom he had thought "plainly the most able and the most educated" when he served among them in the Free State Senate. The Irish Senate from now on would be dominated by men chosen by the vulgar ballot box.

Capping the whole was the Constitution's dedication of the country to the Holy Trinity and its recognition of the Roman Catholic Church "as the religion of the great majority."

It is hardly surprising that Yeats now concluded that the ideal life was six weeks in England and six weeks in Ireland. For most of September and all of October 1937, he was in England, alternating between his London club and his two Sussex retreats. George often did not know at which place to write to him and thought he was at Penns in the Rocks more often than he actually was. Life at Penns was once more disturbed: Dorothy had suffered another breakdown when her Great Dane, Brutus, had had to be put down.

The other unstable woman in his life surfaced once again. Margot Ruddock was taking part as a reader in his BBC broadcasts. Her essay and poems about her Barcelona madness had been published as *The Lemon Tree* and reviewed on the whole favorably. The critical praise for certain verses showed once again that Yeats's enthusiasm for her talent, while excessive, was not misplaced. The *Irish Times* compared her to the great Italian mystics and to J. M. Synge.[47] Yeats himself was loyal still and had recruited her for the BBC work, which meant renewed contact at many rehearsals. He was somewhat surprised that George approved of his choice. But "of one thing you may be quite certain," Yeats wrote Dulac, conveying George's strong views on a musical matter, "she means exactly what she says."[48]

But Margot was more trouble than she was worth. She sulked and threatened that if she was to be allowed to read only the "Curse of Cromwell," she would not read at all. Dulac, more than ever the go-between, sent her four guineas (the equivalent of the BBC fee) to buy her out of the program, and implored Yeats to accept the compromise.[49] Evidently he did not, for she appeared anyway. Yeats's friend Walter Turner, who had set some of the poems to music, thought she was a disaster and told Yeats so: her performance, he wrote Yeats, was "downright bad; in fact horrible—a mere whining."[50] Barnes, the producer, was more tolerant. He indulged Yeats's insistence on including Margot as far as he could; she had, Barnes conceded, a vivid low contralto and a remarkable facility for shifting from speech to song. He admired the way Yeats taught her to speak "Ah, dancer; ah, sweet dancer" in a lilting voice.

After the final performance together, Yeats invited Margot and Barnes out to dinner. Finding The Ivy shut, they went to an Italian restaurant Yeats remembered as good, only to find it under new management. It no longer served drink, or very much else. They dined on white coffee and hard-boiled eggs in a dreary celebration that was probably the last time Yeats ever saw Margot Ruddock.[51]

The October broadcast, "My Own Poetry Again," was not the last of Yeats on the BBC that year. On November 22 the "Experimental Hour" of its National Program put out *The Words Upon the Window-Pane* as the second of a series of radio plays begun with Archibald MacLeish's *The Fall of the City*. Radio remarkably conveyed the atmosphere of the Dublin séance invaded by the crabbed voice of Jonathan Swift. But, said *The Times*'s review, "the first laurels must go to Mr. Yeats for the magnificent flow of Swift's language. We felt the authentic ring of the passionate indignation of that great and tragic figure."[52]

Cocooned by his dream of Edith and Monte Carlo, he shuttled back across the Irish Sea to rescue the Cuala Press from deep trouble. He saw the Press (rather than his relations with women) as the "great problem of my life." He considered that he had given Lolly more than two thousand pounds,[53] yet the overdrafts on Cuala's two bank accounts were now running into many hundreds of pounds. Creditors were pressing; the National Bank, College Green, Dublin, was threatening to foreclose on the Sligo family shares held as security. Yeats did not expect to live forever. He was determined to set Cuala straight so that it could continue after his death without being a burden on George. (Once the reorganization was achieved, he observed to Dorothy, "I can fold my hands and be a wise old man and gay.")[54]

The obstacle was Lolly. Lily, now more or less housebound, was still his favorite sister; happily she submitted to his authority and undertook only those embroidery commissions for which he gave his approval. Lolly, however, remained an adversary. The two of them exchanged words as harsh as any to be found in Yeats's correspondence.[55] He swore at her and ordered her to stop writing to the bank manager, to stop paying money into the bank without telling him. As her elder brother, he said haughtily, he believed the world considered him responsible for her debts.

There are two sides to any family row. Yeats had legitimate grievances. The Cuala Press's reputation was built on his name (and, to a lesser extent, on Jack's). Again and again he had been irritated by sloppy misprints, late and disordered proofs, unanswered letters. He had personally handed over £350 only two years before to pay off the Cuala embroidery department's debt, yet Lolly had not managed to stop the rot. It is small wonder that he and George spoke of the Press as a "bloody nuisance." Even the quiet, good-natured Jack, who had done a great deal of drawing and illustration to help his sisters, had got fed up as early as 1926 and declared Cuala too much of a drag on his time and reputation.[56]

On the other hand, Lolly was also right to feel hard done by. Yeats held more control than he should have. Part of Cuala Press's weakness was his insistence on choosing all the books himself, and choosing mainly his own. Thirty-six of Cuala's 82 publications between 1903 and 1945 were his work. When his health faltered and output declined, Cuala's income dried up, yet he vetoed other commercial possibilities. He kept the Press, as he explained to Olivia when rejecting a book proposal from the Swami, "like an old family magazine. A few hundred people buy them all and expect a common theme."[57]

Recent books on the Yeats sisters have made Lolly into a minor feminist icon—a woman of talent and ability, belittled by the men around her, her ambitions and energy dismissed as neurosis and bad temper.[58] The manager of the National Bank, College Green, with the villainous name of Mr. Scroope, treated Lolly as the unreliable sister of a famous man. He would not take her word for anything and unfairly suspected her of concealing the overdraft on the second account from her brother.[59] The reality was more complicated. Lolly did suffer from depression and explosive temper. On the other hand, she kept, and understood, the balance sheets, while Willie was too preoccupied with his other interests to attend to the weekly figures she sent him. However, the real cause of the difficulty lay in the fall in the value of the Pollexfen family shares to one-fifth of their former worth—thus wiping out the security against the mounting overdrafts that had kept the bank quiet.[60]

At seventy, Elizabeth Yeats, as she was known professionally, was well dressed, amusing, sophisticated, and well connected in Dublin. She was recognized as the main force behind the Cuala Press, whose beautifully printed books and *Broadsides,* with strong illustrations by Jack Yeats, were popular, especially with rich Irish Americans (and are collectors' items of considerable value today).* At the same time she kept up an active teaching career: she wrote short textbooks on teaching painting to children and gave lessons in painting until the end of her life. In any event, Lolly herself had been begging Yeats to appoint a new or an additional editorial director, simply to save himself the strain, as he had always said he had no interest in the practical affairs of the business.

In the end, the reorganization was achieved on schedule, with visits to the bank and lawyers, and signatures all round. It was hardly a triumph of business acumen. Yeats appointed in his place only adjuncts to himself: his wife and Higgins, his friend with the racy stories.

---

*A full list of the 82 publications of Cuala Press appears in Gifford Lewis's *The Yeats Sisters and the Cuala* (Dublin: Irish Academic Press, 1994).

Higgins, in the United States with an Abbey tour at the time of his appointment, was hardly ready to play an active part (and botched it when he did get back).

One thing is clear. With his failing health, Yeats at the end of 1937 ought not personally to have undertaken to write something that would put the Cuala Press in the black. But who else but "my sister's handpress" would have published the intemperate *On the Boiler?*[61]

Telling Ethel Mannin about his plans for Monte Carlo, he said he would remain there until April and "do an abominable thing."[62] That *On the Boiler* is an abominable thing many of his readers will agree. The tract was a statement of authoritarian racist views extreme even for 1938 when it was published. The title is possibly the best thing about it. From his youthful hanging around the Sligo docks, Yeats remembered a mad ship's carpenter who used to climb up on the ship's steam tank and make crazed speeches: hence the happy image of the boiler as pulpit for a madman.

He began the work on November 11, intended to produce an occasional booklet that might make an annual £150 for the Press. Its subject was to be a statement of his political beliefs, and was addressed to the youth of Ireland.

By climbing onto his boiler, he was setting himself up as an eccentric version of John Ruskin (whose breakdown he had been so anxious to avoid). Between 1871 and 1884 Ruskin published an audacious irregular series of letters addressed "to the Workmen and Labourers" of Great Britain"—a de haut en bas sermon from the artist to the lower orders for their betterment, drawing on his personal experience, setting events from contemporary history against the nobler background of literature and art.

Yeats's essay adopts a jauntier, conversational tone. Yet the not very hidden subtext was his dismay at the new Constitution, which represented the final defeat of the Anglo-Irish by the "fumblers in the greasy till." He was angry and, being old, prepared to shock.

As he worked at Rathfarnham with his books around him, longing for Edith and wishing she could see him in his agreeable domestic setting, he sent her a word picture of his study: the Burne-Jones window separating the house from the conservatory, the paintings by his father, brother, and Robert Gregory over the low bookcases, two Chinese paintings (the gift of Dulac) on either side of the window overlooking the bare apple trees and last flowers in the garden. Although tensely awaiting Lolly's arrival to hear what he had decided about Cuala, he declared, "I have shaken off depression as a dog shakes off water."[63]

Ireland was entering its winter darkness. Looking out at the snow-covered fields, Yeats mused that his health might require a villa at Monte Carlo every year. That George would replace Edith as his caretaker was always part of the plan. She would come as soon as Michael's school holidays were over.

Late in 1937 the sixteen-year-old Michael was finishing at Saint Columba's, both parents unhappy with the rigid rote way he had been taught *The Aeneid*, line by numbered line.[64] They were thinking of sending him to the Sorbonne for a year. Until then George felt tied to home.

More than ever, Yeats felt competitive with his children. His letters often refer to their beating him at chess or croquet; he was particularly distant with his son. Although he expected the young man to cope with Europe on his own, he did not give the boy credit for his increasing sophistication. (Indeed, he hardly spoke to his son.) When Michael corrected his father's explanation of the situation in Czechoslavakia, for example, Yeats was dumbfounded that "the boy had read something."[65]

George, as if trying to build a bridge between father and son, wrote Yeats after one of the BBC programs (its broadcasts receivable, then as now, throughout much of Ireland) that Michael, hearing Yeats's recite in his normal (rather than his chanting) voice, said that he preferred the poems read like that. She was surprised that the boy (who had declared as a child that he "hated poetry")[66] seemed to know the verses by heart. Perhaps, she speculated, Michael had been furtively reading the Oxford anthology.[67]

As for Anne, Yeats continued to hobble her moves to independence. That year he had opposed her wish to go to Paris to study stage design, saying that London would be better. Frank O'Connor, visiting when the argument was in progress, declared that going to London was a waste of time: Anne should go to Paris. (O'Connor had visited Joyce in Paris and knew that the Irish profile was higher there than in London.) George, accompanying O'Connor to the door, did a little dance step in the hall and said, "That old bully! It's about time someone stood up to him. He's always trying to push people around."[68] As things worked out, Anne went to both cities.

At the same time, he keenly followed Anne's professional progress, and news of her various triumphs and disappointments occupied much space in the letters George wrote him. So did a discussion of her appearance; George and Yeats both wished that their daughter were more stylish. Yeats scolded her if she went around with runs in her stockings and urged her to wear gold nail polish and to dress exotically—like a character in one of his plays, she felt.[69] (Her fond aunts in Dundrum felt the same.)[70] Their concerns probably masked anxiety that she might not find the well-born husband who would "bring her to a house / Where all's accustomed, ceremonious." (In the event, Anne Yeats never married and has said she found "A Prayer for my Daughter" very hard to live up to.)

The emptying nest left George increasingly solitary in the creeper-covered house in Rathfarnham. Her old companion Lennox Robinson was not only married, but shattered by drink. Yeats did appreciate the strain his wife was under; he told Dorothy that "her children and her house weigh her down, and there is so much to do between theatre and Cuala."[71] And, he might have added, in corresponding with him. His frequent absences abroad required many exchanges of letters between "My dear Dobbs" (as he still called her) and "My dear Willy."

Depression returned. One cause may have been Margot Ruddock, who had relapsed. She was now in a mental institution, but he had no idea which.[72] Intent on the Monte Carlo trip, he put off requests from the BBC to set dates for more broadcasts. He even turned down an invitation to appear on its experimental television service. He wanted nothing on his schedule that might wear him out before the trip.

Nervous and suppliant with Edith, he confessed that he lived in fear that she would forget him. He pleaded with her to fix the date for their departure; he reminded her how quickly trains got booked up for holiday periods.[73]

Lightening his tone, he regaled her with his dreams of having affairs with three women—Dorothy Pound and two strangers, one of Eastern appearance. But as he was not in Tibet, he said gaily, he was not accountable for his sleeping mind.

George noticed his darkened mood. Attributing it to fatigue and insomnia, she suggested that she take him to the south of France right away, and wait with him until Edith arrived. He vetoed that idea on the grounds that he needed to be near his library for several weeks more.[74] Then came the suggestion from Edith that she might go out to Monte Carlo ahead of him.

A terrible idea, he wrote back, shaken. They were going to travel together. That arrangement was definite and unalterable. In a moving letter to Edith (from which much of the emotion has been drained in the highly censored version published in Wade's *Letters of W. B. Yeats*) he described his vision of sharing with her the joy of boarding the train in dark Victoria Station and emerging in the warm sun of Monte Carlo.[75] Humbly he thanked her for her willingness to travel so far to devote herself to him. His only sadness was that their time together would be so short.

But he had to take work with him. Never overly sentimental about Christmas, on Christmas Day he wrote to the Eugenics Society asking for two articles on racial decline to be sent to him at the Athenaeum before the sixth of January. Some statistics on the intelligence quotient of the leisured classes would also be useful, he said.[76]

The great day came at last. Fortified with his holiday reading, with his sleeping compartment booked, with his beloved at his side, Yeats got onboard at Victoria and slid off to Monte Carlo, to begin the astonishing final year of his life.

16

A Working Year

(January 1938–January 28, 1939)

THE FOOLISH SIDE of Yeats flourished in the sun. At Monte Carlo he threw himself into his political pamphlet arguing the case for a governing class for Ireland. Poring over the papers from the Eugenics Society, he found what he wanted. "The Causes of Racial Decay" (C. J. Bond's 1928 Galton lecture) particularly impressed him for its conclusion that steady deterioration was inevitable because of the tendency of the most physically and mentally defective stock to breed with those just slightly higher on the social scale. (Among those whom Bond categorized as not-quite rock bottom were "unskilled labour, the habitually poor and the slum-dweller.")[1] As Yeats had already predicted the collapse of civilization, notably in "The Second Coming," this demographic underpinning for his vision was gratifying.

He badgered the Eugenics Society for more data. Having asked for information about the mental abilities of the leisured classes, he had been sent statistics on the performance of the professional classes, and this was not what concerned him at all. "Is there any record," he asked the society's secretary, C. P. Blacker, "of the intelligence quota [*sic*] among people living upon inherited money? One would expect it to be pretty high."[2]

This time Blacker could not help. "I know of no observation as to the intelligence quotient among the leisured classes living on unearned income," he wrote back to Monte Carlo on January 17, 1938. He went on to explain what may not have been obvious to a poet accustomed to leveled lawns and graveled ways: "Such persons would be very difficult to get hold of in any organised body."[3]

Yeats was not to be put off. His next request was for a definition of intelligence. "The men who made the tests must have had some clear idea of what they were testing," he insisted. "Is it power of attention and coordination? Or is it a sense of the significance and affinities of objects?"[4] Blacker began to feel bombarded. Once more, however, respectful of the Nobel laureate's great reputation, he gathered more material and sent it on, allowing himself the terse comment that there was no definition of intelligence comparable to that provided by the Royal College of Physicians for physical diseases.[5]

In the end, Yeats was not overly constrained by statistics. *On the Boiler*, published by Cuala in October 1938, draws openly from the Bond lecture and even more from Cattell's *Fight for Our National Intelligence* (from which the Eugenics Society had recoiled),[6] and mixes in anecdote and speculation with an insouciance bordering on irresponsibility. The main thesis of *On the Boiler* is straightforward.

Since about 1900 the better stocks have not been replacing their numbers, while the stupider and less healthy have been more than replacing theirs. Unless there is a change in the public mind every rank above the lowest must degenerate, and, as inferior men push up into its gaps, degenerate more and more quickly.[7]

Having failed to gather evidence that the idle classes were brighter than the rest, Yeats said so anyway: "Somebody has written, 'There can be no wisdom without leisure.'"[8] He then drew on a bag of favorites from Castiglione to Swift to prove his hunch about rich men's special gift for culture and governance.

The resulting snobbish, reactionary pamphlet—one Yeats scholar has called it "repellent"[9]—is redeemed only by its incoherence. In his most rambling after-dinner speech, Yeats could not have foisted on an audience such an outrageous jumble of hearsay, meaningless statistics, and racist nonsense. In a sequence of unrelated sections that read like gulps for breath, he praises violence. He calls for war. He calls for a ruling class, and military families, from which would spring a small efficient army to "throw back from our shores the disciplined uneducated masses of the commercial nations." He reports the Irish as ranking bottom on American intelligence classification of immigrants, and he claims that Ireland leads Europe in "madmen."[10] Gaily he dismisses any need for public education. Once Ireland undergoes the kind of revolution that he is outlining, all that the government will need to teach the great majority of schoolchildren is:

> nothing but ploughing, harrowing, sowing, curry-combing, bicycle-cleaning, drill-driving, parcel-making, bale-pushing, tin-can-soldering, door-knob polishing, threshold-whitening, coat-cleaning, trouser-patching, and playing upon the Squiffer, all things that serve human dignity, unless indeed it decide that these things are better taught at home, in which case it can leave the poor children at peace.[11]

There would be no need for an informed citizenry, for the farce of democracy would be gone. His own experience in the Senate showed him all that the ballot box could be expected to produce: "Some typical elected man, emotional as a youthful chimpanzee, hot and vague, always disturbed, always hating something or other."[12]

Throughout *On the Boiler*, Yeats's prejudice is based on class, not religion. Anti-Catholic he certainly sounds, but his rage is more against the shop owner than the papist. At the same time he vents a savage distaste for the misshapen and the unfit and declares that only those "sound of body and mind should be suffered to marry." Remarkably, considering the rampant bigotry of the time—Maud Gonne MacBride was among those who fulminated against Jewish usury and England's conspiracy with Jewish bankers[13]—anti-Semitism plays no part in his rantings. A whiff of his own class snobbery appears in a gibe at Lord Nuffield (the motorcar manufacturer William Morris). *On the Boiler* accuses Nuffield of being a "self-made man" who was corrupting Oxford University with gifts of money that would "substitute applied science for ancient wisdom."[14] (In fact, Nuffield's donations to Oxford went chiefly to medical research.)

Yeats finished this polemic at the end of February and sent it off to the Cuala Press, where it was prepared for publication with a strong cover illustration by Jack Yeats of an old sailor climbing on a boiler to deliver his tirade. Understandably, Yeats was worried that liberal friends such as Ethel Mannin might not speak to him after reading it. He might have worried as well about how far the pamphlet could go toward putting Cuala into the black. For all his long-winded self-indulgence, the resulting pamphlet is only forty-six pages long. Indeed, *On the Boiler* would be even flimsier were it not padded out by several poems and an eight-page play, which are of a different order altogether.

In late life, Yeats's poetic gift had never been so much at his command. In his poetry he could now say what he wanted, using colloquial, even vulgar language, in sentence fragments and imperfect rhymes. By the end of his first month at Monte Carlo, he had corrected the proofs of *New Poems* and had sent them off to Lolly. There were thirty-five in all, strong poems, written from mid-1936 to the autumn of 1937, ranging from "The Gyres" and "Lapis Lazuli" to "The Municipal Gallery Revisited" and "Are You Content?" Uninterrupted by other commitments, he was working on still more.

A violent attack of food poisoning from what he called "bad cabbage" and the doctor called "hotel infection" precipitated a move from Monte Carlo across the bay to Menton.[15] His time with Edith was running out; she had to leave to join her sister in Paris. He suggested to George, who was soon to come, that she might prefer a flat to the hotel. If so, he and Edith would find one.

No, George would not like a flat. She was tired of housekeeping; she now disliked temporary flats with their inadequate crockery and linen, and unreliable servants. However, she said, she could come out to Menton anytime now that Michael had gone back to school. Should she wait until Edith had left or did Yeats wish them to overlap?[16]

She need not have asked. In a non-English-speaking environment, Yeats did not want one moment without protection. Accordingly, when George arrived at Monte Carlo on February 4, Edith was waiting at the station with a taxi, and the handover occurred.[17] Thus began a year of joint stewardship. Yeats had assured Edith that she had won his wife's good will—a promise borne out by the subsequent amiable correspondence between the two women.

In Yeats's letters to friends, there is no sign that he was any less happy with one caretaker or the other. George's arrival allowed him to dictate the untyped part of *On the Boiler.* The stream of letters to Edith that started as soon as she left tell a different story. He missed her dreadfully; his ideal life would be to be there alone with her. Devotedly he reported what he had accomplished since she had left: two poems, one a nursery rhyme to end *On the Boiler,* the other about a coat on a coat hanger. Once his pamphlet was done, he promised, he would write nothing but verse.[18] He occasionally relayed bits of news—the British consul at Nice had been rude to George because she had an Irish passport; an Englishwoman whose signature he had sought for a legal document thought "I was trying to pick her up."[19] But the burden of his letters to Edith was always the same: love and longing. Counting the days until he could see her again, he was already looking forward to their next winter together in the sun.

By the first of March, George, so good at organizing his life, had found a cheaper and quieter hotel. It was perfect, he wrote to Edith. The two of them should come there the next year.[20] The hotel was at the steep medieval village of Cap Martin, which lies at the extreme eastern end of the Riviera. Prettily named Idéal-Séjour, it faced the sea, had a garden at the back over which hung the huge brown rock, the Roquebrune, one of the great features of the coast, and served excellent food cooked by the patron: all for three pounds ten a week each (tips included, he added, with his usual punctiliousness about money). Then, in a burst of feeling, he said Edith could have no idea of the difference she had made to his life; his only wish was to be with her.[21] There were only three weeks to wait for the joy of reunion.

Longing was tempered by realism. Passing himself like a parcel among his women took considerable management. He had planned that when they returned to England, George would put him on a train at Victoria and send him directly to Edith, while she went home to Ireland. Dorothy Wellesley, however, spoiled this plan. She and Hilda had to leave Penns in the Rocks at the end of March for some weeks. Yeats, therefore, should come to her first and bring his wife if she was free to come. Then, at the end of the visit, her chauffeur would drive him down to Steyning.

Yeats did not wish to offend his titled friend or to forgo the comforts of her splendid house. Balancing his allegiances with exquisite tact, he asked Edith if she would dine with him in London the night he arrived, but then forgive him for postponing his visit to Steyning for a few days. He really could not refuse Dorothy; she needed help with her poetry. And when he did get to The Chantry House, he would stay for a long time—so long that Edith might grow bored with him.

Once he was with her, he wrote, there was a good deal he wished to write in the total seclusion only she could provide. He did not want to see anyone—not even Dulac. A one-act play of tragic intensity had formed in his head. He would begin it at Steyning. Relaying all this, he reminded Edith (with superlatives rare in his letters) that her position in his life was supreme. She was all he lived for; his only fear was losing her; he was her lover and her friend. "O my dear," he closed, "I want your arms to make me sleep."[22]

The tone of this and his many other passionate letters written to Edith over succeeding months is difficult to gauge. Are they the words of a yearning eager lover? Or of an old man in love with his nurse?

After a full week at Penns in the Rocks, he reached The Chantry House at the end of March and stayed for six weeks. A rather sharp plea from George asked that one of them let her know how he was.[23] There was family news: Michael was miserable with chicken pox and an infected leg; George was totally occupied with putting on and taking off his dressings. Anne's hair was looking like a savage's, but she refused to get it cut. There was gossip too. Frank O'Connor had gone off with somebody else's wife—an escapade that, George remarked tartly, might give other people notions about deserting their patient spouses of many years.

Happy as Yeats was with Edith, he prepared himself for death at her house. The poems he wrote there were not love poems. While not ill, he saw himself declining. The death dreams he had been having for five years were troubling him again. One apparition—a coat hanger traveling across a room, the same one that had so amused Virginia Woolf—was "extraordinarily terrifying."[24]

Out of this terror came "The Apparitions": an aged man proclaiming that he needs all his courage to face "the increasing Night / That opens her mystery and fright." Each stanza ends with the remorseless refrain: *"Fifteen apparitions have I seen; / The worst a coat upon a coat-hanger."*

The Chantry House that spring produced another important poem. Yeats still believed with Pythagoras that "all is number." He wished to express his deep sense that Greek statues, sculpted to Pythagorean ideal proportions, marked the beginning of Western civilization. He intended also, linking his aesthetic and eugenic philosophies, to declare that the Greek physical ideal had changed the direction of European desire, in art and in sex.

He was now a master of syntax. "The Statues" begins in the vernacular with a confidence that permits a poignant reference to the loneliness of adolescent masturbation.

Pythagoras planned it. Why did the people stare?
His numbers, though they moved or seemed to move

In marble or in bronze, lacked character.
But boys and girls, pale from the imagined love
Of solitary beds, knew what they were,
That passion could bring character enough,
And pressed at midnight in some public place
Live lips upon a plummet-measured face.

The poem goes on to present ill-thought-out ideas about the victory of Western over Eastern civilization.

Divided opinions about "The Statues" fill Yeats criticism. Harold Bloom hates the poem, Richard Ellmann loves it; Elizabeth Cullingford calls it a "eugenic love poem" because, concluding its argument that sexual choice is the foundation of civilization, it urges the Irish to choose their mates by physical perfection and bravery:

No! Greater than Pythagoras, for the men
That with a mallet or a chisel modelled these
Calculations that look but casual flesh, put down
All Asiatic vague immensities,
And not the banks of oars that swam upon
The many-headed foam at Salamis.
Europe put off that foam when Phidias
Gave women dreams and dreams their looking-glass.

One image crossed the many-headed, sat
Under the tropic shade, grew round and slow,
No Hamlet thin from eating flies, a fat
Dreamer of the Middle Ages. Empty eyeballs knew
That knowledge increases unreality, that
Mirror on mirror mirrored is all the show.
When gong and conch declare the hour to bless,
Grimalkin crawls to Buddha's emptiness.

When Pearse summoned Cuchulain to his side,
What stalked through the Post Office? What intellect,

What calculation, number, measurement, replied?
We Irish, born into that ancient sect
But thrown upon this filthy modern tide
And by its formless, spawning, fury wrecked,
Climb to our proper dark, that we may trace
The lineaments of a plummet-measured face.

It seems fair to say that seldom does Yeats's phenomenal command of technique outstrip his intellectual abilities more than in "The Statues." Amazingly, this does not dim the power of the poem. Declan Kiberd, in *Inventing Ireland*, acknowledges that "many of Yeats's most striking lines (like the end of 'The Second Coming') are remarkable without being lucid. . . . This need not necessarily be a bad thing, for great poetry often has the capacity to communicate before it is fully understood."[25]

What can be understood, imperfectly or not, is that the opening lines of the last verse—"When Pearse summoned Cuchulain to his side, / What stalked through the Post Office?"—intend to link classical sculpture with the statue of Cuchulain newly placed in the renovated General Post Office. The entire poem boldly puts modern Ireland in the context of a pre-Christian past. Whether this link of politics with literature is justified, or whether Yeats, like Pearse, was "inventing Ireland," remains a subject of continuing dispute.[26]

At The Chantry House that spring, with Edith's arms to help him sleep, he wrote his finest play. *Purgatory*, which rounds off *On The Boiler*, displays the difference between the pamphleteer and the playwright. In just 223 lines, all the preceding sloppy thinking about degeneration and miscegenation is transformed into a stunning statement of the universal hatred between the generations and of the power of the dead over the living.

The "Persons in the Play" are simply "A Boy" and "An Old Man." The setting is a bare stage with a stone and a tree, and the suggestion of a ruined house—the minimalism learned from the Japanese that Yeats handed on to Samuel Beckett. (Beckett, then thirty-two, living in Paris, had not yet begun to write plays.)

The action of *Purgatory*, such as it is, shows an old peddler, accompanied by his son, visiting the ruins of his ancestral home. The peddler (the Old Man) declares that his mother was the daughter of this great house and landowning family who married her rough stablekeeper. She died giving birth to their only child—himself. As a consequence of this disastrous misalliance, the house now stands wrecked, its great library gone, the uncouth stablekeeper having set fire to it while drunk. For this crime, their son, having reached sixteen, killed his father.

The Old Man relates this sorry saga to his own son, a coarse lad of sixteen, who jeers that nothing was wrong: "My grand-dad got the girl and the money." But as the Old Man tries to explain the offense of having killed a great house and a distinguished lineage, a window in the house lights up. Through it, to his horror, he sees the ghosts of his parents re-enacting (or, in Yeats's *Vision* parlance, "dreaming back") their wedding night. They are reliving the act of begetting him, a murderer. Watching, the Old Man is appalled to see his mother show desire: "She is mad about him." He watches the couple mount the stairs. "Do not let him touch you!" he screams to his mother. But the sexual act is consummated; his own birth will inevitably follow, as will his murder of his father. Thus bad blood is passed on from generation to generation.

As he contemplates this ruinous replication, the Old Man sees the boy trying to steal his money. Bringing out the same jackknife with which he killed his father ("That knife that cuts my dinner now"), he kills his son. The window goes dark. The murderer then dementedly sings to himself:

'Hush-a-bye baby, thy father's a knight,
Thy mother a lady, lovely and bright.'
No, that is something that I read in a book,
And if I sing it must be to my mother,
And I lack rhyme.

The Old Man congratulates himself. Had his own son lived, "He would have struck a woman's fancy, / Begot, and passed pollution on."

But hoofbeats are heard, again and again. The unstoppable sound ("How quickly it returns—beat—beat—!") tells him that the sacrifice of his son was futile. A family can never purge itself of a crime inherited in its blood. The drama will perpetually recur. The powerful play ends in despair: the Old Man can do nothing to give his mother peace:

> O God,
> Release my mother's soul from its dream!
> Mankind can do no more. Appease
> The misery of the living and the remorse of the dead.

Purgatory cannot be read simply as a lament for the decline of the Irish Ascendancy class. The stark oedipal drama could well be called "A Prayer for My Mother": Yeats's final expression of his helpless wish to rescue his suffering mother from his irresponsible, bullying father. It casts in a eugenic light his long-standing fear of inherited Pollexfen madness. It conveys also an infantile desperation to halt his parents' endless begetting—and an aged man's resentment at the burgeoning of his own son, then sixteen. The Chantry House was an appropriate setting for its composition. Edith and Nora Heald too had sheltered a mother from a father cast as the villain of the family triangle.

As Yeats's visit to England came to a close in May 1938, George feared he would try to pack too much into the final week and exhaust himself. From Rathfarnham she wrote Edith (treating her as the substitute wife John Quinn once told Yeats that he needed), "Do please extract from him his prescription for the digitalis mixture and make him take it twice a day."[27] When Edith replied to say, of course, she had remembered the digitalis, George apologized. "He needs so much intellectual stimulus that you and others can give," she said, "but he unfortunately also needs that heart stimulus." Then, uncharacteristically, she burst out, "And nobody can feel more passionately than I that he has to return to this desolate place."[28]

Desolate? The lovely little creeper-covered house with the book-lined study? George's outburst reveals the dark side of two very separate lives. That she should call their home desolate gives an idea of what life in Rathfarnham must have been like in the many weeks when Yeats was abroad, Michael at school, and Anne at the Abbey. George suffered from many colds and retained her old faith in bed rest. There is no evidence that the "Communicators," so persistent in the early days of her marriage, favored her any longer with their company.

Shyness at least was one feature that she shared with her famous husband. She knew what fears his gregarious public facade covered. Yeats held back from being introduced to many people he would have liked to meet—Arnold Toynbee, for instance. Hilda Matheson offered to bring the two together, but Yeats did not dare.[29] He confessed to Edith that even the telephone "makes me timid and scared."[30]

Yeats's uneasiness with sophisticated strangers may have stemmed from his lack of university education. He was eloquent when holding forth uninterrupted, but the cut-and-thrust of debate was not to his taste. One day that spring at Penns in the Rocks, when the conversation was heatedly political, he found his mind wandering off. The result was the poem "Politics," composed on May 23.

> How can I, that girl standing there,
> My attention fix
> On Roman or on Russian
> Or on Spanish politics?
> Yet here's a travelled man that knows
> What he talks about,
> And there's a politician
> That has read and thought,
> And maybe what they say is true
> Of war and war's alarms,
> But O that I were young again
> And held her in my arms.

The poem's epigraph, from Thomas Mann, *"In our time the destiny of man presents its meanings in political terms,"* was taken from an article by Archibald MacLeish in the spring 1938 issue of the *Yale Review* in which MacLeish complimented Yeats for his "public" language. In the poem Yeats gratefully acknowledges MacLeish's recognition that he is "public" in his own fashion.

However, what now is conspicuous in this poem (usually placed last, after considerable scholarly disagreement, in most post-1983 editions of Yeats's collected poems)* is the absence of any reference to German politics. In May 1938, when London was recruiting air raid wardens, it was Hitler, and not Mussolini, Stalin, or Franco, who was the cause of talk of "war and war's alarms."

That Edith, despite her age, was "that girl" is suggested by a letter Yeats wrote her the day after finishing the poem. He said he was not expecting war, ominous as the news was. But should it come, perhaps he and she could escape to Cornwall and shut it out.[31]

Spurning George's kind offer to cross over to Holyhead and escort him back across the Irish Sea, Yeats made the trip home at last but did not stay long. Ireland was rainy, and the doctor called in and gloomily pronounced that all the winter's benefit to Yeats's health had worn off. Early in July, in spite of having renounced all public life, he took the chair at an Abbey board meeting ("usual storms," he wrote Dorothy)[32] and satisfied himself that the Cuala Press was in good shape. He then sped back to his room at The Chantry House. George could tell how happy and well he was from his handwriting: there were fewer misspellings than usual. He must have been happy, for just before returning he had told Edith, "I do not want henceforth to be away from you for any great length of time. I am always afraid you will forget me."[33]

Typically, he kept his infatuation with Edith from the other women in his life. Writing to Maud from Steyning, he offered a very distanced view of his hostess.

---

*The re-ordering was done by Professor Richard J. Finneran in *The Poems: A New Edition* (New York: Macmillan, 1983) on the basis of persuasive evidence that this was Yeats's preferred arrangement. For a full discussion of this contentious bibliographical matter, see Warwick Gould's "Appendix Six, the Definitive Edition: A History of the Final Arrangements of Yeats's Work," *Yeats's Poems*, 706–49.

I am staying now with an old friend Miss Shackleton Heald,
once the best paid woman journalist in the world. She found
she had no leisure & so gave up most of it. On Tuesday I go to
Penns in the Rocks and stay with Lady Gerald Wellesley,
another good friend, then back here and then to Ireland for the
first performance of my one-act play *Purgatory.*

When he did manage a few days with the other "good friend," her
butler was alarmed to hear loud moans from Yeats's room. The sound,
Dorothy explained, was of a poet at work. Yeats seemed very frail; he
could not walk ten paces without stopping for breath. Determined to
show him the folly she was having constructed—a small classical
"Temple of the Muses"—Dorothy got a small car to transport him
over the fields.

The opening of *Purgatory* on August 10, 1938, at the Abbey was the cause
of religious controversy and much debate in the *Irish Times.* In construct-
ing his play, Yeats had helped himself to a central Roman Catholic dogma
and remade it to his own purposes, ignoring *Purgatory's* function as a
place of purgation and redemption. This nicety hardly bothered Yeats. His
theology was slapdash, like his eugenics, and his idiosyncratic view of
what happened after death was set out in *A Vision:* the recently dead do
not know that they are dead and hover between the two states in a curious
half-life (called, in *A Vision,* "The Shiftings"). For how long do souls remain
in that state? Dorothy asked him. "Perhaps some twenty years" was the
instant answer.[34] And then? Perhaps the souls went to Purgatory, then per-
haps they returned to God. When Dorothy pressed him to be more pre-
cise, he laughed.

In spite of his audacity in putting parricide, filicide, and parental
intercourse on a Dublin stage, Yeats had a hit. The *Irish Independent's*
report on the opening of *Purgatory* was that "even to hardened playgo-
ers the effect was uncanny"; in London the *Times* called it "the out-
standing event of the first week of the Abbey Theatre Festival."[35]
Describing the play as "almost a monologue," the *Times* said it was

beautifully acted. . . . the spare dignity of the lines stood out
with gaunt nakedness against the shell of the ancestral house.
The design for the stage by Miss Ann [sic] Yeats, daughter of
the poet, made it possible to bring the ghostly visions of the
pedlar's mind before the audience with startling vividness.

The review went on to sum up both Yeats's curtain speech and the
play's meaning:

So far as may be gleaned, his message is that humanity is born
into the world at haphazard, educated at random, and then left
to drift whither the winds may determine. It would appear to
carry a definite eugenic message: so that the poet has turned
sociologist in his eighth decade. The "Big house" had been
brought to ruin by the misguided alliance of a love-sick girl.
All that the demented son could do was to ensure that the
strain should not be perpetuated. Thus does Mr. Bernard Shaw
come to the Abbey Theatre through the medium of Mr. W. B.
Yeats.[36]

The curtain speech from the Abbey stage was Dublin's last public
look at the man who on such an occasion was not shy, but rather (in
Frank O'Connor's description of Yeats in good form) "all alert, dra-
matic, amazingly brilliant . . . the head thrown back . . . his whole face
lit up as from within."[37] This time the message was grave and valedic-
tory: he said that into his little play he had put his thoughts about this
world and the next.

After the play's triumph, Yeats retreated to Rathfarnham. With his
new affluence, he sent a car to bring Maud Gonne MacBride to tea.
They had resumed their friendship, after a long period when, Maud
said later, "politics had separated us . . . we got on each other's nerves
over them."[38] Now both were mellower, and Yeats gave her permission
to quote his poems in the autobiography she was writing, cautioning
her that "if you do not want my curse do not misprint them. People

constantly misprint quotations."[39] Maud was now living in large, gaunt Roebuck House in the countryside south of Dublin. Although they had now been friends almost fifty years, Yeats had not named her by name in a poem until the previous year. "Beautiful Lofty Things" tells of "Maud Gonne at Howth station waiting a train, / Pallas Athena in that straight back and arrogant head."

He had done more, however. Another poem, "A Bronze Head," iconized her in her decrepitude, capturing in words, as the cast by Lawrence Campbell in the Municipal Gallery could not do, the double image of a woman in youth and in age:

> Human, superhuman, a bird's round eye,
> Everything else withered and mummy-dead.
> . . . .
> But even at the starting-post, all sleek and new,
> I saw the wildness in her.

In old age, the physical similarity between the two was stronger than ever—the towering frame, the aquiline gaze, the prominent cheekbones. Yeats, who wore carpet slippers more often than shoes in those days, rose with difficulty from his armchair in his study to greet her. He was wearing, Maud noticed, a silk dressing gown of his favorite fawn color, which set off the attractive brown of his skin. He said as she left, "Maud, we should have gone on with our Castle of the Heroes, we might still do it."[40] He seemed ill to her but was talking of things they would do together when he got back from Monte Carlo in the spring.

For Yeats, Maud's marriage in 1903 to the drunken little MacBride had epitomized the evils of misalliance. Yet the only child of that marriage was not turning out too badly. Sean MacBride was now thirty-four and his mother's pride. He had retired as chief of staff of the IRA (having spent half his life in its service), completed his law studies, and established himself as a Dublin barrister with a lively practice in defending IRA men threatened with execution by the de Valera government.[41]

Yeats had not forgotten Iseult. He kept her portrait on an easel in his study. Her marriage to Francis Stuart had failed completely, and her youthful beauty had vanished under the strain. Stuart had made a half-hearted attempt to get a Catholic annulment on the grounds that he had been only seventeen at the time of the wedding. But he soon gave up the attempt to free himself and concentrated instead on drinking, womanizing, gambling, traveling, and building a career as a novelist, his reputation boosted by glowing words of praise from Yeats. (In 1939 Stuart settled in Germany, where, igniting a controversy that was to endure for the rest of his very long life, he spent World War II working in Nazi radio propaganda.) Iseult remained in Ireland, living with their two children and her mother-in-law in Laragh Castle, a converted eighteenth-century barracks near Glendalough.

Yeats lampooned Francis Stuart unforgettably in "Why Should Not Old Men Be Mad?," the poem that introduces *On the Boiler.* The lines are: "A girl who knew all Dante once / Live to bear children to a dunce." Yeats was very far from thinking that Stuart was a dunce. Indeed, he had declared his belief that Stuart had the most majestic prose style of anyone writing in English,[42] and might become "our great writer," and he wrote extravagant phrases for the jackets of at least five of Stuart's books; in *The Coloured Dome,* he found "a style full of lyrical intensity, a mind full of spiritual passion."[43] However, having been so involved in trying to save the marriage in its early days, Yeats cannot have approved of Stuart's flamboyant neglect of his family. Besides, "dunce" is a good rhyme for "once"—too good, apparently, to resist.

Yeats once said, famously, "Out of the quarrel with others, we make rhetoric; out of the quarrel with ourselves, poetry."[44] Three new poems revealed that the internal quarrel was still going on. Several years later, W. H. Auden was to write, in his moving elegy for Yeats, that "poetry makes nothing happen."[45] In "The Man and the Echo," written between July and October 1938, Yeats asks what his poetry might have made happen. In a searing examination of conscience, expressed dramatically as a man shouting questions into a deep, rocky cleft high on Knocknarea, one of the mountains overlooking Sligo, he puts three blunt questions to himself in words mainly of one syllable. Highly specific, they are at the same time, like the best of Yeats, universal:

> All that I have said and done,
> Now that I am old and ill,
> Turns into a question till
> I lie awake night after night
> And never get the answers right.

The questions follow:

> Did that play of mine send out
> Certain men the English shot?
> Did words of mine put too great strain
> On that woman's reeling brain?
> Could my spoken words have checked
> That whereby a house lay wrecked?

The first of these raises a charge that will forever hang over Yeats. Was he responsible for romanticizing blood sacrifice, luring ardent Irish nationalists to respect the gun over the ballot box for a large part of the twentieth century? "That play of mine" refers to *Cathleen ni Houlihan*, in which a young Irishman spurns his fiancée in order to join the Irish patriots supported by the French in the doomed rebellion in 1798. Yet the sense of culpability extends also to "Easter 1916," with the brilliant oxymoron, "A terrible beauty is born," suggesting that violence can be beautiful.

Accusations were leveled against Yeats in the mid-1930s. In his *Irish Literary Portraits*, written in 1935, John Eglinton says that Yeats and his literary believers in ancient mystical Ireland "may be said to have conjured up the armed bands of 1916."[46] In *Irish Literature and Drama in the English Language* in 1936, Stephen Gwynn recalls that *Cathleen ni Houlihan* so disturbed him when he saw it in 1902 that "I went home asking myself if such plays should be produced unless one was prepared for people to go out to shoot and be shot."[47]

The question hangs in the air. Yeats scholars, when they mount a public platform are liable to be asked, guilty or not?

Absolutely not, says Denis Donoghue, University Professor at New York University. At the Yeats International Summer School in Sligo in August 1996, he was contemptuous of the postcolonial theory that Yeats, like Patrick Pearse, bears some responsibility for the post-1969 killings in Northern Ireland. To Donoghue, Yeats's texts do not support the charge: any young person who takes up a rifle as a result of reading Yeats, he said, "is guilty of bad reading." R. F. Foster, Carroll Professor of Irish History at Oxford and official Yeats biographer, also emphatically rejects the proposition of Yeats as political conjuror. At the Hay-on-Wye Literary Festival in 1997, he argued that so much in Irish history, not least Britain's involvement in World War I, led to the 1916 Rising that Yeats's words cannot be seriously considered an influence on actual events.

On the other hand, Robert Tracy, Professor of English and Irish Literature at the University of California at Berkeley, believes that Yeats may possibly have something to answer for. At Sligo in 1996 Tracy interpreted *Cathleen ni Houlihan* as effectively telling young Irishmen that violent death in the nationalist cause is preferable to dull domestic life. Indeed, he said, the common personification of the Irish nation as a beautiful young woman gives Ireland a Dracula quality— that of a vampire who is rejuvenated by the blood of young men.

For Ireland's leading postcolonialist theorist, Declan Kiberd, Professor of Anglo-Irish Literature and Drama at University College, Dublin, there is no doubt. He answers Yeats's question "Did that play of mine send out / Certain men the English shot?" with a resounding "Yes." Kiberd, in Sligo in 1995, observed that the entire Rising, staged in its symbolic but indefensible location, with Pearse reading out the proclamation of the Republic before the Ionic columns of the Post Office, was "street theatre in the manner of Yeats": men consciously acting for dramatic effect. Yeats, said Kiberd, answering Auden, intended his poetry to make things happen.

Perhaps Yeats needed to believe that his words could alter the course of history. What "The Man and the Echo" shows indisputably is that his conscience was not clear.

The poem's second question—"Did words of mine put too great strain / On that woman's reeling brain?"—needs no exegesis. Only Yeats knew exactly what passed between him and Margot Ruddock. He could not know what part his affair and subsequent rejection, or even his overpraise of her poetry, had played in her ultimate collapse. Continuing to make efforts on her behalf, in August Yeats wrote a long letter to the Swami in India, asking him to repay Margot fifty pounds of his debt.[48] Yeats himself waived fifty pounds that the Swami owed him in order to make the repayment possible. When the Swami did as he was asked, he was hurt to get no reply.[49]

The third question—"Could my spoken words have checked / That whereby a house lay wrecked?"—is generally understood to relate to Coole Park.[50] The house still stood when Yeats wrote these lines and was not demolished by a contractor until 1941. Its fate, however, had been clear since 1928 when Margaret Gregory remarried and sold the estate to the Free State Department of Forestry, with the provision that her mother-in-law, Lady Gregory, could live there until her death. Yeats could not have stopped that. But "The Man and the Echo" is a poem, not a legal document. Yeats obviously felt residual guilt over some part of his association with Coole. The phrase "my spoken words" recalls the many angry confrontations he had with Margaret Gregory. Perhaps if he had not argued with her, perhaps (what may also have been in the back of his mind) if he had not usurped so many of Robert Gregory's privileges at Coole, the house might have been kept in the family.

The truth seems to be that, as with the 1916 Rising, Yeats felt responsibility for events that his words had made into legend. The rest of this bleak interrogatory poem runs through the great mysteries of existence. Is there any meaning in intellect, in love, in life? "Echo" suggests that there is not; the last words it throws back are "Into the night." "Man" then wanders off. Just as in the poem "Politics," he cannot focus on abstractions: "A stricken rabbit is crying out, / And its cry distracts my thought."

*   *   *

"The Circus Animals' Desertion," written between November 1937 and September 1938, shows Yeats counting once again: "What can I but enumerate old themes?" He makes another list. First, he looks at Oisin, the mystical ancient Irish hero of "The Wanderings of Oisin," his first long narrative poem, and sees a dream sprung out of sexual frustration: "But what cared I that set him on to ride, / I, starved for the bosom of his faery bride?"

Next he repudiates his Fenianism: "'The Countess Cathleen' was the name I gave it." But when nationalist politics turned ugly, the dream that took its place—the Irish theater—was just another evasion of reality: "Players and painted stage took all my love, / And not those things that they were emblems of."

Having knocked over all his cherished illusions in a row, like a child with his old toys, he is left with the question of where they came from, the mystery that had perplexed him since youth. Now, at life's end, he knows:

> A mound of refuse or the sweepings of a street,
> Old kettles, old bottles, and a broken can,
> Old iron, old bones, old rags, that raving slut
> Who keeps the till. Now that my ladder's gone
> I must lie down where all the ladders start
> In the foul rag and bone shop of the heart.

Yeats worked hard to find the right scraps for this rubbish pile. He tried out "old orange peel" and "old bits [of] newspaper" before settling on his melodious list.[51] There was no hesitation, however, about the "raving slut." This designation, constant through the poem's composition, represents the final appearance of Yeats's madwoman-muse, Crazy Jane. Less clear is whether the poem's terrible solipsistic conclusion—that all his symbols came from his own imagination, the human junk shop—is a defeat or a triumph.

The man who wrote the letters, as distinct from the narrator of the poems, did not despise the human heart. In early September, having been away from Edith for all of six weeks, Yeats wrote, "I have great need of you, needing you as earth needs Spring . . . I begin to hold you, gently, timidly at the top of your head and then—having got so far, my dear, it is best to close this letter with

Yours affectionately W. B. Yeats[52]"

A week later brought another love letter, almost adolescent in its inarticulateness.

> I am longing for you in body and soul . . . O my dear—I want to say all those foolish things which are sometimes read out in breach of promise cases. I know what it is to think what transcends speech and what speech transcends, that is perhaps what savage tom toms are for.[53]

From the examination of conscience and the discarding of dreams, it was a short step to the epitaph. Beginning *On the Boiler* earlier that year, Yeats had hoped that setting down his political views would increase the power of his poetry. "Under Ben Bulben," written in the late summer of 1938, shows that the hope was not misplaced.

He had done a lot of work on the poem before going to England. The famous last lines—"*Cast a cold eye / On life, on death. / Horseman, pass by!*"—were inspired by reading Rilke during the summer, written by August (in a preliminary version, with the word *Huntsman* in place of *Horseman*)[54] and sent to Ethel Mannin, who, with her new husband, was coming to Dublin for a visit. Yeats told her that he had chosen his burial place, Drumcliffe, a village north of Sligo, where his great-grandfather (John Yeats) had been rector. Ethel brushed off morbidity. "I like your epitaph," she said, but added, looking forward to their dinner at the Shelbourne Hotel, "I don't want to talk of death, but rather of life and ideas."[55]

The poem is best known for its final verse (which starts "Under bare Ben Bulben's head / In Drumcliff churchyard Yeats is laid"). But the penultimate stanza, with its irresistible rhythm and pounding rhymes, is more revealing, biographically and politically. It is *On the Boiler* poeticized and detoxified; the landed gentry and the peasantry are idealized, the growing middle class dismissed with the finest phrase the dubious science of eugenics is ever likely to enjoy: "Base-born products of base beds." Condescending as it may be, the stanza offers a unifying vision of "Irishry," a people linked by common inheritance of an ancient tradition of superlative warriors. (Some would draw the snobbish sting from the poem by arguing that the riders who are asked to cast a cold eye on the modern world are not the hunting-fishing Anglo-Irish aristocracy but rather the horsemen of the mythical Queen Maeve.) The opening couplet issues an order that, by general agreement, continues to ring, perhaps too loudly, in the ears of every Irish poet since Yeats:

> Irish poets learn your trade,
> Sing whatever is well made,
> Scorn the sort now growing up
> All out of shape from toe to top,
> Their unremembering hearts and heads
> Base-born products of base beds.
> . . . .
> Sing the lords and ladies gay
> That were beaten into the clay
> Through seven heroic centuries;
> Cast your mind on other days
> That we in coming days may be
> Still the indomitable Irishry.

A cold look at the great poems of Yeats's last two years of life will show him vacillating to the end. He can be found facing East and West, embracing the meaning and the meaninglessness of life. The joyful stoicism of "Lapis Lazuli's" "All things fall and are built again, / And those that build them again are gay" is counterbalanced by the bitterness of "But I am not content" and the anger of "Why should not Old Men be Mad?" Even such a Yeats-lover as Ellmann, whose admiration for the poems was boundless, almost protective, concludes, in *The Identity of Yeats,* that Yeats "does not offer a set of fixed positions even at the end of his life."

Yeats never hid his ambivalence. Summarizing what he called his "private" philosophy for Ethel, he wrote, "To me all things are made of the conflict of two states of consciousness." To his fellow student of Indian mysticism, Lady Elizabeth Pelham, he also tried to clear up the muddle: "When I try to put all into a phrase I say, "'Man can embody truth but he cannot know it.'" In other words, he seems finally to have accepted what his father had told him long before—that he was a poet, not a philosopher. That is how most readers also accept him.

Lily Yeats was family historian. Learning of her brother's plans for his grave, she chided him for breaking with Yeats tradition. There had not been a tombstone in the Yeats family since the eighteenth century. "The family," she declared, "has always been very gay."[56] Yeats's memorial plans, along with the imminent death of their unmarried aunt Jane Grace Yeats, born in 1846, sent Lily's thoughts racing back to the Great Famine when their grandparents, the Reverend William Butler Yeats, a Protestant clergyman in County Down, and his wife, "drew down the blind before they sat down to a meal. Any moment the face of staring men or women might look in at the window, and they were living on just the bare necessities, and working hard at relief work." Lily, in what sounds like a defense of their nonstarving ancestors, wrote that "Grandfather Yeats and the grandfather of the present Archbishop Gregg were sent together preaching through England to collect money for relief."[57]

In October Yeats was prevented by lumbago from returning to England as soon as he had planned. Confined to his room at Riversdale, he heard that Olivia Shakespear had died in London of a heart attack, following gallbladder trouble. He was shaken and called it "tragic news." Although he had been less in touch with Olivia in recent years, he wrote to Dorothy (but, significantly, not to Edith), openly acknowledging perhaps for the first time Olivia's importance to him:

For more than forty years she has been the centre of my life in London. . . . When I first met her she was in her late twenties but in looks a lovely young girl. When she died she was a lovely old woman. . . . For the moment I cannot bear the thought of London. I will find her memory everywhere.[58]

At Olivia's Kensington mansion flat, as her son-in-law, Ezra Pound, packed up her things, he got in touch with George to ask if Yeats still wanted an embroidered portiere of Olivia's, as he had once mentioned. "If he remembers and wants it I am deputed to see that he gets it," said Ezra. Olivia's will, published a month later, helps to explain the source of her grace and independence maintained through so many years alone. The estate of the widow of Henry Hope Shakespear was valued at £23,377—the equivalent of £670,000 in 1998—and several times the sum Yeats had received for his Nobel Prize. The family solicitors recognized this as an inheritance of "substantial means." As Ezra later said of himself and his wife, Dorothy, still living in Rapallo, "We had money from then on."

Late in October Yeats left for England, heedless of Dorothy Wellesley's warning that if war broke out he would find himself unable to travel through London. He would not even be able to come to Penns in the Rocks, she spelled out, as the estate would be full of children from London. (The Home Office's Committee on Evacuation had been working since April to draw up plans to reduce the population of densely populated areas in the event of air raids.) However, Yeats—and not only he—put faith in the accord that Neville Chamberlain had just reached with Hitler at Munich. King George VI offered public thanks to the Almighty "for His mercy in sparing us the horrors of war."[59]

Yeats thus spent a tranquil month with his Sussex hostesses. At The Chantry House, he wrote the draft outline of *The Death of Cuchulain*, concluding the cycle of five Cuchulain plays begun with *On Baile's Strand* in 1904. The plot, in which the great hero, Yeats's alter ego, is beheaded by the Blind Man who had profited from his foolishness in the first play, suggests a valedictory state of mind. The play was complete when, on November 26, George met him in London and escorted him on his winter journey south. The first of December saw them reinstalled at the Hôtel Idéal-Séjour at Cap Martin.

The nursing roster of the previous year was reversed. George was now to stay with Yeats until the end of January, when Edith would take over. Spelling this out in a letter to Edith before Christmas, he added, "My son is expected. He should have been here at 2 P.M., then it was to be at 4. Now it is to be 12 P.M. at the earliest."[60]

Yeats blamed the weather for this delayed arrival, but there is impatience in his curt phrasing. Overall his letters display little feeling for his son, now seventeen—a marked contrast to the many affectionate references to his daughter and her activities. Both before and after Christmas, he mentioned without comment to Edith that Michael was in Corsica by himself. (Anne Yeats remained in Dublin over the holidays and spent Christmas Day with the extended family at the home of Aunt Fanny Yeats.) His paternal aloofness was mixed with admiration and envy; he saw his son as tall, elegant, and mathematically gifted. He also recognized that their political views were opposed. From the age of ten Michael had described himself defiantly as "a Dev man," and as he grew older he sided with de Valera's Fianna Fáil.[61]

Thanks to Yeats's pulling power or the climate, a number of his friends found themselves wintering in the same corner of the Côte d'Azur, and in a position to pay social calls. The president of the Royal Hibernian Academy of Arts, Dermod O'Brien, and his wife, Mabel, were at Cap d'Ail. Dorothy and Hilda settled in for the winter in a villa at Beaulieu. Yeats dined with them every second or third day, Dorothy sending a car over the ten-mile distance to fetch and return him each time.[62] Their friend Walter Turner, with his wife, was also in the neighborhood. It made a convivial scene. All dined together one evening with the pianist Artur Schnabel and his wife; Christmas dinner saw Dorothy, Hilda, Yeats, George, and Michael around the table.

These and other pleasant details of the last month of Yeats's life were recorded by Dorothy in *Letters on Poetry from W. B. Yeats to Dorothy Wellesley* in 1940 and by Joseph Hone's biography in 1942. However, the actual atmosphere is unlikely to have been as serene as described. Not recorded is the background of illness, lesbian rivalry, and alcoholism. Hilda, exhausted from writing a survey of Africa and suffering from thyroid malfunction, was to die the following year. Dorothy was drinking heavily.[63] Also, there was a tussle between Dorothy and Edith for Yeats's company. The two were bitter enemies.[64] Dorothy's detailed account of those crucial weeks omits any mention of Edith Shackleton Heald. Yet Dorothy and her lover would not have been free to dance attendance on Yeats for two months had Edith, rather than George, been in charge of his timetable.

Edith's arrival was set for January 27. On New Year's Day, 1939, Yeats wrote to her saying how eagerly he looked forward to her arrival and to their month alone together. When she came, he said, not only George but Dorothy and Hilda would be leaving. He described himself as suffering from too many journeys to Dorothy's villa. He complained also of "too much chess in which I am always beaten by my son."[65] Once again he signed himself (in a phrase excised before publication) as her lover and friend.

If his health was failing, he gave no hint, apart from a mention of fatigue. His letters carry none of the recitatives of diagnoses, injections, and temperature readings that mark those written in his other periods of illness in foreign parts. As January dragged itself along, Yeats advised Edith what her duties were to be when she came: to take him for long drives and to keep him awake during the day so that he would sleep when he went to bed. Saying that he felt better than he had for years, he signed off with familiar wistful effusions implying desire.

To Elizabeth Pelham, however, he wrote the very opposite: "I know for certain that my time will not be long."[66]

That he was facing his own death shows clearly in the somber new poem begun as a sequel to *The Death of Cuchulain*. George did not like the play, with good reason. It is not a strong play; it never recovers from a jokey start in which an old man walks on, introduces himself as an antiquated producer, and addresses the audience directly about the small number of people who appreciate "Mr. Yeats." The poem, for which Yeats began dictating a prose draft on January 7, was, once again, a work of a different order.

A dead warrior, unnamed except in the title, "Cuchulain Comforted," arrives in the country of the dead. The other shades tell him to put aside his arms and, as they are doing, to sew himself a shroud. As they thread the needles for his winding sheet, they tell him that they are "convicted cowards all." They then begin to sing:

> **They sang but had nor human tunes nor words,**
> **Though all was done in common as before;**

> *They had changed their throats and had the throats of birds.*

"Cuchulain Comforted" is an eerie, almost cinematographic depiction of Yeats's concept of "the Shiftings," the soul immediately after death entering a dream of the life it had not lived. In the poem, Cuchulain, the great shape-changer, changes form for the last time. By laying down his arms and beginning to sew his shroud, he becomes all that he was not: a woman, a coward, and finally—all that is left of a dead poet—a voice.

That Yeats had considerable strength and audacity on January 13, 1939 (the day he put the prose draft of the poem into verse), shows in his use of *terza rima*, a metric form he had never used before. This rhyme scheme—an intricate interweaving of rhyme through a three-line pattern—is a conspicuous borrowing from Dante, and a sign that Yeats was preparing his journey into the next world.

On Saturday, January 21, 1939, he wrote "The Black Tower." He had one week to live. Again, the setting is pictorial: a wind-swept Irish hilltop where a tower (black, the color of death) is guarded by besieged men who wait for a king who will not return. They are, with echoes of 1916, "oath-bound men"—that is, bound to a hopeless cause. Near them is a tomb where (in a reference to the last pagan king of Ireland) the dead are buried upright, their bones rattling in the wind. The refrain, even when read silently, carries the sound of Yeats's chanting voice:

> *There in the tomb the dark grows blacker,*
> *But wind comes up from the shore:*
> *They shake when the winds roar,*
> *Old bones upon the mountain shake.*

The last week of his life began with the usual socializing. The Dermod O'Briens stopped by the hotel and had tea. George was out; Yeats held court from bed, in his small room with its single large window looking out at the sea. He did not seem to be ill. He talked animatedly of the Abbey and his friend Higgins. He was so busy working, he said, that he had even given up reading detective novels. When Dorothy and Hilda stopped to see him, they found him dressed and full of talk, ready to praise, with the kind of words she liked to hear, a song Dorothy had written for the Cuala *Broadsides*—"Yes, yes, it has great poetical profundity."[67] Later that evening, back at his hotel, he sat in the lamplight and read aloud "The Black Tower." Dorothy, taking in the light brown suit, the blue shirt and matching handkerchief, and the silver hair, thought to herself, "What a beautiful man!"[68] When he had finished, he asked Hilda to try to set the poem to music. It was not a request easily refused. Hilda and Dorothy went outside, walked up and down until they constructed a singable tune and went back in and performed it. Yeats (whom they knew to be tone deaf) said he liked it.

In those days he did all the talking. Dorothy tried to memorize his words as he uttered them. She caught observations on the unmatched perfection of Greek drama; also, "Shakespeare is only a mass of magnificent fragments" and "I feel I am only beginning to understand how to write."[69] He looked as well as she had ever seen him.

He looked well also to a professional eye. His doctor was so impressed with Yeats's vigorous work that he told George her husband might live another six months.

A few days later Yeats was dying. A man full of vitality and fun suddenly turned into a pain-racked, semi-conscious invalid gasping for breath. He was slipping fast and knew it. He instructed George that if he died, she was to wait a year until the publicity had subsided and then ship him back to Sligo.[70] He did not want the kind of big funeral that George Russell, "AE," had had.

George wondered how to let the family in Dublin know that the end was near. A public telegram would have the news all over Dublin within hours. When Dorothy and Hilda came to visit on Thursday, January 26, it was decided that Hilda would send a telegram to Vita Sackville-West in Kent and ask her to deliver the message by telephone. The request was duly relayed to Sissinghurst Castle in Kent, where Sackville-West, former lover of both Hilda and Dorothy and a woman unacquainted with any of the Yeats family, thought this a curiously roundabout way of doing things.[71] Nonetheless, she did as she was asked.

George remained calm. She invited Dorothy to visit again, saying poetically (so Dorothy remembered), "Come back and light the flame."[72] Dorothy did return and found Yeats under sedation, scarcely able to speak. He gathered enough strength to ask her if she was writing poetry. The answer was yes. "Good, good," he said, kissed her hand, and drifted off again.

The following day, Friday, he was in a coma. In the small hours, however, he seemed to rally, and on Saturday morning he was awake enough to add some corrections to "The Black Tower." At two o'clock in the afternoon he died. George telephoned the O'Briens, who came with an Anglican clergyman. O'Brien too was struck by Yeats's appearance; he said he had never seen such a beautiful face.[73]

The month alone with Edith, so long dreamed of, was not to be. As Yeats lay dying, a friend from Steyning drove her to the South of France and she arrived before he breathed his last. The night of his death she sat in vigil over his body. She later set down her thoughts: "I watched over him until 4 A.M. His features had become even more noble and beautiful than I had known them. It was a wonderful southern night of stars and I remembered that 'the heavens themselves blaze forth the deaths of princes.'"[74]

George's thoughts are not on record. Yet on her honeymoon in the Ashdown Forest she had taken down Yeats's description of just such a scene. The loyal queen in *The Only Jealousy of Emer* invites her husband's mistress, Eithne Inguba, to watch with her over the body of Cuchulain:

> Come hither, come sit down beside the bed;
> You need not be afraid, for I myself
> Sent for you, Eithne Inguba.
> . . . .
> Of all the people in the world we two,
> And we alone, may watch together here,
> Because we have loved him best.

The selfless wife, the latest love, side by side mourning the dead hero: the scene invented in 1917 staged itself at the Hôtel Idéal-Séjour in 1939. That life should imitate art was no more than Yeats expected. That it should do so at his deathbed was a fitting finale for a man who believed so passionately that between dream and reality there is no great divide.

Epilogue: Laid to Rest?

YEATS'S GRAVE is one of Ireland's great tourist attractions.[1] The deep sense of communion felt by the thousands who every year make the pilgrimage to Drumcliffe Churchyard outside Sligo would not be dimmed by knowing they had been manipulated into doing exactly what the poet wished. A modernist in that he put his message into multiple media, Yeats intended his grave, like his tower, like his book jackets, like his clothes, to make a statement, and he carefully controlled its look.

With geological precision, he specified the stone for his marker: "No marble . . . / On limestone quarried near the spot." He chose the backdrop for the inevitable photograph; the right camera angle can catch the gravestone and Ben Bulben in the same shot. And he wrote the caption:

> *Cast a cold eye*
> *On life, on death.*
> *Horseman, pass by!*

What else to see once obeisance has been paid to the grave? "By the road an ancient cross," the poem helpfully specifies. Otherwise, the carved tenth-century cross at the side of the N15 would be easy to miss. The whole scene is an exercise in self-iconization, well prepared in advance. "Under Ben Bulben" was first published in the *Irish Times* and *Irish Independent* on February 3, 1939, five days after Yeats's death.

Would visitors to the grave be less moved if they thought that Yeats's body was not in it? There is a fair chance that it is not. Getting his remains from France to the selected spot was a matter over which the poet had no control.

Yeats was buried on January 30, 1939, with Anglican prayers, in the Catholic cemetery at Roquebrune. Among the mourners, as reported by the Paris correspondent of the *Times,* were Mrs. Yeats, Mr. Dermod O'Brien, the president of the Royal Hibernian Academy of Arts, and Lady Gerald Wellesley, the poetess.[2]

In his last days, Yeats had instructed his wife that he wished to be reburied in Sligo after a year. He had not anticipated, however, that the war with Germany would now take place. After September 1939, repatriating dead poets took low priority in French affairs.

The war was not the only complication. Like James Joyce, who died in Zurich two years later, and D. H. Lawrence, who died in Vence in 1930, Yeats had the mischance to end his life in an expensive part of the world accustomed to having visitors coming to fight for their health and losing. The problem of burial space was chronic in the spas and resorts of the South of France and Switzerland. A permanent plot of valuable ground was a waste, as families of foreign deceased seldom visited. A common solution was the temporary grave; the remains of both Joyce and Lawrence were eventually moved.

After the war, as Europe got back to normal, Joyce's widow, a native of Galway living in Zurich, hoped that the Irish government would bring home the remains of a towering figure of Irish literature. However, after making inquiries, the eminent Dublin lawyer Constantine Curran reported that sadly the body would not be welcome.[3] The author of

Ulysses, who had never wished or dared to set foot in the Free State, was far from being Erin's favorite son.

Yeats was another matter. As soon as he died, the Irish government wired George about repatriation. Maud Gonne herself wrote to Eamon de Valera and also to the Irish president, Douglas Hyde, and to F. R. Higgins, of the Abbey Theatre, asking for the remains to be brought to Ireland.[4] Higgins wrote back that every effort was being made: "While various appeals are being made to us for a burial in St Patrick's Cathedral, Glasnevin or Mount Jerome, because of their association with W. B.'s work, I know personally that he had a passionate desire to rest in Sligo."[5]

From Zurich, Joyce sent a wreath to the funeral, and conceded to a friend that Yeats had been the greater writer, because of his imagination.[6] From England, George Bernard Shaw found a practical way of paying his last respects. In July 1939, he sent three hundred pounds to Lolly as a gift to the troubled Cuala Press.[7] The finest tribute to Yeats from a fellow writer came from W. H. Auden, freshly arrived in the United States. In the magnificent elegy "In Memory of W.B. Yeats," dated "Jan. 1939" as if to mark the death of the thirties as well as of the poet, he addresses the question of the relation of art to history. With the assertion "poetry makes nothing happen: it survives / In the valley of its saying," he accepted Yeats's view that the poet's duty lies not in political action but in the affirmation of language and imagination:

> Follow, poet, follow right
> To the bottom of the night,
> With your unconstraining voice
> Still persuade us to rejoice.

George herself began making immediate plans for the reburial. Upon her return to Ireland she and Jack went to Sligo and made inquiries with the Sligo Steam Navigation Company, which had so often transported Yeats as a boy. The company said it would be simple to bring the body from Liverpool to Sligo, and Constantine Curran offered her his help in case there were Customs difficulties.[8] The repatriation was to take place that September—sooner than Yeats had wanted, she conceded to her dear friend Tom MacGreevy. He had wanted a year to go by, until the newspapers had forgotten him.

Instead, as Yeats's friend Joseph Hone wrote in his biography published in 1942, "the War came in September. Yeats still lies at Roquebrune. His grave is on second terrace of the cemetery, and is marked by a small flat stone at the head, with 'W. B. Yeats, 1865–1939' on it in simple letters." A photograph of the gravestone shows it beside that of A. G. Hollis.

Edith Heald took a long time to recover from Yeats's death. In 1947, when the British who could afford it were slowly returning to the luxury of Continental travel, under severe currency restrictions, Edith Shackleton Heald and her partner of four years, Hannah Gluckstein, went to Monte Carlo as if finally to exorcise the ghost of Edith's famous lover. On June 10 they made the pilgrimage to Roquebrune and looked for the grave at which Edith had stood heartbroken eight years earlier. It was not there. Edith was distraught. Gluck, as she insisted on being called, took charge.[9]

Gluck (rhymed with *luck,* not *look*), ten years younger than Edith, was the daughter of the wealthy Gluckstein family, owners of the London caterers J. Lyons and Co. Financially independent, indifferent to convention, Gluck was almost a caricature of a 1930s lesbian. Like the notorious novelist Radclyffe Hall, she dressed like an elegant man in a time when no woman wore trousers. According to her biographer Diana Souhami, she had her hair clipped at a gentlemen's hairdresser's on Bond Street and her shirts made on Jermyn Street; John Lobb, Bootmaker, of Saint James's had a last of her foot.

Gluck had taken over Edith's life. As brusque and dominating as her cross-dressing was meant to suggest, she had moved into The Chantry House at Steyning against the strong objection of Nora Heald, who was disgusted by her sister's flaunted lesbianism. There were many angry scenes, and tears (Nora's). Gluck took the hallowed "Yeats room" for her study, and made a shed in the garden into her studio. She hired the servants, organized the garden, chose the guests, ordered for the wine cellar, and sat at the head of the table in a dinner suit. It was with the same manly decisiveness that at Roquebrune she set herself to find out what had happened to Yeats's missing grave.

Educated by a Swiss governess and by the rigorous St. Paul's Girls' School in London, Gluck spoke excellent French. She closely questioned Abbé Biancheri, the local priest at Roquebrune, who checked with the Maison Roblot, the Menton undertakers who had handled the funeral. Biancheri reported back that there was no Yeats grave—for good reason.

At the time of the death, according to the abbé's findings, Yeats's widow had been given three choices: a permanent grave, a plot for ten to fifteen years, or a *fosse commune*. She had chosen the last of these. Over succeeding years the *fosse* had been cleared, in part in 1941, then fully in January 1946 to make room for new arrivals. The removed bones had been placed in the *ossuaire*.

The atavistic horror of a loved one unburied sent Edith into fits of weeping. She cried all night, moaning over and over (so Gluck recorded), "I would know his bones anywhere."[10]

Gluck pushed the abbé for more information. Five days later, after consulting the records of the Mairie de Roquebrune and the cemetery official in charge of graves and exhumations, he offered firmer information to the same effect. No permanent site had been acquired in Yeats's name. He had been buried instead in a communal grave, which had been partly cleared in 1941, the rest by 1946. All the bones were put in the ossuary. The spot that had been occupied by Yeats in 1939 was now the resting place of a Madame Victoire Lanteri. The whereabouts of the remains had been hard to trace because Yeats's death had been registered at the *mairie* under the name of Butler. The cemetery's exhumer, however, had volunteered a vague recollection that the Yeats body had had a surgical truss circled with thin strips of steel. In any event, reassembling a particular skeleton would not be easy, as the ossuary's practice was to separate skulls from limbs, and new additions were made daily.

Edith and Gluck went back to England and poured out their macabre discovery to a horrified Edmund Dulac and his partner, Helen Beauclerk. Dulac instantly fixed on two things: that George Yeats must not know about the missing grave, and that the matter must be kept out of the press. He himself wrote to Abbé Biancheri, stressing the need for absolute secrecy.

The trio's determination to deal with the matter themselves reopened an old conflict. Yeats had effectively been leading a double life. So much did Dulac, Beauclerk, and Edith see themselves in charge of the English side of his life that on occasion at The Chantry House, they would introduce their famous guest as a widower.[11] They saw George's penny-pinching as the cause of the problem.

Vowing silence, they arranged for a headstone, designed by Dulac, to be erected at the cemetery, appropriately enough, up against the ossuary, in a permanent spot for which they paid five thousand francs. They would tell the world, and George Yeats, that, as friends, they had merely donated a more lasting monument.

Satisfaction in their quiet conspiracy was shattered by a short item in the *Times* on January 6, 1948: YEATS'S LAST WISH: REMAINS TO BE BROUGHT FROM FRANCE. The newspaper reported that the poet's widow had informed the mayor of Sligo that the family was arranging to have the remains brought back from France that summer. They would be laid to rest at Drumcliffe, as Yeats had specified in "Under Ben Bulben." The story went on to explain how the war had intervened to prevent the widow from carrying out the poet's express wish that the reburial take place a year after his death.

Shaken, Dulac felt obliged to write and tell George the terrible truth. His concern, he told the widow, was that a sham burial not take place. He sent a copy to Edith, with his own comments on George.

He did not think kindly of George. In a possible reference to her fondness for drink,[12] Dulac told Edith that he thought that George had "enough wits left" to try to prevent a scandal.

If she now spreads the news about, she will undoubtedly cut a very poor figure as we have definite proof that she could have done something during all these years; the grave was not touched for eighteen months from the Liberation and she had nearly 10 years in which to extend the concession. Eire was neutral all that time.[13]

George Yeats wrote back instantly. For all her tolerance of Edith, she must have been aware that Dulac had forged and fostered the affair, and she was, moreover, not kindly disposed to Beauclerk, a highly attractive woman whom Yeats himself is said to have fancied. What is more, George did have her wits about her. She slapped Dulac down with a terse letter saying that her receipts proved that the grave was for ten years, not five, that the body had certainly not been placed in a communal grave, and that a French government representative in Ireland had assured her that returning the body would be a simple matter.[14]

By February 1948, with the wheels of repatriation in motion, the French authorities woke up to the potential embarrassment on their hands. A police inspector was sent from Paris to Roquebrune. After his visit, and a comparison of the funeral registers of Menton and Roquebrune, Abbé Biancheri wrote again to Dulac. It was certain that Yeats had had only a five-year place in a communal grave; this had definitely been emptied and the bones removed to the ossuary. A possible explanation for the confusion could be a clerical mistake; perhaps Mrs. Yeats's document specified a lease of ten years, while that held by the register of funerals granted five years only. A sight of her document would help to sort out the discrepancy. In any event, before the skeleton could begin to be reassembled, full medical and dental records—with details of illnesses, fractures, fillings, and measurements of the circumference of the skull and other bones—would be necessary.

All this was conveyed to Dulac in a masterly piece of clerical prose, which translates as:

> *One fact is certain: the bones of the late poet were placed in the ossuary. There is no doubt whatsoever on this subject. Is it possible to find the bones of the poet Yeats in the ossuary? Yes! If we empty the entire contents of the ossuary and if we have details of distinctive characteristics which will enable us to reconstruct the skeleton after painstaking research carried out under the direction of a medical*

expert. . . . The researches would be long, expensive, extremely difficult,
but not impossible. The results would remain subject to the laws of
probability. Absolute certainty is in my view impossible.[15]

Yeats's death had not meant the end of George's unpleasant letters
from aggressive women. In early March, a letter arrived from Gluck
that was scarcely polite. Gluck listed her meticulous researches at
Roquebrune, mentioning acidly that "my enquiries were the first in
eight years."[16] To explain her own intense involvement, as a total out-
sider, she presented herself as a humble seeker after truth. As the iden-
tity of the remains would always be in doubt, "I cannot view this
reburial with equanimity."[17] She asked George to set her mind at rest
by reconsidering the plans.

Beneath all this seemingly dispassionate recital of facts lay an
implicit threat to go to the press.

This letter caused a split between Dulac and Gluck. Dulac com-
plained about Gluck's interference, saying that if she did not stop, he
would wash his hands of the whole affair. Edith apologized gently and
said that "W. B. might not have disliked his no-grave, but it would have
distressed him to think it might diminish our friendship—and I do not
see why it should. Love from Kosh."[18]

Tiny Edith was a feminist in print but not in practice. That same
month she had allowed Gluck to drive the sixty-five-year-old Nora
from The Chantry House. Having failed to protect her sister, at sixty-
five, from eviction from their beloved home, she could not curb Gluck
even to please Dulac.

If the long list of medical details requested by the cemetery was
assembled in Dublin and sent to Roquebrune, it was done quickly. On
March 17, in the presence of the mayor of Roquebrune, officials from
Paris, and the local police, an array of bones purported to be "Yeats's
body" was assembled and put into a coffin, and the original nameplate
attached. The good Abbé Biancheri found himself unable to be pres-
ent, owing, he explained to Dulac, to a call to a sickbed "in a distant
part of town."[19]

From then on, the return to Sligo was on a par with Siegfried's Rhine journey. In August 1948 a small vessel of the Irish Navy, the *Macha*, left Cork harbor for Dublin, where she was inspected by Ireland's minister for external affairs—none other than Sean MacBride, now, with his new party Clann na Pobla chta, a member of the interparty coalition government which had forced de Valera out in February. The ship then went via Gibraltar to Villefranche, to await the body.

If Roquebrune had been inattentive to the remains of its honored guest in the past, it made up for its neglect now. A guard of honor from the French Alpine Infantry escorted the coffin from Roquebrune Cemetery to the square of the town for a lying-in-state. The coffin was then taken to the ship at Nice, where, draped in the Irish tricolor, it was carried aboard to the accompaniment of "La Marseillaise" and "A Nation Once Again."

Back on the west coast of Ireland, the military vessel docked at Galway; the port of Sligo was ruled out, owing to tidal conditions. There Mrs. Yeats, with the poet's children and his brother, went on board and, to the sound of pipes and popping flashbulbs, the coffin came ashore. Taken by road through Galway and Mayo, with bystanders blessing themselves as it passed, the cortege was escorted into Sligo by the James Connolly Pipe Band with draped drums.[20] On September 17, 1948, in the square in front of the town hall, with local dignitaries, waited Sean MacBride and Yeats's old adversary, Eamon de Valera. A military guard of honor stood by the coffin for an hour as it lay in state. Then, at last, out at Drumcliffe, in a gravesite near the church porch, the coffin was interred, watched by a silent crowd that included Edith and Gluck.

The matter seems not again to have troubled George. When she died in Dublin in 1968, she was buried beside her husband. The churchyard, however, was not the resting place for Yeats's brother and sisters. Lolly, who died in 1940, was buried in the Saint Nahi Anglican churchyard at Dundrum, and Lily, failing to escape from Lolly even in death, was laid beside her in 1949. Jack, who died in 1957, was buried in Mount Jerome Cemetery, Dublin. John Butler Yeats's grave remains in upstate New York, Susan Yeats's in west London.

*   *   *

Ireland being Ireland, irreverent speculation about the actual contents of the sealed box began the moment it was carried ashore in Galway. Louis MacNeice, who was present in a jovial mood, informed a friend that they were witnessing the burial of a "Frenchman with a club foot."[21] Thirty-eight years were to pass, however, before the rumors were treated as more than a joke.

On August 19, 1986, an article in the *Times,* inspired by remarks of the novelist Anthony Burgess in a lecture in Monaco, reported speculation in France that the wrong body had been dug up and that a certain Capitaine Guillaume had ended up in Ireland.[22] Quelling the rumors was difficult because, the story said (just as Abbé Biancheri had told Gluck), the death certificate at the Mairie at Cap Martin was in the name of "Butler, Yeats William" and also because all references to the burial had disappeared.

In 1988, with the publication of the Gluck biography imminent, the story gathered strength. The *Daily Telegraph* saw a news peg: "Thousands of admirers of the poet W.B. Yeats who will make the pilgrimage to his grave in County Sligo for the 50th anniversary of his death next year, will almost certainly be paying their respects, not to his remains but to those of several anonymous Frenchmen."[23] The *Irish Times* put on its front page, "Claim that Yeats was buried in pauper's grave," and repeated the Souhami evidence.[24] (When she read this Nuala O'Faolain, its well-known columnist, wrote that she would undoubtedly visit Yeats's grave again "even though I now don't believe that he's there at all."[25]

Immediately Yeats's distinguished son, a former senator, and former member of the European Parliament, dismissed the rumors as "the greatest nonsense" and "cheap publicity." The body had been moved, he acknowledged, but to a temporary gravesite where those waiting to be transported were kept. He himself held the documents containing precise measurements of the bones, which proved beyond a doubt that the right body had been returned. "My father was a big man," he commented.[26]

In a joint letter to the London *Independent* on October 4, 1988, Anne and Michael were more forthcoming. The suggestion of a pauper's grave was ridiculous; the body had been placed in a ten-year grave—with the intention of its eventual return to Ireland. They stressed that their mother was extremely competent in business affairs, having handled all of Yeats's dealings, and that her French was excellent. They acknowledged, all the same, "It appears that at some stage the body was moved." When she had learned of the exhumation, their mother had gotten in touch with the French authorities and was assured that there would be no problems when the body was eventually transferred to Ireland. Upon the occasion of what they called "the official exhumation" in March 1948:

> Careful measurements were made of the remains (Yeats had a particularly massive bone structure) and the task of certification was made easier by the fact that, due to a long-term hernia problem, our father wore a truss. The exhumation took place in full conformity with the rigorous French laws on these matters, and in the presence of the mayor of Roquebrune, senior police officers, a medical expert, the superintendent of graves and other persons of expert and official standing.[27]

The Yeats children were, therefore, satisfied, as their mother had been, that the identity of the remains was established beyond all possibility of error. They hoped not to have to contribute further to the discussion.

Alas, four days later another letter appeared in the *Independent*, from a Madge Cockman of Oxford. She was the niece of Alfred Hollis, who had been buried in the grave next to Yeats. With her family, she too had gone to Roquebrune in 1947. They too found that the grave was gone and that their uncle had been exhumed. And, such is coincidence, their uncle also had been buried wearing a truss. Later they learned that identification of the body sent to Ireland "rested on it being encased in a steel corset." Thus, wrote Mrs. Cockman, "amongst

my family it is the belief that the body which lies in Drumcliffe ceme-
tery is that of my mother's brother, Alfred George Hollis."[28] The infor-
mation about the truss had been conveyed to Michael Yeats, she said.
However, both families had agreed not to pursue the investigation fur-
ther because of mutual distress.

There the matter rests, so to speak.

Obviously doubt will never be dispelled until the glaring discrepancies
in various accounts have been resolved. The precision of the details
made public by the Gluck and Hollis researches has not been matched
by corresponding openness and detail on the Yeats side. Some ques-
tions cry out for answers.

Why, if the grave had been leased for ten years, was the grave dis-
turbed after five years? Where was the exhumed body (or coffin)
stored between 1946 and 1948, if not in the ossuary? If the location,
either of the coffin or of the remains, was known, why were Gluck
and Heald not told, and why did the abbé and the *mairie* report confi-
dently that these could not be traced? Why, if there was absolute cer-
tainty about their identity, did the Yeats family need to have the bones
measured? And why were so many officials necessary as witnesses to
eliminate the possibility of error? Above all, if a surgical prosthesis was
the main criterion for identification, what was the size of the truss
worn on the remains sent to Ireland? Hollis's must have been the
larger of the two, because his niece described it as "a kind of steel
corset," designed to support a frame nearly bent double by disease.
Yeats suffered from no such deformity.

Rumor inevitably follows iconic remains, from Jesus to Elvis. And the
disturbed grave must be one of the most powerful in the Anima
Mundi. D. H. Lawrence's ashes, for example, are widely believed not
to lie at his ranch above Taos but to have been tipped out somewhere
along the journey from Vence to New Mexico, in the process of being
transported from Europe to the United States by his widow's not
overly respectful third husband.

Edith Heald, in the end, set up her own memorial: a plaque on The Chantry House proclaiming WILLIAM BUTLER YEATS 1865–1939 WROTE MANY OF HIS LATER POEMS IN THIS HOUSE. The stone designed by Dulac was set in the wall of the ossuary at Roquebrune in 1953.

What was once a mystery, however, is now a soluble problem. An analysis of the DNA of the bones buried at Drumcliffe would swiftly settle the matter with absolute finality. Honesty in tourism, one might argue, demands that this be done.

In the awkward circumstances, many words of the great, quotable poet suggest themselves. "Tread softly because you tread on my dreams"? Or, simply, the name of one of his his plays *The Dreaming of the Bones*? Most appropriate of all may be his apocryphal comment upon being told that he had confused Mussolini with Missolonghi: "But . . . does . . . it . . . really . . . matter?"

Abbreviations and Short Forms

By W. B. Yeats

Au	*Autobiographies*
AV	*A A Critical Edition of Yeats's "A Vision"* (1925), George Mills Harper, ed.
AV B	*A Vision* (1937)
CL1	*The Collected Letters of W. B. Yeats*, vol. 1, 1865–1895, John Kelly and Eric Domville, eds.
CL2	*The Collected Letters of W. B. Yeats*, vol. 2, 1896–1900, Warwick Gould, John Kelly, and Deirdre Toomey, eds.
CL3	*The Collected Letters of W. B. Yeats*, vol. 3, 1901–1904, John Kelly and Ronald Schuchard, eds.
Exp	*Explorations*, selected by Mrs. W. B. Yeats
LDW	*Letters on Poetry from W. B. Yeats to Dorothy Wellesley*
Mem	*Memoirs*, Denis Donoghue, ed.
Myth	*Mythologies*, London and New York: Macmillan, 1959
OBMV	*The Oxford Book of Modern Verse, 1892–1935*

OTB	*On the Boiler*
P	*Yeats's Poems*, A. Norman Jeffares, ed., 1989
SS	*The Senate Speeches of W. B. Yeats*, Donald R. Pearse, ed.
UP1–2	*Uncollected Prose by W. B. Yeats*, 2 vols., John P. Frayne, ed.
VP	*The Variorum Edition of the Poems of W. B. Yeats*, Peter Allt and Russell K. Alspach, eds., 1960
VPlays	*The Variorum Edition of the Plays of W. B. Yeats*, Russell K. Alspach, ed., 1966
Wade	*The Letters of W. B. Yeats*, Allan Wade, ed.
YVP1–3	*Yeats's "Vision" Papers*, George Harper, ed.

By Other Authors

Carpenter Humphrey	Carpenter, *A Serious Character: The Life of Ezra Pound*
Coogan	Tim Pat Coogan, *De Valera: Long Fellow, Long Shadow*
EDL	Omar Pound and A. Walton Litz, *Ezra Pound and Dorothy Shakespear: Their Letters 1909–1914*
Ellmann NB	Richard Ellmann, notebook, "Interviews with Mrs. Yeats, Frank O'Connor and others about W. B. Yeats, 1946"
FS	William M. Murphy, *Family Secrets*
Harwood	John Harwood. *Olivia Shakespear and W. B. Yeats: After Long Silence*
Hone	Joseph Hone, *W. B. Yeats 1865–1939*
Jeff	A. Norman Jeffares, *W. B. Yeats: A New Biography*
LDW	Dorothy Wellesley, *Letters on Poetry from W. B. Yeats to Dorothy Wellesley*
Lewis	Gifford Lewis, *The Yeats Sisters and the Cuala*
LG50	*Lady Gregory: Fifty Years After*, Saddlemyer, Ann, and Colin Smythe, eds.
LTWBY 1–2	*Letters to W. B. Yeats*, Richard J. Finneran, George Mills Harper, and William M. Murphy, eds.
McHugh	*Ah, Sweet Dancer: W. B. Yeats, Margot Ruddock, A Correspondence*, Roger McHugh, ed.

MM	Richard Ellmann, *W. B. Yeats: The Man and the Masks*
MYV1–2	George Mills Harper, *The Making of Yeats's "A Vision"*
PF	William M. Murphy, *Prodigal Father: The Life of John Butler Yeats (1839–1922)*
Pierce	David Pierce, *Yeats's Worlds* New Haven: Yale, 1995
Reid	B. L. Reid, *The Man from New York: John Quinn and His Friends*
RF.	R. F. Foster *W. B. Yeats: A Life*.
Souhami	Diana Souhami, *Gluck: Her Biography*
V Moore	Virginia Moore, *The Unicorn: William Butler Yeats' Search for Reality*
TLS	*Times Literary Supplement*
White	*The Gonne-Yeats Letters 1893–1938: Always Your Friend,* Anna MacBride White and A. Norman Jeffares, eds.
YA	*Yeats Annual*
YAACTS	*Yeats: An Annual of Critical and Textual Studies*
YH	George Mills Harper, *W. B. Yeats and W. T. Horton: The Record of an Occult Friendship*
YO	*Yeats and the Occult,* George Mills Harper, ed.

Correspondents

BM	Brenda Maddox
DW	Dorothy Wellesley
EM	Ethel Mannin
EP	Ezra Pound
ESH	Edith Shackleton Heald
JBY	John Butler Yeats
JQ	John Quinn
LG	Lady Gregory
Lily	Susan Mary (Lily) Yeats
LR	Lennox Robinson
Lolly	Elizabeth Corbet (Lolly) Yeats
MD	Mabel Dickinson
MG	Maud Gonne
MR	Margot Ruddock

OS	Olivia Shakespear
RE	Richard Ellmann
SY	Susan Yeats
TM	Thomas MacGreevy
WBY	W. B. Yeats

Manuscript Locations

Bancroft	Bancroft Library, University of California at Berkeley
Beinecke	Beinecke Rare Book and Manuscript Library, Yale University
Berg	The Henry W. and Albert A. Berg Collection, New York Public Library
BL	British Library
Burns	John J. Burns Library, Boston College
Emory	Robert W. Woodruff Library, Emory University, Atlanta, Georgia
Houghton	Houghton Library, Harvard University
Huntington	Henry E. Huntington Library, San Marino, California
Indiana	Lilly Library, Indiana University, Bloomington, Indiana
Kansas	Kenneth Spencer Research Library, University of Kansas
NLI	National Library of Ireland
NYPL	New York Public Library (Astor, Lenox, and Tilden Foundations)
Princeton	Firestone Library, Princeton University
Sligo	Sligo County Library
TCD	Trinity College Library, Trinity College Dublin
Texas	Harry C. Ransom Humanities Research Center, University of Texas at Austin
Tulsa	McFarlin Library, University of Tulsa
UCD	Archives Department, University College Dublin
USB	State University of New York at Stony Brook
Wellesley	Wellesley College Library

Notes and Sources

The abbreviations and short forms of the names of frequently cited books, journals, libraries, and people appear under *Abbreviations*. Full reference to books and articles is in the bibliography. Speculative information (chiefly where a letter's date of composition has been ascertained by postmark) is indicated by square brackets; uncertain dates are indicated by [?]. I have tried to indicate the source and date of cited unpublished letters. As the Yeats archive appears in various libraries, sometimes in duplicated form, I have given the name of the library where I studied the material.

I have not put in page references to the poems where the title is found in the text. Otherwise, page references refer to *Yeats's Poems*, edited by A. Norman Jeffares, with an appendix by Warwick Gould (London: Macmillan, 1989).

Introduction

1. BM, "Relative Values," *Sunday Times Magazine*, April 1, 1984.

2. W. H. Auden, "Yeats as Example," *The Kenyon Review* 10:2 (Spring 1948): 187–95.

3. Curtis Bradford, "George Yeats: Poet's Wife," *Sewanee Review* (July–Sept. 1969): 402.

4. Sean O'Faolain to Gwyneth Foden, Oct. 21 [?], Houghton.

5. *AV B* was not published until 1937. Yeats wrote this passage, dated "November 23rd 1928 and later" when preparing a revised edition of *AV A*, published in 1925.

6. Cullingford, *Gender, and History in Yeats's Love Poetry*, 111.

7. *MM*, 5.

8. *YVP1*, 18.

9. Ibid., 21.

10. Ibid., 18.

11. Andrew Motion, *Keats* (London: Faber, 1997).

Chapter 1. *An Astrological Deadline*

1. This incident is described in *MYV1*, 44 and 273 n9, and *YVP1*, 9; also in Edmund Dulac, "A Report on a visit paid to Mr David Wilson at St. Leonard's on Sea on the 22nd of March 1917 by Dr. E. D. Ross, W. B. Yeats and myself for the purpose of testing his 'chemical' medium." Texas.

2. For testimonials to Yeats's good company, see Oliver St. John Gogarty's *Irish Times* obituary, Jan. 30, 1939; Thomas MacGreevy's "A Generation Later," 10–11; and John Quinn, quoted in Reid, 418. Gogarty's view—that Yeats was the best conversationalist he had ever met—was no mean compliment, coming from one who might have merited the title himself.

3. *The Times*, March 22, 1917, 1.

4. Edmund Dulac, "A Report," p. 10.

5. *YVP1*, 9, and Dulac, "A Report," p. 10.

6. Ibid.

7. Yeats derived the concept of the Anima Mundi from the seventeenth-century Cambridge Platonists, particularly Henry More. See "Swedenborg, Mediums and Desolate Places," *Exp*, 60–61.

8. *Au*, 272.

9. WBY to John O'Leary, May 7 [1889], *CL1*, 163. In Yeats's enthusiasm for Blake, he made the erroneous claim that Blake had an Irish grandfather.

10. *Au*, 116.

11. Blake, prose preface and plate 77 of "Jerusalem."

12. WBY to LG, Jan. 29, [1917], Berg, NB6–26.

13. Hyde, "Yeats and Gogarty," 159.

14. *RF*, 103.

15. For a concise history of the Golden Dawn, see *CL1*, 486–87.

16. V. Moore, *The Unicorn*, 134.

17. *RF*, 106.

18. Sir Oliver Lodge, F.R.S., *The Survival of Man: A Study in Unrecognised Human Faculty* (London: Methuen, 1909).

19. *YVP1–2*.

20. *MYV1*, 269, n16.

21. WBY's "The Manuscript of 'Leo Africanus,'" edited by Steve L. Adams and George Mills Harper, *YA1*, 21 and 42, n40.

22. WBY to Sir William Barrett, Dec. 17, 1917, *MYV1*, 75.

23. *Exp*, 51.

24. WBY to LG, April 25 [1900], *CL2*, 514–15 and ibid., n2, provide a detailed account of this colorful episode. The Hammersmith Rare Book Entry lists Mr. Wilkinson, a builder, as occupant of the property in 1900.

25. "Mr. W.B. Yeats and Ghosts," *Irish Times*, Nov. 3, 1913; *UP2*, 407.

26. MacGreevy, "A Generation Later," 13.

27. WBY to LG, May 4, 13, [1914], Berg; also, George Mills Harper, "'A Subject of Investigation': Miracle at Mirabeau," and MG to WBY, April 20, June 8 [1914], White, 340–42.

28. WBY to LG, May 13, 1914, Berg, and *RF*, 517–19.

29. Harper, "'A Subject of Investigation,'" 172–189.

30. *Au*, 103–5; Katharine Tynan, *Twenty-five Years; Reminiscences* (New York: Devin Adair, 1913), 209.

31. RF, 463.

32. Kelvin I. Jones, *Conan Doyle and the Spirits: the Spiritualism of Sir Arthur Conan Doyle* (Wellingborough, Northants.: Acquarian Press, 1989), 119.

33. WBY to LG, Jan. [n.d., 1917], Berg. The ghost of Hugh Lane was a popular figure on the séance circuit. Appearing to Hester Dowden and Lennox Robinson in Dublin in January 1918, it relayed details of the sinking of the *Lusitania* and also his wish that his codicil be honored. Bentley, *Far Horizon*, 38–41.

34. TLS, Feb. 7, 1918, 66.

35. Carpenter, 492. Pound was speaking after the publication of these theories in *AV A*.

36. WBY to LG, Jan. 24 [1917], NLI, and WBY to Lily, Sept. 26, [1910], Burns.

37. Interview with Brigid O'Brien Ganly, March 26, 1997.

38. *FS*, 387.

39. JBY to Frank Yeats, Sept. 8, 1910, *FS*, 386.

40. Reid, op. cit. 248.

41. *CL3*, xlv.

42. *Exp*, 49.

43. Elizabeth Heine, "Yeats and Maud Gonne: Marriage and the Astrological Record, 1908–09," *YA*13, 4.

44. Elizabeth Heine, "'W. B. Yeats' Map in His Own Hand,'" *Biography* 1:3 (1978): 41. This article provides a thorough astrological analysis of Yeats's horoscope.

45. *John Sherman & Dhoya*, 40.

46. MG to WBY, Aug. 26 [1914], White, 347.

47. MG to JQ, July 15, 1915, Reid, 217.

48. MG to WBY, Aug. 26 [1914], White, 348.

49. MG to WBY, Sept. 25 [1914], White, 350.

50. *CL2*, lxxii.

51. *Au*, 354.

52. Stuart, *Black List*, 17, and WBY to LG, Dec. 1, 1915, Berg.

53. WBY to EM, Dec. 11 [1936], Wade, 872.
54. WBY to Lily, June 15 [1915], Burns.
55. *PF,* 377–78.
56. *FS,* 247–48.
57. Lily to JQ, Dec. 13, 1915, NYPL.
58. "Song of the Wandering Aengus."
59. "He Tells of the Perfect Beauty," written in 1895.
60. PASL in *Exp,* 344.
61. WBY to LG, June 27, 30, [1917], Berg.
62. Heine, 41.
63. Heine, 48.

Chapter 2. Counting

1. WBY to JBY, May 12, 1917, Wade, 624.
2. WBY to LG, Jan. 29, [1915], Berg.
3. Ibid.
4. George Moore, *Vale,* 119, 113–19.
5. George Moore, *Ave,* 242.
6. George Moore, *Vale,* 113–15.
7. Ibid., 114.
8. Amory, *Lord Dunsany,* 75.
9. JBY to WBY, Feb. 20, 1914; *PF,* 419.
10. WBY to LG, written on board the *Lusitania,* dated "Thursday," Berg.
11. First published as "Notorious," *VP,* 320, now as *[Closing Rhymes]* in *Responsibilities.*
12. *Mem,* 71–72.
13. *Mem,* 88. Even in his first draft, Yeats concealed Olivia Shakespear's identity under the pseudonym of "Diana Vernon."
14. *Mem,* 88.
15. Ibid., 101.
16. Ibid., 125.
17. Ibid., 126.

18. Harwood, 55.

19. *Mem*, 127.

20. Ibid., 134.

21. Ibid., 171.

22. WBY to LG, Jan. 13, 1913; Longenbach, 19.

23. *EDL*, 302.

24. WBY to Lily, Nov. 11, 1914, Burns.

25. T. S. Eliot, 'Yeats' in *On Poetry and Poets*. London: Faber and Faber, 1957.

26. JBY to Lily, May 17, 1916, NLI.

27. JBY to Lolly, May 17, 1916, NLI.

28. WBY to MD, May 11, 1908, Bancroft.

29. WBY to MD, July 6, [1908], Bancroft.

30. WBY to MD, Aug. 17 [1910], Bancroft.

31. Interview with Brigid O'Brien Ganly, March 26, 1997.

32. WBY to MD, June 20, [1908?].

33. MG to WBY, [June ?, 1913], White, 321.

34. RF, 485.

35. WBY to MG, [July?, 1913], White, 322.

36. *MYV1*, 280 n58, gives June 6, [1913], as the date.

37. *YVP2*, 376 gives May 1913 as the date when "the emotion of paternity was begun."

38. WBY to MG, [July? 1913], White, 322–23.

39. WBY to LG, April 30, 1914, and May 4, 1914, to LG, Berg.

40. Bradford, *Yeats at Work*, 53–58.

41. Of the 337 questions in Yeats's poems, 185 are rhetorical, according to Phillip Marcus, *YAACTS6*, 42.

42. V Moore, *The Unicorn* 239.

43. Derek Patmore, *My Friends When Young: The Memoirs of Brigit Patmore* (London: Heinemann, 1968), 80.

44. WBY to LG, March 11, [1914], Berg. See also Reid, 74, *PF*, 348, and RF, 407.

45. "Journal," in *Mem*, quoted in White, 35.

46. Interview with Anne Gregory de Winton, July 23, 1996.

47. *LG50*, 79–81.

48. Lolly to JBY, [n.d.], Lewis, 72.
49. JQ to WBY, Dec. 8, 1907, Alan B. Himber (with the assistance of George Mills Harper), *The Letters of Quinn to William Butler Yeats* (Ann Arbor: UMI Research Press, 1983), 95.
50. *LG50,* 129.
51. *Mem,* 160–61.
52. Ibid., 72.
53. Harwood, 118, says that George Yeats placed a second affair with Olivia around 1903.
54. WBY to LG, March 9, [1917], Berg.
55. Collis, *Somerville and Ross,* 129.
56. WBY to LG, Aug. 10, [1913], Berg.
57. Lolly to JBY, June 26, 1910, NLI.
58. JBY to WBY, April 25, 1915, *LTWBY2,* 312–13.
59. WBY to LG, June 16, [1917], Berg.
60. WBY to JBY, May 12, [1917] Wade, 624.
61. Ibid.
62. WBY to LG, June 28, [1917], Berg,

Chapter 3. *Mother or Daughter*

1. WBY to Lily, June 10, [1924], Burns.
2. White, 389–91, describes some of Yeats's wartime Channel crossings.
3. WBY to Florence Farr, March 5, 1917, *YA9,* 253.
4. "The Lover Speaks," and *MYV1,* 5.
5. *Mem,* 40.
6. *Mem,* 40, White, 10.
7. RF, 115–17.
8. "No Second Troy."
9. White, 36.
10. RF, 308.
11. Arthur Symons to JQ, Oct. 13, 1918, Cardozo, *Maud Gonne,* 320.
12. White, 517.

13. *EDL*, 338.
14. Stuart, *Black List*, 12, 20, and 24; also interview with BM, Feb. 2, 1996, in which he said the details in his fictionalized autobiography are factually accurate.
15. White, 369–70.
16. Iseult Stuart, interview at Glendalough, Feb. 16, 1949, in "Memories of W.B. Yeats," National Sound Archive, T7655R.
17. White, 280.
18. Ibid., 325, 328, and 335.
19. Ibid., 334.
20. Ibid., 376.
21. Ibid., 344, 302, and 366.
22. Ibid., 367.
23. Ibid., 232.
24. Ibid., 247, says that Maud learned of the crime in October 1904 and went to lawyers in London in December.
25. MG to WBY, [Nov. 1905], White, 217.
26. See White, 208, 212, and 214.
27. Ibid., 204.
28. Ibid., 32, 220, and 228.
29. See Perloff, "Between Hatred and Desire," *YA7*, 35.
30. Cardozo, *Maud Gonne*, 93.
31. White, 39.
32. WBY to LG, May 9, 1916, Wade, 613.
33. Lily to JQ, May 8, 1916, Reid, 230.
34. JBY to Lolly, May 12, 1916, NLI.
35. WBY to JQ, May 18, 1916, Reid, 231.
36. WBY to LG, May 9, 1916, Wade, 613.
37. WBY to LG, May 25, [1916], Berg.
38. WBY to MG, [May 1916], White, 378.
39. WBY to LG, May 25, [1916], Berg.
40. WBY to LG, June 21, [1916], Berg.
41. MacBride, *Servant of the Queen*, 319.
42. MG to WBY, Nov. 8, [1916], White, 384.

43. Stuart, *Black List* 17. The Gonne women's belief that they had talked WBY out of a knighthood was unfair. He had no inclination for the title and knew that his family would be shocked, as he explained to LG, Dec. 1, 1915, Berg.

44. WBY to LG, [?], 1917, Berg.

45. WBY to LG, [?], 1917, Berg.

46. WY to LG, Aug. 18, [1916], Berg.

47. GY to RE, Oct. 8, 1946, Ellmann NB, 31.

48. Amory, *Lord Dunsany,* 132–33.

49. Moore, *Vale,* 131.

50. WBY to LG, Aug. 12, [1917], Wade, 630.

51. WBY to T. Sturge Moore, July ?, [1917], Bridge, 28.

52. WBY to LG, Aug. 15, [1917], Wade, 620.

53. WBY to LG, Feb. 7, 1913, Berg. *En famille,* the Gonnes agreed that his French was abominable; he could not manage even a line; White, 391.

54. WBY to LG, Sept. 8, [1917], Wade, 631.

55. White, 391.

56. WBY to LG, Aug.? [1917], Berg.

57. WBY to LG, Sept. 22, 1917, *LG50,* 233.

Chapter 4. Soror and Frater

1. Lolly to JBY, Sept. 2, 1917, NLI.

2. WBY to Lolly, Sept. 30, 1917, *The Yeats Sisters,* Burns.

3. Lolly to JBY, Sept. 2, 1917, Hardwick, 203.

4. Pierce, 197.

5. Ibid.

6. WBY to JBY, "Monday," [prob. Oct. 8 or 15?], [1917], *PF,* 637 n81; full letter in NYPL.

7. Ibid.

8. JBY to JQ, Nov. 6, 1917, NYPL.

9. *Marriage and Divorce Statistics, Historical Series, 1836–1983,* London: Her Majesty's Stationery Office, 1990.

10. *EDL*, 308–9.
11. Ibid.
12. WBY to LG, April 20, [1914], Berg.
13. Dorothy Shakespear to EP, [Feb. 13, 1914], *EDL*, 306.
14. Grace M. Jaffe, "Vignettes," *YA5*, 139. In the same article, p. 152, Jaffe speculates whether George Yeats's "abnormal reticence" about her past meant that she had been "mistreated" during early childhood.
15. Ibid., 139.
16. Harwood, 139–40, suggests that Hyde-Lees may have died of drink.
17. WBY to JQ, Nov. 19, 1918, NYPL.
18. *EDL*, 57.
19. *EDL*, 59.
20. RF, 437.
21. GY to RE, Dec. 8, 1948, Ellmann NB, 39.
22. For example, GY to TM, [Aug. 1923], TCD; to Dorothy Pound, Feb. 2, 1928, Beinecke; to EP, Sept. 8, 1927, *YA7*, 10; and to Dorothy Pound, Aug. 20, [1930], *YA7*, 16.
23. WBY to JBY, Nov. 30, [1917], USB.
24. MG to WBY, [October ? 1917], White, 392.
25. Yeats's poem "Broken Dreams" refers to Maud's dazzling beauty; of Iseult, an old Irish woman in Dublin told John Quinn's friend Jeanne Robert Foster, "I met Iseult Gonne in the street and I fell on my knees, she was so beautiful." Reid, 353–54.
26. *OBMV*, 1936 ed., xi.
27. For example, Oates, "At Least I Have Made a Woman of Her," 16–19, and Cullingford, *Gender*, 210.
28. MG to WBY, [October ? 1917], White, 392.
29. Jeff, 220.
30. V Moore, 229.
31. Harwood, 130.
32. *YO*, 140–41, and Ann Saddlemyer, "George, Ezra, Dorothy and Friends: Twenty-Six Letters, 1918–592," *YA7*, 4.

33. Reid, 307–8.
34. V. Moore, 134.
35. Ibid., 150.
36. Raine, *Yeats, the Tarot and the Golden Dawn* 71.
37. *YVP2*, 235 and 560 n67, and *MYV2*, 247.
38. V. Moore, 178.
39. *YVP3*, 129, n60.
40. Jeff, 40; *YVP3*, 39; and White, 39.
41. WBY to LG, Sept. 19, [1917], Wade, 632–33. Uncut version, Harwood, 156.
42. Ibid.
43. Harwood, 156.
44. WBY to LG, Sept. 22, [1917], Berg.
45. Ibid.
46. E. E. Tucker to LG, Sept. 30, 1917, Harwood, 157–58.
47. Ibid.
48. V. Moore, 253.
49. WBY to GY, Oct. 4, [1917], USB.
50. WBY to LG, Oct. 13, [1917], *LG50*, 234.
51. WBY to GY, Oct. 5, [1917], USB.
52. MG to WBY, "Wednesday," (probably Oct. 1917), White, 392.
53. WBY to GY, Oct. 6, [1917], USB.
54. The courtship letters of WBY to GY of early Oct. 1917 are at USB.
55. Nelly Tucker to LG, Oct. 9, 1917, Harwood, 158.
56. Harper, *W.B. Yeats and W.T. Horton,* 57–58.
57. Ibid.
58. WBY to LG, Oct. 13, 1917, Berg.
59. *LG50*, 234.
60. Ibid.
61. Reid, 307.
62. *Freeman's Journal,* Oct. 23, 1917, p. 3, col. 7.
63. *PF,* 477.
64. JBY to WBY, Nov. 5, 1917, *LTWBY2*, 337–38.
65. *PF,* 477.

66. Niall Montgomery, Sept. 1948, Ellmann NB, 26.

67. Gordon Bottomley to T. Sturge Moore, Dec. 14, 1917, *YA4*, 178.

68. Arthur Symons to JQ, Nov. 11, 1917, Cardozo, 320.

69. Charles Shannon to JQ, Nov. 7, 1917, Reid, 306.

70. George Russell to JQ, Feb. 1918, Reid, 438.

71. Reid, 197.

72. Ibid., 307.

73. WBY to LG, Sept. 8, [1917], Wade, 631.

74. I am grateful to Anna MacBride White for supplying the hitherto unknown date of Iseult's letter: October 26, [1917]. White to BM, Jan. 22, 1996.

75. Iseult Gonne to WBY, Oct. 26, 1917, White p. 392. His Majesty's Postal Service was so swift that Yeats expected that his letters posted from London before 6:00 P.M. would reach Ireland next morning.

76. The Automatic Script of March 30, 1919 (*YVP2*, 224), says that GY's "Critical Moment" was "when you told of letter." Yeats's Card Files, *YVP3*, 349, further describe GY's "moment of greatest disquiet" as "caused by me . . . through letter & IG." Yeats later corrected this card file entry to give the date of the starting of the Automatic Script as Oct. 24–25, 1917, misdating the event to correspond with the date he gave in *AV B*, 8, when he misdated the day of his wedding. What is significant, however, is that he related his new wife's shock over Iseult's letter to the first appearance of the Script.

77. *MM*, xvi.

78. George Mills Harper, in his introduction to *YVP1*, 10, suggests that Saturday, October 27, was the date because on October 29 Yeats wrote to Lady Gregory that "two days ago" the automatic writing had begun. As Anna MacBride White now confirms that the critical letter from Iseult was written on Friday, October 26, the October 27 starting date seems to be confirmed.

Chapter 5. *Folie à Deux*

1. The horoscope on the jacket covers to *Yeats's Vision Papers* shows the time of day as 6:40 P.M.
2. WBY to LG, Monday, Oct. 29, [1917], Wade, 633.
3. Ibid.
4. Ibid.
5. Elizabeth Radcliffe to WBY, Nov. 13, 1917, *LTWBY2*, 339.
6. *AV B*, 2.
7. Stopes, cautions against over-exerting a husband, *Married Love*. 24.
8. "Parting."
9. *YVP1*, 55.
10. Ibid., 71.
11. For example, *YVP2*, 486: "There were about 3 months before Anne was coming when sun-in-moon was impossible & yet there was script."
12. *AV A*, xii.
13. *YVP1*, 64.
14. "Visions Induced by an Oriental Powder," *Occult Review* [?] (1906), USB.
15. *MM*, xvii.
16. Ibid., xxi.
17. Grace M. Jaffe, *Years of Grace*, 36.
18. Marcia Keith Schuchard, "Freemasonry, Secret Societies and the Continuity of the Occult Traditions in English Literature" (Ann Arbor, Mich.: Xerox University Microfilms, 1975), 639.
19. Reid, 420.
20. Marjorie Perloff, "Between Hatred and Desire," *YA7*, 29–50.
21. *CL2*, 23 n2.
22. *YVP1*, 369.
23. V. Moore, 150.
24. *MM*, xvii, and GY to RE, Jan. 17, 1947, Ellmann NB, 42.
25. Collis, *Somerville and Ross*, 164.
26. OS to WBY, July 17, 1932, Harwood, *YA6*, 88.

27. Bentley, *Far Horizon,* 42–59.
28. "Introduction to 'The Words upon the Window-Pane,'" *Exp,* 365.
29. "Solomon and the Witch."
30. *YVP1,* 81.
31. Ibid., 76–78.
32. George Mills Harper, "'Unbelievers in the House': Yeats's Automatic Script," *Studies in the Literary Imagination* 14:1 (1981): 1–15.
33. *YVP3,* 110.
34. Thomas Parkinson, "Yeats and the Love Lyric," *James Joyce Quarterly* 3:2 (Winter 1996): 109–23.
35. *AV B,* 211.
36. "Mr De Valera to Irish Volunteers," *The Times,* Sat., Nov. 3, 1917.
37. MG to WBY, [Oct. ? 1917], White, 393.
38. *YVP1,* 67.
39. W. T. Horton to WBY, Nov. 14, 1917, *YH,* 63–64.
40. WBY to JQ, Nov. 29, [1917], Reid, 307.
41. *P,* 539. Also, WBY to Lolly, [n.d.], from Stone Cottage, Burns, folder 13, item 6, asks her to ask Lily whether "free of the six and four" is the right term for their ancestor who married Mary Butler.
42. LG to WBY, Nov. 28, 1917, Berg.
43. Ibid.
44. *YVP1,* 109.
45. Ibid., 110.
46. *Au,* 116.
47. The doctoral candidate, Eliot Dole Hutchinson, won his degree and later quoted Yeats's response in *Psychiatry* 4:33 (1941), according to Dr. J. D. Mollon, departmental archivist, University of Cambridge Department of Experimental Psychology.
48. *YVP1,* 78.
49. Letters from the builder Rafferty to Mrs. Yeats for windows, pipes, starting Jan. 15, 1918, are in NLI, 30663.

50. WBY to LG, Dec. 16, [1917], Wade, 634.
51. Ebbutt, *Hero-Myths & Legends of the British Isles*, 184.
52. *YVP1*, 72, and *MYV1*, 26.
53. *YVP1*, 80 and 159.
54. *YVP1*, 177, Dec. 23, 1917.

Chapter 6. An Adventure

1. WBY to LG, Jan. 4, 1918, Wade, 643–44.
2. WBY to LG, Feb. 22, [1918], Wade, 646.
3. Moberly, *An Adventure*, 25.
4. *YVP1*, 179.
5. *YVP1*, 209.
6. Ibid., 216.
7. Ibid., 522 n52.
8. Ibid.
9. Gregory, *Seventy Years*, 554.
10. LG to WBY, Feb. 2, [1918], USB.
11. WBY to LG, April 29, [1919], Berg.
12. *UP2*, 429.
13. *YVP1*, 89.
14. WBY to LG, Jan. 4, [1918], Wade, 644.
15. John Wyse Jackson and Bernard McGinley, *James Joyce's "Dubliners": An Annotated Edition* (London: Sinclair-Stevenson, 1993), 21.
16. *YVP1*, 196.
17. *MYV1*, 202.
18. C. A. E. Moberly to WBY, March 20, 1918, *LTWBY2*, 346–47.
19. *PF*, 548 n9.
20. George Russell to JQ, March 20, 1911, RF, 435.
21. *EDL*, 91 and 348.
22. *YVP1*, 371, and *YVP3*, 78 in which Yeats reviews this day's important communication in his "Sleep and Dream Notebooks."
23. *YVP1*, 372.

24. *YVP1,* 539 n65.
25. *YVP1,* 378.

Chapter 7. *What Rough Beast?*

1. Lily to JBY, Jan. 31, 1918, Lewis, 142.
2. Ibid., and full text in NLI.
3. Lily to JBY, March 13, 1918, Lewis, 142–43.
4. Lily to JQ, March 13, 1918, Reid, 308–9.
5. Lolly to JBY, June 14, 1918, NLI.
6. Lily to JBY, Aug. 8, 1916, NLI.
7. WBY to LG, Jan. 17, [1915], Berg.
8. Lily to JBY, April 26, 1918, *PF,* 487.
9. JBY to Rosa Butt, Feb. 19, 1908, *FS,* 351; JBY to Rosa Butt, Feb. 1, 1910, *FS,* 352; JBY to Rosa Butt, Feb. 19, 1908, *FS,* 350–51.
10. Lily to JBY, Jan. 3, 1919, NLI.
11. *YVP1,* 379.
12. *YVP1,* 381.
13. The intense series of questions at Glendalough and Glenmalure took place between March 14 and April 2, 1918, and can be found in *YVP1,* 379–418.
14. *YVP1,* 390.
15. Ibid., 406.
16. Ibid., 407.
17. Ibid., 414.
18. Ibid., 394.
19. Ibid., 388.
20. LG to WBY, Nov. 28, 1917, and Anne Gregory de Winton to BM, Dec. 6, 1996.
21. Hardwick, *The Yeats Sisters,* 98. Also, Lolly to JBY, June 26, 1910, and Lilly to JBY, Aug. 16, 1916, NLI, and GY, Aug. 17, 1946, Ellmann NB, 21.
22. *YVP1,* 420.
23. Lily to JQ, Sept. 2, 1920, NYPL.

24. *YVP3*, 81.

25. *YVP2*, 254, question 4.

26. *YVP1*, 467 and notes, 548 n3.

27. MG to WBY, June 14, [1918], White, 395.

28. WBY to MG, Oct. 4, 1918, White, 397.

29. WBY to MG, Aug. 18, [1918], White, 396.

30. WBY to JQ, July 23, 1918, Wade, 651.

31. Ibid.

32. WBY to MG, May 13, [1918], White, 393.

33. Lolly to JBY, June 14, 1918, NLI.

34. Lolly to JBY, June 4, 1918, NLI.

35. Lily to JBY, June 13, 1918, NLI.

36. GY to EP, May 28, 1918, Beinecke.

37. *YVP2*, 7.

38. *YVP2*, 15.

39. *YVP2*, 486.

40. *YVP2*, 30.

41. WBY to LG, Aug. 14, [1918], misdated 1917 at Berg. See WBY to MG, Aug. 18, [1918], White, 395.

42. EP to WBY, March 10, 1918, C. F. Terrell, "Ezra Pound Letters to W. B. Yeats," *Antaeus* (Spring/Summer 1976): 36.

43. *YVP2*, 45.

44. *YVP2*, 44.

45. *YVP2*, 65.

46. *YVP2*, 63.

47. Lily to JBY, Sept. 19 and 22, 1918, NLI.

48. *YVP2*, 5.

49. *YVP2*, 31.

50. Ibid., 33.

51. WBY to GY, Oct. 3, [1918], USB.

52. WBY to MG, [Oct. 1918], White, 396.

53. *YVP2*, 67.

54. *MYV2*, 207.

55. MG to WBY, Nov. 1 [1918], White, 399.

56. EP to JQ, Nov. 15, 1918. *Selected Letters of Ezra Pound, 1907–1941*, ed. D. D. Paige (London: Faber and Faber, 1950), 140–41.

57. Ibid.

58. *YVP2*, 128.

59. Ibid., 129.

60. Ibid., 114.

61. Ibid., 119.

62. Strong, *Green Memory*, 209.

63. Lily to JQ, Dec. 15, 1918, NYPL, WBY to LG, Dec. 14, [1918], Berg.

64. Cardozo, *Maud Gonne*, 330.

65. EP to JQ, Dec. 12, 1918, *Maud Gonne* [Cardozo, 330.]

66. WBY to LG, Jan. 5, [1919], Berg.

67. WBY to EP, Feb. 3, [1919], *MYV2*, 216.

68. Goldring, *The Nineteen Twenties*, 118.

69. *YVP2*, 195.

70. *YVP2*, 196.

71. *YVP2*, 199.

72. Lily to JBY, Feb. 11 and 25, 1919, NLI.

73. WBY to LG, Feb. 26, [1919], Berg.

74. Bradford, "George Yeats: Poet's Wife," 404, says that as a girl GY had dreamed of having six children, all boys.

75. WBY to LG, Feb. 26, [1919], Berg.

76. *Black List*, 25, Carpenter, 316, and White, 42.

Chapter 8. Only One More

1. Lily to JBY, April 20, 1919, NLI.

2. Lily to JBY, April 21, 1919, NLI.

3. *YVP2*, 201.

4. Ibid.

5. Ibid.

6. *YVP3*, 226.

7. *YVP2*, 205.

8. *YVP2*, 256.

9. Ibid., 222.

10. Ibid., 292.

11. Ellmann, in *MM*, 82, traces Yeats's separation of himself into two parts to his creation in 1894 of two contradictory symbolic persons, Michael Robartes and Owen Aherne.

12. "The Stage Society," *The Times*, May 28, 1919, 15.

13. Lolly to JBY, May 18, 1919, NLI.

14. *YGD*, 130–31.

15. *YGD*, 128. Chapter 9 and its notes describe this 1917–20 row within the Order in great detail.

16. *YVP2*, 296–97 and 566–67.

17. *YGD*, 306–7.

18. *YVP2*, 296.

19. *YGD*, 136.

20. *YVP2*, 298.

21. WBY to JBY, July 16, 1919, Hone, 319.

22. T. Sturge Moore to WBY, Feb. [?], 1919, Hone 317, Bridge 38.

23. GY to Gogarty, Jan. 6, [1928], *The Dream I Knew* ed. Jim McGarry (Sligo: Collooney, 1990), 4.

24. WBY to JBY, [Sept. 1919?], Burns.

25. Ibid.

26. *YVP2*, 299.

27. WBY to JQ, July 11, 1919, Wade, 659.

28. Lily to JBY, April 20, 1919, *PF*, 495 and 640 n188.

29. Joyce Carol Oates. "At Least I Have Made a Woman of Her," 7–30.

31. Cullingford, *Gender and History in Yeats's Love Poetry*, 137.

32. *YVP2*, 300.

33. Bloom, *Yeats*, 233.

34. *YVP2*, 349.

35. Conor Cruise O'Brien, "Passion and Cunning," *In Excited Reverie*, pp. 207–78.

36. *YVP2*, 349.

37. Ibid.

38. Stopes, *Married Love*, 24, 62–63.

39. *YVP2*, 367.

40. *YVP2*, 268.

41. WBY to LG, Dec. 6, 1919, Berg.

42. *MYV2*, 319

43. *YVP2*, 389.

44. Ibid.

45. *VP*, 822–23.

46. *YVP2*, 411.

47. *YVP2*, 382.

48. WBY to JQ, Nov. 7, 1921, NYPL. Also, Amory, *Lord Dunsany*, 197, cites Lord Dunsany's remark that long afternoon naps were a family habit of George Yeats's that Yeats gave up.

49. *YVP2*, 411.

50. *YVP2*, 434.

51. *YVP2*, 485.

52. Ibid., 472.

53. *YVP2*, 477 and 482.

54. Ibid., 453.

55. Ibid., 482, 487, 484.

56. Ibid., 486.

57. Ibid., 487.

58. Marjorie Perloff, "Between Hatred and Desire," *YA7*, 40.

59. Lily to JBY, Nov. 18, 1919, NLI.

60. Ibid., 485.

61. Ibid., 507.

62. *YVP2*, 519.

63. Ibid., 519.

64. *VP2*, 510, 523.

65. *VP2*, 530.

66. WBY to LG, Dec. 29, 1919, Berg.

67. Lolly to JBY, March 1920, NLI; *FS*, 83; and WBY to LG, Dec. 6, 1919, Berg.

68. JBY to Isaac Yeats, Feb. 20, 1920, *PF*, 505. *PF*, 505–7, gives an excellent description of the meeting of WBY and GY with JBY.

69. Reid, 17, 418.

70. *VP2*, 532.

71. JBY to WBY, April 27, 1918, *PF*, 485.

72. WBY to LG, Feb. 28, 1920, Berg.

73. See *FS*, 343–44.

74. JBY to Isaac Yeats, Oct. 26, 1920, *PF*, 509.

75. *PF*, 506.

76. WBY to LG, Feb. 28, 1920, Berg.

77. GY to Miss Bates, May 12, 1920, Wellesley College Library.

78. Hone, 322.

79. *YVP3*, 8.

80. Ibid.

81. *YVP2*, 533.

82. WBY to OS, March 14, [1920], Wade, 661.

83. *YVP3*, 8.

84. *YVP2*, 535.

85. *YVP*, 9.

86. *YVP3*, 8.

87. *YVP2*, 539.

88. Ibid., 540.

89. *Los Angeles Sunday Times*, March 28, 1920.

90. *San Antonio Evening News*, April 14, p. 10; April 15, 1920, p. 2.

91. *New Orleans Times-Picayune*, April 16, 1920, p. 1; "'Irish Republic' Head Is Awarded Degree by Loyola," April 17, pp. 1 and 10.

92. *VP3*, 14 and 12.

93. *YVP3*, 14.

94. WBY to LG, May 18, 1920, Berg.

95. WBY to LG, May 18, 1920, Berg.

96. For background to Stuart, see Geoffrey Elborn's biography, and White, 43.

97. WBY to LG, May 18, 1920, Berg.

98. *PF*, 642 n17, and Reid, 419.

99. JBY to GY, May 24, 1920, NLI.

Chapter 9. *Waiting for J. B.*

1. WBY to LG, June 14, [1920], Berg.
2. Lily to JBY, June 12, 1920, NLI.
3. WBY to LG, June 15, 1920, Berg.
4. *YVP3*, 31.
5. MG to WBY, July 1920, White, 407.
6. GY to WBY, Aug. 4, 1920, USB.
7. WBY to GY, Aug. 6, 1920, USB.
8. WBY to GY, Aug. 1, [1920], USB, and MG to WBY, Aug. 10, [1920], White, 407–9.
9. WBY to Dr. Bethel Solomons, Aug. 4, [1920], BL.
10. WBY to LG, July 29, [1920], Berg.
11. Lily to JBY, Oct. 17, 1920, NLI.
12. GY to WBY, Aug. 4, 1920, USB.
13. WBY to Dr. Bethel Solomons, Aug. 4, 1920, BL.
14. GY to WBY, Aug. 8, 1920, USB.
15. Ibid.
16. *YVP3*, 31.
17. WBY to GY, Aug. 10, 1920, USB.
18. GY to WBY, Aug. 6, 1920, USB.
19. Lily to JBY, Aug. 2, 1920, NLI.
20. Lily to JBY, Aug. 7, 1920, NLI; GY to WBY, Aug. 6, 1920, USB.
21. GY to WBY, July [31?], 1920, USB. Also, *YVP2*, 567.
22. *YVP3*, 31, 41.
23. Ibid., 49, 48.
24. Ibid., 48.
25. *YVP3*, 51 and 53; for other cat dreams see also 55–56.
26. Ibid., 42–43.
27. Ibid., 43.
28. Ibid., 56.
29. WBY to JQ, Oct. 30, 1920, Wade, 663.
30. *YVP3*, 55.
31. Jaffe, "Vignettes," *YA5*, 145.

32. Strong, *Green Memories,* 242.
33. Ibid., 245, 246.
34. Frank Tuohy, *Yeats: An Illustrated Biography* (New York: New Amsterdam Books, 1976), 176.
35. Donald D. Pearce, "Hours with the Domestic Sybil," *Southern Review* 28:3 (July 1992): 485–501, noticed on a visit to Mrs. Yeats in 1949 that the *Vision Papers* bore the stains of wine glasses.
36. WBY to George Russell, March 29, [1921], Wade, 667.
37. *Au,* 123.
38. Lily to JBY, Nov. 23 and 29, 1920, NLI.
39. *YVP3,* 247, 65.
40. Lolly to JBY, Jan. 8, 1921, NLI.
41. WBY to Lolly, Feb. 25, [1921], Burns, and *PF,* 256.
42. *YVP3,* 85.
43. Ibid.
44. WBY to LG, March 13, [1921], Berg.
45. WBY to OS, April 9, [1921], Wade, 667.
46. WBY to Iseult Stuart, April [? 1921], Elborn, 48–49.
47. Lolly to JBY, Mar. 8, 1921, NLI.
48. Lolly to JBY, May 24, 1921, Lewis, 155, and NLI.
49. Lily to JBY, May 4, 1921, Lewis, 153.
50. *YVP3,* 74.
51. Ibid., 89.
52. Ibid., 92.
53. Ibid.: 75, 87 75;
54. Ibid., 76.
55. Ibid.
56. WBY to JQ, May 30, 1921; WBY to Lily, June 21, 1921, Burns.
57. WBY to Lily, June 21, [1921], Burns.
58. Lolly to JBY, June 24, 1921, NLI.
59. JBY to WBY, June 24, 1921, *PF,* 529.
60. WBY to Lolly, July 5, [1921], Burns.
61. WBY to Lolly, July 13, 1921, Burns.
62. WBY to Lily, Sept. 1, 1921, Burns.

63. WBY to JQ, Aug. 25, 1921, Wade, 673.
64. Gibbon, *The Masterpiece and the Man,* 38.
65. *AV B,* 18, and *YVP3,* 95.
66. JBY to GY, Sept. 28, 1921, NLI.
67. Lily to JBY, Sept. 19, 1921, Lewis, 161.
68. WBY to JQ, Sept. 30, [1921], NYPL.
69. WBY to JBY, Sept. 30, 1921, *PF,* 532.
70. WBY to GY, Oct. 27, [1921], USB.
71. GY to WBY, [Oct. ? 1921; postmark illegible], USB.
72. WBY to JQ, Nov. 7, 1921, NYPL.
73. Lolly to JBY, Nov. 27, 1921, NLI.
74. WBY to OS, Dec. 22, [1921], Wade, 675.
75. WBY to Lolly, [Dec. 23, 1921] Burns, and *PF,* 530.
76. WBY to Lolly, Jan. 12, [1922] Burns.
77. Bradford, "Poet's Wife," 395.
78. WBY to OS, Feb. 17, [1922], Wade, 677.
79. JBY to Lily, Feb. 1, 1922, *PF,* 537.
80. *YVP3,* 107.
81. Ibid., 109.
82. Grace Jaffe, "Vignettes," *YA5,* 148.
83. *YVP3,* 6.
84. Jeff, 265.
85. *YVP3,* 117.

Chapter 10. The Silent Woman

1. James Joyce, *A Portrait of the Artist as a Young Man* (New York: Viking Portable Edition, 1947), 512.
2. "A Dialogue of Self and Soul."
3. GY to RE, June 11, 1946, Ellmann NB, 1.
4. The MS of "Among School Children" shows that the poem originally opened with the image of the mother assessing the value of her aged child.
5. JBY to Lily, Dec. 19, 1913, Lewis, 23.

6. *FS*, 439.

7. WBY to Katharine Tynan, [Dec. 2, 1891], *CL1*, 273.

8. WBY to Mabel Dickinson, May 11, 1908, RF, 385.

9. MG to WBY, [early 1916], White, 366–67.

10. "Under Saturn."

11. *Au*, 11, 6.

12. Ibid., 31.

13. Ibid.

14. Ibid., 472.

15. *Mem*, 31.

16. *FS*, 27.

17. JBY to SY, [1863], Lewis, 11.

18. JBY to SY, April 17, 1863, Lewis, 13.

19. See Lewis, 10–11. JBY's courtship letters to Susan Pollexfen "Papa's Letters to Mama Before Their Marriage," are in NLI, labeled, presumably by Lily.

20. JBY to SY, Feb. 16, 1863, NLI.

21. *PF*, 37.

22. Paul Ferris, *Dr. Freud*, 106.

23. *PF*, 74.

24. *PF*, 95.

25. Miss Mechin, [n.d.], Ellmann NB, 5.

26. WBY to OS, April 15, [1926], Wade, 712.

27. Monk Gibbon, in *The Yeats We Knew*, ed. MacManus, 46–47.

28. *Au*, 27.

29. Louisa Dowden to SY, [1873], USB.

30. Deirdre Toomey, "Away," *Yeats and Women* 151–55.

31. See WBY to Edward Clodd, Nov. 6, [1898], *CL2*, 292.

32. *Au*, 32.

33. *PF*, 110–12.

34. *PF*, 56.

35. *Mem*, 71–72.

36. *Au*, 66.

37. RF, 50.

38. WBY to Katharine Tynan, June [c. 15], [1888], *CL1*, 72.

39. WBY to Katharine Tynan, Dec. 21 [1888], *CL1,* 118 n6, 118, 121.

40. *Mem,* 43.

41. WBY to Katharine Tynan, Jan. 31, [1889], *CL1,* 136.

42. Ernest Rhys, "W.B. Yeats: Early Recollections," Mikhail, *W.B Yeats: I,* 35.

43. RF, 11.

44. JBY to JQ, [c. April 1919], *PF,* 464.

45. Full accounts of the mental illnesses of the Pollexfens appear in *PF,* 174, 183, and in *FS,* 22.

46. WBY to Lily, [Nov. 15, 1892], *CL1,* 332.

47. *FS,* 28.

48. Arnold, *Jack Yeats,* 186–91

49. *Mem,* 156–57.

50. *CL1,* xxxv.

51. WBY to Katharine Tynan, July 2, [1888], *CL1,* 77.

52. Toomey, "Away," 153.

53. *Au,* 62.

54. *PF,* 184.

55. See *CL2,* 276 n5.

56. WBY to Richard Le Gallienne, [c. Oct. 15, 1892], *CL1,* 321, and 321 n3.

57. *Mem,* 75.

58. WBY to George Granville Leveson-Gower, Jan. 8, 1900, *CL2,* 488.

59. WBY to LG, Jan. 4, 1900, *CL2,* 485.

60. *FS,* 278, although Arnold, *Jack Yeats,* 89, suggests that the hiatus in Jack's sketchbooks may have been caused by pressure of work.

61. WBY to OS, [May 20, 1900], *CL2,* 529.

62. Ibid.

63. WBY to MD, on, March 9, [1911]. Bancroft.

64. *Mem,* 160–161.

65. Webster, *Yeats,* 60.

66. Cullingford, *Gender and History, in Yeats's Love Poetry* 142, 148, 151–52.

67. "Crazy Jane on God."
68. *FS*, 389.

Chapter 11. Politics and Potency

1. Standish O'Grady to WBY, Jan. [1924], *LTWBY*, 446.
2. For example, WBY to GY, Nov. 29 and 30, [1922], USB.
3. Private information based on a long interview with Dolly Travers-Smith Robinson.
4. WBY to GY, dated "Thursday," [1930], USB.
5. Geoffrey Elborn to BM, Aug. 11, 1998, based on 1984 interview material unused in Elborn's *Francis Stuart: A Life;* also, Frank O'Connor, *My Father's Son,* 186.
6. See TM and GY correspondence, TCD, and GY to LR, Huntingdon. Also, Frank O'Connor, Oct. 13, 1946, Ellmann NB, 32.
7. Elborn to BM, Aug. 11, 1998.
8. GY to TM, [Summer 1926?], TCD.
9. Cronin, *Samuel Beckett,* 87, 344.
10. See Pierce, 302 n61.
11. Geoffrey Elborn, to BM. Aug. 11, 1998.
12. WBY to GY, Nov. 29, [1922], USB.
13. GY to WBY, Aug. 23, [1924], USB.
14. WBY to GY, Aug. 28, [1924], USB.
15. "Sailing to Byzantium."
16. WBY to Lolly, Feb. 16, [1923], Burns.
17. WBY to GY, June [?, 1930?], USB.
18. WBY to OS, May 26, [1924], Wade, 705.
19. "The Bounty of Sweden," in *Au,* 541.
20. Lily to JQ, July 8, 1922, *LTWBY2,* 425.
21. Hone, 349.
22. WBY to JQ, Oct. 19, 1922, NYPL.
23. GY to WBY, Nov. 28, 1922, USB.
24. Arnold, *Jack Yeats,* 218.

25. GY to WBY, Nov. 24, 1922, USB.
26. Ibid.
27. Ring, *Erskine Childers*, 289.
28. White, 437.
29. Elborn, *Francis Stuart*, 58–59.
30. WBY to GY, Jan. 21, 1923, USB.
31. WBY to GY, Feb. 3, 1923, USB.
32. Cullingford, *Yeats, Ireland and Fascism*, 167.
33. "No Question of Disloyalty: Mr. Yeats on Objection to the Oath," *The Times*, April 4, 1932, p. 14.
34. WBY to GY, Feb. 10, [1923], USB.
35. *The Times*, Wednesday, Jan. 31, 1923.
36. "Remorse for Intemperate Speech."
37. See Cullingford, *Yeats, Ireland and Fascism*, 174.
38. WBY to OS, Dec. 24, 1922, Wade, 698.
39. WBY to Edmund Dulac, Dec. 1, 1922, Wade, 694.
40. FitzGerald, *An Autobiography*, 10; Ellmann, *James Joyce* 531.
41. Jeff, 272.
42. Lolly to JQ, July 31, 1923, NYPL.
43. Lily, [c. Feb. 1924], *LTWBY2*, 449–50.
44. *FS*, 240, Hardwick, *The Yeats Sisters*, 234–35.
45. GY to TM, Oct. 27, 1925, TCD.
46. WBY to LG, Jan. 13, [1924], Wade, 701. This account of the immediate spending of virtually the whole of the prize money suggests that Yeats and his wife were comfortably off from his own earnings, from the Senate and from writing, his Civil List pension, combined with George's private income.
47. WBY to OS, June 28, [1923], Wade, 698.
48. Elborn, 60.
49. WBY to OS, June 21, [1924], Wade, 706–7.
50. See "Leda and Rape," Cullingford, *Gender*, 140–64.
51. GY to TM, [Dec. 31, 1925], TCD.
52. TM to GY, Oct. 19, 1926, UCD, NB15–22.
53. *MM*, 324.
54. O'Brien, "Passion and Cunning", 246.

55. WBY to OS, July 13, [1933], Wade, 812.

56. *SS*, 52.

57. Arensberg and Kimball, *Family and Community in Ireland*, 154.

58. Lyons, *Culture and Anarchy*, 157.

59. *SS*, 92.

60. Ibid., 93.

61. Ibid., 98.

62. Ibid., 99.

64. See Fay, *The Abbey Theatre*, 147, Jeff, 283, and Robinson, 140.

65. WBY to JQ, June 5, 1922, Wade, 683.

66. Harwood, *Olivia Shakespear and W.B. Yeats*. 190, attributes this change in their relationship to George's loss or surrender of her powers as a medium.

67. Gould, "A Lesson for the Circumspect."

68. WBY to OS, May 25, [1926], Wade, 715.

69. WBY to OS, July 2, [1926], Wade, 716.

70. The Yeats family was very proud of this precocious saying, which found its way into "Father and Child." GY quoted it to LR, in a letter from 82 Merrion Square dated "Maundy Thursday," Huntington.

71. Janis Tedesco Haswell, in *Pressed Against Divinity*, 1998, argues at this point Yeats became "double-voiced" and his daimon became "gendered," or female.

72. GY to TM, March 26, 1926, Pierce, 222 and 303 n82.

73. GY to TM, [letter beginning "I grovel," undated, c. early 1927], and GY to TM, April 24, 1926, re her play, TCD.

74. WBY to OS, April 15, [1926], Wade, 712.

75. Coogan, *De Valera*, 400.

76. WBY to OS, [April 1933], Wade, 809.

77. WBY to OS, [July or Aug. 1927], Wade, 727.

78. WBY to MG, Oct. 3, [1927], White, 436.

79. WBY to MG, Oct. 3 [1927], White, 437.

79. MG to WBY, [? October 1927], White, 443.

80. Ann Saddlemyer showed this short film at the International Yeats Summer School, Aug. 12, 1997.

81. GY to LR, Nov. 29, [1927], Huntington.
82. WBY to OS, Nov. 27, [1927], Wade, 733.
83. GY to LR, Nov. 29, [1927], Huntington.
84. GY to LR, Nov. 27, [1927], Huntington.
85. GY to LR, Nov. 29, [1927], Huntington.
86. GY to LR, [1927] TCD.
87. WBY to OS, Jan 12, [1928], Wade, 735.
88. EP to GY, Jan. 20, [1928], USB.
89. GY to Dorothy Pound, Aug. 20, [1930], *YA7*, 16.
90. WBY to OS, July 9, [1928], Wade, 744.

Chapter 12. *Politics and Potency, Cont'd.*

1. Gogarty to WBY, June 17, 1930, *LTWBY2*, 510.
2. Porter, *The Greatest Benefit to Mankind*, 611.
3. WBY to OS, Jan. 12, [1928], Wade, 734.
4. WBY to Nora McGuinness, [n.d., postmark Rapallo], Sligo.
5. GY to TM, March 15, 1928, TCD.
6. GY to TM, Feb. 11, 1929, TCD.
7. Carpenter, 463.
8. WBY to OS, March 29, [1929], Wade, 760.
9. *P*, 605.
10. *AV B*, 3.
11. GY to LR, [Nov. ?, 1929], Huntington.
12. WBY to OS, Dec. 12, 1929, Wade, 771.
13. WBY to OS, cited in Keith Aldritt, *The Poet As Spy: The Life and Wild Times of Basil Bunting* (London: Aurum Press, 1998), 63.
14. GY to LG, Feb. 9, 1930, Berg.
15. Pearce, "Domestic Sibyl," 138.
16. GY to LR, Feb. 13, 1930, Huntington.
17. GY to LG, Feb. 9, 1930, Berg.
18. WBY to OS, June 1, [1930], Wade, 775.
19. Ibid.
20. WBY to LG, April 1 [1928], Wade, 739.

21. O'Connor, *My Father's Son*, 99–100.
22. Gogarty to WBY, April 9, 1930, *LTWBY2*, 510–11.
23. *MM*, xvii.
24. *AV B*, 8.
25. Ibid., 23.
26. *MM*, 164–65.
27. Harry Clifton to WBY, Aug. [?], 1932, *LTWBY2*, 541.
28. *AV B*, 26.
29. Carpenter, *A Serious Character*, 492.
30. *AV B*, 19.
31. *AV B*, 24.
32. Hone, 424.
33. H. Montgomery Hyde, "Yeats and Gogarty," *YA5*, 157.
34. Iseult Stuart, interview, Ellmann NB, 27–28, Tulsa,
35. "People and Their Doings," *Daily Mail*, Oct. 31, 1928, p. 10.
36. Francis Stuart, "No Baleful Influence: W. B. Yeats Meets Mercedes Gleitz," *YA7*, 210.
37. WBY to OS, Oct. 23, [1930], Wade, 777.
38. WBY to OS, Dec. 27, [1930], Wade, 781.
39. *P*, 601.
40. *AV B*, 279.
41. Ellmann, *The Identity of Yeats*, 221–22.
42. Carpenter, 463.
43. WBY to OS, Dec. 27, [1930], Wade, 780.
44. *P*, 599.
45. WBY to GY, July [?, 1931], USB; WBY to OS, Aug. 30, [1931], Harwood, "Olivia Shakespear: Letters to W. B. Yeats," *YA6*, 78 n4.
46. GY to WBY, Oct. 15, [1931], USB.
47. Hardwick, *The Yeats Sisters*, 235.
48. GY to WBY, Feb. 29, 1923, USB.
49. WBY, "Ireland 1921–31," *The Spectator*, Jan. 30, 1932, *UP2*, 487.
50. Anne Gregory de Winton, interview with BM, July 23, 1996.
51. GY, Dec. 8, 1946, Ellmann NB, 6.
52. WBY to OS, July 25, [1932], Wade, 799.
53. T. J. K. Kierney to WBY, Oct. 21, 1932, NLI.

54. GY to WBY, [July 1932], USB.

55. WBY to OS, Sept. 15, [1928], Wade, 747.

56. Coogan, *de Valera* 453.

57. James Joyce to WBY, Oct. 5, 1932, Stuart, Gilbert, *Letters of James Joyce* (New York: Viking, 1957), 325.

58. GBS to WBY, Sept. 20, 1932, *LTWBY2*, 545.

59. George Russell to WBY, [April 5, 1932], *LTWBY2*, 532.

60. Carroll F. Terrell, "A Biographical Footnote on Yeats," *Yeats-Eliot Review* (Winter 1994): 3, 134.

61. WBY to OS, [Feb. 3, 1933], Wade, 804.

62. WBY to OS, Feb. 21, [1933], Wade, 805.

63. WBY to OS, Jan. 1, [1933], Wade, 803.

64. Coogan, *de Valera* 456.

65. Pierce, 242.

66. WBY to OS, July 13, [1933], Wade, 811–12.

67. Cullingford, *Yeats, Ireland and Fascism*, 205.

68. WBY to OS, Sept. 20, [1933], Wade, 815.

69. WBY to OS, Aug. 18, [1933], Wade, 814.

70. Ibid. *A New Commentary on the Poems of W. B. Yeats*, Jeffares.

71. *NCPWBY*, 499.

72. Ibid., 500.

73. Manning, *The Blueshirts* 249.

74. *OTB*, 20.

75. "A Dialogue of Self and Soul."

76. O'Brien, "Passion and Cunning," 278: 4 Oct. 53–74.

77. WBY to OS, July 13, [1933], Wade, 813.

78. WBY to MR, *LMR*, Nov. 26 [?27], 1934, McHugh, 32.

79. WBY to OS, Jan. 3, [1932], Wade, 790.

Chapter 13. *"This Is Baghdad"*

1. Hone, 437.

2. Virginia D. Pruitt and Raymond D. Pruitt, "Yeats and the Steinach Operation: A Further Analysis," *YAACTS* 1 (1983): 107 n1.

3. Hyde, *Yeats and Gogarty, YA5,* 158.
4. Ellmann, "Four Dubliners," 28; Harwood, 189.
5. Robert Nye, "Regards to a Gland Old Man," review of *W. B. Yeats: A Life,* by Stephen Coote, *The Scotsman,* July 19, 1997.
6. Porter, *The Greatest Benefit to Mankind,* 568–70.
7. Paul Ferris, *Dr Freud* 104–6.
8. Pruitt and Pruitt, 107 n1.
9. Mannin, *Young in the Twenties,* 64.
10. Ellmann, "Yeats's Second Puberty," *Four Dubliners,* 28.
11. "Theme for a Poem," Gould, "Portrayed Before His Eyes," *YA6,* 215.
12. WBY to EM, [April 8, 1936], Wade, 850.
13. WBY to EM, Dec. 30, [1934?], Sligo, quoted in Jeff, 338.
14. Haire to Blacker, April 30, 1934, and Haire papers, Eugenics Society, Wellcome Institute for the History of Medicine, London.
15. William O'Donnell, "Yeats as Adept and Artist," *YO,* 67.
16. WBY to OS, April 10, [1936], Wade, 852.
17. WBY to OS, [postmark May 10, 1934], Wade, 823.
18. WBY to OS, Aug. 25, [1934], Wade, 827.
19. WBY to Edmund Dulac, [? Dec. 10, 1934], Wade, 830.
20. Deirdre Toomey to BM, June 15, 1998.
21. WBY to OS, Feb. 27, [1934], Wade, 820.
22. WBY to Sean O'Faolain, [possibly 1934], Wade, 822.
23. Coogan, *de Valera,* 501.
24. Ibid., 503.
25. *Irish Press,* Oct. 2, 1934, Coogan, 504.
26. WBY to OS, Feb. 21, [1933], Wade, 806.
27. WBY to Frank Sturm, Jan. 7, 1935, and Sturm to WBY, March 30, 1935, Taylor, *Frank Pearce Sturm,* 105 and 106.
28. WBY to OS, [June 1, 1934], Wade, 823.
29. Harwood, 176–77.
30. Gwyneth Foden, *A Wife's Secret,* author's foreword, 6.
31. WBY to OS, June 28, [1933], Wade, 804.
32. Harwood, 175.

33. Carpenter, 465.

34. WBY, "Preface to *The King of the Great Clock Tower*," *VPlays*, 1310.

35. Ellmann, *Eminent Domain*, 81.

36. Carpenter, 504.

37. WBY to OS, July 24, [1934], Wade, 824–25.

38. Ellmann, *Four Dubliners*, 28.

39. WBY to MR, Oct. 5, [1934], McHugh, 21.

40. GY, Sept. 24, 1946, Ellmann NB, 30.

41. "Future of the Theatre, Mr. Yeats Denounces Stage Propaganda," *The Times*, Oct. 16, 1934.

42. WBY to MR, [? Oct. 30, 1934], McHugh, 24.

43. WBY to MR, Nov. 13, [1934], McHugh, 24.

44. WBY to MR, Nov. 26 [? 27], 1934, McHugh, 31.

45. MR to WBY, [undated, Feb.–March 1936], McHugh, 77.

46. McHugh, 14.

47. McHugh, 33–34.

48. WBY to Edmund Dulac, [? Dec. 19, 1934], Wade, 830.

49. OS to WBY, Nov. 25, 1934, John Harwood, "Olivia Shakespear," *YA6*, 97.

50. WBY to OS, [Dec. 1934], Harwood, 189.

51. EM, *Confessions and Impressions*, 184.

52. Ibid, 158.

53. EM, *Privileged Spectator*, 81.

54. Ibid.

55. WBY to GY, Dec. 26, 1934, USB.

56. WBY to MR, Feb. 25, [1935], McHugh, 35.

57. WBY to EM, March 4, [?1935], Wade, 832.

58. WBY to MR, Nov. 26 [?27], 1934, McHugh, 32.

59. Iseult Stuart, Sept. 21, 1946, Ellmann NB, 27–28.

60. WBY to DW, July 26, [1935], Wade, 838.

61. Richard Eberhardt, "Memory of Meeting Yeats," Mikhail 1, 193.

62. O'Faolain, *Vive Moi!*, 308–9.

63. GY to WBY, Jan. 1, [1935], and WBY to GY, Jan. 3, [1935], USB.

64. GY, Oct. 28, 1946, Ellmann NB, p. 24.

65. Private information based on interview, July 1996.

66. Geoffrey Elborn to BM, Aug. 11, 1998, based on taped interviews, 1984, with Francis Stuart.

67. Iseult Stuart, Sept. 21, Ellmann NB, 28.

68. Iseult Stuart, Sept. 21, 1946, Ellmann NB, 28.

69. Quentin Bell was criticized in 1972 for mentioning Gerald Duckworth's sexual assaults on his half-sister, the young Virginia Woolf.

70. See WBY's letters to GY, USB.

71. Curtis Bradford, "George Yeats: Poet's Wife," 391.

72. V. Sackville-West, "Wellesley, Dorothy Violet," *Dictionary of National Biography, 1951–1960,* 1041.

73. Frank O'Connor, Aug. 15, 1946, Ellmann NB, 18–19.

74. WBY to OS, [1935], Wade, 833.

75. WBY to DW, Aug. 5, [1936], *LDW,* 94.

76. "If I were Four-and-Twenty," *Exp,* 274–75.

77. Michael Carney to BM, Sept. 19, 1997, drawn from an unpublished life of Hilda Matheson.

78. Ellmann, "W. B. Yeats's Second Puberty," 28, restores the phrase excised from WBY to DW, June 17, [1935], *LDW,* 6.

79. WBY to OS, June 16, [1935], and WBY to EM, June 24, [1935], Wade, 835.

80. James Bryant Conant to WBY, May 25, 1935, NLI.

81. WBY to DW, July 6, 1935, Wade, 837.

82. WBY to EM, June 24, [1935], Wade, 836.

83. WBY to Ethel Mannin, June 26, [1935], Sligo, contains celibacy reference excised from Wade, 835.

84. WBY to DW, Aug. 11, [1935], Wade, 839.

85. WBY to Gwyneth Foden, July 6, [1935], Texas.

86. W. B. Stanford, *Enemies of Poetry,* 111.

87. Frank O'Connor, "The Old Age of a Poet," *The Bell* 1:5 (Feb. 1941).

88. WBY to DW, Sept. 8, [1935], *LDW,* 24.

89. WBY to MR, Aug. 11, [1935], McHugh, 42–43.

90. DW to WBY, Oct. 1, 1935, *LDW,* 35.

91. McHugh, 56.
92. Ibid., 58.
93. EM, *Privileged Spectator*, 81.
94. *LTWBY2*, 593.
95. GY to WBY, Dec. 9, 1935, USB,.
96. WBY to DW, Nov. 28, [1935], Wade, 843.
97. MR to WBY, Nov. 30, [1935], McHugh, 63.

Chapter 14. O My Dears

1. WBY to ESH, [Aug. 2, 1937], Wade, 895.
2. WBY to GY, [Nov.-Dec. 1935], USB.
3. OS to WBY, July 18, 1935, *YA6*, 101.
4. John Harwood, "Olivia Shakespear: Letters to W. B. Yeats," *YA6*, 105.
5. Harwood, "Appendix," "Yeats, Shri Purohit Swami, and Mrs. Foden," 102–107. *YA6*, 105.
6. Harwood, *YA6*, 105.
7. WBY to DW, [Jan. 19 or 20, 1936], and Jan. 26, [1936], *LDW*, 54–55.
8. WBY to DW, Jan. 26, [1936], 56.
9. WBY to EM, Dec. 11, [1936], Wade, 872.
10. WBY to DW, [Jan. 19 or 20, 1936], *LDW*, 54.
11. GY to Lily and Lolly Yeats, March 2, [1936], USB.
12. Gwyneth Foden to GY, Dec. 11, 1936, USB.
13. WBY to OS, April 10, 1936, Harwood, *YA6*, 106.
14. Gwyneth Foden to GY, [May 1936], and Dec. 11, 1936, USB.
15. Harwood, *YA6*, 106.
16. WBY to EM, [April 8, 1936], Wade, 850.
17. WBY to Ernest Rhys, May 3, [1934], Wade, 821.
18. WBY to OS, [April 8, 1936], Wade, 852.
19. WBY to MR, [early April 1936], McHugh, 81.
20. Graves, *Crowning Privilege*, 117.
21. "Maeve," *Dublin Evening Mail*, May 16, 1936.

22. Gwyneth Foden to GY, June 8, 1936, USB.

23. WBY to Shri Purohit Swami, May 25, [1936], Mokashi-Punekar, *The Later Phase in the Development of W. B. Yeats,* 263.

24. WBY to MR, [c. June 9, 1936], McHugh, 103.

25. WBY to DW, May 3, [1936], *LDW,* 68.

26. Ibid.

27. WBY to DW, May 22, [1936], *LDW,* 69.

28. WBY to DW, June 30, [1936], *LDW,* 73.

29. DW, "Personal notes," *LDW,* 197.

30. Nov. 9, 1934, *Harold Nicolson, Diaries and Letters, 1930–39,* 188.

31. WBY to DW, July 21, 1936, *LDW,* 89.

32. WBY to DW, Dec. 21, [1936], *LDW,* 125.

33. WBY to DW, Nov. 28, [1936], Wade, 868.

34. DW to WBY, Nov. 25, [1936], *LDW,* 116.

35. WBY to DW, [July 1936], *LDW,* 81.

36. O'Connor, *My Father's Son,* 266.

37. WBY to DW, Aug. 5, [1936], *LDW,* 95.

38. Bloom, *Yeats,* 438.

39. WBY to DW, [July 1936], *LDW,* 81.

40. WBY to DW, July 21, 1936, *LDW,* 90.

41. GY to DW, Sept. 19, 1936, *LDW,* 107.

42. "Modern Poetry," *The Times,* Oct. 12, 1936.

43. GY to WBY, Sept. 39, 1936, USB.

44. WBY to DW, [Oct. 29, 1936], *LDW,* 109.

45. WBY to DW, Nov. 8 [1936], *LDW,* 109.

46. Huxley lecture cited in Bradshaw, "The Eugenics Movement," *YA9,* 191–92.

47. Turner knew that Yeats would be criticized for his choices: see W. J. Turner to WBY, Nov. 24, 1936 *LTWBY2,* 586.

48. *OBMV,* xxxvii.

49. H. A. Mason, "Scrutiny," March 1937, in *Yeats: The Critical Heritage;* 385–87; John Sparrow, "The Welter Out of Which Great Poetry Has Emerged," *TLS,* Nov. 21, 1936, in *Yeats: The Critical Heritage,* "Modern Poetry—Mr. W. B. Yeats on a Period Rich in Lyrics," *The Times,* Oct. 12, 1936, p. 10.

50. W. H. Auden, "The Public v. the Late Mr. W. B. Yeats," *Partisan Review* (Spring 1939). Although he reviews the arguments to be made against Yeats, Auden defends a poet whose politics lie in his words.

51. *OBMV*, xi.

52. The case is stronger now that the diaries may have been genuine, but the question remains unresolved. See Roy Foster, "Forgeries or not? Never a Black and White Case," *The Times,* Dec. 11, 1997, p. 41.

53. WBY to EM, April 10, 1936, Wade, 851.

54. WBY to DW, Feb. 18, [1937], *LDW,* 141.

55. WBY to DW, Dec. 21, [1936], *LDW,* 125.

56. WBY to EM, Dec. 11, 1936, Wade, 872.

57. Ibid., 872–173.

58. WBY to EM, Nov. 15, [1936] and Nov. 30, 1936, Wade, 868, 870.

59. WBY to DW, Dec. 10, [1936], *LDW,* 122.

60. Cullingford, *Gender,* 279.

61. OS to DW, Dec. 8, 1936, Harwood, 179.

62. WBY to Shri Purohit Swami, March 21, 1937, Shankar Mokashi-Punekar, *The Later Phase in the Development of W. B. Yeats,* Jeffares, *A New Commentary on the Poems of W. B. Yeats,* 264–65,

63. *MM*, xxix.

64. "Athenaeum Elections," *The Times,* Feb. 16, 1937, p. 19.

65. Garrett Anderson, *"Hang Your Halo in the Hall": The Savile Club from 1868.* (London: Savile Club, 1993), 67.

66. WBY to DW, Feb. 18, [1937], Wade, 883.

67. WBY to George Barnes, Jan. 27, [1937], Wade, 878.

68. WBY to EM, Dec. 11, [1936], Wade, 872.

69. WBY to EM, March 1, [1937], Wade, 885.

70. WBY to EM, Feb. 17, [1938], Wade, 904.

71. Kenner, *A Colder Eye,* 41.

Chapter 15. *Such Friends*

1. The quote is from Yeats's *Journal*, Jan. 23, [1909], now in *Au*, 463, 144. ESH could have read it in *Estrangement: Being some fifty thoughts from a diary kept by William Butler Yeats in the year nineteen hundred and nine* (Dublin: Cuala, Aug. 1926), in *The London Mercury*, Oct. & Nov. 1926, or *The Dial*, Nov. 1926.

2. ESH, "Middle Age Without Weeping. How to Be Forty and Not Think it Ghastly." *Sunday Express,* June 20, 1926, pp. 9.

3. Ibid.

4. Ibid.

5. ESH, "Second Thoughts On First Nights," *Evening Standard*, Jan. 13, 1928.

6. Diana Souhami, *Gluck* (London: Pandora, 1988), 206; this fine piece of literary detective work is the source of biographical details of ESH unless otherwise indicated.

7. "Miss Edith Shackleton," *The Times,* Nov. 10, 1976, p. 18.

8. Souhami, *Gluck*, 215–16.

9. Jeremy Silver, "George's Barnes's 'W.B. Yeats and Broadcasting' 1940," *YA5*, 190.

10. WBY to Mrs. Llewelyn Davies, March 19, [1937], Wade, 885–86.

11. Ottoline Morrell to WBY, March 10, [1937], Seymour, *Ottoline Morrell*, 405.

12. WBY to EM, March 24, [1937], Sligo.

13. *Au*, 463 and 489.

14. David Bradshaw, "The Eugenics Movement and the Emergence of *On the Boiler*," *YA9*, 194, 195.

15. Ibid.

16. Ibid., 197.

17. *SS*, 99.

18. WBY to GY, April 15, [1937], USB.

19. WBY to GY, April 25, [1937], USB.

20. WBY to ESH, May 4, [1937], Wade, 877.

21. WBY to DW, May 4, 1937, *LDW*, 149.

22. WBH to ESH, May 24, [1937], Souhami, 216.

23. WBY to ESH, May 29, [1939], Souhami, 216.

24. WBY to ESH, May 18, [1937], Wade, 888.

25. Edmund Dulac to WBY, June 3, 1937, *LTWBY2*, 589.

26. WBY to ESH, June [?] 1937, Houghton.

27. WBY to ESH, June 22, [1937], Houghton.

28. H. Montgomery Hyde, "Yeats and Gogarty," *YA5*, 158.

29. WBY to GY, Oct. 30, [1937], USB.

30. GY to WBY, June 13, 1937, USB, cited in Pierce, 263.

31. WBY to GY, July 15, 1937, USB.

32. "Poem of Lancelot Switchback," Pearce, "Domestic Sibyl," 141.

33. Asa Briggs, *The History of Broadcasting in the United Kingdon,* vol. 2 (London: Oxford University Press, 1965), 262; also H. Matheson, "Listener Research in Broadcasting," *Sociological Review* 27 (1935): 408–22.

34. WBY to GY, [?], 1937, USB.

35. WBY to GY, July 15, 1937, USB; Michael Carney, unpublished biography of Hilda Matheson, chap. 7.

36. WBY to ESH, June 19, 1937, Houghton.

37. ESH, "'Mannish' Woman the Product of Prudery," *Sunday Express,* Nov. 22, 1925; "Day of 'Surplus' Men," *Sunday Express,* Aug. 23, 1925.

38. Deirdre Toomey to BM, Aug. 16, 1998.

39. Recorded in Hannah Gluck's diary as a comment Yeats made to ESH, Souhami, 218.

40. WBY to ESH, Aug. 2. 1937, Souhami, 217.

41. James D. Mooney to WBY, April 7, 1937, NLI.

42. WBY to ESH, Aug. 6, [1937], Wade, 895.

43. "King George V and the Lane Pictures," *The Times,* Aug. 18, 1937, p. 8.

44. WBY to James A. Healey, Sept. 7, [1937], Wade, 898.

45. WBY to DW, Aug. 13, 1937, *LDW,* 157.

46. From "Cherishing the Diaspora," presidential speech given to the Irish Parliament (Oireachtas) on Feb. 2, 1995, in *Mary Robinson,* by Olivia O'Leary and Helen Burke (London: Hodder and Stoughton, 1998), 196.

47. McHugh, 128.

48. WBY to Edmund Dulac, [? July 1937], Wade, 893.

49. Edmund Dulac to WBY, June 24, 1937, *LTWBY2*, 589–90.

50. W. J. Turner to WBY, July 9, 1937, and ibid, 590.

51. Silver, "George Barnes 'W.B. Yeats and Broadcasting' 1940," *YA5*, 194, and McHugh, 112.

52. "Queen's Hall Concert," *The Times*, Nov. 24, 1937.

53. WBY to Lolly, Oct. 6, [1937], Burns.

54. WBY to DW, Sept. 5, 1937, *LDW*, 159.

55. WBY to Lolly, many letters concerning Cuala finances, Nov. 1937–Jan. 1938, Burns. For full details of Cuala's financial difficulties in these years, see Lewis, *The Yeats Sisters and the Cuala* 170–77.

56. Lewis, 175, 170.

57. WBY to OS, March 9 [1933], Wade, 807.

58. See Lewis, and Hardwick, *The Yeats Sisters*.

59. T. C. Scroope to Lolly, [June 1938], Lewis, 177.

60. Lewis, 179.

61. WBY to C. P. Blacker, Dec. 25, 1937, cited in David Bradshaw, "The Eugenics Movement in the 1930s and the Emergence of *On the Boiler*," *YA9*, 201.

62. WBY to EM, Dec. 13, [1937], Wade, 902.

63. WBY to ESH, Nov. 28, [1937], Wade, 901.

64. WBY to GY, Oct. 13, [1937], USB.

65. GY, June 17, 1946, Ellmann NB, 4.

66. Hone, 432.

67. GY to WBY, April 3, [1937], USB.

68. O'Connor, *My Father's Son*, p. 186.

69. Anne Yeats, British Library National Sound Archive record, 1CA0012476, S2 BD2 and 4, 1974.

70. Lolly's inscription on the back of the photograph of the Yeats children on bicycles at Gurteen Dhas comments that Anne was simply at the age when she didn't care what she looked like. Princeton.

71. WBY to DW, Dec. 17, 1937, *LDW*, 166.

72. McHugh, 134.

73. WBY to ESH, Nov. 14, [1937], Houghton.

74. WBY to ESH, Nov. 28, [1937], Houghton.

75. WBY to ESH, Dec. 10, [1937], Houghton; Wade, 901.

76. Bradshaw, "The Eugenics Movement," *YA9*, 201.

Chapter 16. A Working Year

1. David, Bradshaw, "The Eugenics Movement in the 1930s and the Emergence of *On the Boiler*," *YA9*, 202.

2. WBY to C. P. Blacker, Jan. 13, 1938, ibid, 209.

3. C. P. Blacker to WBY, Jan. 17, 1938, ibid, 209.

4. WBY to C. P. Blacker, Feb. 20, 1938, ibid, 210.

5. C. P. Blacker to WBY, March 8, 1938, ibid, 210.

6. In *OTB*, 18, Yeats recommends the Cattell book to his readers, saying in a footnote, "I have taken most of the facts in this section, and some of the arguments and metaphors that follow, from this book."

7. *OTB*, 18. *OTB* can also be read in *Exp*, 407–53.

8. *OTB*, 23.

9. Stanley Sultan, "Yeats at His Last," *New Yeats Papers*, no. 11 (Dublin: Dolmen Press, 1975), 13, cited in Bradshaw, 211.

10. *OTB*, 29–30, 20.

11. Ibid., 27–28.

12. Ibid., 12.

13. Cardozo, *Maud Gonne*, 391.

14. *OTB*, 18.

15. WBY to GY, Jan. 23, [1938], USB.

16. GY to WBY, Jan. 20, 1938, USB.

17. WBY to GY, Jan. 27 and 29, [1938], USB.

18. WBY to ESH, Feb. 5 [1938], Houghton.

19. WBY to ESH, Feb. 21, [1938], Wade, 905.

20. WBY to ESH, March 2 [1938], Houghton.

21. WBY to ESH, letters, Feb.–March [1938], Harvard, part cited in Souhami, 217.

22. WBY to ESH, March 15, [1938], Souhami, 217.

23. GY to WBY, April 18 and 20, 1938, USB.

24. *P*, notes, 640.

25. Kiberd, *Inventing Ireland*, 312–13.

26. Colm Tóibin, "Playboys of the GPO," *London Review of Books*, April 18, 1996, pp. 14–15.

27. GY to ESH, May 6, 1938, Souhami, 217.

28. GY to ESH, May 12, 1938, cited in Souhami, 217.

29. GY, "A Fishing Excursion with Yeats," BL National Sound Archive, Feb. 16, 1949, T76255V.

30. WBY to ESH, July 21, [1938], Wade, 912.

31. WBY to ESH, May 24, [1938], Houghton.

32. WBY to DW, July 3, 1938, *LDW*, 187.

33. WBY to ESH, June 28, [1938], Souhami, 217, deleted from Wade, 911.

34. WBY to MG, June 16 [1938], Wade, 910.

35. Toomey, "Away," *Yeats and Women*, 166, n47, quoting *Irish Independent*, Aug, 13, 1938; "Abbey Theatre Festival, Mr. Yeats's New Play," *The Times*, Aug. 16, 1938, p. 10.

36. "Abbey Theatre Festival," p. 10.

37. Frank O'Connor, "The Old Age of a Poet," *Bell*, Feb. 1941, p. 8.

38. MG to EM, Nov. [?], 1945, White, 453.

39. WBY to MG, June 16, [1938], Wade, 910.

40. MG, "Yeats and Ireland," *Scattering Branches, Tributes to the Memory of W.B. Yeats,* ed. Stephen Gwynn (New York: Macmillan, 1940), 25.

41. Anthony J. Jordan, *Willie Yeats and the Gonne-MacBrides* (Dublin: The Central Remedial Clinic, 1997), 190.

42. WBY to Iseult Stuart, July 19, 1932, Kansas.

43. Elborn, *Francis Stuart,* 91. WBY wrote many effusive letters of praise to Stuart, such as that of Sept. 6, [1933], Kansas.

44. *Myth*, 331.

45. W. H. Auden, "In Memory of W. B. Yeats," *Collected Poems [of] W.H. Auden,* ed. Edward Mendelson: Faber and Faber), 1976.

46. John Eglinton, *Irish Literary Portraits* (London: Macmillan, 1935), 26.

47. Stephen Gwynn, *Irish Literature and Drama in the English Language; A Short History* (1936), 158; cited in *NC*, 423.

48. WBY to Shri Purohit Swami, draft letters [n.d., and Aug. 23, 1936], NLI.

49. Shri Purohit Swami to WBY, Aug. 27, 1938, *LTWBY2*, 603–4.

50. *P*, 641.

51. Keane, *Yeats's Interactions with Tradition*, 74.

52. WBY to ESH, Sept. 5, 1938, Souhami, 217.

53. WBY to ESH, Sept. 12, 1938, Souhami, 217.

54. WBY to EM, Aug. 22, 1938, Sligo.

55. EM, *Privileged Spectator*, 312.

56. WBY to EM, Oct. 20, [1938], Wade, 611 918.

57. WBY to Lady Elizabeth Pelham, Jan. 4, 1939, Wade, 922.

58. EP to GY, Oct. 9, [1938], Terrell, "Ezra Pound: Letters to W. B. Yeats" Carpenter, *A Serious Character*, 556.

59. "Evacuation in War," *The Times,* Oct. 28, 1938, p. 8, and "Parliament Today: Mr Chamberlain's Critics; The King to His People; A Message of Thanks," *The Times,* Oct. 3, 1938, p. 12.

60. WBY to ESH, Dec. 19, 1938, and Jan. 9, 1939, Houghton.

61. Arnold, *Jack Yeats*, 312.

62. WBY to ESH, Dec. 19, [1938], Houghton.

63. Michael Carney to BM, Sept. 17, 1998.

64. GY, Oct. 28, 1946, Ellmann NB, 35.

65. WBY to ESH, Jan. 1, [1939], Wade, 922.

66. WBY to Lady Elizabeth Pelham, Jan. 4, 1939, Wade, 922.

67. *LDW*, 213.

68. "Last Days," *LDW*, 213.

69. Ibid, 214.

70. GY to Thomas MacGreevy, March 6, 1939, TCD.

71. Glendinning, *Vita*, 299.

72. "Last Days," *LDW*, 214.

73. Brigid O'Brien Ganly to BM, April 25, 1998.

Epilogue: Laid to Rest?

1. *Bord Fáilte Visitor Attractions 1991–1996,* published by Bord Fáilte/Irish Tourist Board, has no figures on visits to Drumcliffe because no fees are charged, but records the number of visitors to Yeats's tower, Thoor Ballylee, as 28, 406 in 1996. *The Guardian,* Dec. 29, 1998 in "Modern Lives to Yeats Church", estimated the grave's annual visitors as 80,000–90,000.

2. "Mr. W. B. Yeats Buried at Roquebrune," *The Times,* Jan. 31, 1939, p. 11.

3. BM, *Nora* (London: Sinclair-Stevenson, 1988), 478.

4. White, 453–54.

5. Ibid.

6. Ellmann, *James Joyce,* 660n.

7. Lewis, 179.

8. GY to Constantine Curran, Feb. 22, 1939, UCD.

9. Souhami, 229; unless otherwise specified, details of the 1947–98 search for Yeats's bones are from Souhami's book. A valuable critical analysis of *Gluck* and the debate about the grave is Warwick Gould's "Diana Souhami, *Gluck 1895–1978: Her Biography.*" YA9, 342–49.

10. Souhami, 229.

11. Warwick Gould, "Diana Souhami, *Gluck 1895–1978: Her Biography,*" YA9, 344.

12. Pearce, "Hours with the Domestic Sibyl." Yeats Eliot Review, Vol. 12, nos. 3 & 4 (Winter 1994) 137; John Montague, "Poetic Widow." *Agenda* 33: 3–4 (Autumn/Winter 1996): 221–26.

13. Edmund Dulac to ESH, Jan. 6, 1948, Souhami, 231–32.

14. GY to Edmund Dulac, Jan. 9, 1948, cited in Souhami, 232.

15. Abbé Biancheri to Edmund Dulac, Feb. 16, 1948, Souhami, 233–34.

16. Hannah Gluck to GY, c. March 2, 1948, Souhami, 234.

17. Ibid., 234.

18. ESH to Edmund Dulac, March 17, 1948, Souhami, 237.

19. Abbé Biancheri to Edmund Dulac, March 31, 1948, Souhami, 237.

20. Jordan, *Willie Yeats and the Gonne-MacBrides,* 194.

21. Maurice Collis, *The Journey Up* (London:, Faber and Faber, 1970), 84.

22. Jillian Robertson, "Yeats Mystery Unearthed." *The Times,* Aug. 19, 1986, p. 8.

23. Jonathan Petre, "Frenchmen's Bones 'Lie in Yeats's Grave.'" *Daily Telegraph,* Sept. 6, 1988.

24. Ella Shanahan, "Claim That Yeats Was Buried in a Pauper's Grave," *Irish Times,* Sept. 6, 1988, p. 1.

25. Nuala O'Faolain, "No W.B. under Bare Ben Bulben's Head?," *Irish Times,* 1988.

26. Kathryn Holmquist, "Reports on Yeats's Grave Dismissed," *Irish Times,* Sept. 7, 1988, p. 3.

27. Anne Yeats and Michael Yeats, "Yeats's Resting Place," *The Independent,* Oct. 4, 1988, p. 17.

28. Madge Cockman, "Whose Grave?." *The Independent,* Oct. 8, 1988, p. 15.

Bibliography

Alldritt, Keith. *W.B. Yeats: The Man and the Milieu*. London: John Murray, 1997.

Allt, Peter, and Alspach, Russell K., eds. *The Variorum Edition of the Poems by W.B. Yeats*. London: Macmillan, 1960.

Alspach, Russell K., ed. *The Variorum Edition of the Plays of W.B. Yeats*. London: Macmillan, 1966.

Amory, Mark. *Lord Dunsany*. London: Collins, 1972.

Arensberg, Conrad M., and Solon T. Kimball. *Family and Community in Ireland*. Cambridge: Harvard University Press, 1940.

Arnold, Bruce. *Jack Yeats*. New Haven: Yale University Press, 1998.

Auden, W .H. "The Public v. the Late Mr. W .B. Yeats." *Partisan Review* (Spring 1939).

Balliet, Conrad A. *W. B. Yeats: A Census of the Manuscripts*. New York: Garland, 1990.

Beckett, J. C. *The Making of Modern Ireland 1603–1923*. London: paperback, 1969.

Bentley, Edmund. *Far Horizon: A Biography of Hester Dowden, Medium and Psychic Investigator.* London: Rider and Company, 1951.

Bloom, Harold. *Yeats.* New York: Oxford University Press, 1970.

Boylan, Patricia. *A Cultivated People: A History of the United Arts Club of Dublin.* Gerrards Cross, Bucks.: Colin Smythe, 1988.

Bradford, Curtis. "George Yeats: Poet's Wife." *Sewanee Review* 77:3 (July–Sept. 1969): 385–404.

———. "Yeats and Maud Gonne." *Texas Studies in Language & Literature* 3:4 (Winter 1962).

———. *Yeats at Work.* Carbondale: Southern Illinois University Press, 1965.

Bradshaw, David. "The Eugenics Movement in the 1930s and the Emergence of *On the Boiler.*" *Yeats Annual* 9, 189–215.

Bridge, Ursula, ed. *W. B. Yeats and T. Sturge Moore: Their Correspondence 1901–1937.* London: Routledge & Kegan Paul, 1953.

Cardozo, Nancy. *Maud Gonne: Lucky Eyes and a High Heart.* London: Gollancz, 1979.

Carleton, William. *Traits and Stories of the Irish Peasantry.* Dublin: 2 vols. 1830.

Carney, Michael. Unpublished biography of Hilda Matheson. *Stoker: The Life of Hilda Matheson.* 1888–1940, 1997.

Carpenter, Humphrey. *A Serious Character: The Life of Ezra Pound.* Boston: Houghton Mifflin, 1988.

Collier, Richard. *Duce! The Rise and Fall of Benito Mussolini.* London: Collins, 1971.

Collis, Maurice. *Somerville & Ross: A Biography.* London: Faber, 1968.

Connell, K. H. *Catholicism and Marriage in the Century after the Famine.* Oxford: Clarendon Press, 1968.

Coogan, Tim Pat. *De Valera: Long Fellow, Long Shadow.* London: Arrow.

———. *The I.R.A.* London: Fontana, 1980.

Coote, Stephen. *W. B. Yeats: A Life.* London: Hodder and Stoughton, 1997.

Coxhead, Elizabeth. *The Thankless Muse.* London: Secker & Warburg, 1967.

Cronin, Anthony. *Samuel Beckett: The Last Modernist.* London: HarperCollins, 1996; Flamingo, 1997.

Cullingford, Elizabeth Butler. "Family Values." *Bullán: An Irish Studies Journal* 2:2 (Winter/Spring, 1996): 120–27.

———. *Gender and History in Yeats's Love Poetry.* Cambridge: Cambridge University Press, 1993.

———. *Yeats, Ireland and Fascism.* London: Macmillan, 1981.

Davis-Goff, Annabel. *Walled Gardens.* London: Barrie & Jenkins, 1990.

Deane, Seamus. "Blueshirts." *London Review of Books,* June 4–17, 1982, p. 23.

———. *Celtic Revivals: Essays in Modern Irish Literature.* London: Faber, 1985.

De Vere White, Terence. *Kevin O'Higgins.* London: Methuen, 1948.

Eagleton, Terry. *Heathcliff and the Great Hunger: Studies in Irish Culture.* London: Verso, 1995.

Ebbutt, M. I. *Hero-Myths & Legends of the British Race.* London: Harrap, 1915.

Edwards, Ruth Dudley. *Patrick Pearse: the Triumph of Failure.* London: Gollancz, 1977.

Elborn, Geoffrey. *Francis Stuart: A Life.* Dublin: Raven Arts Press, 1990.

Ellis, Havelock. "A New Artificial Paradise." *Contemporary Review,* no. 73 (1898): 130–41.

Ellmann, Richard. *Eminent Domain: Yeats among Wilde, Joyce, Pound, Eliot and Auden.* New York: Oxford University Press, 1967.

———. *The Identity of Yeats.* London: Faber, 1954.

———. "Interviews with Mrs. Yeats, Frank O'Connor and Others about W. B. Yeats, 1946." Clothbound notebook, McFarlin Library. University of Tulsa.

———. *James Joyce.* Rev. ed. London: Oxford University Press, 1982.

———. "W. B. Yeats's Second Puberty." In *Four Dubliners: Wilde, Yeats, Joyce, Beckett.* London: Hamish Hamilton, 1987.

———. *Yeats: The Man and the Masks.* London: Macmillan, 1948; Oxford University Press, 1979.

———. "The Yeatses at Home." In *Riverrun.* London: Hamish Hamilton, 1988.

Fahy, Catherine. *W. B. Yeats and His Circle.* Dublin: The National Library, 1989.

Fay, Gerard. *The Abbey Theatre.* London: Hollis & Carter, 1958.

Ferris, Paul. *Dr. Freud.* London: Sinclair-Stevenson, 1997.

Finneran, Richard J., George M. Harper, and William M. Murphy, eds. *Editing Yeats's Poems: A Reconsideration.* London: Macmillan, 1983, 1990.

———. *Letters to W. B. Yeats.* 2 vols. London: Macmillan, 1977.

———. *Yeats Annual.* Vols. 1–2. London: Macmillan, 1982, 1984.

———. *Yeats: An Annual of Critical and Textual Studies.* Vols. 1–8. Ithaca, N.Y.: Cornell University Press. 1983.

FitzGerald, Garret. *An Autobiography.* London: Macmillan, 1991.

Foden, Gwyneth. *A Wife's Secret.* London: Arthur H. Stockwell, 1926.

Foster, R. F. *Modern Ireland 1600–1972.* London: Allen Lane, 1988.

———. "Protestant Magic: W. B. Yeats and the Spell of Irish History." *Proceedings of the British Academy* 75 (1989): 243–66.

———. *Yeats: A Life: The Apprentice Mage.* London: Oxford University Press, 1997.

———, ed. *The Oxford Illustrated History of Ireland.* Oxford: Oxford University Press, 1989.

Gibbon, Monk. *The Masterpiece and the Man: Yeats as I Knew Him.* London: Hart-Davis, 1959.

Glendinning, Victoria. *Vita: The Life of V. Sackville-West.* London: Penguin, 1994.

Goldring, Douglas. *The Nineteen Twenties.* London: Nicholson & Watson, 1945.

Gould, Warwick. "Diana Souhami, *Gluck 1895–1978: Her Biography.* *Yeats Annual* 9, 342–47.

———. "'A Lesson for the Circumspect': W. B. Yeats's Two Versions of *A Vision* and the *Arabian Nights.*" In *The Arabian Nights in English Literature.* Edited by Peter L. Caracciolo. London: Macmillan, 1988.

———. "Yeats, Mescal and Visions." *Times Literary Supplement,* July 13–19, 1990, p. 762.

———, ed. *Yeats Annuals, 3–8, 10–13.* London: Macmillan, 1985–88.

Graves, Robert. *The Crowning Privilege: The Clark Lectures 1954–1955.* London: Cassell & Company, 1955.

Gray, Tony. *A Peculiar Man: A Life of George Moore.* London: Sinclair-Stevenson, 1996.

Gregory, Anne. *Me and Nu.* 1970. Reprint, Gerrards Cross, Bucks.: Colin Smythe, 1990.

Gregory, Lady. *Diaries 1892–1902.* Edited by James Pethica. Gerrards Cross, Bucks.: Colin Smythe, 1996.

———. *The Journals, vol. 1, books 1–29.* Edited by Daniel J. Murphy. Gerrards Cross., Bucks.: Colin Smythe, 1978.

———. *Seventy Years: Being the Autobiography of Lady Gregory.* Edited by T. R. Henn and Colin Smythe. Gerrards Cross, Bucks.: Colin Smythe, 1973.

Grosskurth, Phyllis. *Havelock Ellis.* London: Allen Lane, 1980.

Hardwick, Joan. *The Yeats Sisters.* London: Pandora, 1996.

Harper, George Mills. *The Making of Yeats's "A Vision."* 2 vols. London: Macmillan, 1987.

———. "Out of a Medium's Mouth: Yeats's Theory of 'Transference' and Keats's 'Ode to a Nightingale.'" *Yeats: An Annual of Critical and Textual Studies* 1. Ithaca: Cornell University Press, 1983, 17–32.

———. "Unbelievers in the House: Yeats's Automatic Script." *Studies in the Literary Imagination, 1981, Vol. 14/1:* 1–15.

———. *W. B. Yeats and W. T. Horton: The Record of an Occult Friendship.* London: Macmillan, 1980.

———. *Yeats's Golden Dawn.* London: Macmillan, 1974.

———, ed. *Yeats and the Occult.* London: Macmillan 1976.

———, general ed. *Yeats's "Vision" Papers.* Vol. 1: *The Automatic Script: 5 November 1917–18 June 1918.* Edited by Steve L. Adams, Barbara J. Frieling, and Sandra L. Sprayberry. London: Macmillan, 1992. Vol. 2: *The Automatic Script: 25 June 1918–29 March 1920.* Edited by Steve L. Adams, Barbara J. Frieling, and Sandra L. Sprayberry. London: Macmillan, 1992. Vol. 3: *Sleep and Dream Notebooks, "Vision" Notebooks 1 and 2, Card File.* Edited by Robert Anthony Martinich and Margaret Mills Harper. London: Macmillan, 1992.

Harper, Margaret Mills. "The Medium as Creator: George Yeats's Role in the Automatic Script." *Yeats Annual of Critical and Textual Studies* 6, 49–72. Ann Arbor: University of Michigan Press, 1988.

Harwood, John. *Olivia Shakespear and W. B. Yeats: After Long Silence.* London: Macmillan, 1989.

———. "Olivia Shakespear: Letters to W. B. Yeats." *Yeats Annual* 6, 59–107.

———. "'Secret Communion': Yeats's Sexual Destiny." *Yeats Annual* 9, 252–80.

Hassett, Joseph M. "Yeats and the Chief Consolation of Genius." *Yeats Annual of Critical and Textual Studies* 4, 55–68.

Haswell, Janis Tedesco. *Pressed Against Divinity: W. B. Yeats's Feminine Masks.* DeKalb: Northern Illinois University Press, 1997.

Heine, Elizabeth. "W. B. Yeats' map in his own hand." *Biography* 1:3 1978, 48–49.

———. "Yeats, Maud Gonne: Marriage and the Astrological Record, 1908–09." *Yeats Annual* 13, 3–33.

Hone, Joseph. *W. B. Yeats: 1865–1939.* London: Macmillan, 1942.

Hood, Connie K. "The Remaking of *A Vision.*" *Yeats Annual of Critical and Textual Studies* 1, 33–67.

Hough, Graham. *The Mystery Religion of W. B. Yeats.* Brighton: Harvester, 1984.

Howes, Marjorie. *Yeats's Nations; Gender, Class and Irishness.* Cambridge: Cambridge University Press, 1996.

Hyde, H. Montgomery. "Yeats and Gogarty." *Yeats Annual* 5, 154–161.

Jackson, John Wyse, and Bernard McGinley. *James Joyce's "Dubliners": An Annotated Edition.* London: Sinclair-Stevenson, 1993.

Jaffe, Grace. "Vignettes." *Yeats Annual* 5, 139–53.

———. *Years of Grace.* Sunspot, N.M.: Iroquois House, 1979.

Jeffares, A. Norman. *The Circus Animals: Essays on W. B. Yeats.* Stanford: Stanford University Press, 1970.

———. *A New Commentary on the Poems of W. B. Yeats.* London: Macmillan, 1984.

———. *W. B. Yeats: A New Biography.* London: Hutchinson, 1988.

———. *Yeats's Poems.* London: Macmillan, 1989.

———, ed. *Yeats the European.* Gerrards Cross, Bucks: Colin Smythe, 1989.

Jeffares, A. Norman, and K. G. W. Cross, eds. *In Excited Reverie: A Centenary Tribute, W. B. Yeats 1865–1939.* London: Macmillan, 1965.

Jordan, Anthony J. *Willie Yeats and the Gonne-MacBrides.* Dublin: The Central Remedial Clinic, 1997.

Jordan, Carmel. *A Terrible Beauty and Yeats's "Great Tapestry."* London: Associated University Presses, 1987.

Kavanagh, Patrick. *Voices in Ireland: A Traveller's Literary Company.* London: John Murray, 1995.

Keane, Patrick J. *Yeats's Interactions with Tradition.* Columbia: University of Missouri Press, 1987.

Kelly, John, general ed. *The Collected Letters of W. B. Yeats.* Vol. 1 (1865–1895). Edited by John Kelly and Eric Domville. Oxford: Clarendon Press, 1986. Vol. 2 (1896–1900). Edited by Warwick Gould, John Kelly, and Deirdre Toomey. Oxford: Clarendon Press 1997. Vol. 3 (1901–1904). Edited by John Kelly and Ronald Schuchard. Oxford: Clarendon Press, 1994.

Kennedy, Robert J. *The Irish: Emigration, Marriage and Fertility.* Berkeley: University of California Press, 1973.

Kenner, Hugh. *A Colder Eye:* London: Penguin, 1983.

Kiberd, Declan. *Inventing Ireland.* London: Jonathan Cape, 1995.

Krimm, Bernard G. *W. B. Yeats and the Irish Free State 1918–1939: Living in the Explosion.* Troy, N.Y.: Whitston, 1981.

Lewis, Gifford. *The Yeats Sisters and the Cuala.* Blackrock, Co. Dublin: Irish Academic Press, 1994.

Lodge, Oliver. *The Survival of Man: A Study in Unrecognised Human Faculty.* London: Methuen, 1909.

Longenbach, James. *Stone Cottage: Pound, Yeats and Modernism.* New York: Oxford University Press, 1988.

Lyons, F. S. L. *Culture and Anarchy in Ireland 1890–1939.* Oxford: Clarendon Press, 1979.

———. *Ireland Since the Famine.* London: 1971; Fontana, 1983.

MacBride, Maud Gonne. *Servant of the Queen.* London: Gollancz, 1968.

MacGreevy, Thomas. "W. B. Yeats—A Generation Later." *University Review* 3:8 (1966).

McHugh, Roger, ed. *Ah, Sweet Dancer: W. B. Yeats, Margot Ruddock: A Correspondence.* London: Macmillan, 1970.

MacManus, Francis, ed. *The Yeats We Knew.* Cork: Mercier Press, 1965.

Mannin, Ethel. *Confessions and Impressions.* London: Jarrold's, 1930.

———. *Privileged Spectator: A Sequel to Confessions and Impressions.* London: Jarrold's, 1939.

———. *Young in the Twenties: A Chapter of Autobiography.* London: Hutchinson, 1971.

Manning, Maurice. "The Authors Were in Eternity—or Oxford: George Yeats, George Harper, and the Making of *A Vision.*" *Yeats' Annual of Critical and Textual Studies* 6, 233–44. Ann Arbor: University of Michigan Press, 1988.

———. *The Blueshirts.* Dublin: Gill and Macmillan, 1970.

———. "Yeats's 'Last Poems': A Reconsideration." *Yeats Annual* 5.

Matheson, Hilda. *Broadcasting.* London: Thornton Butterworth, 1933.

Mikhail, E. K. *W. B. Yeats: Interviews and Recollections.* 2 vols. London: Macmillan, 1977.

Moberly, C. A. E., and Eleanor F. Jourdain. *An Adventure.* London: Faber, 1931.

Mokashi-Punekar, Shankar. *The Later Phase in the Development of W. B. Yeats.* Dhawar, India: Karnatak University, 1966.

Montague, John. "Poetic Widow." *Agenda* 33:3–4 (Autumn/Winter 1996): 221–26.

Moore, George. *Hail and Fairwell!* 3 vols.: *Ave, Salve,* and *Vale.* 1914; London: Heinemann, 1919 and 1947.

Moore, Virginia. *The Unicorn: William Butler Yeats' Search for Reality.* New York: Macmillan, 1954.

Moynahan, Julian. *Anglo-Irish: The Literary Imagination in a Hyphenated Culture.* Princeton: Princeton University Press, 1995.

Murphy, William M. "The Ancestry of William Butler Yeats." In *Yeats and the 1890s.* Edited by Robert O'Driscoll and Lorna Reynolds. Shannon: Irish University Press, 1971.

————. *Family Secrets.* Dublin: Gill and Macmillan, 1995.

————. *Prodigal Father: The Life of John Butler Yeats (1839–1922).* Ithaca, N.Y.: Cornell University Press, 1978.

Nichols, Beverley. *Twenty-Five.* London: Penguin, 1985.

Nicolson, Harold. *Diaries and Letters 1930–1939.* Edited by Nigel Nicolson. London: Collins, 1966.

Oates, Joyce Carol. "'At Least I Have Made a Woman of Her': Images of Women in Twentieth-Century Literature." *The Georgia Review* 37 (1983): 7–30.

O'Brien, Conor Cruise. *Ancestral Voices.* Dublin: Poolbeg, 1994.

————. "'Passion and Cunning': An Essay on the Politics of W.B. Yeats." In *In Excited Reverie.* Edited by A. Norman Jeffares and K. G. W. Cross. London: Macmillan, 1965.

O'Connor, Frank. *My Father's Son.* London: Macmillan, 1968.

————. "The Old Age of a Poet." [By Michael O'Donovan.] *Bell,* Feb. 7–18, 1941.

O'Connor, Ulick. "The First New Age Lovers." *Sunday Independent,* March 2, 1997.

————. *Oliver St. John Gogarty: A Poet and His Times.* London: Jonathan Cape, 1964.

O'Faolain, Sean. *Vive Moi!: An Autobiography.* London: Sinclair-Stevenson, 1993.

Owen, Alex. *The Darkened Room: Women, Power and Spiritualism in Late Victorian England.* London: Virago, 1989.

Paige, D. D., ed. *Selected Letters of Ezra Pound 1907–1941.* London: Faber and Faber, 1982.

Pearce, Donald D. "Hours with the Domestic Sibyl: Remembering George Yeats." Yeats Eliot Review, vol. 12, Nos. 3 & 4, (Winter 1994), 136–43.

————. *The Senate Speeches of W.B. Yeats.* Bloomington: Indiana University Press, 1960. London: Faber, 1961.

Perloff, Marjorie. "Between Hatred and Desire." *Yeats Annual 7,* 29–50.

Pethica, James, ed. *Lady Gregory's Diaries 1892–1902.* Gerrards Cross, Bucks.: Colin Smythe, 1996.

Pierce, David. *Yeats's Worlds: Ireland, England and the Poetic Imagination.* New Haven: Yale University Press, 1995.

Porter, Roy. *The Greatest Benefit to Mankind: A Medical History of Humanity from Antiquity to the Present.* London: HarperCollins, 1997.

Pound, Omar, and A. Walton Litz. *Ezra Pound and Dorothy Shakespear: Their Letters 1909–1914.* London: Faber, 1985.

Pruitt, Virginia D. "Yeats and the Steinach Operation." *American Imago* 34 (Fall 1977): 287–96.

Pruitt, Virginia D., and Raymond D. Pruitt. "Yeats and the Steinach Operation: A Further Analysis." *Yeats: An Annual of Textual and Critical Studies* 1, 104–25.

Raine, Kathleen. *Yeats: The Tarot and the Golden Dawn.* Dublin: Dolmen, 1976.

Regardie, Israel. *The Golden Dawn.* St. Paul, Minn.: Llewellyn Publications, 1971.

Reid, B. L. *The Man from New York: John Quinn and His Friends.* New York: Oxford University Press, 1968.

Ring, Jim. *Erskine Childers.* London: John Murray, 1996.

Robinson, Lennox. *Curtain Up.* London: Michael Joseph, 1942.

Russell, George. *The Avatars.* London: Macmillan. 1933.

Saddlemyer, Ann. "George, Ezra, Dorothy and Friends: Twenty-six Letters 1918–59." *Yeats Annual* 7, 4–28.

———, and Colin Smythe, eds. *Lady Gregory: Fifty Years After.* Gerrards Cross, Bucks.: Colin Smythe, 1987.

Said, Edward. *Culture and Imperialism.* London: Chatto and Windus, 1993.

Scheper-Hughes, Nancy. *Saints, Scholars, and Schizophrenics: Mental Illness in Rural Ireland.* Berkeley: University of California Press, 1979.

Schuchard, Marsha Keith. "Freemasonry, Secret Societies, and the Continuity of the Occult Traditions in English Literature." Ann Arbor, Mich.: Xerox University Microfilms. 1975.

Seymour, Miranda. *Ottoline Morrell: Life on the Grand Scale.* London: Hodder & Stoughton, 1992.

Silver, Jeremy. "Yeats and Broadcasting." *Yeats Annual* 5, 181–203.

Souhami, Diana. *Gluck: Her Biography*. London: Pandora, 1988.

Smith, Thomas R. "The Double Aim of Yeats's *Autobiography*." *Yeats Eliot Review* Vol. 10. No 4, Fall 1990, 95–101.

Smythe, Colin. *A Guide to Coole Park*. Gerrards Cross, Bucks.: Colin Smythe, 1995.

———, ed. *Robert Gregory 1881–1918*. Gerrards Cross, Bucks.: Colin Smythe, 1981.

St. John, Ervine. "Portrait of W.B. Yeats." *The Listener,* Sept. 1, 1955.

Stallworthy, Jon. *Between the Lines: Yeats's Poetry in the Making*. London: Oxford University Press, revised 1971.

Stanfield, Paul Scott. *Yeats and Politics in the 1930s*. London: Macmillan, 1988.

Stanford, W. B. *Enemies of Poetry*. London: Routledge & Kegan Paul, 1980.

Steinach, Eugen. *Sex and Life: Forty Years of Biological and Medical Experiments*. New York: Viking, 1940.

Steinman, Michael. *Yeats's Heroic Figures: Wilde, Parnell, Swift, Casement*. London: Macmillan, 1983.

Stopes, Marie. *Married Love: A New Contribution to the Solution of Sex Difficulties*. London: Hogorth Press, 1934.

Strong, L. A. G. *Green Memories*. London: Methuen, 1961.

Stuart, Francis. *Black List: Section H*. London: Martin Brian & O'Keeffe, 1975.

———. "No Baleful Influence: W. B. Yeats meets Mercedes Gleitz." *Yeats Annual 7*, 209–210.

———. *Pigeon Irish*. London: Gollancz, 1932.

———. *Things to Live For: Notes for an Autobiography*. London: Cape, 1934.

Swami, Shree Purohit, and W. B. Yeats. *The Ten Principal Upanishads*. London: Faber, 1937.

Taylor, Richard. *A Reader's Guide to the Plays of W. B. Yeats*. London: Macmillan, 1984.

———, ed. *Frank Pearce Sturm: His Life, Letters and Collected Work*. Carbondale: University of Southern Illinois Press, 1969.

Terrell, Carroll F. "A Biographical Footnote on Yeats." *Yeats Eliot Review* 12:3 and 4 (Winter 1994): 134–15.

———, ed. "Ezra Pound: Letters to William Butler Yeats." *Anteus* (Spring/Summer 1976): 34–49.

Toomey, Deirdre. "Away." In *Yeats and Women*. London: Macmillan, 1992.

———, ed. *Yeats and Women*. (First published as *Yeats Annual 9*.) London: Macmillan, 1992.

Torchiana, Donald. *W. B. Yeats & Georgian Ireland*. Evanston, Ill.: Northwestern University Press. London: Oxford University Press, 1966.

Travers-Smith, Hester. *Voices from the Void: Six Years' Experience in Automatic Communications*. London: Rider and Sons, 1919; reprint, Mokelumne Hill, Calif.: Health Research, 1972.

Tuohy, Frank. *Yeats: An Illustrated Biography*. London: Herbert Press, 1976; paperback 1991.

Vendler, Helen. *Yeats's Vision and the Later Plays*. Ithaca, N.Y.: Cornell University Press, 1961.

Wade, Allan, ed. *The Letters of W. B. Yeats*. London: Macmillan, 1955.

Ward, Margaret. *Maud Gonne: Ireland's Joan of Arc*. London: Pandora, 1990.

Watson, G. J. *Irish Identity and the Literary Revival*. London: Croom Helm, 1979.

Webster, Brenda. *Yeats: A Psychoanalytic Study*.

Wellesley, Dorothy. *Letters on Poetry from W. B. Yeats to Dorothy Wellesley*. London: Oxford University Press, 1940.

White, Anna MacBride, and A. Norman Jeffares, eds. *The Gonne-Yeats Letters 1893–1938: Always Your Friend*. London: Hutchinson: 1992.

Yeats, John Butler. *Early Memories*. Dublin: Cuala Press, 1923.

Yeats, W. B., *Autobiographies*. London: Macmillan, 1955.

———. *Collected Plays*. London: Papermac 1982.

———. *Collected Poems*. London: Macmillan, 1949.

———. *A Critical Edition of Yeats's "A Vision" (1925)*. Edited by George Mills Harper.

———. *Essays and Introductions*. London: Macmillan, 1961.

————. *Explorations*. Selected by Mrs. W. B. Yeats. London: Macmillan, 1962.

————. *John Sherman and Dhoya*. Edited by Richard J. Finneran. Detroit: Wayne State University Press, 1969.

————. *Memoirs*. Edited Denis Donoghue. London: Macmillan, 1972.

————. *Mythologies*. London: Macmillan, 1959.

————. *On the Boiler*. Dublin: Cuala Press, 1938.

————. *The Oxford Book of Modern Verse. 1892–1935*. Oxford: Clarendon Press, 1936.

————. *Per Amica Silentia Lunae*.

————. *The Speckled Bird*. Toronto: McClelland and Stewart, 1976.

————. *Uncollected Prose by W. B. Yeats*. Vol. 1 edited by John P. Frayne. London: Macmillan, 1970; Vol. 2 edited by John P. Frayne & Colton Johnson. London: Macmillan, 1975.

————. *The Variorum Edition of the Poems of W. B. Yeats*. Edited by Peter Allt and Russell Alspach. London: Macmillan, 1960.

————. *The Variorum Edition of the Plays of W. B. Yeats*. Edited by Russell Alspach. London: Macmillan, 1966.

————. *A Vision*. London: Macmillan, 1937.

————. *Yeats's Poems*. Edited by A. Norman Jeffares with an appendix by Warwick Gould. London: Macmillan, 1989.

Index

Brenda Maddox's work has been translated into ten languages. Former Home Affairs editor of the *Economist* and media columnist for the *London Daily Telegraph* and the *Times*, she is a contributor to the *New York Times Book Review*, a regular reviewer for the *London Observer* and *Literary Review*, and frequent braodcaster on the BBC.

Her 1988 biography of James Joyce's wife, Nora, won the *Los Angeles Times* Award for biography, the British Silver P.E.N. Award for nonfiction, the French Prix du Meilleur Livre Étranger, and was nominated for the National Book Award. Her 1994 biography of D. H. Lawrence won the Whitbread Award in biography and was nominated for the Critics Circle Award.